NEGATIVITY AND POLITICS

'This book offers a highly nuanced and productive reading of the play of negativity, and its link with politics, within the modern and late-modern continental tradition of political theory, providing new insights into the likes of Kant, Marx, Nietzsche, Adorno, Merleau-Ponty, and Kristeva. ... Both the student and scholar of contemporary philosophy and political theory will find much to engage with, and learn from, in this brave and ambitious study.'

Keith Ansell Pearson, University of Warwick

Although frequently invoked by philosophers and political theorists, the theory of negativity has received remarkably little sustained attention. *Negativity and Politics: Dionysus and dialectics from Kant to poststructuralism* is the first full length study of this crucial problematic within philosophy and political theory. Diana Coole clearly and skilfully shows how the problem of negativity lies at the heart of philosophical and political debate. First, she explores the meaning of negativity as it appears in modern and postmodern thinking. Second, she sets out the significance of negativity for politics and our understanding of what constitutes the political.

A key theme of *Negativity and Politics* is the recurring hostility between the dialectical use of negativity found in Hegel and running through Marxism and critical theory, and the Dionysian use of negativity as developed by Nietzsche and found in important strands of French thought. Diana Coole shows how the appropriation of negativity in both cases threatens but also informs our understanding of politics and the political. A fascinating and bold intervention in political theory and philosophy, *Negativity and Politics* will be of interest to all those in politics, philosophy and contemporary social theory.

Diana Coole is Senior Lecturer in Political Theory and Head of Department at the Department of Politics, Queen Mary and Westfield College, University of London. She is the author of *Women in Political Theory* (1988; 2nd edn, 1993).

NEGATIVITY AND POLITICS

Dionysus and dialectics from Kant to
poststructuralism

Diana Coole

London and New York

First published 2000
by Routledge
11 New Fetter Lane, London EC4P 4EE

Simultaneously published in the USA and Canada
by Routledge
29 West 35th Street, New York, NY 10001

Routledge is an imprint of the Taylor & Francis Group

© 2000 Diana Coole

Typeset in Times by Taylor & Francis Books Ltd
Printed and bound in Great Britain by St Edmundsbury Press, Bury St Edmunds,
Suffolk

British Library Cataloguing in Publication Data
A catalogue record for this book is available from the British Library

Library of Congress Cataloging-in-Publication Data
Coole, Diana H.
Negativity and politics : Dionysus and dialectics from Kant to
poststructuralism / Diana Coole.
p. cm.
Includes bibliographical references and index.
1. Negativity (Philosophy) 2. Political science–Philosophy.
I. Title.
B828.25.C66   2000
149–dc21   99-052690

ISBN 0–415–03176–1 (hbk)
ISBN 0–415–03177–X (pbk)

CONTENTS

CONTENTS

CONTENTS

NOTE ON TEXTUAL SOURCES

I have tried to keep footnotes to a minimum. Because I have made extensive use of primary texts, I have incorporated the main references into my own text. These are given as abbreviations followed by page number, in parentheses. Lists of abbreviations and the bibliographic details of editions can be found at the beginning of the notes for each chapter. The references given are for English translations. I have not included a bibliography, but references to all material that has been explicitly used, plus selected references to texts of particular relevance to my arguments, are included in the notes.

ACKNOWLEDGEMENTS

I'm indebted to the friends and colleagues who read and commented on chapters of the book during its various stages. Keith Ansell Pearson, Gary Browning, Kimberley Hutchings, Iain MacKenzie, Stewart Martin, Carrie Noland, Peter Osborne, Maurizio Passerin D'Entrèves, Jacqueline Rose, Mark Warren, Margaret Whitford and Caroline Williams all helped enormously with their perceptive criticisms and suggestions and I'd like to thank them once again for their time and enthusiasm. I have tried to incorporate their comments into my arguments; any flaws remaining are, of course, my own responsibility.

I'd also like to thank my colleagues in the Politics Department at Queen Mary and Westfield College for continuing to provide a congenial and stimulating environment for research; for their interest and support and for their patience with my often distracted state and need for research time, despite my being Head of Department during much of the period it took to complete the manuscript. Tony Bruce at Routledge was an understanding and receptive editor, for which I was indeed grateful. I must also thank the Fulbright Commission, which granted me a Fellowship 1995–6. This enabled me to spend a year teaching at the University of California, Irvine, where I also undertook the research for the discussions of Nietzsche and Freud. Southern California proved to be the perfect place for thinking about their contributions to negativity and granted me a perspective I'd never have achieved in London.

More generally, I'd like to thank the many friends and students who have listened with a mixture of incredulity and fascination to my ramblings about negativity over the past few years. I often suspected that their support was intensified by a belief that writing about negativity must be a profoundly depressing experience; I hope at least some of them will now understand my insistence that negativity is affirmative. Finally, mere thanks are inadequate for expressing my gratitude to Bob and Lucien, my fellow adventurers. This book is dedicated to them with love.

INTRODUCTION
Negativity and politics

Exploring negativity

This book emerged from a fascination and two questions: what is 'negativity' and how does it relate to politics? Frequently appearing in political theory or continental philosophy, the term negativity seemed to suggest something profound if elusive, yet in many cases it was used rather promiscuously, even casually, by these traditions' expositors. Rarely deployed with precision, much less defined, it seemed that there was both a vague and rather general way in which the term was being used and a constellation of meanings that supported this. Although an association with political radicalism was often implicit, occasionally negativity would be violently denounced as inimical to socially-transformative processes. My initial plan was accordingly to pursue the sort of careful analytical procedure I associate with a British tradition of the history of political thought, seeking out the concept's appearances and adducing its meaning(s) within an evolving intellectual and historical context.[1]

Something of this approach undoubtedly remains, but the impossibility of such an undertaking, as well as its particular inappropriateness in the case of negativity, quickly became apparent. The most obvious obstacle here was an insistence on the part of those who use the term that it is neither a concept nor amenable to definition. To track its appearances in order to pin it down would not merely do an injustice to the negative's many and incommensurable senses (as an essentially-contested concept); it would be an enactment of the very stabilising, classifying logic that negativity is invoked to defy and which its practitioners reject. To name it would be to destroy it; to render it positive, ideal, and thus to fail at the very moment of apparent success. In this sense negativity bears connotations of alterity, the non-rational and unrepresentable; to ask what it 'is' or 'means' is already to find oneself implicated in the questions and paradoxes it provokes.

This aura of alterity persists in the chapters that follow. At first it suggested to me a secret and volatile life of subjects or objects, hence an enchanting project. But negativity cannot be ontologised as some veiled or marvellous Other for which no adequate conceptual schema or vocabulary (yet) exists, despite the seductiveness of the fantasy and occasional gestures in this direction by its dreamers. Its real or discursive status is and must remain, I will conclude, undecidable. For the ambiguities of the term and the enigma of what, if anything, it represents are not separable dilemmas. Even articulating the conundrum in this way presupposes a subject–object relation that negativity defies and denies. Exploring such questions introduces all the questions of metaphysics, ontology, epistemology and representation that the negative implicates and is implicated in. Indeed even using the term negativity is a dangerous and hazardous undertaking. For it tempts one to treat it as a sign for some referent, or in despair to prune it into an empty signifier or discursive convention, where either option would be to prejudge what negativity problematises.

The term negativity gains its most obvious sense from its opposition to the positive. I have insisted on retaining something of this emphatic distinction because this is where its political significance lies. It suggests criticism and negation, resistance and transgression, absence and lack, and thus an opposition that is political in more than a simply linguistic sense. But the limits of this binary formula quickly became apparent in my study, not least due to a need to distinguish between negativity and negation, where the former is also affirmative and de(con)structive of the positive–negative dualism. This renders negativity a more complex term and the necessity for its internal differentiation should be evident by the end of chapter 2, where I consider poststructuralist critiques of Hegelian dialectics. Nor do the processes I have come to recognise as negativity necessarily go under that name in the texts I consider. For it has, to borrow Derrida's phrase, many non-synonymous substitutes: dialectics, non-identity, difference, *différance*, the invisible, the semiotic, the virtual, the unconscious, will to power, the feminine. These cannot be reduced to the various signifiers of a common referent, but I will show how they are all implicated in the negative. Rather than describing the latter's exponents as theorists refining a concept, it has seemed more appropriate to speak of adventurers exploring, producing, a 'motif'. I have followed them in their struggles both to convey the dynamism and heterogeneity of this negativity that defies yet provokes philosophical rendition, and in refusing its subordination to aims of rational identification. Like them, I have found myself groping for words or phrases where none is adequate, yet persevering because negativity is not nothing.

While such struggles remain both a permanent challenge and fecund incitement for negativity's adventurers, they have provoked widespread accusations of performative contradiction, the paradox of self-referentiality, from their critics. The charge has been levelled against them especially in the wake of Habermas's criticisms of his critical theory predecessors and of their poststructuralist and postmodernist successors, all of whom I associate with negativity.[2] For how can rational discourses speak of the very processes they deny themselves access to, without contradiction or madness? I have been obliged to take this problem very seriously in the chapters that follow, both because it poses a challenge that goes to the heart of philosophies of the negative and because the exponents of clear, communicative language often seem to think its very invocation suffices to dismiss such philosophies as nonsense. But the latter's exponents also take this puzzle of representation seriously since it is integral to their explorations of negativity. In negotiating it, they typically deploy what I will elicit as a dual strategy: one that combines the discursive and the performative while defining philosophy and politics as practices of negativity. One of the questions I have then addressed is what the political version of this practising might look like.

It would be inappropriate here to prejudge the performances of negativity that will emerge across ensuing chapters, but it is necessary to mention my own involvement in this process. Because of the negative's resistance to any positive formulation, it must be approached circumspectly: through allusion, metaphor, invocation. If my book were to elicit, clarify and explain these elusive provocations and hesitant performances, it would itself do an injustice to its topic and its texts. Yet equally, it would be fairly pointless if it offered no clarification or indication of the negative and its implications. (This is indeed the conundrum evident in the literature I discuss, which is why its exponents are driven to a provisional exposition of the negative even while they deny its feasibility and aspire to its performing or practising instead.) Moreover a strong assertion of negativity is needed if its incitement is to be politically efficacious, since its recognition is part of a rational appeal for reflecting upon and changing political practice. If, unlike (most of) the writers I discuss, I have not utilised a performative strategy myself – in particular I have not experimented stylistically – I have tried to remain faithful to the negative by combining critical exegesis and analysis with a certain undecidability, ambiguity and openness, as well as recognising the differences and discontinuities between negativities which refuse assimilation into any simple narrative of a term's coming to consciousness.

My strategy was to begin with a general intuition of the negative, which allowed the identification of key texts and a provisional recognition of relevant arguments. Then I reworked each chapter (often several times) more critically and precisely in light of the deeper grasp of negativity that my readings had yielded. I came to think of this as a dialectical process and if I assumed from the start that the most fertile route to negativity would be through its textual invocations, my choices here also evolved dialectically. As I became more confident through my readings in ascribing negativity, my identification of its exponents broadened and their contributions in turn enriched my understanding of it. Hegel seemed an obvious starting point, since he explicitly introduces the term negativity into modern thought as well as giving it a political *frisson*, while subsequent explorations have been closely related to his alleged successes and failures. Some of Hegel's successors – Marx, Kojève, Merleau-Ponty, Adorno – would define their task as rescuing negativity from Hegelian positivism, while continuing to insist on its dialectical nature. They explicitly associate such a negative dialectics with political radicalism. They were therefore attractive candidates for inclusion in my own adventure, one of whose motivations has been to rescue dialectics from the often crude way it is interpreted and rejected by postmodernists. I regret that I did not have space to include Marcuse here, but would commend Richard Bernstein's excellent article on his negativity, in its absence.[3]

Somewhat to my surprise, the book concludes with an endorsement of dialectics and a call for some re-instantiation of a dialectical approach as politically fertile, albeit one that has been reworked in the crucible of more Nietzschean and postmodern sensitivities. The surprise arises because the book was originally envisaged, in part at least, as a defence of postmodernism and poststructuralism: as harbouring a radical politics and an affirmative ethics and thus as immune to charges of being 'merely negative', de(con)structive and nihilistic.[4] This defence is indeed developed and relies on what might at first seem an odd assertion: that negativity is affirmative, productive as well as destructive (a claim that will become clearer by chapter 3 where I discuss Nietzsche). But if I have retained some sympathy for an equation between postmodern strategies and political transformation, it has been tempered by my conclusion that this needs to be put within a dialectical context. Again, this judgement must be allowed to unfold across the following chapters and can only be anticipated here.

This concern with poststructuralism meant however that my exploration of negativity could not be confined to dialectical theories, which would anyway have rendered my discussion rather one-dimensional. I am grateful for Keith Ansell Pearson's insistence from the start that I could not possibly write a book about negativity without discussing Nietzsche, despite the virtual absence of, and lack of enthusiasm for, the term in his work. My ascription of negativity to Nietzsche and his followers, Deleuze in particular, has been one of the book's challenges and I will offer an initial defence of it shortly. Reading Nietzsche and his epigones as adventurers in negativity posed its own methodological difficulties, too. For if my readings of dialectical thinkers would call for an interpretation of their references to negativity which always courted the danger of being too positive, the challenge now was to elicit negativity where the term was absent or rejected without being overly enigmatic.

A somewhat similar problem, if from a different perspective, was summoned in what is now the first chapter, on Kant. Kant is no adventurer in negativity and it had not therefore been my initial intention to include a whole chapter on his work. However by the time I came to discuss Adorno's negative dialectics, it became obvious that so much of Kant needed to be appreciated, both as source and target of such dialecticians' work, that some serious consideration of the critical philosophy would be required. As I pursued this, it became evident to me that Kant was deeply implicated in the question of negativity precisely because of his denial of it: he incites it in order to keep it off-limits. Kant's clear and eloquent rejection of voyages on the high seas of the negative called for a deconstructive reading of his *First Critique*, to show its absent presence in the fissures and productivity of his text.

A further problem that influenced my choices and organisation for the book concerned the temptations inherent in any history of ideas. Tracing the twists and turns of a concept in emergence risks participating in the sort of idealist phenomenology that marks Hegelian dialectics. It may seem that a vague idea or recalcitrant referent comes to consciousness, acquiring identity and richness as it is synthesised, mediated, until it appears in all its resplendent, sparkling completeness. Not only has it been necessary to avoid identifying the negative in this way, but a historical rendition of its adventures risked becoming the sort of teleological grand narrative that today attracts both incredulity and hostility.

In part I tried to resist this narrative structure by re-ordering the chronology of my discussions. Instead of considering Derrida or Deleuze in the last chapter, implying some higher stage of the negative's evolution or transcendence, I integrated their thinking into chapter 2 as responses to Hegel. Yet I ascribe inspiration for Derrida's approach to dialectics to Deleuze's reading of Nietzsche and thus to the negativity explored in chapters 3 and 6. Regrettably I have not had space to do anything like justice to Deleuze's thinking here; like Foucault he merely haunts the text, resisting and enriching it but confined to footnotes and brief allusions.

It is Kristeva's psychoanalytical summoning of negativity that now ends the book: an appropriate, if provisional conclusion to its exploration in as much as she draws on many of the writers cited earlier and still insists on an inherent connection between negativity and politics, despite moving in the more postmodern direction where the relationship becomes more tenuous. Indeed Kristeva's work offered the opportunity to explore politically radical dimensions and strategies associated with the postmodern and I pursued these in the context of her ambivalent relationship to feminism. Kristeva's work also allowed me to consider more explicitly the connections between negativity and subjectivity, where my earlier focus had tended to be on negativity and the 'object'. I included material in this last chapter that had originally been intended for a fourth chapter on Freud where, had space permitted, his ambiguous status as an adventurer in negativity – as unhappily both Kantian and Nietzschean – would have been discussed more fully. For in Freud's ruminations on the status of his psychoanalytic theory, as physics or metaphysics, and in his historical positioning at that moment when classical physics was succumbing to the new physics, the ontological status of negativity was thrown into question with unusual clarity, if unde-cidability.

Despite my resistance to a phenomenology of negativity's appearing, a metanarrative or conceptual clarification and definition, a persistent sense of negativity does emerge from my readings: as *generativity*. It is in this sense, I will argue, that it is affirmative: a creative–destructive force that engenders as well as ruins positive forms. In this sense negativity does tend to operate as (a surrogate for) ontology, although it is far too mobile, too negative, to serve as a foundation for what follows. In the spacings, intervals, differences, gaps and non-coincidences with which the positive is riven, the latter's becoming, its self-productivity, is provoked. It is this restlessness that haunts all positive forms and although metaphysical theories sympathetic to this negativity can be traced back to Heraclitus, it is their political, opposi-tional resonance that has for me defined more recent interrogations as theories of negativity. What divides their exponents is only the rhythms, the tempo, the choreography, of its becoming: whether its flows are more logical or musical, more lawful or wild. I will not pursue this as yet cryptic distinc-tion further here, but it is in such differences that the relation between negativity and politics will come into relief and provide a critical perspective on their interface.

Nor have I wholly rejected all sense of plot. Because those who have tarried with the negative have not done so in isolation, but have been influ-enced by or critical of their predecessors, there is a certain internal logic to their work. I would even ascribe a trajectory to this dialectical process, whereby repeated invocations of the negative, and criticisms of its provoca-teurs' infidelities, has resulted in its becoming increasingly negative. This judgement may again seem cryptic, but it too will be important for my conclusions regarding the relation between negativity and politics. For in order for the relation to be an efficacious one, I will argue, negativity must be implicated in the positive: at that place where positive and negative, form and excess, reason and its other, are imbricated; where they meet and clash or incite one another. Aware of the dangers of contamination by the posi-tive, negativity's defenders have tended to push it increasingly in a transcendental direction, where it becomes pure process: mobility, flows, the virtual. This poses a significant problem regarding the political, since in saving negativity from infection by the positive, its exponents also deny their engagement until it becomes difficult to imagine or enact a politics. In the course of writing the book, I indeed became aware of a certain weariness among those of us who have been fascinated by this extreme negativity; a suspicion that its political promise is irredeemable. This has been, then, the greatest challenge of *Negativity and Politics*: to grasp and insist upon their relationship.

Pursuing the political

A compelling motivation for writing this book was indeed my dissatisfaction with the way recent discourses have understood the political. As far as most recent continental philosophy is concerned, which is also where the most defiantly negative processes are invoked, it has become virtually impossible to elicit any meaningful sense of the political or any efficacious politics. This lacuna is frequently noted even among sympathetic critics.[5] The Anglo-American approach that dominates political theory, on the other hand, offers a more precise sense of the political but a narrow one, while its own analyses are themselves peculiarly uncritical, abstract and apolitical. Their formality accommodates little sense of politics as a dynamic, conflictual, process and is accordingly antipathetic to negativity. Despite the antagonism between the two approaches, these shortcomings can equally, I think, be traced to their shared Kantian roots, where they are respectively wary of invoking the real, because it is non-discursive, or the empirical, because it is contingent. In this context I suggest that a return to Hegel might be timely since it encourages a more dialectical sense of the relation between the real and the conceptual; between the sociological content of everyday life and its political forms or analysis.

Politics is primarily, I will contend here, the domain of *collective life*. As such it concerns the shared institutions, rules, customs, values and practices that facilitate coexistence. Equally, however, it is about the strife, the unruly processes and normative disagreement that the engendering and imposition of such power structures entails. While the consensus and conflict involved in collective life are partially formalised in a domain defined as the political, its legitimacy and effects are under continual negotiation at all levels of intersubjective life, so politics is practised here, too. This negotiation renders politics an unstable, dynamic process; one whose strategies and contingencies may be constrained, but never wholly contained, by the more formal institutions of the political which are therefore themselves in process.

The general claim that politics concerns the guarantee and practising of collective life is common to many strands of political theory. Among the ancients, the political concerned that domain where equal citizens would consider together their common destiny. It was considered a natural, if noble, expression of what it meant to be human. For social contract theorists, the political is instituted artificially at that moment when individuals agree to surrender some portion of their natural rights and powers to a higher jurisdiction, which will henceforth have the right to legislate rules and instantiate procedures that are necessary for peaceful coexistence. It is evident from this liberal model that collective life need not necessarily entail democratic practices or social solidarity, that is, active expressions of political association. However the passive aggregation facilitated by the political, where we become subject to the law and to objective criteria of justice, has often been linked by political theorists to models of more participatory citizenship, whether in Rousseau's notion of the continuous and active consent expressed by the General Will or Habermas's descriptions of the public sphere and communicative action.

While all the theories cited above ascribe the facilitation and procedures necessary for collective life to the political, they are not equally amenable to the negative. The social contract model, for example, tends to perceive political order as a positive, stable edifice, as symbolised by the great Leviathan. Formalised under constitutional regulations and institutional procedures, this liberal order is insulated from and indeed intended to transcend the conflictual, contingent negotiations and adversities of collective life. The latter are relegated to a private sphere that is both managed and declared apolitical. It is here that difference and sociological dynamism belong, as opposed to the equality and immobile objectivity realised in and by the state. Such thinking is hostile to the idea of politics as an irreducibly violent and hazardous process occurring throughout the social fabric and inimical to any sense of political order as a merely provisional balance of forces. The latter sense of politics is more conducive to negativity and is caught to a greater degree in theories that focus on the ways shared institutions emerge from democratic negotiation (thus, for example, in Habermas as opposed to Rawls). However in so far as their ideal is one of consensus and their focus is on formal procedures for acquiring it, their negativity is limited to the differential perspectives of discussants whose aim is to trump negativity with agreement.

A Machiavellian or Foucaultian sense of politics is more congenial to negativity here, in so far as these thinkers describe an unstable process of strategies, negotiations and fragile political compromises without any terminal fantasy. Rather than distinguishing between public and private; between the formalities and everyday practices of collective life; between a political order and the fluctuations of power, they describe flows of power which constantly create and destroy the possibilities and limits of coexistence. As one critic puts it, the

> modernist view, from its roots in Hobbes, traces a world of eurhythmic (as in harmoniously ordered and proportioned) power … . The contrasting view from Machiavelli ['"post-modern" before even modernity'] is of a world far more dissonant and difficult to play upon, which is characterized by strategic manoeuvres made in contingent circumstances, is bereft of any overall harmonic, and is without the guidance of any overall conductor.[6]

In this sense one might provisionally contend that such a politics is thought from the perspective of the negative, or understood as a process caught up in the rhythms of negativity. To put it otherwise: this manner of thinking politics, which focuses on the ubiquitous strategies and multiplicitous strands of cohesion and dissolution that criss-cross collective life, to some extent corresponds with, or expresses, the mobilities and flows that philosophies of negativity invoke. Collective life from this perspective involves all the strategies of subversion, negation, opposition, resistance, transgression, that positive institutions provoke when they exclude, discriminate, dominate or oppress in the name of harmonious stability or political order. As such, populations do not require formal rights to democratic participation in order to have political effects.

If however more formal, liberal models are unable or unwilling to accommodate such negativity, philosophies that begin with heterogeneity and flux, with 'pure' processes of negativity, are inimical to the subsequent derivation of a politics. As I will argue: precisely because the political is the domain of collective life, it necessarily engenders, and indeed requires, shared practices, habits, norms, languages, no matter how diverse its participants. Conflict and dissonance alone merely describe a pre-political state of nature. In other words, the political must entail relatively enduring structures and practices, as well as negation and critique. For politics means carving up the flux of social life, imposing boundaries, limits, laws that its apparatus then polices. These may be experienced as coercive but, also, as empowering. As such, the political cannot be conceived as a direct expression of negativity in its more evanescent and wild modulations. For it is impossible to understand or interpret the rhythms of this more turgid realm – where power and inertia as well as desire conspire to fix the positive, and where the given necessarily changes according to the rather slow tempo collective action and structural imperatives entail – if the choreography of generativity is understood in too mobile a fashion. As Simon Critchley for example remarks, 'there is an impasse of the political in Derrida's work, and ... deconstruction fails to offer a coherent account of the passage from ethical responsibility to political questioning and critique.' He asks how one could enact the decision-making, action, judgement that politics demands, on the basis of the 'undecidable terrain' Derrida offers and wonders whether it amounts to a 'refusal of politics'.[7] It is then attention to the specific rhythms of negativity that the political enacts which is missing from much post-Nietzschean thinking and it is into this lacuna that I will insinuate a more dialectical appreciation. Otherwise, politics tends to be reduced to aesthetics or ethics.

An analogous problem, and one especially acute regarding politics, concerns the question of political agency. While liberalism's strong claims regarding the individual make it difficult to locate the glue that would hold society together in any convincing way, an emphasis on heterogeneity has tended to reduce political actors, whether individual or collective, to an unstable flux of shifting identities and desires. Political efficacy is hard to explain on this basis. For how is politics to be enacted, and by whom or for what ends? Important political criticisms of metaphysics, bourgeois individualism and humanism have tended here to become confused with distrust of the sort of closures, criteria and concerns that the political legitimately expresses. Again, some relatively enduring (inter)subjective forms, as well as the processes of their dissolution and the illusions that sustain their identity, call for recognition.

In considering politics, is it not then necessary to emphasise and interpret the formative, as well as the destructive, dimensions of change; to *engage* with its positive structures? A major challenge for political theories of negativity is accordingly to envisage how criticisms of obsolete or oppressive intersubjective systems might also countenance a transformative political process that would perform negativity without itself lapsing into absolute negation or a renewed reification. This question will resound throughout the ensuing discussions.

I previously justified placing a variety of philosophies under the sign of the negative in so far as they invoke a generativity that has political resonance. I can now be more specific about this inflection. Despite the differences between critical modern and poststructuralist discourses, they are all finally motivated, I suggest, by an unambiguous *political* opposition to the positive. The positive here refers to those institutions – language, subjectivity, metaphysics, positivist knowledge as well as mode of production, state structures, social stratifications, modern culture – that have become reified, ossified, totalised. The positive is the given; what has presence. As far as philosophers of negativity are concerned, the structures of modernity deny their own genesis and contingency in order to preserve themselves unchanged. They may advance ideological assertions regarding their own excellence and immutability or sheer inertia and exhaustion might sustain them. But they must deny and suppress negativity *qua* the restless movement – of forces, flow, flux; contingency, adversity, difference; opposition, resistance, conflict – that engenders yet assaults them. As such they enact a certain violence and blindness, a mystification and closure, that renders them dysfunctional for collective life and forces them into strategies of domination and control (in Machiavellian terms one might say that they lack *virtú* because they deny *fortuna*).

Philosophies of presence and correspondence theories of truth; the ascetic ideal, the ego, the liberal state, capitalism, binary sexual difference, the culture industry, even grammar and law: all have been identified as structures of power that deny their own mediations or genealogies in order to sustain themselves and related parts of the system as unequivocal, self-identical, immutable. They claim universality both to mask their own particularity and to subordinate what is particular, non-identical, to their own ordering principle. In more politically explicit theories these closures are associated with specific structures of modernity; in some poststructuralist versions a more generalised equation between institution and violence is entertained. But it is this antipathy towards the positive that lends all philosophies of negativity their radical political ethos and allows me to bring some quite disparate approaches under the sign of the negative.

The critical theorists explicitly used this oppositional language. Marcuse writes: 'Negation is the Great Refusal to accept the rules of the game in which the dice are loaded.'[8] Adorno insists that

> [d]own to the vernacular of praising men who are 'positive,' and ultimately in the homicidal phrase of 'positive forces,' a fetish is made of the positive-in-itself. Against this, the seriousness of unswerving negation lies in its refusal to lend itself to sanctioning things as they are.[9]

But Foucault also typifies this orientation when he writes in 'What is Enlightenment?' that

> if the Kantian question was that of knowing what limits knowledge has to renounce transgressing, it seems to me that the critical ques-tion today has to be turned back into a positive one: in what is given to us as universal, necessary, obligatory, what place is occu-pied by whatever is singular, contingent, and the product of arbitrary constraints? The point, in brief, is to transform the critique conducted in the form of necessary limitation into a prac-tical critique that takes the form of a possible transgression.[10]

For the mid-career Foucault, at least, subjectivity was an effect of disci-pline on the fluidity of organs, pleasures, desires, while for Deleuze it is an 'anti-production' that closes down 'desiring-production' and 'lines-of-flight'. Lyotard fears the present age is one of 'slackening', where experimentation is discouraged in the name of realism; where language would be re-anchored solidly in the referent and culturally there is 'an identical call for order, a desire for unity, for identity, for security'. He challenges it in the name of the postmodern, a sublime denial of 'the solace of good form' in favour of the 'jubilation' of invention and a war on totality.[11] Drucilla Cornell explains the title of her book *Transformations* as exhorting 'change radical enough to so dramatically restructure any system – political, legal, social – that the "identity" of the system is itself altered' along with the subjects who would be open to it.[12] Stephen White catches this postmodern orientation when he concludes that, in revealing dissonance, poststructuralism enacts 'an experi-ence that has an unsettling effect on our modern, deep-rooted quest for harmony and unity, for a world of problems finally solved.'[13]

To invoke negativity is thus to exhort political intervention while already performing a political act: it destabilises illusions of perfection, presence and permanence by associating the positive with petrified and illegitimate struc-tures of power. As such it has strategic significance. Yet such performances cannot substitute for the political as such, nor do they offer paradigms for politics as the reproducing of collective life. In this sense theories of negativity that go too far in their desire to purge themselves of all positivity, and to keep their hands clean, end up with the same apolitical vacuousness as more positivist Anglo-American liberalisms. Although I think some sense of politics as collective life is implicit within most theories of negativity, I will then use it as a critical perspective against versions that fall short of their political aspirations. I will also use it as an interrogative tool to ask what sort of process and model of politics can be derived from negativity. How does its generativity take political form and how does its perspective change our understanding of the political? It is not then a question of stitching together, or drawing arbitrary links between, negativity and politics but of asking how negativity yields the political and whether it might describe any exemplary process for its undertaking.

1

NEGATIVITY AND NOUMENA
Critical reason at the limit

Succeeding chapters of this book will follow some of negativity's adventurers. Is Kant among them? Deleuze has commented that he 'is the analogue of a great explorer – not of another world, but of the upper and lower echelons of this one.'[1] An explorer, then, rather than an adventurer: one who maps a familiar but previously uncharted terrain, presenting himself as cartographer and gate-keeper rather than venturing into the perils of the unknown. Does he encounter negativity in this world he explores, or banish it to a beyond he eschews? Kant will be presented here as an ambiguous figure: as one who engendered or succumbed to negativity in his attempt to exile it, but in whose project of critique a certain negativity is nevertheless embraced.

In this chapter significant aspects of the *Critique of Pure Reason*[2] will be sketched in, with allusions on the way to places where negativity insinuates itself within Kant's text. Since negativity as such is not a concern of the critical philosophy, and the senses in which it will emerge in modern thought and in this book have yet to appear, there is an obvious danger of anachronism in attributing an unwitting or pale summoning of it to Kant. At this stage only a gentle provocation is then in order: an immanent critique and a temperate deconstruction, which will elicit certain metaphorical and metaphysical gestures, as well as lacunae and leakages, within the dry formalities of the transcendental method. Crucially, I will leave open the question of whether it is the limitation placed on reason, which Kant believed a self-grounding philosophy requires, that itself engenders negativity in the joints and lining of his thinking, or whether negativity irrupts there with the irrepressible ontological force of something he tried in vain to suppress. This question of negativity's status, as immanent to reason or its other, will be played out repeatedly but variously in subsequent discussions.[3]

Kant's transcendental method and the limits of theoretical reason

Kant begins the *Critique* by opposing his critical philosophy to all previous metaphysics. He speaks of the latter as an outcast matron, a deposed Queen whose philosophical reign was equivalent to barbarism and anarchy; to a nomadic assault on the settled life of civil society. Her powers must once and for all be rejected in a mature age of criticism which respects only what survives the test of free and open examination (CPR: Aviii–xi). For such metaphysics yields but 'illusory knowledge'; 'a completely isolated speculative science of reason' associated with the 'darkness and contradictions' into which reason falls when it ventures beyond the limits of experience (CPR: Axi/Bxiv). Reason is thus summoned to that most difficult task of self-knowledge: 'to institute a tribunal which will assure to reason its lawful claims, and dismiss all groundless pretensions', not via despotic decrees but 'in accordance with its own eternal and unalterable laws' (CPR: Axii).

Kant's political metaphors here are not gratuitous, since challenges to indefensible metaphysics and to arbitrary power structures are complementary processes that define an enlightened age. As the little essay 'What is Enlightenment?' makes clear, maturity involves the duty of all rational persons to think autonomously and critically, thereby transforming the self-incurred tutelage to authority that the less courageous endure.[4] Kant nevertheless insists on the limits that any responsible challenge must recognise, lest disorder ensue: argue but obey. In this sense he is aligned with the cautious political negativity of liberalism, where criticism might challenge the closures of the given but only within limits wherein order is sustained and legitimacy restored. The critique of reason operates within equivalent parameters.

The purpose of the critical philosophy is then to establish the principles, and thus also the limits, of reason in order to yield a version that is self-reflexive and critical as opposed to dogmatic or sceptical. Although Kant acknowledges that speculative thinking about such things as freedom or totality is natural and even desirable for reason, he insists on a distinction between such ideas and knowledge, the latter being tied to objects of possible experience and the faculty of understanding. His chief question is accordingly: 'what and how much can the understanding and reason know apart from all experience?' (CPR: Axvii). Although Kant adds that his answer will have the positive consequence of releasing practical reason from the limits of sensibility (thereby leaving scope for morality and freedom beyond the mechanical determinations of nature), 'a critique of pure reason ought properly to be only negative' (CPR: Bxxiv, B25). This sense of the negative, as the determination of a limit, is then central to the *First Critique*. It forbids the transgression of certain boundaries and the exploration of certain spaces, because it establishes 'our unavoidable ignorance of things in themselves' and limits what we can legitimately claim to know, to appearances. As Adorno describes it, Kant's is a 'system of stop signals'.[5]

Such limitation is a consequence of the revolutionary strategy Kant deploys in trying to defeat scepticism, which he associates with dogmatic or empirical ('problematic') idealism. Rather than seeking confirmation of knowledge in things as they exist independently of us, where their true, unmediated nature, or even proof of their existence, remains inaccessible, he turns to the cognitive faculties that construct them. Because we can never cross the divide between subjectivity and a subject-independent reality, the pursuit of certainty through appeal to the latter seems to rely on a questionable inference. As Kant summarises his alternative: 'we can know *a priori* of things only what we ourselves put into them' (CPR: Bxviii). In legislating against pre-critical metaphysics, he both rejects speculative forays into ontology and aims to displace the epistemological aporias they produce.

It is important at this stage to be clear about what Kant's transcendental method entails and excludes. He is not concerned with specific (empirical, *a posteriori*) knowledge about experience, but with the necessary conditions for the possibility of such knowledge. He does not therefore offer a phenomenology of meaning, but a formal analysis: of the logical conditions experience must satisfy if we are to know it and of the cognitive faculties that provide them. Issues concerning semantics or ontology are thus irrelevant to his approach and should remain absent from it. Will it be possible to honour this prohibition?

The idea of a limit is especially provocative here in that its very meaning seems to rely upon something beyond it which is excluded. As Hegel will write,

> great store is set by the barriers to thought, to reason, and so forth, and those barriers are said to be impassable. Behind this contention lies awareness that by its very definition as a barrier a thing is already passed. For a definite thing, a limit, is defined as a barrier – opposed to its otherness at large – only against that which it does not bar; the otherness of a barrier is its transcending.[6]

This otherness is summoned by the act of naming, in order to exclude, that which makes a limit necessary. The question raised once again is whether it is reason's own act of exclusion that produces this negativity, as reason's necessary corollary and the discursive condition of its possibility, or whether negativity resides in some ontological alterity of which knowledge is both denied and assumed. The latter arises most obviously during Kant's consideration of noumena, which remain for him beyond the frontiers of any possible knowledge. But the spatial metaphorics this barrier sets in motion will also oblige him to deploy a number of ambiguous and problematic dualisms. While the grounding of reliable knowledge requires that these remain only analytically distinct, Kant is forced into an unwelcome textual productivity in attempting to fill the discontinuities and gaps that open in their midst: an intrusive negativity that threatens transcendental reassurances regarding the truth of phenomenal knowing.

These dualisms and hiatuses that proliferate within the deduction of knowledge's conditions of possibility are spawned by the question of subject–object relations. This question will echo through succeeding chapters, where it will acquire considerable existential, as well as epistemological, resonance. Kant explicitly rejects their ontological severance as an index of faulty thinking, but it is an opposition that nevertheless remains on the horizon of his own thought, enframing his responses to the challenge of scepticism.

The problematic engendered by scepticism aligns it with negativity in that it undermines epistemic confidence in the truth or accessibility of the given (the positive), sustaining an interrogative and doubting attitude towards it. Things are not what they seem. A sceptical attitude invokes the possibility, at worst, of a void (outside the mind there is nothing; objective reality is an illusion; what seems to be present may be absent) or, at best, of a slippage between subject and object, with its attendant uncertainties concerning misrepresentation and error, where knowledge might dissolve into contingency or fantasy. Such epistemological conundra are attributed by Kant to pre-critical, and hence illegitimate, metaphysical assumptions regarding a fundamental opposition between subject and object. He refers here to a 'crude dualism' between thinking and extended substances and warns against filling the gap where knowledge is unavailable with 'paralogisms of reason', via an 'imaginary science' that confuses appearances with unknowable things in themselves (CPR: A392, 395). He then displaces this problematic by proposing two alternative dualisms. The first is between phenomena and noumena: between appearances we indubitably know and things in themselves which are beyond experience and thus unknowable. The correct question regarding knowledge does not then concern the communion between the soul and a materiality heterogeneous to it, which is an ontological question, but the lawful connections between representations of inner sense and modifications of outer sensibility (CPR: A386). This displacing of subject and object onto inner and outer senses, both attributable to mind, then yields a second dualism between its two faculties: one receiving content and the other imposing form upon it. Do these alternative dyads then avoid the gaps, doubts and speculations that haunt the various idealisms and empiricisms that Kant rejects? To address this question one must turn to the Transcendental Aesthetic and the first part of the Transcendental Logic, where the conditions necessary for knowledge are deduced.

Although temporal, spatial or architectural metaphors are inappropriate to the formalism of the transcendental method, it is difficult for Kant, in what Adorno refers to as his 'topographical zeal' and Körner as his 'impressive design in logical geography', to avoid invoking, even trading upon, them.[7] There is a sense of a painstaking labour of bridge building, whereby he would deduce every brick, every stage, in order to reconstruct a seamless linkage between subject and object that would be without missing parts where doubt or contingency might surface. For if any gap remains, we will again face the dizzying prospect of peering into the abyss of uncertainty; the realisation that representations cannot be guaranteed to correspond with what they purport to organise and that inner and outer might fall out of joint.

Accordingly, one might expect the first and crucial stage in this construction to lie in Kant's establishing the passage of external matter into mind, but this phase is in fact barely mentioned.[8] He relies upon an implicit theory of causality whereby something affects our senses, causing them to change and thereby to register 'mere' – subjective and contingent – sensations (such as heat, sound or colour). 'Apprehension by means of sensation occupies only an instant', he writes, and it does not necessarily tell us anything about the effective thing (CPR: A167/B209; A28/B44–5). It will be necessary to return to the question of this first causality, but Kant's transcendental idealism cannot in principle begin with the passage of objects in themselves (or more consistently, of something) into mind, since it already entails that no one 'can have the right to claim that he knows anything in regard to the transcendental cause of our representations of the outer senses' (CPR: A391).[9] Perception, which is produced by the synthesis of apprehensions and defined by Kant as 'representations accompanied by sensation' (CPR: B147), glosses over the mind/body and inner/outer interfaces, playing a role similar to the imagination's later occult mediation between their internalised interplay within the faculties.

Kant insists that any appeal to causal material forces would be illegitimate here, since causality and materiality are themselves categories of understanding. Thus 'matter, the communion of which with the soul arouses so much questioning, is nothing but a mere form' (CPR: A385). Matter, in other words, is an *a priori* construct and we cannot begin by assuming a precognitive reality comprised of hard chunks of material or bits and pieces of sense data; as particles of stuff or an outer skin of objects or even as strings or forces. Although any of these may correspond to something in itself, we are obliged to remain agnostic on this question and even posing it in these terms relies upon matter's deceptive property of seeming to 'hover' outside the mind. As appearance, matter remains but a 'thought in us'; the distinctive way in which unknown things appear to us as spatial, or outer (CPR: A385). 'This gap in our knowledge can never be filled' (CPR: A393). To pursue such material antecedents would involve an infinite regress and catch reason in antinomy (CPR: A516/B544). Kant points out that it would be unreasonable for us to object that he allows us no insight into the inner (material) nature of things, since we could not grasp matter except in so far as the word corresponds to something accessible through our sensibility.

The absolutely inward [nature] of matter, as it would have to be conceived by pure understanding, is nothing but a phantom; for matter is not among the objects of pure understanding, and the transcendental object which may be the ground of this appearance that we call matter is a mere something of which we should not understand what it is, even if someone were in a position to tell us.

(CPR: A277/B333)

Accordingly, even if science were able to 'penetrate to nature's inner recesses', it still could never know it in itself. These comments on matter must be borne in mind in subsequent chapters when adventurers in negativity insist on their – and its – materialist credentials, as well as later in this chapter in the discussion of things in themselves. Transcendental philosophy is not however a causal narrative and Kant's interest only concerns the ordering of effects once their content is available to the mind.

In order to know objects, as opposed either to suffering inchoate sense impressions, or thinking in a purely formal but empty manner, Kant reasons that we must require the operation of two faculties, sensibility and understanding: the first to produce representations of the contents they receive from the senses (perception) and the second, to subsume them beneath concepts (judgement). Together they provide the content and form on which knowledge depends. The senses, then, yield only the undetermined object of sensible intuition, although, because there is no temporal process of coming-to-knowledge, this is an only analytically distinct phase for Kant and it is not possible to stop at this primitive level of the sensuous manifold.

Although intuition is for him our immediate relation to objects, the latter already have the status of appearances, or representations, since they are structured by the *a priori* rules of space and time. Kant insists over and again that these 'appearances are not things in themselves, but are the mere play of representations' (CPR: A101). In other words, space and time are empirically real but transcendentally ideal, and no amount of clarification could breach this distinction since it would necessarily operate under its conditions (CPR: A30, 36, 43, 539/B49, 51, 54, 60). For 'what we call outer objects are nothing but mere representations of our sensibility ... . The true correlate of sensibility, the thing in itself, is not known and cannot be known, through these representations' (CPR: A29). Kant is equally insistent, however, that this ideality of space–time leaves the 'certainty of empirical knowledge unaffected', since we are equally sure of it whether forms inhere in things in themselves or in our intuitions of them (CPR: A39/B56). It is then vital to his case that appearances should not be equated with illusions (CPR: B69–70). Without this spatiotemporal structuring, experience could not be possible. There is then no creative phenomenology or dialectics of perception at work here: sensibility is a universal and non-contingent faculty which defines the possibility and limits of human perception.

If sensible intuition provides the content for knowledge, this must also be given form. Kant accordingly turns next to the cognitive faculty of understanding, although it is again important to emphasise that perception and judgement are only analytically, not chronologically, distinct processes for him. Nevertheless, having taken them apart it is difficult to reunite them. All the important subject–object links are now reconstructed, but within the subject, between its sensible and intellectual faculties, so that while the transcendental approach aimed to avoid the epistemological problems such ontological dualism caused, these are now replicated internally.[10] The distinction between the two faculties yields a series of equivalent dualisms – passive/active, receptivity/spontaneity, intuition/concepts, the object as given versus the object of thought – and two respective sets of rules: aesthetic and logical (CPR: A50–1/B74–5).

How, then, are these two aspects of the mind to be integrated? This question constitutes the central problematic of Kant's philosophy in as much as the sceptical challenge that arises from Cartesian dualism is displaced by him onto the possibility of connecting the sensible and intellectual conditions of knowledge. There must, Kant reasons, be some 'third thing', a 'mediating representation', that is both sensible and intellectual, and this is the imagination. It brings the manifold of intuition into the form of an image and then reproduces a series of images which it associates according to rules (schemata) (CPR: A120). Kant describes this labour as a blind and unconscious but essential function of the soul. Yet this capacity, which is necessary for valid knowledge, cannot, he concedes, be explicated further: it is 'an art concealed in the depths of the human soul' of which nature is unlikely to allow us a glimpse (CPR: A138, 141/B177, 180–1).

The role accorded the imagination, and the dualistic problem to which it is a response, addresses yet engenders a hiatus that interrupts Kant's text at this point. First, it gives the impression of being an inference rather than a deduction, called upon (imaginatively? As a 'paralogism of reason'?) to complete the connection between content and form which a critical philosophy must make. Surely its *natural* obscurity cannot legitimately excuse *transcendental* ignorance. Its derivation, as well as its own art, remains occult. As Deleuze notes, the internalisation of the subject–object relation has merely shifted the problem of their connection: 'the imagination and the understanding themselves differ in nature, and the accord between the two faculties is no less "mysterious" (likewise the accord between understanding and reason).'[11] The problem remains the fundamentally dualist structure of Kant's thinking: for him there can be no new third term, no *process*, that synthesises, but only a formal joining of two parts whose interface is never negotiated quite convincingly. In other words, a certain negativity – a difference and non-coincidence – insinuates itself here: one which Kant seeks to expurgate, to heal, but which acquires a disruptive fecundity within the text at the same time as the imagination is denied any generativity of its own, since it is accorded only the most formal of powers.

Yet if it is difficult to reassemble the active and passive faculties, their analytical severance in the first place is also questionable. 'Nothing in the world is composed – added up so to speak – of factuality and concept.'[12] For Kant's dialectical successors in particular, even their formal splitting will suggest confusion and historical blindness at the heart of the epistemological account. Adorno suggests that the block between the sensual and intellectual is both pre-critically dogmatic and a reflection of contingent (bourgeois) social conditions.[13] On the other hand, it is precisely such gaps that for him save Kant from the totalisation Hegel will enact: 'the Kantian discontinuities register the very moment of nonidentity' that will be needed to re-energise dialectical negativity.[14]

Second, Kant is unable wholly to insulate the imagination, despite its transcendental status, from the psychological weight the term bears and it seems unlikely that it could play even the formalistic role he ascribes it, were its empirical activities not assumed. The difficulty of sustaining a boundary between the transcendental and empirical is an enduring problem in the *Critique*, especially where the subject is concerned. In this instance it draws attention to the very attenuated role imagination is called upon to perform in the production of knowledge, inspiring Kant's critics to comment upon the latter's resulting impoverishment in his account. For as he will summarise imagination's cognitive function in the *Third Critique*, 'in apprehending a given object of the senses, imagination is tied down to a definite form of this object and to this extent does not enjoy free play.'[15]

In the later work imagination will be accorded a more creative capacity, whereby it actively composes forms in a more open and artistic manner, but the question then arises as to whether the cognitive and aesthetic, as well as the two modes of the imagination, can be separated even analytically in the way Kant suggests. Deleuze notes that the imagination 'sometimes dreams rather than schematises'[16] and, although Kant finds no place for the meanderings of fantasy within knowledge, it is such dreaming that constantly pushes reason to speculate beyond its legitimate limits. Are those limits sustainable? Adorno claims that in its obsession with the apriority of synthetic judgements, Kant's epistemology 'tends to expurgate any part of cognition that does not bow to their rules', so that a scientific thinking monopolises truth and leaves cognition a very scant affair in comparison with the experience of living.[17] In this sense it gestures more in the direction of positivism than negativity and exponents of the latter will insist, even demonstrate, that knowledge cannot be insulated from the negativity of a playful imagination and the aesthetic in the way the transcendental method claims.

Moving on now to the understanding itself, Kant tells us that its 'whole power' consists in bringing the synthesis of the manifold, which it derives from intuition via the imagination, to the unity of apperception. Through acts of judgement it synthesises, connects and legislates, although in so doing it 'merely combines and arranges' material, applying to it formal rules, or categories (CPR: B145). It is thus an active imposition of identity and unity upon the particularity and difference of the manifold, which *must* succumb to such organisation but evinces none itself. Understanding's categories are pure concepts which apply *a priori* to all objects, constituting them according to necessary and universal, transcendental, laws and so rendering them intelligible and non-contingent. They comprise the *a priori* foundation of knowledge, which thereby achieves objective validity despite its subjective source (CPR: A97/B130). Understanding, then, is constitutive but automatic; active but uncritical. As Adorno notes, the 'subject is said to have power to shape immediacy insofar as it is autonomous and spontaneous; but to be powerless insofar as the directly given thing flatly exists.'[18] Again, it is condemned to a positivist relation with a phenomenal world to which it grants universal form. It cannot change it (its freedom operates elsewhere) and nor can Kant countenance any suggestion that the categories might themselves change, shifting as experience does.

The understanding's deduction is thus haunted by some of the same difficulties as the imagination's. It is again difficult to insulate its formal properties from the empirical operations of subjectivity, while its powers too seem to be dogmatically presented and exercised rather than critically deduced. As Kant concedes:

> This peculiarity of our understanding, that it can produce *a priori* unity of apperception solely by means of the categories, and only by such and so many, is as little capable of further explanation as why we have just these and no other functions of judgment, or why space and time are the only forms of our possible intuition.
>
> (CPR: B146)

He seems here almost to anticipate Nietzsche's pithy commentary on his faculties. 'Kant asked himself: how are synthetic judgements *a priori possible*? – and what, really, did he answer? *By means of a faculty* ... . But is that an – answer? An explanation? Or is it not rather merely a repetition of the question?'[19]

Within the work of understanding, there is a cognate of negativity: negation features as an act of judgement, a logical act by the judging subject. Kant distinguishes between logical negation indicated by 'not', which refers only to a formal relation between concepts and acts as a negative criterion of truth that says nothing about content (CPR: A60/B84, A574/B602); and transcendental negation, which 'signifies not-being itself'. This latter does refer to content, but only to signify 'a mere want', 'the abrogation of all thinghood'. Kant distinguishes it from the transcendental affirmation which expresses reality and yields the only transcendental ideal of which reason is capable: the thing in itself as completely determined (an unknowable totality). Negations can then for him be 'nothing but limitations', thinkable

21

only as a lack of something positive. It is this distinction between negation and transcendental affirmation that will underlie the division between negative and positive noumena. It is also such negation that guides the critical philosophy as an establishing of reason's limits. But its formal properties align it with an emptiness devoid of content and as such, it is quite at odds with any negativity that might be accorded ontological or discursive generativity.

The ambiguities of the subject and the refutation of idealism

Two related but problematic areas of Kant's presentation now require further consideration. The first concerns the subject which thinks in terms of the categories and the relation between its transcendental and empirical status; the second concerns the object and the internal and external worlds that relate to the subject's own inner and outer senses. Although both raise questions regarding subject–object relations, and there seems to be some (inevitable) confusion in the way Kant finesses them, it is nevertheless important to keep in mind his intention of distinguishing between transcendental and empirical operations here. Thus, on the one hand, he presents a correlation between the transcendental unity of apperception and the possible object of cognition, as a formal unity; on the other, he describes a correspondence between empirical self-consciousness (inner experience of one's existence as determined in time) and the experience of spatially-arranged objects (of outer experience).[20] In other words, subject–object relations are dealt with on two separate levels, the first focusing on the transcendental subject and the second, on the doubts sceptics provoke regarding the actuality of the objects known.

The divided subject

Let us consider the subject first. Unless the self-identical and unified 'I' of apperception were able to give continuity to representations over time, Kant reasons, no objects could endure beyond fragmented and discontinuous images. Unless it endures self-identically itself, the subject cannot know a persistent object: 'the unity which the object makes necessary can be nothing else than the formal unity of consciousness in the synthesis of the manifold of representations ' (CPR: A105). To hold onto its representations in order to subsume them beneath concepts, consciousness must thus be 'unitary', having continuity and memory (CPR: A104–7). It operates in time but is itself atemporal. Indeed it is in the transcendental subject's (ontological, temporal) difference from the space–time of causally-determined nature that its freedom and the possibility of reason lie. It is not a self as such, but an incision, a difference, within the mechanistic regularity of objects; an 'I think' that is a formal condition of experience but itself devoid of all empir-

22

ical particularity. It needs self-awareness in order to identify objects but it does not have self-knowledge; it can be thought but not known. It is a logical fiction engendered by the imperatives of deducing the possibility of knowledge.

Kant accordingly cautions against hypostatising this logical subject in order to advance metaphysical claims about it, in particular as a thinking substance in itself. It is only analytically distinct from the empirical self, which is an object of knowledge for itself in its inner sense, although only in its phenomenal form. Can this analytic distinction be sustained? Allison notes that 'apperception is something more than a transcendental principle or reference point. It is ... "something real" (B419); namely, it is a real mode of self-consciousness. This is the point on which the ontologically oriented interpreters of Kant rightly insist.'[21] Kant's subject – a 'strange empirico-transcendental doublet' as Foucault calls it[22] – seems to waver between a formal foundation for knowledge and a psychological subject with its attendant contingencies.

The subject presented here is then a divided one. Formally it needs self-awareness for knowledge as such to occur, while empirically it achieves knowledge about its own mental states through self-reflection. This distinction yields a series of related dualisms in Kant's thinking: methodologically, the subject has both empirical and transcendental status (whereby it enjoys inner sense and apperception, respectively); regarding its own self-knowledge, it is both phenomenal and noumenal. To be consistent, Kant tries to equate the first terms of these three dualities and to oppose them to the second, where alignment should also occur. The two parts of the self are supposedly distinct yet complementary.[23] However so many ambiguities, confusions and transgressions occur that one must become suspicious about the thinking behind the transcendental subject. Deleuze, for example, charges that

> Kant traces the so-called transcendental structures from the empir-
> ical acts of a psychological consciousness: the transcendental
> synthesis of apprehension is directly induced from an empirical
> apprehension, and so on. In order to hide this all too obvious
> procedure, Kant suppressed this text in the second edition.
> Although it is better hidden, the tracing method, with all its
> 'psychologism', nevertheless subsists.[24]

Once this psychology is allowed, however, it opens the cognitive subject to the sort of disruptions Freud will find intruding between subject and object, such that Kant's orderly transcendental capacity will become riven by negativity: one where desire and fantasy line knowledge, the boundaries between inner and outer become mobile, and non-identity unsettles conceptualisation as well as the thinking self. From this perspective transcendental idealism's initial presupposition, that knowledge is guaranteed but needs its pre-conditions spelling out, is already a dogmatism: critical reason must begin by asking whether knowledge is indeed possible and what knowledge is.

The challenge of scepticism

The second problematic area I identified returns us to Kant's attack on the idealisms that yield scepticism, which I earlier associated with negativity in its throwing the certainties of knowing into doubt. This concerns the empirical relationship between knower and known and is more insistent regarding the status of the object. Now, although Kant's critical philosophy introduces a sceptical attitude *vis-à-vis* metaphysical claims to Truth, he was eager to refute any doubt regarding the truth of knowledge claims about the empirical world. Of course, he recognised the possibility of error as far as specific experiential claims were concerned, but his Copernican Revolution was intended to overcome any uncertainty about the veracity of phenomenal knowledge in its formal structuring. Here he presents a correspondence theory of truth wherein the formal properties of the natural world (which conforms with the account Newtonian science offers of it) coincide with the categories the subject imposes. 'The nominal definition of truth, that it is agreement of knowledge with its object, is assumed as granted' (CPR: A58/B82). Or again: the principles of pure understanding 'are indeed the source of all truth (that is, of the agreement of our knowledge with objects)' (CPR: A237/B296). Here, in other words, Kant wants to seal up phenomenal knowing (the only kind whose legitimacy he accepts) against negativity; against any possible fissure or heterogeneity between knower and known.

This assertion of truth does not however look especially convincing, since it seems to depend upon a circular argument. It is after all hardly surprising that the subject should know objects indubitably, if it has itself constituted them (unless of course the divided self were to fall apart, but this is not a possibility within Kant's horizons). Kant is in fact aware that his resolution might be interpreted as merely tautological, leaving him open to sceptical claims that he has not guaranteed knowledge of real things but only described a circuit of idealistic construction. He thus pauses periodically to engage directly with his putative critics.

The question that immediately springs to mind is this. With what justification can we presuppose that the objects of intuition (which do lie, Kant insists, outside the mind) are amenable, without excess or hiatus, to categorical classification? As far as the thing in itself is concerned, such classification might be wholly alien to it. If its own nature remains unknowable, this must also apply to any presupposition that mind represents it faithfully. If we are not actively sceptical, we must at least remain agnostic. If on the other hand the categories refer only to external *phenomena*, then again there is the problem that mind seems to know only what it has itself constructed, i.e. representations. It appears to be locked within a self-referential, ideal, analytic totality, while the nature of objects' externality remains unclear. In short, the critical philosophy seems itself unable to avoid either dogmatic metaphysics or scepticism here.

I will begin by considering this latter, phenomenal, domain since Kant's aim in the *Critique of Pure Reason* is clearly to limit all epistemological questioning to it. His initial response to the challenge of idealism is accordingly to circumscribe the legitimate sphere of knowledge more precisely by attributing confusion to linguistic ambiguities. Thus Kant acknowledges the ambiguity of the term 'object', which has a twofold sense of thing in itself and appearance (CPR: Bxx), and he distinguishes the transcendental object (unknowable ground of appearances) from empirical objects which are experienced as spatially-arranged and thus as experientially external (CPR: A367–80). Analogously, he distinguishes between his own transcendental idealism, which is also an *empirical realism* (it 'allows to matter, as an appearance, a reality that does not permit of being inferred, but is immediately perceived'), and transcendental realism (which would include metaphysical materialism) which is idealist and dogmatic in assuming objects independent of the senses as 'self-subsistent beings, existing outside us' (CPR: A371). Again, the latter relies on unwarranted ontological claims. Kant goes on to say that we may admit that 'something, which may be (in the transcendental sense) outside us, is the cause of our outer intuitions', but then draws attention to the unavoidable ambiguity attached to the phrase 'outside us', which also involves equivocal senses of the real.

In sum, the material, corporeal things we think of as outside are already representations, but they do have externality as spatially-ordered, as outer appearance, and this is, Kant sets out to prove, 'the real itself', the actual (CPR: A375, 376), even if it is underlain by the transcendental thing (the Real, as later theorists will term it). Given these clarifications, the question nevertheless remains whether the Real is real and in what sense the real is actual.

As we have seen, two competing subject–object distinctions are implicitly at work here, and these are aligned with the clarifications offered above. There is the ontological one of the sceptics, which Kant dismisses as irresolvable but predicated on faulty premises, and the representational one internal to the mind whereby the still life of nature as science conceives it, and the formal powers of the legislating subject, are rendered coincident via the relation between the faculties. In order to claim true knowledge, the empirical mind must nevertheless be assured that the objects it knows, and whose content it grants form, are real, and it must therefore be able to distinguish between real and imagined objects; between outer and inner.

In the second edition of the *Critique of Pure Reason* a more elaborate refutation of idealism is attempted, probably in recognition that the former clarifications alone were insufficiently compelling. Kant now insists that inner experience (empirical self-consciousness), of which he assumes that we (like Descartes) harbour no doubts, relies upon outer reality (spatiality as discerned by outer sense) as its necessary condition. This apparently realist proof is strange in that it reverses the thrust of the rest of the *Critique*, which makes the synthesis of appearances dependent on the unity of the self rather than vice versa (CPR: A123). The crux of Kant's argument involves the difference yet mutual dependence of time and space. The subject is conscious of its existence as being determined in time and thus of change and permanence. However it cannot perceive its own permanence, but depends upon something distinct from it: the spatial enduring of outer things whose coexistence and succession occur in a register against which the self can measure itself. Formal subject–object *correspondence* thus relies upon an empirical subject–object *distinction*, whereby inner sense depends upon outer sense of 'an external thing distinct from all my representations.' It is this distinction that guarantees 'experience not invention, sense not imagination, which inseparably connects this outer something with my inner sense' (CPR: Bxl–xli, B275).

But does it? Even Kant admits that how external existence 'should be possible', he is incapable of explaining further.[25] Ultimately he seems to have taken empirical realism, and the immediate presence of objects to us which it implies, as self-evident. It follows that if the permanence, inertia and otherness of the outer (phenomenal, Newtonian) world were to fall into doubt then so, according to this second version, would the identity and continuity of the transcendental subject. As Christine Battersby remarks, it is essential to Kant's system that matter should be passive and dead since the self depends on distinguishing itself from this changeless substance. The ego knows itself only because it constructs the world as other.[26]

If Kant promises us objectivity, it is not then through proof that our knowledge is verified by some independent external domain, but in the sense that it has objective necessity (since the self-knowledge that all knowing requires cannot be deduced otherwise and since the forms it imposes are *a priori*). If this formal analysis remains unconvincing, Kant implies, this is because we wrongly seek some ontological proof, and this presupposes verification by the object that it cannot, at least within his own terms, grant. From a materialist perspective the difficulty is however that transcendental idealism is incapable of achieving any contact with the objectivity of things without reducing them to thought, other than in that brief and unexplained moment when the senses are affected by something. It cannot conjure up anything with a convincing semblance of actuality or externality, since it has dismissed any possible communication or criterion as illusory. Since it is impossible to acquire merely sensuous knowledge without its conceptualisation, even the sensuous manifold has a quasi-noumenal quality. Yet our 'mode of intuition is dependent upon the existence of the object, and is therefore possible only if the subject's faculty of representation is affected by that object' (CPR: B72). Concepts require content, but the efficacy of the object and the nature or status of knowledge's content still remain ambiguous. Perhaps more light will be shed on this problem by turning to the other aspect of subject–object relations I identified, which concerns things in themselves.

Negativity and noumena

The discussion so far has established Kant's aims in the *First Critique* as twofold: to deduce the conditions that are necessary for (synthetic *a priori*) knowledge and to establish the limits of that knowledge. Together they are intended respectively to refute scepticism and to legislate against the inappropriate knowledge claims of hallucinatory metaphysics. Both rely, as does the critical philosophy as such, upon a distinction between knowable phenomena and unknowable noumena (that is, between appearances we 'really' know and things in themselves we cannot, given our human constitution, ever know). It is this idea of the noumenal that is the most evocative part of the *First Critique* as far as negativity is concerned, since it appears to involve the positing of an outside to reason: an other beyond its boundaries that is inaccessible to sensibility or understanding although not to thought. Indeed (the positing of) this domain bereft of phenomenal quality seems to be a pre-condition of the knowledge that excludes it, sometimes obliging Kant to advance what look like illicit ontological claims and sometimes catching him in the sort of discursive aporias that critical reason is intended to avoid.

In defence of Kant's transcendental idealism it is often suggested that some of the confusion his dichotomy provokes can be deflected by recognising it as two ways of considering the objects of human experience, rather than as two distinct types of entity.[27] While this is helpful in clarifying what seems to have been Kant's intent, however (and he is fairly unequivocal about this regarding what he will call positive noumena (CPR: A255/B311)), it leaves unresolved certain ambiguities and lacunae in the text. The important question from the perspective of negativity is whether these are engendered by the critical enterprise itself in its quest for reason's limits and knowing's guarantee. In considering that enterprise at the beginning of this chapter, I mentioned the problems which the spatial metaphorics of the limit created, and it is Kant's insistence on topographical imagery that conveys a sense of two antithetical realms here. Even if these were only referring to a dual perspective on experiential objects, this would merely locate hiatus within reason rather than on its borders.

In introducing the chapter of the *Critique of Pure Reason* entitled 'The Ground of the Distinction of all Objects in General into Phenomena and Noumena', Kant suddenly leaps into an uncharacteristically lyrical justification for legislating reason's limits, as necessary for sustaining clear boundaries between order and chaos. This shift in style should alert us to a movement within the text into a more speculative and transgressive space: a movement that is in fact consonant with reason's own natural desire as Kant defines it.

Having concluded the account of pure understanding and the 'territory' it has explored, he presents himself as an intrepid cartographer. He has mapped a safe island beyond whose limits lie only storms, fogbanks and icebergs (i.e. wreckage, illusion and hidden danger). We abandon at our peril the dry land he has 'carefully surveyed' and 'measured', putting everything 'in its rightful place'. For this is an island circumscribed by 'unalterable limits'; a 'land of truth' surrounded by a 'wide and stormy ocean' which is in turn the 'native home of illusion' with its mirages of more distant shores (an other knowledge) that 'delude' adventurers (metaphysicians) with empty hopes (CPR: A235–6/B294–5).[28]

This geography then imposes a clear distinction between legitimate and illegitimate domains of knowledge, with the watery wastes of the noumenal off-limits to it. Yet at the same time, and despite Kant's contention that he only defines a realm already 'enclosed by nature itself within unalterable limits', it is not after all possible for him to sustain his insularity. He must venture out into the stormy seas in order to engage with the 'natural and inevitable' imperative of reason constantly to transgress its limits (CPR: A298/B354–5). For the objective character of the subjective faculties encourages the transcendental illusion that they grant us knowledge of things in themselves, with the connection of concepts wrought by understanding wrongly being extended to claims that a fully-determined (metaphysical) totality can be known, and known completely beyond any particular perspective.

> There exists, then, a natural and unavoidable dialectic of pure reason – not one in which a bungler might entangle himself through lack of knowledge, or one which some sophist has artificially invented to confuse thinking people, but one inseparable from human reason, and which, even after its deceptiveness has been exposed, will not cease to play tricks with reason and continually entrap it into momentary aberrations ever and again calling for correction.
>
> (CPR: A298/B354–5)

If the limits of knowledge are objectively fixed, they are thus subjectively fragile; if transcendental reflection is definitive, then critique is an ongoing process; if the limits to reason are natural, so is their transgression. Moreover the ambition of Kant's method is itself limited since on the one hand 'we are not satisfied with the exposition merely of what is true, but likewise demand that account be taken of that which we merely desire to know', while on the other there remains one task to which understanding is unequal: that of establishing its own limits and knowing 'what it is that lies without its own proper sphere' (CPR: A237, 238/B296, 297). In all these senses reason, as well as its own self-critique, is irredeemably charged with negativity; that is, with gaps and desires that carry it beyond what it can legitimately establish. Kant nevertheless casts himself in the heroic role of doing battle with reason's delusions and, to succeed, he must be able to sustain an unambiguous boundary between appearances and things in themselves. When he sets sail it is not as adventurer but as legislator.

Toward the end of the second edition of the Transcendental Analytic, Kant tries to clarify his ideas about noumena by identifying two different senses, negative and positive. In its negative sense, he explains, the noumenon is 'a thing so far as it is *not an object of our sensible intuition*' whereas in its positive sense, it is 'an *object* of a non-sensible intuition' (CPR: B307). The first implies merely an absence whereas the second suggests a presence (albeit an illegitimate, impossible one from the point of view of knowledge). I suggest that they relate within Kant's thinking to two rather different concerns. In the negative case, the noumenon's presentation seems to be no more than an example of the sort of negative judgement that logical negation permits in setting limits. However this gets entangled in Kant's response to metaphysical idealism regarding the underlying cause of phenomena. In the positive case, the noumenon's invocation and denial is integral to his taming of reason's desire and its yearning for the absolute.

Let us take this latter case first, since positive noumena seem to engender less textual problems. These mark the ambitions of speculative thinking for an object of non-sensible intuition whose properties could be known intellectually as they are in their essence without the mediation of the senses; an immediate coincidence of subject and object. They can be thought without contradiction but they cannot be known since they are impossible for us to experience. They imply some radically other mode of communion but Kant is quick to point out that 'we cannot comprehend even the possibility' of it, since pure intellectual intuition forms no part of our faculty of knowledge (CPR: B307). It does oblige him nevertheless to concede the latter's contingency and to acknowledge that it is the faculty's limitations, rather than the definitive absence of positive noumena, that deny access.

> Doubtless, indeed, there are intelligible entities corresponding to the sensible entities; there may also be intelligible entities to which our sensible faculty of intuition has no relation whatsoever; but our concepts of understanding, being mere forms of thought for our sensible intuition, could not in the least apply to them.
>
> (CPR: B308–9)

Since access *is* impossible, knowledge of positive noumena remains an unsupportable ambition and they are reducible to the negative variety. Nevertheless they will reappear elsewhere as legitimate, if hypothetical, regulative ideas deployed by theoretical and practical reason and Kant also speaks affirmatively of their worth in curbing the pretensions of sensibility to omniscience.[29] In this sense, somewhat paradoxically, his thinking can be claimed as supportive of negativity in that, against for example the explicitly negativist Hegel, he refuses totality while acknowledging our desire to think beyond the merely positivist, static self-identity of phenomena and the limits of experience. As Adorno writes: the 'mind thinks what would be beyond it. Such metaphysical experience is the inspiration of Kantian philosophy, once that philosophy is drawn out of the armor of its method.'[30]

It is however the ambiguity that surrounds negative noumena that is more fecund *vis-à-vis* negativity, and it is this variety that the logic of Kant's epistemology must summon yet deny. Here he wants to refer only to a logical deduction: if the senses represent mere appearances, then we infer that these must be appearances of something (effects of some prior cause); a something which is abstracted from all intuition, as a general object X, even though we can know nothing of it once we abstract from its phenomenality (which is why a general ontology which speculates on things in general is ruled out). In the first edition of the *Critique* this negative noumenon appears in the guise of the transcendental object ('we are constrained to think a transcendental object as underlying appearances, though we know nothing of what it is in itself' (CPR: A540)). Here Kant argues that this indeterminate thought of something in general cannot be called a noumenon since he saves the latter term for claims to knowledge about a non-sensible *object* (the positive noumenon of the second edition) (CPR: A253). In the second edition this indeterminate something is, however, summoned as a negative noumenon.

Kant tries to disarm any ontological liveliness this underlying something might possess by insisting upon its merely logical sense. It is inert; 'the domain that lies out beyond the sphere of appearances is for us empty.'

> The concept of a noumenon is thus a merely *limiting concept*, the function of which is to curb the pretensions of sensibility; and it is therefore of only negative employment. At the same time it is no arbitrary invention; it is bound up with the limitation of sensibility, though it cannot affirm anything positive beyond the field of sensibility.
>
> (CPR: A255/B310–11)

If it is indispensable, there is no special object corresponding to it. It can be thought without contradiction but only as 'an unknown something' (CPR: A256/B312). Or again, 'the problematic thought which leaves open a place for them [noumena] serves only, like an empty space, for the limitation of empirical principles, without itself containing or revealing any other object of knowledge beyond the sphere of those principles' (CPR: A259/B315). In this inert sense negation is not negativity since it lacks any generative or disruptive force.

While, however, the positive noumenon turned out to be reducible to the negative variety because it was an empty category, the negative noumenon seems to become enriched with a more affirmative sense as Kant works through the implications of our need to ask about the lineage of phenomena. While the positive noumenon involves a non-sensible but merely intelligible object, the negative noumenon seems to attract both categorial definition and sensible quality. These acquisitions occur due to the discursive imperatives inherent in references to noumena but, also, because of the excursions into ontology that the engagement with scepticism entails. As but the consequence of logical inference and negation, the negative noumenon remains within the subject's judgement and in this sense it enjoys no autonomy as an independent alterity, but is recouped for reason (as both internal to yet outside it). As the underlying cause of appearances, however, it seems to possess an efficacy that both is and is not reducible to the category of causality. As J. McTaggart pointed out, the

> thing-in-itself as conceived by Kant, behind and apart from the phenomena which alone enter into experience, is a contradiction. We cannot, we are told, know what it is, but only that it is. But this is itself an important piece of knowledge relating to the thing. It involves a judgment, and a judgment involves categories, and we are thus forced to surrender the idea that we cannot be aware of the existence of anything which is not subject to the laws governing experience. Moreover, the only reason which can be given for our belief in things-in-themselves is that they are the ground or substratum of our sensuous intuitions. But this is a relation and a relation involves a category.[31]

Although Kant denies us knowledge of things in themselves, this then entails advancing several claims on their behalf. On the one hand, we might extrapolate them negatively in terms of what they categorically lack (space, temporality, substance, causality and so on), thereby advancing propositions about their identity. Here we glimpse a discursive paradox inherent in negation itself. On the other hand, more positive inferences follow once things in themselves are invoked as underlying appearances. This catches Kant in a further paradox. His philosophy must be self-grounding if it is to remain critical, yet in grounding knowledge as such, he is drawn ineluctably both towards illicit ontological allusions and towards the antinomy that the pursuit of totality via antecedent chains of cause and effect induces.

The ambiguity of noumena is then especially apparent when Kant acknowledges that, although we cannot know things in themselves, we must be able to think them, 'otherwise we should be landed in the absurd conclusion that there can be appearance without anything that appears' (CPR: Bxxvi–xxvii). Although he presents this as a logical imperative, it also returns us to the discussion I earlier left incomplete regarding the movement from things to representation. What is it that appears and what is its relation to the appearance it engenders? The implication, which Kant seems to accept, is that the relation must be a causal one. Since causality is a category it applies only to phenomena, yet in order to avoid scepticism or dogmatism, it seems that Kant must critically deduce some efficacy that lies outside the circuit of representation. This surely can neither be of the sort he ascribes to practical reason (free spontaneity, the self-determination of the will), nor merely a regulative idea, since it concerns the availability of things to the senses and thus implies some sort of sense data with material or energetic potency. It may be impossible ever to know definitively or to prove the empirical nature of this force, but it cannot guarantee the circuit of representation or fulfil its logical function unless some non-ideal productivity is ascribed to it. Any means for doing so seems however to rely on forms of representation ('motion', for example, 'is not the effect of this unknown cause, but only the appearance of its influence on our senses' (CPR: A387)). This in fact reinforces Kant's point about the inescapability of representation, yet at the same time some leakage beyond its boundaries is invoked. The spatial imagery of within and without becomes undecidable at this point and the boundary between phenomena and noumena becomes ambiguous and unstable.

Such difficulties are again evident when Kant offers a gloss on his position in the *First Critique*'s sequel, the *Prolegomena*. Defending himself once more against charges of idealism there, he insists that:

> things as objects of our senses existing outside us *are* given, but we know nothing of what they might be in themselves, knowing only their appearances, i.e., the representations which they *cause* in us by *affecting* our senses. Consequently, I grant by all means that there are bodies without us, that is, things which, though quite unknown to us as to what they are in themselves, *we yet know* by the representations which *their influence on our sensibility procures us*, and which we call bodies. This word merely means the appearance of the thing, which is *unknown to us but is not therefore less real*.[32]

Elsewhere in the same work he similarly writes that although the 'object in itself always remains unknown', representations of it are 'given by the object to our sensibility' (*Prolegomena*: 42); that our sensibility is 'in its special way affected by objects which are in themselves unknown to it and totally distinct from those appearances' (*Prolegomena*: 60). Or again, 'we indeed, rightly considering objects of sense as mere appearances, confess thereby that they are based upon a thing in itself, though we know not this thing as it is in itself but only know its appearances, viz., the way in which our senses are affected by this unknown something.' By accepting phenomenal limits, the understanding 'grants also the existence of things in themselves' and thus, too, their representation as the 'basis of appearances'. 'Our critical deduction by no means excludes things of that sort (*noumena*)' but it does limit the Aesthetic to experience, because otherwise everything would be an appearance (*Prolegomena*: 57).

The implication of such claims is that the possibility of cognition does involve some causal passage between the transcendental object and subject, not merely an internal relation between outer and inner sense. While I agree with Allison that Kant's transcendental concern lies with the non-empirical ground of appearances, and that this would ideally render unnecessary any metaphysical claims about their empirical origin, my point is that Kant cannot sustain this prohibition. The necessity of responding to sceptical idealists; of sustaining his claims to realism; of dealing with the question of appearances' grounding and the status of the contents of knowledge, all drive him beyond the limits that his method may legitimately work within. Underlying such transgression is still the inability of transcendental idealism to link subjects and objects successfully, so that while their hiatus was reproduced internally, between the faculties, it also remains unresolved at that point of the rational subject's incision within an objective world. What remains occult is the conditions of possibility that lie on the interface between things and their appearance. Were the body to be intruded as a 'third term' that mediated via an active–passive, aesthetic process here, then some transposition or becoming might be proposed. But this is to anticipate a dialectical resolution that is unavailable to Kant.

Nevertheless, since it is the senses which are affected first, does this not suggest that things in themselves must possess some efficacy that is material and that the body might play a part in the constitutive activity (of form giving) that Kant saves for understanding? Perhaps then there is a non-representational 'knowing' that Kant's sensibility/understanding configuration denies, where knowledge is more fragile and opaque than the transcendental method allows. In the long quote from the *Prolegomena* cited above, for example, he refers to (theoretically) unknowable bodies 'we yet know' because we have immediate experience of them via sensibility. Unlike positive noumena, which are intellectual ideas unknowable to sensibility, these negative noumena might then be available to the senses but not (yet) to understanding. In other words, the faculties would be more than just analytically distinct. Where Kant begins with the (dogmatic) premise that true knowledge and objective identity exist, indeed correspond, and then enquires about their necessary conditions, the rift between things in themselves and appearances might then prompt a reverse approach which begins by asking whether such knowledge is indeed possible and about the generativity of the object. Such will be the phenomenological project: 'a study of the advent of being to consciousness, instead of presuming its possibility in advance.'[33]

Hiatus emerges within Kant's text because the noumenal is deduced by him as a solution to several different concerns: to limit knowledge (in order both to exile speculative metaphysics from knowledge claims *and* to overcome the limits on truth claims that are tied to the natural, mechanical world, so that room is left for faith) and to ground it. The postulation of limits that would exile negativity simultaneously engenders it, while acknowledgement of the thing in itself's productivity both insists on its necessity and compromises its unknowability by representing it via categories which render it phenomenal. It remains unclear whether Kant believes that noumena (*qua* an indeterminate something, the Real) exist but are unknowable, or do not exist but must be negatively summoned by the logic of a philosophy of limits.

Yet I think he is unavoidably ambivalent here, since the necessity of positing noumena requires some belief in their independent existence (otherwise there would be, as Nietzsche points out and Kant fears, only one world of appearances), while it is we who infer the thing in itself, from within our representational realm. To pursue the question explicitly would involve the sort of regressive analysis and antinomy that Kant is eager to avoid, and there is a genuine representational problem that occurs whenever negativity is invoked, which subsequent adventurers will have to finesse. Because Kant is not among them, however, the ambiguities and contradictions that negativity engenders remain as awkward lacunae in the text which he struggles in vain to expurgate via intermittent exercises in clarification. It is likely however that the noumenon's status is genuinely undecidable within the terms of the epistemological problematic as Kant presents it. He must remain ambiguous as to whether things in themselves have real efficacy we experience virtually, or remain necessary inferences (that is, whether they are positive or negative), because while the transcendental and ontological become confused at this point, Kant's method relies on their separation.

Ontology and transcendentalism become entangled because the latter cannot be self-grounding, and should not even seek grounds, yet if it does not it remains uncritical and dogmatic. Deleuze refers here to the essential ambiguity of Kant's project, drawn on the one hand towards the representation it grounds and on the other, towards a beyond: 'as though it vacillated between a fall into the grounded and an engulfment in a groundlessness [*sans fond*]' that resists all forms and is unrepresentable.[34] Of course Kant tries to foreclose all such concerns as a legacy of pre-critical thinking (CPR: A277/B333, A393)[35], but the crucial questions are still whether the 'not' has ontological or merely logical standing and whether it is inert or generative. In this sense it is important to mark a distinction between the noumenon as a product of logical negation (as limit, inert, empty space, a region denied), which Kant would like to sustain (although even this introduces a dissonant productivity into his thinking), and the noumenal as negativity (an other place – a stormy sea – of material fragments and indigenous forces with a non-categorical, heterogeneous generativity of its own), which he wants to resist. Whether it is inert noumena, the orderly empirical realm of phenomena, the merely mechanical operations of imagination and understanding, or the formal universalism of the categories, there is no room in Kantian knowledge for the enchanted, the non-rational or the non-identical. His explicit target is anyway positive phenomena and it is to these metaphysical creations that he is most eager to deny causal power.

Totality and disintegration

In adumbrating the challenge to truth posed by sceptical idealisms, I suggested earlier that this might occur on two levels: one of phenomenal knowing, discussed above, and one that concerns broader questions about the adequacy of phenomenal knowledge to things in themselves. The final part of this chapter must now address the latter. Kant admits that the entire critical edifice would become 'empty and useless' were we to accept that appearances are 'but a confused representation of things' (CPR: A43/B60). For knowledge would then lack any stability, criteria or sustainable limits. As he concedes, that 'nature should direct itself according to our subjective ground of apperception, and should indeed depend upon it in respect of its conformity to law, sounds very strange and absurd' (CPR: A113–14). But his response is predictably transcendental: as 'merely an aggregate of appearances, so many representations of the mind', we can find only a nature that is the possible object of experience and this can be discovered nowhere but in the unity of apperception as formally deduced. To seek an apparently more realist reply would be to return once more to speculative metaphysics and to pursue an impossible guarantee that knowledge corresponds with things in themselves.

Kant must nevertheless have felt dissatisfied with this response since he returned to it in his *Critique of Judgement*: a third critique summoned because the dualisms that had proliferated within and between the first two (in particular regarding cognition versus desire and nature versus freedom) threatened to pull the critical edifice apart. While still insisting on the *a priori* lawfulness of appearances which the categories yield, he acknowledges that the understanding has no guarantee that these can in turn be legitimately subsumed under the higher empirical laws that render nature an interconnected system rather than simply an aggregate. For it would never be possible to unify these empirical laws themselves under a common principle, were it the case (which is perfectly possible, so far as the understanding can tell *a priori*) that the variety and dissimilarity of these laws, and also of the corresponding natural forms, were infinite and that we were confronted by a crude, chaotic aggregate totally devoid of system, though we had to presuppose a system in accordance with transcendental laws.[36]

Even if phenomenal knowledge remains true, it may be trivial or menaced; a small and local ordering in a sea of heterogeneity. Again, this provokes the sceptical problem that transcendentalism was supposed to suppress regarding the relation between subjective classification and the Real. Because knowing for Kant is not a *process* of verification, it is either guaranteed by the deductive proofs regarding the faculties and their self-sufficiency, or it becomes vulnerable to disintegration if any efficacy or resistance is suspected of things in themselves (or, indeed, of phenomena). As we have seen, he tries to rule out such efficacy by insisting upon noumenal (and phenomenal) inertia, although it insinuates itself once he ascribes causal powers to the thing in itself. Now he tackles the possibility of a resistance or incommensurability of the non-subjective domain via a series of speculative assumptions, regulative ideas and 'as ifs'.

> ... it is a subjectively necessary, transcendental *presupposition* that this dismaying unlimited diversity of empirical laws and this heterogeneity of natural forms does not belong to nature; that, instead, nature is fitted for experience as an empirical system through the affinity of particular laws under more general ones.[37]

He cannot demonstrate that nature is in itself lawful, but we must assume that knowledge is in more than a merely fortuitous or imaginative correspondence with it. That nature comprises a totality is a necessary principle of reason for Kant, although one which is heuristic rather than explanatory. For 'were we not entitled to assume this ... all reflection would be carried on at random and blindly, and as a result with no sound expectation of its agreement with nature.'[38] This seems to concede the sort of species pragmatism that Nietzsche will proclaim, but not to guarantee it against the kind of flux he will associate with Life.

What the *Third Critique* has however added is the necessity for aesthetic judgements that find universals for particulars, thus organising the latter into forms which do not pre-exist them and which are applied '*artistically*' rather than 'mechanically, like a tool'.[39] Kant suggests that this forming relies on an inner harmony, or pre-conceptual logic, of parts, whose coming together yields a sense of beauty and with it, a pleasurable feeling that

nature and our mental capacities must be attuned if the spontaneous organising of nature's parts resonates so well with our predilection for form. We
feel as if nature must have been devised according to some plan or purpose.
'Purposiveness is conformity to law on the part of that which is itself contingent.'[40] We thus experience the satisfaction of desire: that subject and
object, sensibility and understanding, are in harmony.

While the actuality of this harmony remains hypothetical (it is only felt
not known) the production of identity, and the way particulars are organised into coherent forms in aesthetic judgements, does suggest a more
creative and unpredictable process than the deductions of the *First Critique*
had accorded knowledge; one more aligned with negativity than with positivism because more open and contingent than necessary. Now reason is at
the service of the imagination and laws are discovered or invented. They are
not imposed upon nature but derived from it by meeting it half way in a
manner more contemplative than mastering, where subject and object meet.
Of course, Kant still insists on maintaining a strict boundary between cognitive and aesthetic judgements, yet knowledge is itself now recognised as
depending upon activities that generate assumptions about the structures of
the Real. 'Under no circumstances can a principle like this be posted to the
account of experience, because only under this assumption is it possible to
order experience in a systematic fashion.'[41] Yet might the categories themselves – and *a fortiori* regulative ideas – not be the *outcome* of such aesthetic
practices? Nietzsche will certainly suggest as much when he writes that
'among the powerful it is the greatest artists in abstraction who created the
categories'.[42]

Two subversive possibilities emerge within the critical philosophy at this
stage, both of which adventurers of negativity will pursue. The first arises
with the implication that knowledge might itself emerge in the more
aesthetic manner the *Third Critique* describes, such that the
cognitive/aesthetic boundary is unsustainable. This opens reason to negativity without by any means rendering it impossible. Indeed it is this route
that dialectical phenomenology and critical theory will take. Then subjects
will no longer be imprisoned in their own categories which they are destined
endlessly, monotonously, to repeat, but will engage with an objective domain
(the only, phenomenal, domain) where such engagement dynamically
produces both subject and object without dogmatically presupposing them.
As Merleau-Ponty will write:

> We have the experience of a world, not understood as a system of
> relations which wholly determine each event, but as an open totality
> the synthesis of which is inexhaustible. We have the experience of
> an *I* not in the sense of an absolute subjectivity, but indivisibly
> demolished and remade by the course of time. The unity of either
> the subject or the object is not a real unity, but a presumptive unity

on the horizon of experience. We must rediscover, as anterior to the ideas of subject and object, the fact of my subjectivity and the nascent object, that primordial layer at which both things and ideas come into being.[43]

Adorno will advance somewhat similar arguments, rejecting Kant's account of the object as a 'web of subjective forms cast over the unqualified something.'[44] For without the possibility of some more reciprocal relation between subjectivity and its material world, it is difficult to see how free subjects might act historically or politically to realise their freedom in other than a highly abstract, formal sense.

The second route concerns a possible incommensurability of knowledge with the Real/real. This is illustrated arrestingly in Sartre's *Nausea*, where the in-itself as he defines it (*en-soi*) forces the novel's main character, Roquentin, to recognise the arbitrary nature of his categorising powers (*pour-soi*) and to experience the world's absurdity.

> *Superfluous*: that was the only connection I could establish between those trees, those gates, those pebbles. It was in vain that I tried to *count* the chestnut trees, to *situate* the Vallada, to compare their height with the height of the plane trees: each of them escaped from the relationship in which I tried to enclose it, isolated itself, overflowed. I was aware of the arbitrary nature of those relationships, which I insisted on maintaining in order to delay the collapse of the human world of measures, of quantities, of bearings; they no longer had any grip on things.[45]

This nauseating annihilation of classification is experienced as the sheer, stubborn *positivity*[46] of things: the relentless and excessive plenitude of existence, 'gumming everywhere up, all thick, a jelly',[47] as opposed to the negativity of the for-itself (the consciousness that withdraws from and questions being).

The threat of a radical heterogeneity is also posed by Deleuze in his commentary on Kant.

> Now, let us suppose that phenomena were subject to the unity of synthesis from a formal point of view, but that in their content they showed radical diversity: once again the understanding would no longer have the opportunity to exercise its power (this time, the material opportunity) ... . It is therefore necessary not only that phenomena should be subject to the categories from the point of view of form, but also that their content correspond to, or symbolize, the Ideas of reason. At this level a harmony, a finality, is reintroduced. *But* here it is clear that the harmony between

38

the content of phenomena and the Ideas of reason is simply postulated.[48]

If reason presupposes a systemic harmony of nature, this indeterminate accord is derived only by analogy with the objects of experience, which Kant has presented as intrinsically inert. While the latter's injunction against speculative or aesthetic incursions within knowledge seems too positivist, then, the regulative metaphysic of a harmonious totality seems too closed and dogmatic.

For all these critics, the distinction between noumena and phenomena (the illusion of worlds-behind-the-scene, as Nietzsche puts it) will be untenable. The culprit here is to a large extent Kant's insistence on the temporal sequence of cause–effect relations (and it was precisely his anxiety over Hume's scepticism on just this point that had awoken him from his dogmatic slumbers), which refuses the possibility of effects without prior causes and thus obliges him to posit the efficacy of negative noumena. (As Sartre will write, following Nietzsche: 'Force, for example, is not a metaphysical conatus of an unknown kind which hides behind its effects … ; it is the totality of these effects … . [N]o action indicates anything which is *behind itself*; it indicates only itself and the total series.'[49]) Once an unknowable alterity is posited by Kant as the cause of appearances, it acquires discursive efficacy while implying ontological generativity. It thereby produces the spectre of reason's contingency or even gratuitousness at the very moment when he is trying to rule out such speculation by legislating the limits of reason. He provokes the very negativity he wants to negate.

But even at the phenomenal level, is Kant warranted in assuming that nature operates 'as if' it were systemic (indeed teleological), or is this the particular metaphysics of the deist and Newtonian; of the classical mind?[50] Can he avoid making illicit ontological claims here? Is his initial presupposition that knowledge *is* possible rather than menaced not a pre-critical one, as the quote from Deleuze suggests? It is to this disintegration of any systemic foundation and to the resulting contingency of classification – and hence the precariousness of identity – that adventures in negativity will increasingly point.

For if reality might plausibly be discerned as (un)structured, a negativity such as for example Nietzsche summarises as will to power (as I will explain in chapter 3), and as generative, hylomorphic rather than inert, then reality would remain immune to universal categorisation or objective knowledge. This is not because it would be beyond (sensuous) experience, but because its fluidity would test the stability and separateness of conceptualisation. It would challenge Kant's claim that it is mind which imposes all form. Then reason might, as Kant says of the sublime, look 'out into the infinite which is for it an abyss.'[51] It would leave room not for faith but for epistemic humility as the legacy of critical reasoning. For self-formative phenomena would also de-centre the transcendental subject and invite a more interrogative stance.

Of reason itself one would then need to ask: what is the secret of its genesis and ambition? Such a genealogy of critical reason must refigure its transcendental status. For if the (noumenal–)phenomenal domain is already active, efficacious but heterogeneous, then Kant possesses no legislative power to proscribe its invasion. The realms of appearance and of things in themselves would indeed collapse into a single reality where the forms and categories of knowledge remain contingent and provisional, promiscuously sensuous and intellectual, as adventurers in negativity will contend. The erection of various limits, and the separations or 'as ifs' on which they rely, would then amount to an active (yet vain) constraint on knowledge and not merely its transcendental clarification.

Conclusion: critical reason and negativity

In the foregoing discussion I have presented Kant as an ambiguous figure as far as negativity is concerned, while I have also invoked a variety of negativities which I suggested he both excludes and engenders. While it is impossible to define negativity, and anyway inappropriate at this stage of the book, I will conclude by bringing together some of its (dis)appearances as alluded to or elicited above.

I began by suggesting that critical reason is itself an example of negativity *qua* process of interrogating rationally-unjustifiable authority, whether philosophical or political. This is the radical legacy of enlightenment which helps define modernity and with which subsequent adventurers in negativity will usually associate themselves.[52] Within Kant's undertaking, however, I suggested a range of negativities that arrive as unwelcome guests, raising the question of whether it is the critical project that itself generates the negativity it must try to expurgate, or whether this irrupts from independent domains Kant tries unsuccessfully to excise. The idea of the limit was especially provocative here, since it yielded a metaphorical topography of spaces that are both off-limits and irresistible to reason, as well as productive of an undecidability that I found especially fecund in Kant's presentation of negative noumena. Here it became unclear whether the unknowable had merely logical and inert, or ontological and efficacious, status. Only in the latter guise would it anticipate and exhibit negativity, as opposed to its highly attenuated form of mere negation (this distinction will become clearer in subsequent chapters). I suggested that such ambiguity was irresolvable given the implicit subject–object dualism that enframes the transcendental method and which disrupts it on various levels, especially where it insists on its own insulation from empirical, psychological or ontological concerns.

In setting limits to reason, I argued, Kant endeavours to guarantee truth and to reject any doubts about knowledge's correspondence with (phenomenal) objects. However while I expressed some scepticism as to his success here, I also suggested that the very attempt forced Kant into a textual productivity in excess of the formalities of his method: one evident in the proliferation of editions, clarifications, conceptual innovations and metaphors. Here is another unwelcome guest: a discursive negativity that nevertheless enriches the *Critiques* even as it disturbs their logic. This generative negativity, like the implications of efficacy that are implied by Kant's concession of noumenal causality, are then to be contrasted with the logic of negative judgements that understanding carries out and to whose inert formality Kant would like to limit both negative noumena and the critical definition of limits itself.

At this level of immanent critique, I invoked irruptions of negativity in Kant's writing via a series of nouns, adjectives and metaphors: gaps, hiatus, lacunae, discontinuities, undecidables, confusions, ambiguities, inconsistencies, transgressions, contradictions, antinomies, unknowables. Negatively, these identify lacks in the text but, positively, they allude to productive gaps that Kant tried to fill, yielding the textual productivity mentioned above. These are the points where proofs fail and deduction stops; where occult processes are invoked; where dualities refuse to be reunited and where the internal unity of the transcendental method leaks into the contingent, empirical domain it has bracketed. The question raised here then was whether the epistemic conditions of knowledge can be deduced independently of empirical, psychological or ontological assumptions, any of which might reintroduce contingency or dogmatism. I suggested not, since the relationship between the transcendental and the empirical to some extent replicates that between subject and object, only now on a meta-critical level. Ambiguity or transgression of methodological boundaries seemed especially evident, in fact, where these two axes of knowledge were under discussion. Thus the Kantian subject is a divided self whose boundaries seem inherently unstable, while the reality of objects and the denial of any co-constitutive role for them in generating knowledge, seemed unsustainable. Negativity thereby invaded subject, object, and the subject–object relation (both internally, *vis-à-vis* the faculties and externally *vis-à-vis* the mind-in-nature).

Kant's presentation here is interwoven with the rejection of speculative metaphysics and idealist scepticisms, which critical reason is to achieve. Although these had no more appealed explicitly to negativity than Kant does, they are aligned, although equivocally, with it. Thus I associated the latter with negativity in that it injects doubt and suspicion, a certain incredulity and undecidability, into the certainties of knowledge and presence of objects even while, as Kant shows, it is a dogmatic metaphysics that grounds such an attitude. As far as speculative metaphysics is concerned, it too is dogmatic in so far as it exemplifies reason's desire for the absolute and proclaims itself to know the Truth. Yet on the other hand, it does preserve that desire for a speculative thinking beyond the monotonous mechanics of knowing and analytics of logic, thereby sustaining reason's openness to desire, imagination and the unknown.

I then suggested that Kant's own thinking is inspired by an analogous ambivalence. His account of knowledge is positivist in that it merely endorses the given, such that its spontaneity in imposing form exhausts itself in uncritical impotence. If practical reason retrieves its freedom, it is only in a domain that is as severed from the objective world as the subjective faculties are themselves. Yet on the other hand the deduction of knowledge's limits refused it omniscience, thereby sustaining a non-identity whose liveliness in generating and destroying concepts will be synonymous with a negative dialectics. Similarly, the later presentation of aesthetic judgements suggested a more reciprocal, creative knowing, whose importance for the possibility of knowledge and for its regulative ideas, perhaps for knowing itself, also anticipates a more negativist epistemic in the space between subject and object.

In yet another reversal, however, Kant's own regulative ideas reinforced the sense in which reason's desire is, according to him, for totality, absolute knowledge. While he never insists that the latter actually corresponds to a fully-determinate system in itself, the orientation of his thinking is towards unity and identity; an overall design, purpose and lawfulness which are exemplified in his 'as ifs'. These reflect Kant's claim that it is natural for reason to think in such terms: to claim a totalising, if hypothetical, metaphysics as a complement to the scientific knowledge of a mechanistic world.

Future adventurers in negativity will purposefully set out for the wilds Kant put out of bounds and will celebrate the transcendence or transgression of the boundaries he instantiated. In many cases they will turn to the object as a source of inspiration.[53] But these adventures, too, will be presented as integral to the critical journey Kant embarked upon. Negatively, critique will be turned against the limits of Kant's own thinking but more affirmatively, his successors will set sail for the dark, supplementary places where excess, desire and heterogeneity refuse yet summon a knowledge whose own conditions and possibility will be put into question. They will struggle to expand the limits of representation while insisting on its limits and in so doing they will enter into, and perform, the paradoxes and aporias of negativity. Thus Deleuze will insist: 'We write only at the borders of our knowledge, at the border which separates our knowledge from our ignorance and transforms the one into the other.'[54] But if they try to resolve the otherness beyond those borders into a reason without limits, as Hegel seems to, then they will again find themselves accused of denying negativity.

2

HEGEL AND HIS CRITICS

Dialectics and difference

It is Hegel's dialectic that introduces negativity explicitly into modern thought and it is to his work that its provocateurs must always return, either to lament his failure to remain faithful to the negativity he discerned or to read him against the grain in order to retrieve it.[1] The dilemma that Hegel poses for negativity is already apparent in his response to Kant. On the one hand, he does away with the distinction between phenomena and unknowable things in themselves and thus with the limits of reason. He points out that their very distinction relies on the category of negation. Knowledge now appears over time via a reciprocity between, which is also a production of, subject and object. Negativity migrates out of the off-limits inertia of noumena and into the dynamics of becoming, wherein its productivity yields both a phenomenology and a logic. Kant's spatial metaphors yield to temporal ones. Yet on the other hand, this process seems itself to culminate in the elimination of all non-identity, since dialectics is a becoming of reason and, when it is realised, movement apparently ceases, otherness is recouped and negativity transcended. As Hegel writes: 'The sealed essence of the universe has no power that could withstand the spirit of knowledge; it is compelled to open itself and to lay out its riches and its depths and offer them for its enjoyment.'[2]

Two pivotal and related questions arise regarding dialectical negativity. One concerns its ontological and historical status: what becomes and what it becomes. The other involves the process itself and concerns the rhythms of its generativity. Broadly speaking, the first question has arisen for those who would try to sustain dialectics as a critical method and mode of political practice. Their interest has lain, following Marx, in rendering negativity historical and material. Poststructuralists have however rejected dialectics itself as inherently inimical to the negative, arguing that the very mode of becoming it entails – via the negation of the negation, the synthetic resolution of binary contradictions, and a teleological trajectory towards totality – is too rationalistic in comparison with the more excessive productivity and multiplicitous antagonisms they invoke.[3] They are thus more concerned with the second question and find inspiration in Nietzsche rather than Marx. Whether their concern lies with materiality or alterity, however, all these thinkers recognise the necessity of returning to Hegel in order to re-appraise, or mark their departure from, his thinking about the negative.

While all agree that Hegel both glimpsed and compromised negativity, the crucial question for his successors is then at what point his infidelity occurred and whether it is fatal to dialectics as such. His critics also agree that the challenge is to resist the totalising of reason and the conceptual mastery of subjects over objects, or of identity over difference, without either abandoning the means of critical intervention or rendering non-reason inert and off-limits. In this sense their struggle is not just against Hegel's errors (the hubris of the Absolute) but also against what they acknowledge as his truth: the recognition that reason does strive towards omniscience and that by approaching negativity or otherness discursively, they participate in and confirm that process even as they refuse it. Adorno catches this conundrum well when he defines philosophy's struggle as 'an effort to express things one cannot speak about, to help express the noniden-tical despite the fact that expressing it identifies it at the same time.'[4] To oppose Hegel, moreover, seems to proffer the very negation that confirms the dialectical process he describes.[5]

The problem is not only philosophical but also political. For Hegel, objective spirit culminates in the modern, constitutional state. It marks the zenith of ethical life but also incorporates two other moments necessary to that life: the patriarchal family and the competitive individualism of the bourgeois economy. Together these constitute the modernity which for Hegel marks the end of history. Since Marx, this history has been perceived by its antagonists as prematurely foreclosed, since a number of contradic-tions (between women and men, rich and poor, rulers and ruled, abstract freedom and material existence) remained unresolved. Subsequent critics have however argued both that Hegel (and Marx) was wrong in envisaging the completability of history as such, not just in the identification of its specific terminus, and that he was unwittingly right in expressing moder-nity's halting of the dialectic and silencing of the negative, even though it has failed to actualise ethical life, freedom or reason, or to overcome the contradictions and alienation that had seemed to guarantee radical progress prior to history's resolution. Releasing and practising the negative, as a crit-ical and social force that would shatter this premature closure, thus becomes imperative for a radical politics as well as for a critical philosophy. Despite his limitations, Hegel bequeaths a critical method that asks about the ratio-nality of the real as opposed to positivistically recording or endorsing the given.

Hegelian dialectics

The rhythms of negativity

In considering Hegelian negativity, I will vacillate between presenting him as a philosopher of identity and re-appraising him as a philosopher of difference. This oscillation actually replicates what I will argue is the undecidability inherent in Hegel's own thinking and in the dialectic itself. It is consonant with Adorno's definition of his work as 'a philosophy of identity stretched to the breaking point.'[6]

Dialectical negativity is for Hegel both a process of becoming and an explanation, which is also an exemplification, of the internal dynamism of that process. It delineates both a choreography and a generative force. It describes both the rhythms of becoming and their ontology, which are in turn inscribed within Hegel's own writing. He uses metaphors of motility and vitality to convey this dynamism of the dialectical process whose impetus is attributed to both logic and life. Hegel speaks of the 'inner self-movement of the content'; the concept's 'immanent process' or 'rhythm' and its 'moving principle'. But he also invokes a 'living principle' and states his ambition to capture the 'rhythm of the organic whole' by articulating 'matter's very soul putting forth its branches and fruit organically'.[7] An analogy with the life cycle is expressed, for example, in the Preface to the *Phenomenology* where Hegel invokes the plant's evolution from bud to fruit, noting that its stages are not merely differentiated and successive since

> the ceaseless activity of their own inherent nature makes them at the same time moments of an organic unity, where they not merely do not contradict one another, but where one is as necessary as the other; and this equal necessity of all moments constitutes alone and thereby the life of the whole.
>
> (Ph: 68)

It is, however, in his *Science of Logic* that the purest rendition of negativity appears. A variety of terms indicative of the negative is to be found there. Nothing, the logical and ontological equivalent of being, is deduced in its opening pages. Further mediations are accomplished via a process of determinate negation (the 'central nerve of the dialectic as a method' according to Adorno[8]), which evolves into the more precise and affirmative negation of the negation ('the master structure of the category of the dialectic' according to Althusser[9]) and the reflective categories of essence ('absolute negativity') and contradiction. Together these senses of negativity are captured within Hegel's account and application of the dialectic itself: the movement of negativity whose labour lends a common choreography, and indeed a single itinerary, to both thought and being, thereby rendering speculative philosophy, ontology, logic and epistemology more or less equivalent.

The *Logic* begins with pure being, which is wholly abstract and indeterminate; simple 'is-ness' without content or predicates. It is thus logically prior to all else. It is (like the sense–certainty with which the *Phenomenology* begins) illusorily and unsustainably immediate: 'it has no diversity within itself nor any with a reference outwards' (Logic: 82). It is empty. In other words, it is nothing and nothing, or non-being, is thereby derived. Nothing is not itself an interesting category for Hegel inasmuch as it is, like being, a vacuous absence of all determination. It is in no sense an Other, perhaps a radical and heterogeneous alterity with a counter-logic or rhythm of its own, such as I suggested might disturb the inertia of Kantian noumena. As far as negativity is concerned, it is the logical relationship between being and nothing that is dynamic and interesting for Hegel, not the abstractness of nothing *per se*.

On the one hand, being and nothing are the same. They are equally indeterminate. But on the other, they are absolutely distinct: nothing is the negation of being, the 'not'. Yet paradoxically as soon as we think it, it 'is' (precisely Kant's problem with the noumenon and indeed the aporia of negativity itself). Thought tries to hold onto this contradiction and to resolve it, resulting in a perpetual oscillation whereby the unity of being and nothing yields an identity of identity and non-identity. In thinking both, each 'vanishes into its opposite' (Logic: 83). This process is then the paradigm of all further developments and this first, albeit abstract, negation will remain immanent within them. They will be 'only more specific and richer definitions of it' (Logic: 74). Indeed Hegel insists that it 'would not be difficult to demonstrate this unity of being and nothing in every example, in *every* actual thing or thought … nowhere in heaven or on earth is there anything which does not contain within itself both being and nothing' (Logic: 84f).

Between being and nothing in their unstable relationship, there is a zone of transition. As nothing moves towards being it comes to be; as being dissolves into nothing it ceases to be. This reversible process yields a third moment, of becoming, which contains its negative within it and something both is and is not. Becoming, the (logical rather than temporal) transition of being and nothing, is a 'movement' wherein they are distinguished but by a difference that immediately resolves itself. Thus we arrive at the first *Aufhebung* (sublation, *relève*[10]), whereby the original moment and its antithesis are negated–transcended–preserved in a higher, synthetic form which both sustains and resolves the opposition. What Hegel demonstrates here is thus the way in which oppositions are mobile, because of their internal relationship of positive and negative, and resolvable in so far as dialectical logic permits a both/and yet eschews its instability. This process 'can only be stated as an *unrest* of *incompatibles*, as a *movement*' (Logic: 91). As Stace

writes, to 'the eye of reason, ... the categories are seen to be alive with movement, to be fluid, to break up and flow into each other'.[11]

In arriving at the category of becoming, Hegel has derived a more determinate form of being and this allows him to move on from the merely
abstract negation posed by nothing to the more specific process of negation
that is involved in determining content (equivalent to perception in the
Phenomenology). Determinate being has specificity that results from its
particular qualities. However this specification occurs only in so far as it is
differentiated from what it is not. It excludes qualities it does not possess: it
is what it is only through its relationship with others. Nothing determinate
exists independently. Identity is thus established through difference, where it
is negation (to not-be other) that is determination. Determinate negation is
specifically dialectical and is to be distinguished from abstract negation,
which suggests an unproductive opposition: annihilation, nihilism, death.
The former is immanent and thus specific to the particular identity it
negates and transfigures. Thus in the matrix A/non-A, the opposition is
specific to a particular A rather than just random not-ness. It is contextual
and delimited, part of an orderly process of synthesis whereby identities
preserve their negations within themselves. This is why the dialectical
thinking that emulates this process is a *critical* reason, engaged and
hermeneutically feasible in its identification of the contradictions and potentialities which drive provisional unities towards disintegration and
self-overcoming according to their internal logic.

In this process, positive and negative (identity and difference) are interwoven: a thing is affirmed as what it is through denial of what it is not. It is
articulated rather than defined; it is not simply given but moves towards its
potential as its relationships expand. That which it negates becomes an integral part of its identity. The other is thus other and not-other; the thing is
self and not-self. In the negation of the negation, the alterity of the other is
taken into the thing as part of its relational identity for-itself. Identity
thereby emerges as a complex and dynamic unity; a differentiated, mediated
phenomenon contingent upon negativity. It is true that the process has its
sadistic aspects, since the negation of the negation cancels otherness by
taking the other into the self (as in Freud's oral phase), while the other is
located only *as* the other of the self rather than possessing genuine alterity.[12]
This is evident in the *Phenomenology*, where recognition is sought through
life and death struggle, and in the *Logic* to the extent that difference is itself
understood (as Deleuze charges) merely as a means for engendering
identity.[13] Yet the process does bring negativity into the heart of identity,
denying the latter any simple and unmediated unity or closure. For the negation of the negation is not simple destruction or colonisation but preserves a
thing in process, whereby it responds to its others through an internalisation
of them that enriches and synthesises (both). This is its affirmative, but
not positivist, moment. It performs the work of Eros, provided there

is reciprocity between terms (ultimately only one autonomous self-consciousness can adequately recognise another (Ph: 229ff))[14] and it overcomes the one-sidedness of partial resolutions or prematurely closed identities (hence the master–slave dialectic).

In the objective world of the first part of the *Logic*, the process of self-mediation prefigures subjectivity and reveals the object always pushing beyond its limits and towards its potential. In Nietzsche's terms, this might be described as its will to power; its self-overcoming and internal restlessness. Negation is not for Hegel simply an unending play of differences or domination, however, but a movement towards actualisation, where each negation results in something more inclusive and affirmative and the earlier identity is transcended. Negation is the principle of systemic integration, not the subversion of system. In this sense the syntax of dialectical forming and de-forming is unlike the genealogy of Nietzschean will to power. The patterning of negativity in its creative–destructive ferment is different.

The discussion of negation brings the *Logic* to the end of the section on Being and into a second phase, of Essence, where reflective determination occurs. That is, being is no longer immediate but turns back upon itself reflexively, such that the relations implicit within it are now rendered explicit. The previous logic recurs then, but repeats the rhythms of negativity already adumbrated, on a higher level. There are nevertheless two new concepts which have significant implications for Hegel's presentation of negativity. One concerns essence itself and the other, the category of contradiction.

Essence, which stands between Being and the Notion according to the tripartite structure of the *Logic*, has implications for the status of negativity since it is essence that is generally accepted as indicative of foundationalist (essentialist) thinking and it indeed retains this sense in Hegelian philosophy according to many of its critics. Stace, for example, asserts that essence 'is a definition of the Absolute. The Absolute is the essence of the world. It is veiled being that lies behind the world as its unseen source.' As such, he adds, it is the underlying unity, or substratum, which merely manifests itself in phenomenal diversity.[15] Difference (content, materiality) is thus relegated to a derivative realm of appearances, with Spirit (*Geist*) orchestrating them in a manner that is analogous to, if less ambiguous than, Kantian noumena. Marx will also attribute this essentialism to Hegel.

Hegel indeed begins this section by explaining that since being is immediate, knowledge cannot be content to rest there and instead 'penetrates it *on the supposition* that at the back of this being there is something else' (Logic: 389, emphasis added). This supposition turns out however to be unfounded, as do the oppositions it entails (where essence is opposed variously to being, appearance, illusion and the inessential). Eventually reflection is forced to recognise that essence is not being's truth or other, but 'the movement of being itself'. The earlier claims were not however simply mistakes but themselves effects of being, whose essence turns out to lie precisely in giving the illusion that it is underpinned by some more profound substance or in-itself.

At first, then, reflection sees the pure being of essence as the (external) negation of everything determinate, such that essence ('lifeless and empty', 'simple negativity') confronts determinate being as its first negation. Next, it sees being itself as nothing; as illusory, inessential, unknowable, the 'remainder'. This is the moment of scepticism and transcendental idealism. But eventually, reflection realises that these are merely abstract oppositions and that the negativity of essence is not alien to being but rather, its own 'infinite movement' as it mediates, and thereby sublates, itself. When being appears as illusory, this is then nothing but the 'negativity of essence', whose 'intrinsic *nothingness* is the *negative nature of essence itself*' (Logic: 397).

Although the rhythms of negativity are similar across being and essence, the latter is thus more radically negative. For whereas being determined itself through relation with an other (being versus nothing and their transition), essence is self-repelling; a self-negating negation which overcomes itself self-reflexively. Essence is thus 'pure mediation or absolute negativity' rather than any 'affirmatively present substrate' (Logic: 399). As such, it is not mediated or produced by anything outside it but *is* the appearing of a being whose essence is to appear. Being is not produced by something more original, but is generativity as such. Stephen Houlgate describes this as Hegel's Nietzschean moment, where 'essence can be nothing but *the very process of seeming as such*'.[16]

In one sense it remains true that this negative process remains ideal ('Essence is reflection') and is but a stage of reason, so Stace (and Marx) is not wrong in discerning in it the appearing of the Idea. But at the same time, Hegel's understanding of essence calls into question any simple foundationalism or essence–appearance dichotomy, suggesting that if being is the appearing of reason (Spirit), then its mode of appearing is that of being's own self-generativity, which is not the appearance *of* something else more true or real. It is in this latter sense that Hegel remains faithful to a non-essentialised but productive negativity.

Within the Doctrine of Essence, the negations operative within being are reflected on as contradictions.[17] Hegel has also been widely criticised here, accused of reducing multiplicitous differences and antagonisms to this apparently binary category. Certainly on the reflective plane, contradiction is the form that the conjunction of identity and difference takes and Hegel writes that '[d]ifference as such is already *implicitly* contradiction' (Logic: 431). Yet contradiction is derived by him as dialectically richer than difference or opposition and he insists that it 'is the root of all movement and vitality; it is only in so far as something has a contradiction within it that it moves, has an urge and activity' (Logic: 439).

For it is ordinary thought, Hegel argues, that abhors contradiction, perceiving it as abnormal while it remains content to oppose indifferent, inert differences to one another. In speculative thinking, contradiction however means recognition of the internal relation and transition between opposites; only here is the blunt (in)difference of diverse terms brought into *lively* opposition (Logic: 441f). Beyond static, binary opposition (the apparently irresolvable antinomies Kant associated with dialectics; Aristotelian logic), reflection comes to recognise that there are no isolated positive/negative oppositions, since each term is itself derived from another opposition, and so on indefinitely (Logic: 436). As Hegel says in the *Phenomenology*, 'we have to think pure flux, opposition within opposition itself, or Contradiction' (Ph: 206). 'These sundered factors have, hence, each a separate being of their own; each is an opposite for an other' (Ph: 208). In the *Logic* he indeed presents this as an ontological principle which is not confined to thought alone but marks the very nature of things, where '*everything is inherently contradictory*'. Contradiction is a more profound determination than identity, he insists here, the latter being 'merely the determination of the simple immediate, of dead being' (Logic: 439). All things or concepts attain a negative unity in transition between the is and is-not, where they are both inherently self-contradictory and the contradiction resolved. 'Only when the manifold terms have been driven to the point of contradiction do they become active and lively towards one another, receiving in contradiction the negativity which is the indwelling pulsation of self-movement and spontaneous activity [*Lebendigkeit*]' (Logic: 442). Dialectics might recognise the sharpness of contradiction (the fecund positive/negative structure of all being), rather than a simple multiplicity and difference of the manifold, but contradictions are ubiquitous, complex and overdetermined.

The dependence of Hegel's terminology on logic (negation, contradiction, etc.) would inspire criticisms that he had failed to recognise a more heterogeneous generativity at work, of which logic is but an effect. I have, however, suggested that even logic is for him a more complex process than it might appear. Moreover sympathetic critics also note a mode of becoming conveyed by the organic metaphors, which seems more aesthetic than logical. Here the whole is more than the sum of its parts yet nothing without them; a whole that unfolds over time without erasing the differentiation of the multiple constituents on which it depends. From this perspective, the unities that evolve synthetically are not accomplished through the application of a logical schema, but emerge through relationships between parts which resolve themselves into provisional wholes. Adorno writes of the whole as the Idea that operates as a centre of force latent in individual moments, which crystallise 'on their own and by virtue of their motion and direction, into a whole that does not exist outside of its particular determinations.'[18] It is in the differentiated and mobile web of relations wherein parts are attracted and repelled – in the spaces and movements between things – that open yet structured dialectical unities are forged out of the manifold. It is in this sense that for example Merleau-Ponty and Adorno will speak respectively of *Gestalten* and constellations, granting to the rhythms of negativity contingent as well as formative, synthetic powers. From this perspective, the self-generating movement of dialectics is not the cunning of any mysterious theological or transcendental force, nor a sclerotic formula derived from formal logic, but the aesthetic of difference as it crystallises into provisional forms unified by a common style: a lawfulness without law such as Kant had attributed to aesthetic unities.

Indeed logic, like Spirit, might be interpreted now as a figurative device designed to present a process that is itself unrepresentable logically or grammatically. For the very dynamism of dialectics, with its fluid conjunction of parts and whole, preservation and transcendence (*Aufhebung*), identity and non-identity, suggests an inconceivable heterogeneity lodged at the heart of dialectics and invoking the negativity of the negative itself. If negativity is equated with alterity here, this is not however in the sense of some alien force (a hidden god or essence), but *qua* the unrepresentable process of becoming in which reason is itself caught and which aesthetics perhaps captures more successfully.

A question of method

In the previous section I elicited the rhythms of negativity that choreograph the dialectic. These yielded a patterning whereby the play of difference acquires an internal logic that produces relatively enduring, and increasingly integral, forms or unities, not just random differentiation or disintegration. During the course of this book I will associate this formative power of negativity with the possibility of critical theory and politics. Nevertheless I also alluded to an ambiguity in the process: between a self-generativity that emphasises difference and a certain contingency, on the one hand, and a teleological procession towards the Absolute that emphasises identity and its necessity, on the other. In this section I will approach this ambiguity from another, albeit analogous, perspective, asking about the relationship between history and philosophy, logic and experience (or ideas and material life, subject and object). As the young Althusser would note, the main controversy regarding Hegel is 'whether the dialectic represents a form which is imposed from without, or one which emerges from its content, whether it is formal or real, whether its schematism is purely mechanistic or the very soul of things.'[19] What is at stake here is the ontology and historicity of negativity as well as Hegel's own fidelity to it. I will however claim that these are not after all alternatives but remain necessarily undecidable.

The key question here concerns the status of Hegel's own intervention. Is he merely describing for us a dialectical process, as a scientist might describe from a distance the way nature mechanically persists, or does he believe that his own work somehow exemplifies negativity and participates in the process it articulates? In order to address this concern it will be helpful to begin with Hegel's own claims regarding his method.

In the *Logic*, Hegel claims to develop a new scientific method (dialectical, or speculative, logic), whose truth lies in the fact that rather than trying to impose abstract, subjective forms upon an alien domain (as Kantian understanding does), it follows a mode of reasoning which emulates, and plays an integral part in the unfolding of, being itself. Accordingly, both objective reality and conceptual development evolve dialectically, with Hegel's own philosophy *necessarily* taking this form since it follows the logic immanent in that of which it writes. There is no form/content or *a priori/a posteriori* dichotomy. Instead there is a single appearing–disclosing; as Kojève puts it, an equivalence of realised concept and conceived reality, the logical/real.[20]

Hegel expresses this dual sense of the dialectic, as simultaneously ontological and methodological, in introducing his various works. Thus in the *Logic* he describes an approach where 'it can be only the nature of the content itself which spontaneously develops itself in a scientific method of knowing, since it is at the same time the reflection of the content itself which first posits and *generates* its determinate character' (Logic: 27). The dialectical movement of negative and positive, particular and universal, is he insists both 'the absolute method of knowing and at the same time is the immanent soul of the content itself' (Logic: 28). If in the *Phenomenology* he concentrates on consciousness as a concrete knowing where externality is involved, he insists nevertheless on its logical form.

> In the nature of existence as thus described – to be its own notion and being in one – consists logical necessity in general. This alone is what is rational, the rhythm of the organic whole: it is as much knowledge of content as that content is notion and essential nature. In other words, this alone is the sphere and element of speculative thought. The concrete shape of the content is resolved by its own inherent process into a simple determinate quality. Thereby it is raised to logical form, and its being and essence coincide; its concrete existence is merely this process that takes place, and is *eo ipso* logical existence. It is therefore needless to apply a formal scheme to the concrete content in an external fashion; the content is in its very nature a transition into a formal shape, which, however, ceases to be formalism of an external kind, because the form is the indwelling process of the concrete content itself.
>
> (Ph: 115)

Here Hegel inveighs against the 'lifeless and inert' determinations fixed by the understanding, insisting instead upon the 'immanent living principle' of existence that dialectics alone grasps. It 'demands abandonment to the very life of the object, or, which means the same thing, claims to have before it the inner necessity controlling the object, and to express this only' (Ph: 112). Although it is Hegel who writes, he is but a scribe: his philosophy is being, or Spirit, speaking itself; the Real reflecting discursively upon itself through him.[21] Accordingly Hegel warns that we 'must abstain from interrupting the immanent rhythm of the movement of conceptual thought; we must refrain from arbitrarily interfering with it, and introducing ideas and reflections that have been obtained elsewhere' (Ph: 117). Categories must be dialectically engendered, not analytically deduced. Thus neither subject (reason) nor object (content) are reified: they evolve reciprocally as two emergent dimensions of a self-mediating being; one that folds back upon itself over time.

This sense of the dialectic is again expressed in 1821, when Hegel writes in the Introduction to his *Philosophy of Right* that his method presupposes the conceptual development already traced in his *Logic* as 'a purely immanent progress, the engendering of its determinations.'

> To consider a thing rationally means not to bring reason to bear on the subject from the outside and so to tamper with it, but to find that the object is rational on its own account; here it is mind in its freedom, the culmination of self-conscious reason, which gives itself actuality and engenders itself as an existing world. The sole task of philosophic science is to bring to consciousness this proper work of the reason of the thing itself.[22]

The aim of the *Logic* is then the (self-)articulation of the intelligible structure of objective reality, which is demonstrated through the rational and necessary unfolding of logical categories. Unlike the understanding, which only knows isolated, abstract things via fixed categories (Kant's uncritical limitation), dialectical reasoning grasps the relationships which sustain concepts and entities within a complex and dynamic whole. Although logic appears to be merely formal – 'the realm of shadows, the world of simple essentialities freed from all sensuous concreteness' (Logic: 58) – Hegel claims that it reveals the universal truth, or inner structure, of all content. The power of such reason resides in its capacity to articulate and participate in the process of totalisation, whereby things' identities emerge only within the network of relations that constitute the whole. Thus the lower, unmediated categories are abstract and one-sided and it is this inadequacy, their instability, that impels their self-overcoming through relations with opposing categories. Any limit acts as but a spur to further knowledge, not as its end point. Only when all these mediations have been worked through do the categories become concrete and the Idea realised. It 'is the inwardness of the content, the dialectic which it possesses within itself, which is the mainspring of its advance' (Logic: 54). 'That which enables the Notion to advance itself is the ... *negative* which it possesses within itself; it is this which constitutes the genuine dialectical element' (Logic: 55). It follows then that objective and reflective being evolve according, and due, to the same rhythm of negativity, since they are dialectically interwoven dimensions of a single process.

But the central question for Hegel's critics, as alluded to by Althusser, is whether Reason (or essence) is merely a name given to the self-reflexivity that being acquires through its self-mediations (such that negativity remains the principle of all movement), or whether it is the hidden instigator and purpose of becoming (such that it is self-identical *Geist*, the cunning of reason, not negativity, which ultimately drives the dialectic). This could again be expressed in terms of Hegel's Marxian or Nietzschean (/Heideggerian), as opposed to his idealist or theological, moments, and it seems to me that the comments cited above concerning his method, like those on essence, leave their relationship unresolved. Thus we return to the question of whether Hegel's own thinking remains integral to the dialectic, or is merely a representation of it from the perspective of the Absolute. Can he both articulate the dialectical process as the truth of being and remain dialectical in his method? This again poses the question of the relationship between difference and identity, but it now raises it on a higher level of reflection: one concerning the relationship between philosophy and non-philosophy.

The undecidability of the Hegelian dialectic

According to Adorno the challenge of dialectical thinking is to represent, but without effacing, non-identity. It is not to reflect on the objective world but to be that world speaking itself. 'Things themselves speak in a philosophy that focuses its energies on proving that it is itself one with them.'[23] From this perspective dialectics is less about the mastery of reason than reason's tragic struggle to articulate that which is alien to it without reducing it to itself, which would render thought merely tautological self-reflection. If the concept is not the thing, then consciousness always mutilates that of which it speaks. But this is precisely why reflection must always remain self-critical, driven by the non-identity that marks the motivation and ruin of its ambition. Negativity remains immanent, not transcendent, to knowledge. Accordingly, Adorno contends that 'the justification of the primacy of negation in Hegel's philosophy is that the limits of knowledge to which its critical self-reflection leads are not something external to knowledge ... ; rather, they are inherent in all moments of knowledge.' He cites Hegel's 'spontaneous receptivity' and the labour the dialectical philosopher must perform if the concept is to be subordinated to the discipline of the thing in itself. 'Hegel is able to think from the thing itself out, to surrender passively, as it were, to its authentic substance'.[24]

Adorno suggests that Hegel struggled to let the real speak through his work by means of a *stylistic* attempt at emulating the very process of a dialectics which is itself unpresentable. Hegel's method is then an attempt at setting the objective in motion (the Absolute is 'pulsation') and exemplifying its flow in a style more musical than clear; one that 'murmurs and rustles'. 'The substance of Hegel's philosophy is process, and it wants to express itself as process, in permanent *status nascendi*, the negation of presentation as something congealed.'[25]

This mimesis is ultimately judged a failure by Adorno, since Hegel paid insufficient attention to language,[26] and it is also true that Hegel's thought failed to challenge the irrational totality of bourgeois society. If he struggled in vain to express the dynamism of dialectical reality, however, his idealism does preserve that distance from the given which critical reason requires. Thus dialectics remains both representationally and politically radical, since it refuses to let the merely given, the positive, be, either conceptually or existentially. It recognises both the reciprocity and the non-identity of subject and object, concept and real. As Marcuse would insist, this is what grants to history its 'energy'.

> Dialectical thought ... becomes negative in itself. Its function is to break down the self-assurance and self-contentment of common-sense, to undermine the sinister confidence in the power and language of facts, to demonstrate that unfreedom is so much at the core of things that the development of their internal contradictions leads necessarily to qualitative change: the explosion and catastrophe of the established state of affairs.[27]

What is, is always confronted with what it is not, yet might become. Negativity and critique are thus intimately related, indeed almost synonymous, since negative thinking is immanent critique. Whatever Hegel's own limitations, dialectics thus remains exemplary as a critical practice. If negativity is ontologically unavoidable, its recognition and reflective practising might allow the political to unfold in a more rational way.

The relationship between subject and object, and (analogously) between Hegel's philosophy and the dialectic, is not then of merely epistemological or methodological concern but has profound political implications. This is why it must also be negotiated by existentialist Marxists and (post)structuralists, where it is implicated in disagreements between humanist and anti-humanist positions. These disagreements to some extent hinge on the relationship between *The Phenomenology of Mind* (1807) and the *Science of Logic* (1812–16, but substantially revised in 1831). Anti-humanists have presented the dialectic as pure, or structural, process. Here the *Phenomenology* is read as an account simply of one manifestation of an onto-logical process whose formal structure the *Logic* lays bare, such that the dialectic is not primarily anthropological. Althusser, for example, would offer a scientific account of this process, salvaging the Hegelian conception of history as a particular kind of process: one *'without a subject'*. 'There is no subject to the process: *it is the process itself which is a subject in so far as it does not have a subject.'*[28] And Derrida insists that the *Phenomenology* (and *a fortiori* the *Logic*) 'is in no way concerned with something which could be called man. A science of the experience of consciousness, a science of the structures of the phenomenality of the mind in reference to itself, it is strictly distinct from anthropology.'[29]

Humanist Marxists have however been more inclined to equate negativity with the historicity of the human species, as exemplified in Kojève's formula: 'Hegelian conception of Man = Action = Negativity'.[30] Now it is the *Phenomenology* that emerges as the key work, reconstructing the history whereby meaning appears in the world, the real becomes rational and alienation is overcome. It tells of a lived, dynamic relation between subject and object, subject and subject, and it is on this level that materialist practitioners of negativity, from Marx on, locate themselves.

The Hegel of 1807 is presented here as more abstract, but hardly more idealist, than Marx.[31] As Merleau-Ponty glosses the early work: the 'truth is not that there is only knowledge or that there is only the in-itself or the object, but that there is the one and the other in a kind of procession, or gravitation, exchange or reversibility.'[32] He describes the *Phenomenology* as an existentialist account of 'man's efforts to reappropriate himself', where Hegel makes interpersonal life the basis of history.[33] The dialectical method is now located within the process of reason's own appearing, with all its lived contingency. But this once more poses the problematic status of philosophy itself and with it, of Hegel's (and the dialectician's) own self-understanding.

For it is only when the process achieves self-consciousness at the end of its journey that Hegel can speak from its vantage point to explain the significance and necessity of what was first experienced only in a confused way. If the process is dialectical, the philosophy that articulates it seems to transcend it and to remain idealist, metaphysical. In naming the dialectic it destroys it. This becomes apparent in the *Logic*, in so far as it is presented as the formal truth of a completed process. Here, Merleau-Ponty says, the 'formulation transforms [the dialectic] into something said, into something positive, and makes the negative disappear in the 1807 sense – it restores the sense of identity' (an itinerary he will find repeated by Marx).[34] The later Hegel is now presented as a rationalist who underwent a shift from the negatively to the positively rational.[35] One way of saving negativity would then be to grant priority to the earlier Hegel, where Absolute Knowledge is understood phenomenologically: not as the Truth of a completed history, but as an expression of the modernity whose particular mode of being-in-the-world is one of rationalism and whose epoch acquires an appropriate, but limited, level of self-understanding. Rationalism, in other words, remains a new type of experience and if the Absolute is knowledge of such experience, it is also an experience of knowledge and cannot step outside this horizon to account for itself. Merleau-Ponty concludes that Hegel deliberately left this ambiguity in 1807, where reason is historical as well as history being rational, and so the openness and provisionality of his system were preserved, only to be surrendered subsequently.[36]

The distinction between Hegel the practising dialectician and Hegel the metaphysician had already been made by Marx and it is again apparent in Kojève's account. According to Kojève, Hegel's method is not dialectical at all but merely phenomenological in the Husserlian sense of being simply descriptive, even positivist. This is because Kojève separates out a number of dialectics superimposed upon one another. First there is the material, existential one: the 'active or *real* negation of the given, effected in Fighting and by Work', which 'constitutes the negative or negating element determining the dialectical structure of the Real and of Being.' This is history as it is lived: humanity changing itself through exchanges with its natural environment. But it also spawns a superstructural dialectic that accompanies it as a 'secondary and derivative movement', a history of philosophy and culture. This is the reflective moment of the first but it is equally one-sided and continually challenged by life's shifting forms, so that there is a productive reciprocity between these symbolic and lived processes, too.

This is where Merleau-Ponty (among the participants in Kojève's now-famous seminars) would like to relocate Hegel's own thinking. However the latter is defined by Kojève as tertiary: it describes history's dialectics but it does not itself engage critically with the real or its idealisations in a dialectical manner. Hegel thus sacrifices the dialectical method to passive contemplation.[37] 'His role is that of a perfectly flat and indefinitely extended mirror.'[38] He reflects, rather than negates, the real. The end of history is presented by Kojève as equally inert and devoid of negativity: equivalent to a new animality – repetition, boredom, passivity and unfreedom – even if it were the ideal achievement of subject–object coincidence. 'In fact, Man can be satisfied only by *action*. Now, to act is to transform what is real. And to transform what is real is to *negate* the given.'[39] For Kojève it is humans who are 'absolute negating negativity'; there is no dialectical generativity within being as such for it is through its desire that humanity introduces nothingness and annihilation into the given, transforming it in pursuit of recognition. The termination of this negativity would spell the negation, not the fulfilment, of freedom; it would mark a return to the static identity of pre-history and brute facticity.

The criticisms of Hegel advanced by Adorno, Merleau-Ponty and Kojève all suggest that he tried to practise dialectics but ultimately failed: either because he finally believed concepts could master reality, or because he believed speculative truth could master history. All try to rescue negativity by re-instantiating it in the volatile space between reality and thought, where it becomes synonymous with a critical method, a hermeneutics and a praxis, rather than Truth. One way of negotiating this solution is to attribute different levels to Hegel's thinking, and these are indeed anticipated by the Being/Essence/Notion structure of the *Logic*. However I now want to argue that these differential levels must themselves be understood dialectically; that, rather than subverting his own dialectical insights, Hegel assigned dialectics an undecidable status, one that is conveyed better by the circular figures of the circuit or spiral than by the more linear or stratified images of narratives and levels.

This claim is best explored via the *Phenomenology*. In reflecting upon the genesis of reason, Hegel begins with sense–certainty. This seems to offer the most immediate knowledge and the most concrete, authentic, 'richest' experience of the object. For it seems to be a knowledge that has not yet 'dropped anything' from the object, which confronts it as complete, true and autonomous (Ph: 151). Yet it is actually the most abstract, dualist and illusory form of knowing, since all that could be known without the mediations necessary for the determination of specific properties would be the object's simple is-ness: a universal devoid of distinction and quite at odds with the sense–certainty intended. Objects which are identified in the here and now, as this and that, require both the determinations perception brings and the specificity that language yields through its universal concepts, since 'what is called unspeakable is nothing else than what is untrue, irrational, something barely and simply "meant"' (Ph: 160). 'In the very attempt to say it, it would, therefore, crumble in their hands.' Hegel is not denying experience of sensuous reality – even animals, he notes sardonically, despair of things *per se* 'and in complete assurance of the nothingness of things they fall-to without more ado and eat them up' – but even the most apparently immediate experience of it depends on the process of determining mediations, formally described in the *Logic*, where identity depends upon the negation and exclusion of differentiated properties. 'The diversity of content is, *qua* determinate, due to relation, and is not inherent; and its restless activity consists in cancelling and superseding itself, or is negativity' (Ph: 805). Even in material activities, like labouring or perceiving, negativity is already at work since they inscribe objects in a field of forces whose vectors and traces grant them a certain ideality because it is their relations that sustain them.

This 'ideality' is then *a fortiori* apparent in more complex intersubjective acts. Hegel is not, any more than Marx, a transcendental realist in the sense proscribed by Kant. But material relations between active sentients and natural objects always involve complex mediations and it is in this web of connections that the material world gains significance and becomes a more concrete totality, more amenable to comprehension, hence more rational. This is why Hegel can write that the object becomes 'a vanishing factor', while self-consciousness becomes 'at home with itself in its otherness as such.' It is in this sense that the dialectical itinerary could be expressed not as a unified metaphysical substance reclaiming itself from its alienated externality, but as the totality coming to self-knowledge. It is the 'totality of its determinate characteristics' that 'makes the object *per se* or inherently a spiritual reality'. It does not cease to exist in its materiality, but it is 'indifferent' to this external form. 'The thing is nothing in itself; it only has significance in relation, only through the ego and its reference to the ego' (Ph: 789–91). The ego must be grasped here not as some reified self, but as the reflexiveness and complexity inherent in being as process. It is the proliferation of such relations that then marks the dialectic, *both as reality and as method*, and Lukács' rendition of this totalising process could equally apply to Hegel or Marx when he writes that:

> If change is to be understood at all it is necessary to abandon the view that objects are rigidly opposed to each other, it is necessary to elevate their relatedness and the interrelation between these 'relations' and the 'objects' to the same plane of reality. The greater the distance from pure immediacy the larger the net encompassing the 'relations', and the more complete the integration of the 'objects' within the system of relations, the sooner change will cease to be impenetrable and catastrophic, the sooner it will become comprehensible.[40]

It is the vibrancy and productivity of these shifting relations that exemplifies negativity: a multiplication of connections and relations, oppositions and differences. Although Hegel anticipates their complete mediation in a final Totality, the totalising process does not itself however necessarily compel this end. The dialectical method might then attempt a provisional reconstruction of the dense web of relations that make sense of superficially isolated and abstract appearances, without necessarily claiming exhaustive knowledge or extricating itself from the force field in which it is situated. In this way it would practise, indeed emulate, rather than ontologise, dialectics.

Any account of the dialectic *per se* would nevertheless remain problematic and this is the difficulty with Hegel's rendition when he writes that the 'process of carrying forward this form of knowledge of itself is the task which spirit accomplishes as actual History' (Ph: 801). For history is then reduced to a 'gallery of pictures', a predicate representing the progress of Spirit. In fully comprehending itself, *Geist* leaves behind its external existence and passes from embodiment to recollection, whence it becomes 'engulfed in the night of its own self-consciousness', although its 'vanished existence' is nevertheless 'conserved therein' (Ph: 807).

But Hegel does not stop here. Having achieved this level of self-knowledge, Spirit must traverse the circle again (sense–perception or indeterminate being were only, after all, origins under erasure: they had but illusory immediacy since, under interrogation, the totality of mediations is already found inherent within them). The process of mediations must start again, 'as fresh as before', negating its ideality and returning to immediacy although on a 'higher level' (Ph: 80). It is in this sense that I think the relation between the *Phenomenology* and the *Logic*, and the question of which level of the dialectic Hegel works on, remains undecidable. A phenomenology of meaning and its recounting are not sequential and definitive, but complementary renditions of the same circuit that is lived–thought on different levels simultaneously, eternally returning as knowledge and material existence are endlessly imbricated and moved by an irrepressible negativity. Totalising and disintegration are always replayed, hence the infinity of the Absolute. Absolute Knowledge itself is then but a brief and unsustainable moment. Philosophy, Hegel insists, need not trouble itself over the question of how distinction or otherness arise from pure essence, since 'the process of disruption has already taken place and in excluding distinction, self-identity confirms it.' Thus unity is 'merely one moment of the process of disruption', an abstraction that cancels itself in excluding its other. Infinitude is not therefore rest, but the 'absolute unrest of pure self-movement' (Ph: 208f). Unity is but a moment in the circulation of difference.

Yet as Deleuze also notes, 'Hegel's circle is not the eternal return, only the infinite circulation of the identical by means of negativity.'[41] Adorno passes a similar judgement: for 'all his emphasis on negativity, division, and nonidentity, Hegel actually takes cognizance of that dimension only for the sake of identity'.[42] In this small space of Hegel's intent a slippage towards the positive thus occurs; he shifts dialectics away from difference and towards identity. But I suggest that the alternative possibility was also inherent in his thinking. The dialectic is undecidable between identity and difference at this vanishing point.

In presenting the Hegelian dialectic I have tried to preserve the sense in which it operates on many, irreducible levels. These could be classified as differential negativities: one whose mobility is unrepresentable yet invoked by stylistic strategies that convey its generativity; one that is rendered more lawful via the deployment of logical categories which structure dialectical dynamics; and finally one that only masquerades as the negative. The first of these is the most elusive and brings Hegel closer to philosophies of alterity and difference than is often acknowledged; the second is associated with a critical hermeneutics and praxis, as well as with a recognisably dialectical rhythm of formation and rupture; the last is where Hegel's infidelity to the negative is located in an idealist, metaphysical move that renders him a philosopher of identity. These three dimensions could again be described respectively as negativity which is affirmative; as negation which mediates negative and positive, and as surrender to positivism.

In terms of my concern about the relationship between negativity and politics, and anticipating subsequent claims, I suggest the following. To the first, most heterogeneous, negativity there clings a politically-radical aura since its generativity promises a relentless destabilising of every reified form, although it is difficult to redeem its promises in any collective action or critique. The latter are more definitively related to the second, where the imbrication of negative and positive occur and where ideas and material practices, positive institutions and their practical negation, occur. The last is a fate always awaiting theories of negativity and the one against which the first two are mobilised. Although all three levels are linked, their relationship is insufficiently mediated, I suggest, in Hegel's texts.

Hegel's thinking then yields various negativities and I have contended that it remains undecidable in terms of privileging any one or fixing any definitive conceptualisation of the negative. This is why adventurers in negativity find his texts fascinating, threatening and flawed; why they must always return to them for inspiration and denial. In the next section I will consider Marx's attempt to rescue the second, dialectical negativity from the third, positivist moment; in a final section I will present more recent attempts at releasing the first, affirmative negativity from either of the other two.

Negativity and materialism: the Marxian dialectic

For Marx the question of the object cannot be simply epistemological or metaphysical, since it concerns the material transformation of the world. He agrees with Hegel that subject and object are co-produced historically, but insists in 1844 that critical thinking must question where it stands *vis-à-vis* the Hegelian dialectic.[43] He had already challenged Hegel's conservative view of the state but now turned his attention to the *Phenomenology*, the 'true birthplace and secret' of Hegel's philosophy, in order to lay bare the work's metaphysical schema. The first negation Spirit enacts is that of its own immediacy: it alienates itself as objectivity, in order to give itself content. Through coming to knowledge of that content, the latter is in turn negated and returned to thought. Absolute Knowledge, as the negation of the negation on this meta-level, is therefore an affirmation of self-conscious Spirit. Not only does the completion of the circle transcend dialectics as such, according to Marx, but the negativity which moved it was only an abstract process. For Hegel, objectification thus meant estrangement: in its self-diremption, Spirit alienates itself as other and its aim is thenceforth to overcome this externalisation by redeeming itself in fully-mediated form. There is a subject–object dialectic (abstract thought mediating sensuous reality), but ultimately it is only a relation of Spirit with itself. The 'result is the dialectic of pure thought.'[44] Or as Marx puts it in *Capital*, it is the Idea that is 'the demiurgos of the real world, and the real world is only the external phenomenal form of "the Idea."'[45] Hegel thus reversed subject and predicate, agency and effect, essence and appearance, which is why Marx thinks he needs inverting. It is because there is no specific content to his dialectic, Marx argues, that its abstract forms can fit any content as logical categories indifferent to real contexts. 'The inexhaustible, vital, sensuous, concrete activity of self-objectification is therefore reduced to its mere abstraction, *absolute negativity*.'[46]

Marx's quarrel with Hegel is not however with negativity as process, modulated and driven by contradiction. Indeed what Marx thinks is worth preserving in Hegel is precisely his sense of negativity: the *Phenomenology* does have a 'thoroughly negative and critical appearance'. Hegel correctly recognised that human self-creation is a process (with 'the dialectic of negativity as the moving and producing principle'[47]) in which alienation is engendered and transcended, but he failed to recognise this as a socioeconomic struggle. Marx thus distinguishes two levels of the Hegelian dialectic: in one the dynamism and rhythm typical of its negativity are played out historically, if abstractly, but in the other a non-dialectical idealism closes over it (in other words, Marx identifies the second and third levels I previously elicited but pays no heed to the first). It is this distinction that is conveyed in the famous seed analogy, where Marx says he aims to rescue the rational kernel (and to deploy it as his own methodology) from its mystical shell.[48]

The implications of this metaphor, and the related project of inversion, are central to the question of negativity's status in Hegel and Marx. If the rational kernel is a process whereby historical meaning appears through contradictions and complex mediations, then it suggests that dialectics is an ongoing movement wherein forms and their significance emerge over time: a subject–object, lived–thought reciprocity that is simultaneously a mode of historicity and a critical engagement within it. As such, it is the medium of existence and is inextricably material and ideal. It is this process, and its implications for critical thinking and praxis, which must then be severed from the metaphysical shell. The seed analogy is in this sense more appropriate than the inversion one about standing Hegel on his feet. For it would be no advance simply to replace the metaphysical idealism of the shell with an equally metaphysical materialism (a pre-critical, transcendental realism in Kant's sense). On the other hand, if the historical process is summed up from a distance in terms of an inevitable logic verging on completion, then the philosopher himself steps outside the dialectic and assumes an ideal stance, even if the narrative he reconstructs is a materialist one. If philosophy is to remain dialectical, it cannot therefore operate at the level of a mystical shell at all. The only question is whether Marx remains faithful to his own insight. But the materialist philosopher does face an additional difficulty which Hegel's idealist (being = reason) ontology had avoided. How can thinking engage with the material world without idealising it and how is it to intervene efficaciously there? How is negativity to be practised? In what sense is it, or can it become, a material force capable of changing the world? It is only on the basis of Hegelian dialectics that Marx can begin negotiating this transgression of what metaphysics had previously presented as two radically discrete substances (matter and mind) or realms (phenomenal and noumenal).

From nature to communism: a materialist history

Marx derides Feuerbach's materialism for being insufficiently dialectical, noting (in the first Thesis on Feuerbach) that previous materialisms had seen the object too passively, failing to recognise objectivity as sensuous human activity and objects as realisations of its practices. As Hegel had noted, 'matter is a sheer *abstraction*. (Matter cannot be seen, felt, and so on – what is seen, felt, is a *determinate matter*, that is, a unity of matter and form.)' (Logic: 450). In 1844, Marx had already insisted that his own naturalism was actually a synthesis of materialism and idealism because the process of the species's self-creation is both objective and constitutive. At this stage he was nevertheless seeking a realist answer to the question of negativity as an effective force: what drives it and what is the source of its momentum? Like Freud, when he thinks about matter, he is influenced by the language of motion inherited from Newtonian physics (his ultimate aim, he insists in *Capital*, is to 'lay bare the economic law of motion of modern society'[49]). However the mechanical and determinist chains of cause and effect running between isolated particles, of which natural science spoke, were of little use to a revolutionary thinker. As Kant had argued, such accounts are still subjective representations, while their causal imperatives are immune to freedom or transformation. As a dialectical thinker, Marx needed a material medium that could both change and understand itself; like Hegel, he needed to show that material and conceptual becoming, content and method, are part of a single process. When he speaks of material objects, he does not then begin with the phenomena of natural science and Kantian philosophy, but with natural things that are internally dynamic: embodied humans on the one hand; natural objects that are laboured upon on the other. The logic of their formative reciprocity yields him a historical narrative that is equivalent to, but more concrete than, the one offered by Hegel in the *Phenomenology*.

Marx (perhaps disingenuously) insists on beginning not with a speculative derivation but with what can be empirically verified: 'real premises' which are 'real individuals' living under particular material conditions; 'real, corporeal *man*, his feet firmly planted on the solid earth and breathing all the powers of nature'.[50] Like Freud, he locates an initial dynamism in the imperatives of need. As sensuous, natural beings, humans enjoy certain vital powers which exist 'as dispositions and capacities, as *drives*.' They need objects in order to exist. 'Passion is man's essential power vigorously striving to attain its object.'[51] It is in this sense (bodily suffering as lack, scarcity, drive, a difference in nature between inside (need) and outside (external objects)) that a rudimentary negativity emerges out of the positivity of the materialist, or naturalist, starting point. Yet since humans are part of nature, this fissure remains internal to the natural. Nature is alien inasmuch as it is a recalcitrant objectivity required for the satisfaction of need, but humans are not yet alienated in the specific sense Marx gives the term. Moreover this splitting might only yield a static circuit of exchanges, as happens in the monotonous repetition of animal satisfaction. But Marx explains its velocity precisely in terms of humanity's not being instinctually programmed and creating itself through the very activities it embarks upon.

For humans do not simply satisfy need, they labour. Nature is objectively 'worked up' in the image of the species through this activity and thereby reflects back to it its own powers, which include aesthetic as well as utilitarian modes.[52] The species 'duplicates' itself in reality; its objects become mirrors for its capacities, such that objectification means not estrangement, as it had for Hegel, but recognition (and also, for critical reason, the potential for a dialectical reading of objects which become knowable not because they express the Idea, but because they are suffused with material, intersubjective relations and practices). Nature is thereby humanised over time as natural objects are recreated as congealed labour. This could be expressed less humanistically as nature recreating itself. But more specifically, it is the self-constitution of the human species through its productive capacities. For if labour changes objects, it also transforms the embodied subjects who work upon them: their social relations, their self-understanding, their needs and desires, even the '*cultivation* of the five senses is the work of all previous history.'[53] Once set in motion, the process is therefore self-sustaining and spiralling, without fixed terms, that is, it is a materialist version of the dialectical generativity which Marx had praised in Hegel. Marx might not have sufficiently developed a theory of the subject, but neither does he reify or ontologise consciousness.[54]

The small space that human need opens within nature is highly productive in terms of the development of subjects, of objects and of their relationship, but the crucial mediation occurs via labour ('an eternal nature-imposed necessity, without which there can be no material exchanges between man and Nature, and therefore no life.'[55]). Labour, as 'a force of nature, human labour power',[56] is also transformed, through the logic of its tasks, into a more general productive process which includes the modes of social cooperation that enhance its efficiency. The social division of labour, and the invention of tools and machines that maximise its production of use values, yield forces of production which are the real momentum driving historical becoming ('the multitude of productive forces accessible to men determines the nature of society'[57]).

Although need, labour and the forces of production inject a formative spacing and momentum into nature, however, this is not yet dialectical negativity in Hegel's sense since it lacks the contradictions that lend the dialectic its particular rhythmic energy. Marx renders it so by explaining how the originally small lacuna of need succumbs to the yawning gulf of alienation and exploitation. For these material forces become increasingly mystified and hierarchical as ideology and class divisions drive a wedge between producers and their productive activity. This process is the domain of history.

The division of labour 'only becomes truly such from the moment when a division of material and mental labour appears.'[58] At first, Marx implies, ideas arise unproblematically – as 'ideological reflexes and echoes', 'sublimates of ... material life-process' – and thus consciousness corresponds to, indeed is only a more rarefied expression of, reality.[59] However with the emergence of a class of mental labourers (priests, philosophers, etc), consciousness gains independence so that not only do bigger ruptures open up between life and its representation, but ideologically-motivated misrepresentations begin to appear. It is in this social imaginary that the first alienations emerge, in the form of idols and idealisms: the 'phantoms' of the human mind take on a life of their own, their social origins obscured, until they come to rule over persons as alien powers. At the same time, each new development of the productive forces engenders a division of labour whose stages are 'just so many different forms of ownership'. Although this always means a hierarchy of producing and appropriating classes, under capitalism the linkage between human labour and its production of use values is itself finally broken since the market now mediates between need and its satisfaction. Production thenceforth takes place under conditions of alienation, where workers are definitively ripped out of nature, out of their species being and out of their creative humanity and sociability.

Thus on the one hand religion, state and ideology (*qua* idealist philosophy) alienate producers from their real, material conditions and interests; on the other, the objective conditions of production themselves come to rule over producers, both mystifying them and really subjecting them to forces they sustain but cannot control. The imperatives of the 'hidden hand' of the market must be obeyed as surely as the originally untamed powers of nature and their projection onto the gods, and they seem equally mysterious. In commodity production, 'a definite social relation between men ... assumes, in their eyes, the fantastic form of a relation between things' analogous to 'the mist-enveloped regions of the religious world'.[60] Ideology, alienation, commodity fetishism and reification are thus closely related. Like Hegelian essence, it is nevertheless of the essence of capital that it should appear as mysterious to its bearers, in its commodity form. It is insufficient merely to understand it, since the productive system really does operate as 'an overriding law of nature'; the overcoming of alienation means both recognising the social relations which underpin it and changing them.

The life-process of society, which is based on the process of material production, does not strip off its mystical veil until it is treated as production by freely associated men, and is consciously regulated by them in accordance with a settled plan.[61]

This is then how Marx's own narrative unfolds: beginning with need under conditions of an external nature, humanity's motivation is to humanise/dominate the objective realm and thereby to achieve both abundance and its thorough rationalisation by recreating it in human form. This is why Communism will be the riddle of history solved: a rational economy that is both transparent in its organisation and planned to satisfy need universally. Without claiming an idealist ontology whereby reason and being are one, it satisfies the Hegelian goal of reconciliation, materially: by reproducing nature through labour such that it is both wholly knowable *in* its objectivity and the real is rendered actually rational.

More importantly for negativity, however, the history between primordial beginnings and Communism is one in which the alienation between humans and nature takes the form of class struggle and so Hegel's dialectical choreography, of incremental progress punctuated by contradictions, is also replicated. For the evolution of productive forces would not yield a *dialectical* negativity if it merely registered the species' ingenuity in transforming nature. The contradictions that drive history are produced by a mismatch between two tempos: the evolution of productive forces, which is a species, universal task, does not map smoothly onto the lurching development of the social relations of production, which move between encouraging and fettering production depending on the interests and powers of the economically-dominant class. Thus the forces of production are not an efficient cause propelling a chain of causes and effects, because their expansion is periodically blocked. This results in contradictions played out through class conflict and a complicated history of shifting dialectical configurations. Such dialectical momentum explains why, when Marx summarises his views in 1859, the static model of hierarchical storeys and correspondences is supplemented by a dynamic account of how the various parts move into conflict.[62] Contradiction is not between false consciousness and reality, subject and object, but between productive forces and the relations of ownership and appropriation. It occurs within the economic foundation whose ideological misrepresentation is functional for its reproduction as well as an expression of its existential horizon.

If an interim summary is offered at this point, it becomes obvious that negativity cannot be pinned down within Marx's thinking to a single force or agency, but enjoys a certain heterogeneity which yields both richness and tension to his thought. Thus it can be discerned as a historical force which originates as a splitting within nature (the aperture of sensuous suffering) but then more significantly translates into labour, whose social division engenders both more elaborate forces of production and social distinctions which will harden into class antagonisms, the former exemplifying history's energy and the latter imposing upon it a pattern of growth and entropy, consolidation and revolution. It is through the negations wrought by oppressed classes that history is saved from the terminal inertia of congealed class interests. Although historical momentum, and thus a certain negativity *qua* becoming, is inherent in the material forces of need and labour, the *dialectical* negativity that underpins Marxism derives from the class differences and contradictions that inscribe it, lending to history its recognisable logic.

At a certain stage, capitalism itself appears to accrue the powers of generativity that natural and social relations had previously exhibited. In this context a certain negativity becomes lodged in the popular imaginary: Marx describes the system's 'rapid development', the 'constant revolutionising' of the means of production and the 'constantly expanding market', in the *Communist Manifesto*. In this immense creative–destructive upsurge, there is 'uninterrupted disturbance of all social conditions and everlasting uncertainty and agitation', where 'all that is solid melts into air'.

It is possible to describe this process as a purely structural one, where individuals are merely the bearers and performers of prescribed roles and negativity works as an anonymous force. Indeed, under the alien and mysterious structures that dominate capitalism, it is appropriate to write in this way if form is to follow content, and it is perhaps unsurprising that Marx should have thought again of the abstract formalism of Hegel's *Logic*.[63] For here is a real, historically-engendered, inversion of subject and predicate. 'It is now no longer the labourer that employs the means of production, but the means of production that employ the labourer.' They 'consume him as the ferment necessary to their own life-process, and the life-process of capital consists only in its movement as value constantly expanding, constantly multiplying itself.'[64]

> ... once adopted into the production process of capital, the means of labour passes through different metamorphoses, whose culmination is the *machine*, or rather, an *automatic system of machinery* (...), set in motion by an automaton consisting of numerous mechanical and intellectual organs, so that the workers themselves are cast merely as its conscious linkages ... . Labour appears ... merely as a conscious organ, scattered among the individual living workers at numerous points of the mechanical system; subsumed under the total process of the machinery itself, as itself only a link of the system, whose unity exists ... in the living (active) machinery, which confronts his individual, insignificant doings as a mighty organism.[65]

A structuralist or machinist account of the system is then appropriate but it is also historically specific; limited in that it participates in the alienation it describes. For capitalism, like Hegelian idealism, must be inverted if alienation is to be overcome, since for all its dynamism it still moves within a broader dialectics of contradiction that will destroy it. Its own dynamic only reproduces more of the same (commodification). Progressive destruction however requires a self-conscious act of negation and, before it can succeed, dialectical agents must make sense of the web of social forces that reproduce this infernal machine.

The politics of negation

What is politically novel about Marx's dialectic is that he associates the negation for which a decadent capitalism is ripe with a particular social force: the proletariat. Thus 'material force must be overthrown by material force. But theory also becomes a material force once it has gripped the masses.'[66] Idealist philosophy, religion, and political theories of the communitarian or rights-based state, are all condemned in the early writings as abstract, fantastic resolutions to (and symptoms of) the isolated and competitive individualism of bourgeois existence. It is civil society whose conditions need negating and this requires a materially-efficacious form of negativity.

Returning to the two-tiered dialectic, it is nevertheless obvious how ambiguous the proletariat's status remains within Marx's thinking. From the perspective of a teleological history, it is at first only speculatively derived: as a class that is already the negation of bourgeois society because, devoid of property or humanity, it represents total lack, generalised wrong, exclusion from civil society.[67] Here it is an idealised negating force as well as history's Truth; the universal class without factional interests that is equivalent to Hegel's bureaucracy. In so far as history is interpreted as guaranteeing proletarian victory as its Truth, the approach is no longer itself dialectical but replicates Hegel's inversion of subject and predicate. On the other hand, Marx does go on to show both that the working class is the necessary precondition and gravedigger of capitalism (because its exploitation yields the surplus value which is reinvested to drive the process forward) and how it is politically forged as a concentrated but exploited mass sharing common interests in the system's overthrow. In other words, it is shown methodologically to have structural privilege, while its sociological condition is also elicited from a wealth of data about the system's evolution. Its historical significance emerges from an analysis of its place within the totality of social and economic forces. As such, its definitive role is contingent on the latter and it no longer represents their merely abstract negation. It is in this sense that the proletariat is derived from the methodological practices commended by the dialectic's rational kernel, rather than metaphysically, and two important indices of negativity follow.

The first concerns the working class's own practices. If it is to negate with the requisite self-consciousness, it must act in awareness of its historical task (otherwise it does not overcome alienation, since the productive process must be restored to rational, social control). Moreover it must act strategically, reading the field of forces to gauge when material conditions are ripe and political conditions propitious. To engage in a praxis is thus to *act* dialectically, where theory emerges from existence as a back and forth between experience and its conceptualisation (as concepts evolved out of content for Hegel via subject–object reciprocity). Theory is no more to be imposed on the masses than abstract categories are to be subjectively imposed upon nature. Rather, it will strike a resonance among the masses if it expresses what they live, inciting practices that change conditions in a theoretically-informed, determinate way. Remove the teleological narrative, and this leaves a field of contingent forces in which no particular outcome is guaranteed although structural trajectories can be deciphered. This subject–object *relationship* is therefore distinct from the sort of subject–object *identity* that thinkers like Lukács had posited. It restores negativity to the contingent processes of negation. (It also shifts the productive ferment of negativity away from contradictions within the economic infrastructure, back towards a more Hegelian reciprocity between life and thought, which had also marked the pre-alienated, pre-ideological relation between material existence and consciousness, for Marx.)

Furthermore, the significance of proletarian victory cannot be limited to an act of negation. It also concerns the political style – practices of liberty – it instantiates thereafter.[68] For if the dialectic is ongoing and history continues with its contingencies and antagonisms, then it is important to ask what sort of politics will be appropriate to it. In other words, the crucial question is whether proletarian victory must be a negation of the negation antecedent to a new phase of positivity – the administration of things; Kojèvean boredom – or whether it simply restores domination-free (yet still agonistic) spaces wherein negativity engenders new forms of coexistence and negotiates power differently. As such, one might speculate that practising liberty might become a process which sustains, indeed exemplifies, negativity, through dialectical political performances that avoid the alternating stagnations and explosions of previous history. (I will explore this further in chapter 4.)

Meanwhile, Marx himself sometimes presents the revolution as a protracted phase in which a ferment of unimaginable creation–destruction occurs; a revaluation of all values where revolutionary experiences of solidarity transform bourgeois egoism as well as rendering redundant the oppressive institutions of liberal-capitalist society. But will the working class then be trapped in its own whirlpool of disintegration, unable to build sustainable institutions and collective practices, or will those practices emerge out of a politics that performs negativity? For if the 'rational kernel' of the dialectic is recognised, does it not call for a politics that might avoid the traumas of contradiction by emulating processes of generativity whose fecundity lies in a play of differences which are not allowed to reach the stage of contradictory opposition? In this sense, a dialectical politics would be interwoven with, and analogous to, a dialectical methodology: two inter-related levels on which subject–object and subject–subject reciprocities are practised to yield a politics whose style and rhythms are those of negativity.

This brings us to the second index of negativity I mentioned, which concerns Marx's own theoretical intervention. Whether or not one believes that Marx followed Hegel in abandoning negativity depends largely on the interpretation and weight that are given to his own later works as a critical intervention deploying a dialectical methodology.

Marx's dialectical method

In *Capital*, Marx aims to reveal the law of a specific mode of production. The core of its development lies in the commodity form, which is both the secret of its productivity and the nexus of its contradictions.[69] Like Hegel's *Logic*, the logic of Marx's own method here will move from simple to complex, abstract to concrete (i.e. fully mediated). To begin with, Marx presents himself analogously to the natural scientist who abstracts micro-scopic cells and then builds up a picture of their real relations, but he is more insistent in a subsequent afterword that he does not make the same mistake as other political economists who seek regularities as the physicist does. More like the biologist, his laws are evolutionary and contextual because like the organism, the abstract parts he begins with are intercon-nected and their actual movement can only be generalised after exploring their different modes of development. A structural and genetic analysis is thus needed because of the complex relations between whole and parts, truth and appearances. In fact, however, the method is more dialectical than these analogies suggest, because body and cell are not just developmental but, as commodity and capitalism, also self-destructive; rent by immanent contradictions. Moreover, the 'scientist' who reveals their law must proceed in a dialectical way, which means deriving concepts and tendencies out of the movement of the material itself and not imposing pre-conceived abstrac-tions upon it.

Nevertheless Marx seems to be arguing, like the scientist, that reality has a certain structure which he can adequately represent. It is only that that structure is dialectical and thus requires a dialectical presentation. 'If this is done successfully, if the life of the subject-matter is ideally reflected as in a mirror, then it may appear as if we had before us a mere a priori construc-tion.'[70] The result seems to be rather positivist (in the sense Kojève attributes to Hegel's third tier) because, epistemologically, the mirror metaphor is usually deployed to suggest an accurate reflection of one static medium by another. A complicated theory and presentation would be needed to achieve this totality, but if it succeeded it would seem to have more to do with truth than with a critical engagement within reality.

A mirror also suggests, however, an infinite series of reflections, and Marx adds that his method 'regards every historically developed social form as in fluid movement, and therefore takes into account its transient nature not less than its momentary existence; because it lets nothing impose upon it, and is in its essence critical and revolutionary.'[71] As in the *Logic*, where every form involved both being and nothing, each is for Marx a combination of identity and negativity: in its rational form it combines a positive acknowledgement of existing things and 'the recognition of the negation of that state, of its inevitable breaking up.' To grasp and convey this fluidity must surely involve a difficult mediation and not merely the induction of a law from the given or the imposition of a formula. For the object is over-determined and both is, and is caught up in, a force field which requires an interpretive (re)construction from within. Because it is in process, both homeostatic and unstable, its conceptualisation must be as lively as it is and this means an ongoing analysis of its internal tendencies. The method is Hegel's but, precisely because the real is not estranged Spirit for Marx, there can be no guarantee that its articulation is accurate. This is why Marx's statement is presented in conditional terms: if the dialectical theorisation is done well, it will *seem* as if the conceptualisation has captured the real in its dynamism. It will appear as if there is a mirroring back and forth between reality and concept precisely because there has been a subject–object dialectic at work methodologically (analogous to, but on a more rarefied level than, praxis). Thus reality is not simply there, awaiting articulation, as the empiricist believes, but relies on the 'reproduction of the concrete by way of thought'. 'The concrete is concrete only because it is the concentration of many determinations, hence the unity of the diverse.'[72] If the dialectic has not completed itself in Absolute Knowledge, then the theorist must engage critically within an open totality in its contingency and mobility and as such, she practises negativity; that is, she repeats on the level of theory, the mediations that occur on an existential level. As Balibar says: what interests Marx is 'the relation of forces in play at any particular moment, determining the direction of its advance.'[73] In order to ascertain internal tendencies, anticipated dialectical developments must be compared with actual historical trends.[74] There is no sense of subsuming the facts under some crude logic of contradiction, although contradiction is not precluded and yields the system's anticipated moment of rupture.

There are also historical parallels between reality and thought here. Just as over time simple forms evolved into more complex unities, so thinking in terms of simple categories builds up to mediated wholes.[75] Similarly, the bourgeois economy is described as an organic system wherein every economic relation presupposes every other. Its development into a totality 'consists precisely in subordinating all elements of society to itself, or in creating out of it the organs which it still lacks. This is historically how it becomes a totality.'[76] It is this totality in its concrete complexity of identity *and* contradiction that the dialectical method tries to convey. This is why the system is observable but not empirical: it is the relation between parts that imparts its momentum and, although the parts can be seen, their connections remain invisible to the non-dialectical voyeur. It is important that theory cannot be the same as the real in its reified material form, otherwise there would be no scope for criticism. But more profoundly, the real is a dialectic of ideal and material relations, not a congealed positivity (like Sartre's *en-soi*), and the dialectical thinker practises this relation only on a more abstract level. It would seem to follow nevertheless that as history itself becomes more complex (in its productive and social relations) and more mystified, so the dialectical method is itself a (necessary) historical product since only it can capture the historically-mediated totality in its dynamic, weblike complexity.

In conclusion, I think there is some lack of clarity on Marx's point as to what he actually does: in part because he wants to defend a narrative abstractly engendered as well as to elicit its historical validity and in part, because there is a genuine problem in applying Hegel's method to a material world. I have nevertheless tried to present an interpretation of his approach that is conducive to seeing it as a practising of negativity and in this sense, the work of the dialectical theorist and the politics of the proletariat, while they must be dialectically interwoven, are also structurally analogous. Both engage critically in a contingent world, struggling to construct meaning, whether symbolic or material, out of its diverse linkages and according to its rhythms as a dialectical ontology, or better phenomenology, describes them. In this sense Marx's actual analysis of capitalism, and the historical studies he undertook, are of more significance than his pronouncements on his method. The important thing is to engage in the open but unfolding relations between subjects and objects, concepts and reality, reading their vectors in terms of progressive forces and potential for change. In this reading of Marx, we can begin to anticipate the negative dialectics practised by Merleau-Ponty and Adorno, which will be explored in chapters 4 and 5. Totality here does not mean totalitarianism, an elision mischievously made by some of Marx's recent critics. It does not imply reduction to the same, false universalism or closure, but engagement in and emulation of a process whereby threads are woven and parts mediated.

From dialectics to *différance*

Before concluding this chapter, I want to introduce a rather different line of criticism of the Hegelian dialectic: one which is broadly identified with post-structuralism and that derives its sense of negativity from Nietzsche rather than Marx. This sense will be explored more fully in later chapters but at this stage, I want to anticipate it by considering the antipathy it has generated towards Hegel (and Marx). What distinguishes it from earlier Marxist and existentialist misgivings is that its target is dialectical negativity itself. Indeed this new reproach often appears to reject the very notion of the negative and so it will be necessary to offer a provisional justification for continuing to associate it with negativity at all.

My own analysis has in fact pushed Hegel more in this direction than his critics generally acknowledge since despite their differences, the thinkers mentioned below agree that dialectical negativity for Hegel remained tied to logical categories which prevented him from approaching that which reason excludes, other than to rationalise it. As negation, negativity belongs to the sphere of judgement and knowing and cannot therefore break out of their circuit. The Hegelian terms that are challenged here are central to the dialectic: negation (and the relationship it entails between identity and difference, self and other), *Aufhebung*, synthesis, contradiction, totality.[77] It is no longer the historical fate of a recalcitrant *materiality* that is at stake, with the attendant aim of rendering these ideal terms practically efficacious, but the question of *alterity*: of a radical otherness heterogeneous to reason and thus to the categories of the negative that dialectics employs. Although this shift is not devoid of political implications, it does generally move the explicit focus of critique from one of changing the real to a questioning of philosophy's own standing.

Hegel is designated here as *the* philosopher of identity, although he is also credited with some intimation of an other mobility at work: one I earlier cited as the first, most elusive dimension of negativity. It is to this generativity that Julia Kristeva gestures when she distinguishes between negation as a logical procedure and negativity as a mobility or energy that underlies, invades and produces reason. Negativity in Hegel, she explains, is what 'reformulates the static *terms* of pure abstraction as a process, dissolving and binding them within a mobile law.'[78] It thus constitutes the impetus *beneath* negation. More explicitly, 'negativity is the liquifying and dissolving agent that does not destroy but rather reactivates new organizations and, in that sense, affirms.'[79] It is a productive force that breaks through reified structures and opens the way to new forms, which it again destabilises against closure. To formalise the dialectic in terms of its triadic structure is then to freeze this fluidity and Kristeva insists that Hegel was himself aware of this dilemma, since he too defined 'this negativity as the *fourth term* of the true dialectic: triplicity is only an appearance in the realm of understanding.'[80]

For Kristeva herself this negativity (whose modulations will be explored in chapter 6) is material, unconscious, semiotic. Its rhythmic pulsing outside the circle Hegel closed irrupts, she insists, to destabilise being, rather than being sublated into becoming. In so far as the 'fourth term' suggested an excessive movement that threatened to overflow the dialectical structure while defying reason's will to full representation and complete knowledge, Hegel suppressed this mobility. He abandoned 'negativity's powerful moment: the scission that exceeds and precedes the advent of thetic under-standing.'[81] Having glimpsed it at work 'beneath all rationality', he subordinated it to Absolute Knowledge by a 'masterly stroke', unable to acknowledge its heterogeneity outside of the system of meaning.[82]

Derrida locates this hiatus in a contradiction between Hegel's writing and his system. 'I believe that Hegel's text is necessarily fissured; that it is some-thing more and other than the circular closure of its representation.' If Hegel tried to suppress this negativity, it is by no means absent: 'his text exceeds its meaning, permits itself to be turned away from, to return to, and to repeat itself outside its self-identity' (P: 77–8).[83] While Hegel might have believed that it is being which writes itself in his philosophy to produce a legible script, there is another productivity that inscribes his text and disrupts the identity he sought to restore. In trying to suppress it, he unwit-tingly admitted that which produces and fractures conceptual effects but which operates according to a 'strange "logic"' that Derrida calls, among other things, différance (P: 40).

It is this movement whose generativity is then evoked, as more originary than the dialectical mode of becoming, by those French philosophers who have been influenced by the rhythms of Nietzsche's will to power. Because of negativity's association with Hegel, its exponents are reluctant to present this heterogeneous and unrepresentable productivity in these terms and it is true that its rhythms are quite different. Yet it is not gratuitous that they should offer it through reference to Hegelian negativity. For if its modula-tions and ontology differ, I suggest that both dialectics and this 'other mobility' (one whose rhythms have been invoked by many recent French philosophers despite their own diversity) yet share certain aspects that warrant their all being brought under the motif of negativity.

Provisionally, I suggest, this arises from a common effort at articulating, invoking or performing the principle of generativity itself: that force or movement which both renders meaning and institution possible yet menaced, and which inscribes their possibilities of endurance or transforma-tion. Negativity thus conveys a restlessness that disturbs the slumbers of the given; that undermines any reified plenitude, presence, power or position, be it representational or political. It is affirmative in its engendering (creative, although sometimes in a destructive mode), yet negating (critical, transgres-sive, subversive, etc) vis-à-vis the positive. As such, the motif of negativity itself refuses definition in terms of any simple binary opposition (positive/negative). Yet in this provisional sketch I have retained a sense of negativity as opposition to the positive and as I insisted in my Introduction, it is this political ethos that justifies retaining this term, which brings along its retinue of oppositional associations. Accordingly, I suggest that what distinguishes Hegel from his later French critics is less their rejection of negativity *per se* than the different logics, tempos, rhythms or economy they ascribe to it. It is the significance of these differences (which will become clearer following my discussion of Nietzsche in the following chapter) for politics that interests me in this book. In order to start exploring the continuity and difference I am claiming here, it will be helpful to begin by looking more carefully at the reasons why philosophers of difference are generally unhappy with the terminology of the negative, which they associate specifically with Hegelian dialectics, although they are not in most cases wholly averse to deploying the term.

While Kristeva does hesitantly retain the term, it is Derrida whom she credits with making the most radical attempt at pushing post-Hegelian 'dialectical negativity further and elsewhere', in his non-totalising conceptions of *différance*, *écriture*, the trace and so on.[84] In what sense(s), then, can negativity be ascribed to *différance* and its 'non-synonymous substitutes', and why does Derrida himself present the term in relation to Hegel? Indeed Derrida confesses that we must incessantly return to Hegel since it is the challenge of approaching an alterity irredeemable by reason, and thus the very possibility of philosophy, that he had posed and exemplified (P: 77). Always aware that arguments which challenge dialectics risk becoming integrated into it, deconstruction must proceed in a novel way.[85]

Derrida introduces *Margins of Philosophy* by referring to philosophy as a discursive project of thinking its other, with the ambition thereby of gaining mastery over its own limit. He asks if this means *aufheben* (the sublation of alterity), or 'does the limit, obliquely, by surprise, always reserve one more blow for philosophical knowledge?' This question is posed, he makes clear, within but against Hegelian phenomenology (M: xf). It is Hegel who tries to ontologise the remainder, the excess, by thinking it within the circuit of logic and by tracing and completing its phenomenology, its coming to meaning. The challenge is then to approach alterity without reducing it to the Logos or ontologising it as philosophy's Other (as nothingness, non-being, noumenon). Derrida approaches this problem by rejecting the oppositions that spatial metaphors of inside/outside suggest, moving instead towards a displacement of the limit between them and turning to the unrepresentable within thinking itself. He conveys this not in terms of a line that proscribes or invites traversal, but as a labyrinth. From this perspective Hegel's aporia is more like Kant's: having engendered alterity by excluding it, he found himself haunted by a return of the repressed.

Derrida's deconstructive move is conveyed in *Margins* by the figure of the tympanum, the thin membrane of the ear that is both inside and outside but obliquely stretched so that it vibrates. By invoking this sonic diaphragm, Derrida intends to avoid any simple form of negation ('opposition in all forms of *anti-*') and to suggest an undecidable limit whose timbre (its beating, pulsations, musical cadences) is other than that of the Logos. Thus 'beyond the philosophical text there is not a blank, virgin, empty margin, but another text, a weave of differences of forces without any present center of reference' and towards whose general economy – an 'inexhaustible reserve, the stereographic activity of an entirely other ear' – the written text 'overflows and cracks its meaning'. It is this cracking that he would then discern within the Hegelian text, but he also presents his own project in distinction from Hegel's. If 'the Hegelian wound [*Beleidigung, Verletzung*] always *appears* sewn up again', then the task is 'to give birth, from the lesion without suture, to some unheard-of partition' (M: xxiii–xxvi). Otherness is not outside or beneath reason, as the quotes from Kristeva seem to claim, but within it.

The 'weave of differences of forces' referred to above is evocative of Deleuze's rendition of will to power.[86] It takes many forms but one of its more accessible indices is discernible semiologically, when Derrida derives his motif of *différance* from Saussurean linguistics even while acknowledging the term's 'relations of profound affinity with Hegelian discourse'. Unable to break with that discourse, *différance* does operate, he claims, an 'infinitesimal, if radical, displacement' of it (M: 14). More definitively, he adds that if 'there were a definition of *différance*, it would be precisely the limit, the interruption, the destruction of the Hegelian *relève* [*Aufhebung*] *wherever* it operates' (P: 40). Since one cannot escape Hegelian logic by negating it, one must disrupt it by other means.

The term *différance* literally incarnates, or exemplifies, aspects of the negativity it invokes. Although provisionally called a concept or word it is neither; it is indicative of what cannot be named (M: 26). Unlike a concept, it does not universalise or identify since it is too mobile, heterogeneous and polysemic to fulfil such functions. Derrida refers to it rather as a 'sheaf'; a complex weaving and interlacing comprised of multiple threads and lines of force which lead in many directions. Yet it is no dialectical totality, since it 'unceasingly dislocates itself' in a chain of substitutions. It operates at the very limits of metaphysical language, by rejecting what the latter aspires to in terms of identification, stability and clarity. It is even marked by its own graphic (but mute) difference (the 'a' which in its French pronunciation is indistinguishable from the 'correct' 'e'), suggesting both a transgression (of the law of spelling) and the silent play that *différance* linguistically involves, where it is the inaudible difference between phonemes that is their condition of being heard. Just as for Merleau-Ponty the invisible was the condition for visibility, so for Derrida this silent play – which has no sensible or intelligible status, no possibility of presence, no ontology – is the condition of language. It is in this sense much more radically negative than any 'occult of nonknowledge' or 'hole with indeterminate borders' (M: 3–6). It is not a sign because it signifies nothing that could be made present (it is no mere absence or substitute) and it plays no legislative role of denial or proscription. If it is more originary than dialectics and reason, *différance* is not *an* origin (it is not, like *Geist*, 'an organic, original, and homogeneous unity that eventually

76

would come to be divided, to receive difference as an event' (M: 14)). Typically, its negativity is thus invoked by explaining what it is not: as Derrida summarises it, '*différance* is *not*' (M: 21).

Although *différance* involves a complex of meanings, two are pre-eminent: the temporalisation of deferral and the spatial distribution of differences. The first defies completion or synthesis, since this *play* (unlike the '*labour* of the negative', as Deleuze had insisted on calling it) is unlike dialectical dynamism: there is no progressive, temporal succession, a coming-to-meaning. 'Play is the disruption of presence ... . Play is always play of absence and presence, but if it is to be thought radically, play must be conceived of before the alternative of presence and absence.'[87]

The second, however, looks more reminiscent of the Hegelian process of engendering identity from difference. Thus, for Saussure, Derrida reminds us, 'the system of signs is constituted solely by the differences in terms, and not by their plentitude.' Signification functions due to the network of oppositions that distinguish and relate elements. In language there are thus 'only differences *without positive terms*' (M: 10). Each so-called present element is related to something other than itself, 'thereby keeping within itself the mark of the past element' and anticipating future ones, hence bearing within itself traces, a 'synthesis of marks' (M: 13). However this is not negative (or positive) in the sense of determinate negation, contradiction and synthesis: it is through the generativity of a non-logical negativity *qua* non-ontologised alterity – intervals, spaces, distances – that sense emerges and dissolves. (Deleuze criticises Saussure for presenting these differences as negative, where everything, he insists, 'points to the contrary': that is, to the 'peculiar thickness' of an affirmative, productive, differentiation.[88]) If for Hegel there is always a negation of the negation – the co-defining other is taken back into the thing to enrich its identity – for Derrida identity is deferred along the chain of signifiers and the other is never assimilated in a synthetic process.

The spacing that produces effects is thick with relations, but it does not obey any logical category in its productivity. It has no location and is no immediacy; rather it is a mobile and genetic operation, an active spa*c*ing, that inscribes alterity within every position. 'Spacing designates *nothing*, nothing that is, no presence at a distance; it is the index of an irreducible exterior, and at the same time of a *movement*, a displacement that indicates an irreducible alterity' (P: 81). It has no identity of its own, but interrupts all identity while producing it (it 'carries the meaning of a productive, positive, generative force', a 'genetic motif' (P: 106f n.42)). Unlike Kantian space it neither metaphorically circumscribes reason *vis-à-vis* an unknowable exterior, not adumbrates any causal and universal Newtonian order. Unlike Hegelian temporality, there is no becoming.

Like dialectics, *différance* indicates an affirmative process of engendering attributable to the negative, but it never engenders unified wholes. Thus we will designate as *différance* the movement according to which language, or any other code, any other system of reference in general, is constituted 'historically' as a tissue of differences. 'Is constituted,' 'is produced,' 'is created,' 'movement,' 'historically,' etc., have to be understood beyond the metaphysical language in which they are caught, along with all their implications.

(P: 104 n.31)

The term designates (in classical terminology) 'the process of scission and division which would produce or constitute different things or differences'; 'the playing movement that "produces" ... differences, these effects of difference' (M: 10,12). It does not therefore mediate given identities in their difference, but is the differentiating process itself: one whose impetus does not arise from the binarism of contradiction but flows promiscuously within and beneath it. Derrida concludes his discussion by calling on us to affirm *différance* in a very Nietzschean (and Deleuzean) way: by dance and laughter, without nostalgia, in an 'affirmation foreign to all dialectics' (M: 27).

It is important to keep in mind that despite the mobility of this process, it does nevertheless produce historical effects: that is, specific differences are contextual, historical and enjoy a certain inertia. If no teleological trajectory can be traced or transcendentally grounded, deferral and differentiation do not just trickle away along endless substitutions within particular historical texts and institutions, for then meaning and communication would be impossible. This is why metaphysics is inescapable and deconstruction, a ceaseless project. It is both why the principle of *différance* bears within itself subversive implications for reified forms that lay claim to natural or metaphysical stability, *and* why semantic and political closures are able to endure. In other words, this is where violence and power become lodged, the site of a (textual) politics. Deconstruction emphasises the mobility of *différance*, but it is in the hiatus between the latter's undisciplined generativity and its production of positive forms that a critical, political interval opens (as I will explain in the next chapter, this is much clearer in Foucault's work).

When invited to clarify his views in the interviews reproduced in *Positions*, Derrida was even more explicit about their relation to Hegel, insisting that his own critical operation – deconstruction – was directed against 'dialectics of the Hegelian type', since that always idealised its other by a spiritual uplifting (*relève*) to a higher level.

Hegelian idealism consists precisely of a *relève* of the binary oppositions of classical idealism, a resolution of contradiction into a third term that comes in order to *aufheben*, to deny while raising up, while idealizing, while sublimating into an anamnesiac interiority (*Erinnerung*), while *interning* difference in a self-presence.

(P: 43)

Nevertheless Derrida clearly found it necessary to pursue clarification via this opposition and it is obvious that there is some internal affinity between the terms. Deconstruction, he explains, must 'avoid both simply *neutralizing* the binary oppositions of metaphysics and simply *residing* within the closed field of these oppositions, thereby confirming it.' This caveat is reminiscent of Hegel's case against understanding: contradiction must be both sustained and gone beyond. One must proceed by way of a double gesture, but one that is now the inverse of dialectics. For oppositions are not simply antithetical for Derrida, but in a 'violent hierarchy' which must first be inverted. The next phase is not then one of synthesis, but a disruption of the dualistic figure of opposition itself (hence: de-synthesis; deconstruction not *relève*; a sort of dialectical regression). What occurs is not a new term that reconciles (becoming), but 'the irruptive emergence of a new "concept," a concept that can no longer be, and never could be, included in the previous régime' (P: 41). Instead of antithesis/synthesis, there is thus inversion/subversion; not the two reconciled by a third, but an irruption of an undecidable that defies identity. (This is for example Derrida's strategy for feminism: to identify and invert the binary opposition of sexual difference, but also to render it unworkable by provoking the heterogeneity that produces yet deconstructs it[89].)

It is not then contradiction, but the multiplicity of the undecidable (the unconscious of philosophical contradiction) that is disruptive and immune to representation or recuperation (P: 101 n.13). Undecidables (like *différance*) are terms which combine several, perhaps incompatible, meanings beneath one signifier and cannot therefore be included within an opposition because they inhabit it, 'resisting and disorganizing it, *without ever* constituting a third term, without ever leaving room for a solution in the form of speculative dialectics' (P: 43). Against dialectical totalising, dissemination 'marks an irreducible and *generative* multiplicity.' Totalisation is always interrupted, Derrida insists, by a 'nerve, a fold, an angle' where closure or reassembly are impossible (P: 45f). In Freudian terms, the difference between negativity *qua différance* and dialectical negation is that between the primary and secondary processes. If Hegelian logic cannot be definitively exceeded, deconstruction is a permanent process of destabilising it: a practising of that most radical negativity which Hegel glimpsed and suffered on the margins, in the fissures, of his thinking yet which he was unable to incorporate within his rational project.

Derrida practises this deconstructive reading on Hegel's own system in *Glas*, drawing it towards those impossible sites where the system is exceeded and dialectical appropriation defied. He reads Hegel's texts according to a rhythm of development and rupture, fits and starts, jolts and jerks designed to disrupt the ineluctable unfolding of the system's triadic development.[90] In other words, he writes according to the agitations of the differently-modulated negativity that *différance* opposes to dialectics. Later, Marx's system would be subjected to a similar treatment. Derrida would in fact like to rehabilitate Marx as a radical thinker, but this again means deconstructing his penchant for totalising thought. He accordingly invokes plural voices, or spirits – an 'irreducible heterogeneity, an internal untranslatability' – within Marx's texts (which Marx himself resisted) in order to subvert their totality. It is in this disjointedness that he then locates a 'spectral asymmetry' whose undecidable status renders it a further substitution for *différance* and which he associates here with non-dialectical difference.

In traditional metaphysical mode, Marx wanted to distinguish between being and non-being; between communism as absent versus its realisation.[91] But, like the promise of democracy to come invoked elsewhere, Derrida summons the spectre that haunts Europe as resistant to this sort of ontology. Communism cannot be brought to presence, it cannot *be* without destroying itself (as permanent revolution, as negativity, as the promise of justice), but neither is it simply absent since its haunting renders it virtually more actual than if it lived: it remains an unfulfilled promise, a spacing,[92] that haunts Europe. The ghost that is undecidably dead and alive, subject and object, mind and body, visible and invisible, intelligible and sensible, is no *Geist*, but enjoys a 'paradoxical phenomenality' which resists opposition or ontology. Derrida's hauntology thus aims to rescue Marx by subverting his belief that alienation can be overcome by distinguishing between appearances (apparitions) and real presence (actuality). But in saving negativity from the positivism of a putative realisation and a politics of presence, does it not evade the audacity and efficacy of political intervention, with its inevitable moments of closure? I will raise this question again in chapter 4, but what I want to indicate here is the way Derrida believes he re-radicalises Marx by prising him away from the dialectical language he owed to Hegel and re-presenting his negativity as an index of *différance*; as more of an ethics than a praxis.

In relating Derrida to Hegel, I have suggested that *différance* has an affinity with dialectics yet gestures towards another modulation of negativity: one glimpsed in yet resisted by and disruptive of his texts. In this context it is worth taking a brief excursion through a recent essay by Jean-Luc Nancy, 'The Surprise of the Event'.[93] Nancy advances some analogous claims to Derrida (and Deleuze) regarding difference, despite a more obviously ontological (and Heideggerian) language, but he is more explicit in his references to negativity here.

At the heart of Nancy's essay there again lies the problematic of a generativity that is more originary, more *negative*, than the dialectic. He seeks 'the dialectical mainspring at the point of which, before being the resources and motivating force, has to be the trigger or investigation, and hence its negativity *itself*.'[94] He speaks in this context of 'happening itself', the '*as such* of the event'; of leap, spacing and rupture; creation and surprise. It is not what happens, but the happening itself that is in question: the heart of a becoming that is both more inaccessible and more decisive (as Derrida also insists of *différance*) than the actual passage of history.

It was indeed this 'logic of happening' [*arriver*] that Hegel himself pursued, according to Nancy, when he spoke in the *Logic* of an 'agitated instability' (*haltungslose Unruhe*). In making this claim Nancy refers us to the section on Essence and its competing interpretations, which I discussed earlier. Opposing readings of essence as the ground of mere appearance, Nancy accords with its interpretation as Hegel's effort to convey the 'being of being' or, as he goes on to call it, the 'unpresentifiable of the present' in its 'structuring difference', the *differend*.[95] As such, negativity is not an even more subterranean and efficacious force than dialectics, whose result, symptom or effect is becoming or being, but the very 'condition of the formation of all forms' that is inherent within them. I previously alluded to this as Hegel's Nietzscheanism, since it is just this negativity which defies cause/effect, reality/appearance models in favour of a self-generativity that is called by Nietzsche, among other things, will to power.

Nancy insists, accordingly, that this negativity must not be confused with an Other which is not yet knowable, or some hidden presence defiant of representation. Much less can it be pursued as the target of a conceptual mission that would render it the object of thought: it is not the 'beyond-knowledge of a mystical negativity'; not *the* unpresentable nor a category of being; not spirit, substance or foundation.

> Empty time, or negativity as time, the event, itself makes up the "in itself" of the "thing in itself": this is no doubt exactly what Kant could not grasp, and Hegel and all of us who came after him ... keep aiming at.[96]

This is no abstract negativity linking successive events but time itself; the 'that there is', the difference and rupture needed for any process since if 'being simply was, nothing would happen and there would not be thought either.' Negativity is affirmative, creative.

Nancy admits that this reading of Hegel pushes him to the limit of viable interpretation but in any case, the latter failed to get a grasp on this negativity and Nancy is adamant (like Derrida) that its creativity is not dialectical fecundity. 'Negativity, here, does not negate itself, and does not raise [*relève*] itself out of itself. It does something else': it obeys 'another mode' which is the tension/extension of being; its happening which is not a narrative of progress, but there where there is a difference between nothing and something; the 'originary excision and chiasmus' that opens time and space to one another. This negativity is then no abyss from whose depth the event comes, but 'the affirmation of ek-sistent tension', the 'surprising tone of existence.'[97] Philosophy's task lies not in an impossible rendering of this affirmative negativity as positive by naming it, but in performing it, exemplifying it in a mode of astonishment, where thought is itself event, creation, an 'interminable game'. In this sense Nancy likens it to Deleuze's 'becoming-surprise of thought'[98], where philosophy is itself generativity. One of the questions I will want to ask is whether a politics might also be envisaged that is an emulation of this negativity.

I mentioned earlier that *différance* pulses with a rhythm redolent of will to power. Derrida himself seems especially influenced by Deleuze's presentation of Nietzsche. This modulation of negativity will be the focus of the next chapter, but it is important here to note how vehemently Deleuze opposed this play of difference to dialectics ('What I most detested was Hegelianism and dialectics'[99]). Because he associates difference with *positivity* and explicitly dissociates it from the negative, he presents a particular challenge to my intention of including all these productive forces under the motif of negativity, although it should already be evident that negativity and positivity are not necessarily exclusive in this context.

In *Nietzsche and Philosophy*, Deleuze insists that Marx's materialist inversion of the dialectic remains irrelevant, since it still deals abstractly with symptoms; with permutations of unreal terms. This is because it remains ignorant of the 'real element from which forces, their qualities and their relations derive.' Like Kristeva, Derrida and Nancy, Deleuze invokes some other generativity – difference – which produces representations and categories and cannot therefore be captured by them. If dialectics cites contradiction as its moving force, this is an unwarranted and abstract formula for the dense and multiplicitous plays of differentiation; for a repetition of the Same that differs without negation.

> Opposition can be the law of the relation between abstract products, but difference is the only principle of genesis or production; a principle which itself produces opposition as mere appearance. Dialectic thrives on oppositions because it is unaware of far more subtle and subterranean differential mechanisms: topographical displacements, typographical mechanisms.[100]

In this sense, dialectical negativity only very crudely approximates the differential games of will to power: 'the living depths, the diagonal, is populated by differences without negation. Beneath the platitude of the negative lies the world of "disparateness"'.[101] Dialectics thus misinterprets the nature of change, where singularities are repeated until patterns, forms, emerge. In this sense Deleuze moves further away from Hegel than the other philosophers discussed here, since he denies that difference relies upon negation.

In *Difference and Repetition*, Deleuze reiterates the sense in which contradiction remains a category whose meaning is tied to identity: it is the greatest difference only from this perspective. The negative in this sense regulates difference within categories of representation, subordinating it to identity by means of limitation (Kant) or opposition (Hegel). As such it tames it, rendering it off-limits because unthinkable, or admissible because only too thinkable; condemned or redeemed. This is indeed central to what Deleuze sees as philosophy's own creative quest of conquering the obscure, which requires 'causing a little of Dionysus's blood to flow in the organic veins of Apollo.' For Hegel this voyage into negativity is however deemed a charade. 'The intoxications and giddiness are feigned, the obscure is already clarified from the outset. Nothing shows this more clearly than the insipid monocentricity of the circles in the Hegelian dialectic.'[102]

In fact philosophy generally lacks any concept for difference *as* difference, as non-identical, according to Deleuze. If it is ontologically designated as non-being, this only introduces the mediations and eventual identity that Hegel's *Logic* revealed. Deleuze suggests that difference is better presented as the being of the problematic, written perhaps as ?-being or 0/0-being.[103] 'Not' here is to be interpreted not as the negative, an absence of being, a hole or outside, but as a fold wherein interrogation, creativity and genesis occur; the 'ideal, differential and problematic element' which is a 'positivity'. 'There is no synthesis, mediation or reconciliation in difference, but rather a stubborn differenciation.'[104]

What we see here is once again then a distinction between negation as a category of reason, and what Hegel's French critics variously call negativity or positivity. Across its variety of names – semiotic, *différance*, happening, difference, will to power, unconscious – it invokes the generative force and wild rhythms of the differential. As such it is too unreserved and excessive to fit within the dynamics of dialectics, but its evocation is still redolent of the effort to cite the modulations and forces which engender, circumscribe and destroy positive forms without replicating them. One can understand why there is a reluctance to associate this process with the negative, *qua* logical forms of negation and contradiction or the spatial metaphorics of holes and hollows, exteriors and limits. But I have suggested that it remains a negativity in a broader sense in that it destabilises the illusion of metaphysical, symbolic or political stability while gaining its powers of affirmation from the repetitive and meandering non-coincidences and spacings of difference. Negativity and affirmation are thus complementary rather than antithetical and if Deleuze captures this by using the term positivity, the latter's semantic association with the terminology of the negative remains apparent. Nevertheless, the way this translates into a politics will sustain a difference between dialectical negativity and that of its Nietzschean-inspired critics.

Indeed there is an additional source of antipathy towards the negative that comes from reading Nietzsche. This arises from its association with the reactive, ascetic, life-denying forces of *ressentiment* that Nietzsche identified with a slavish, nihilistic herd mentality. Thus Derrida refers to the guilt, nostalgia, mourning (for presence, immediacy, totality) of the 'saddened negative', whose other side would be the Nietzschean *affirmation* 'of the play of the world' and a surrendering to 'the *seminal* adventure of the trace.'[105] And Deleuze claims that the negative's labour and sad passions detract from the affirmative power of creation and decision which determine problems and also, from the real processes of politics.

> History progresses not by negation and the negation of the nega-
> tion, but by deciding problems and affirming differences. It is no
> less bloody and cruel as a result. Only the shadows of history live
> by negation: the good enter into it with all the power of a posited
> differential or a difference affirmed.[106]

Contradictions are not resolved in history, since they are only the penumbra of deeper, more complex problematics that are dissolved: 'Practical struggle never proceeds by way of the negative but by way of difference and its power of affirmation.'[107] In re-playing the positive/negative opposition, Deleuze thus invokes another rhythm of the political than that inherent in Marx's thinking.

In beginning to explore the similarities and differences between dialectical and post-Nietzschean difference, I have already anticipated the theme, or tension, that lies at the heart of this book, while alluding to its political significance. However there are still many adventures to be undertaken before the relationship between politics and negativity can be considered more explicitly. In particular, the experiments of those who would lead dialectics in a more resolutely negative direction call for consideration. And Nietzsche, whose importance has now been alluded to several times, must also be interrogated more fully. It is then to his will to power and the sense in which it is an allusion to negativity that the next chapter turns.

3

NIETZSCHE

Negativity as will to power

Such an experimental philosophy as I live anticipates experimentally even the possibilities of the most fundamental nihilism; but this does not mean that it must halt at a negation, a No, a will to negation. It wants rather to cross over to the opposite of this – to a Dionysian affirmation of the world as it is, without subtraction, exception, or selection ... . The highest state a philosopher can attain: to stand in a Dionysian relationship to existence – my formula for this is *amor fati*.[1]

Nietzsche is an important figure in the adventures of negativity, both because of his influence on subsequent adventurers, dialectical as well as postmodern, and because he often thinks in terms of negative versus affirmative: terms which emerge in his work with considerable existential resonance. He condemns values and forces associated with the negative – nihilism, metaphysical no-saying, dialectical negation, reactive forces, will to nothingness, guilt and *ressentiment* – which are for him symptoms of descending life and characteristic, even constitutive, of history, at least since the pre-Socratic Greeks. His revaluation of these negative orientations points to an affirmation such as the ancient Greek nobles allegedly practised and which *Übermenschen* (over-men) might again enjoy in a future beyond the nihilism of late modernity, where they would say Yes to life and its eternal recurrence.

The antithesis needs however to be qualified in two directions. First, although Nietzsche uses the opposition for critical and rhetorical purposes, affirmative and negative forces are in no sense foundational for him (as for example in a life versus death force or a moral imperative to good over evil). They are simply strengths or directions of one force – will to power – which has many intensities and manifestations. Moreover, the revaluation he has in mind would move beyond the negative figure of opposition itself, where one part is defined only through denial of its other. As the analysis of the noble–slave relation in *The Genealogy of Morality* concludes: 'Whereas all noble morality grows out of a triumphant saying "yes" to itself, slave morality says "no" on principle to everything that is "outside", "other", "non-self"'. Its 'action is basically a reaction' (GM I: 10); a resentful denying of life as such. The strong-spirited affirmers of life avoid such heteronomy: they celebrate their distance from the weak but do not define themselves in terms of it. The noble method of valuation

> acts and grows spontaneously, seeking out its opposite only so that it can say 'yes' to itself, thankfully and exultantly, – its negative concept 'low', 'common', 'bad' is only a pale contrast created after the event compared to its positive basic concept, saturated with life and passion, 'We the noble, the good, the beautiful and the happy!'
>
> (GM I: 10)

If this noble affirming were a simple positivism or celebration of plenitude then there would be no sense of *negativity* in Nietzsche's work. Great characters do not, however, praise a self-identical given or indulge a fullness too replete further to change. On the contrary, what they affirm is the differentiations and plays, the openness and openings, of a becoming in whose effulgence they participate. In this they are perfect nihilists, postmodernists *avant la lettre*, since they embrace the world's dissonance and flux without nostalgia for some lost unity.[2] The 'ascertaining of "truth" and "untruth," the ascertaining of facts in general, is fundamentally different from creative positing, from forming, shaping, overcoming, willing' (WP: 605). In this differentiation without opposition, this affirmation without positivism, there is an overcoming of the yes/no of judgement; a new *economy of life beyond negation*. Here are singularities which move beyond relational, mediated specificity – beyond identity spawned by negation of the other – to become *sui generis* and generative of their own normativity. In his interpretation of Nietzsche, Deleuze makes much of this distinction between the yes and the no and the indebtedness of his rejection of the negative to Nietzsche should already be apparent.[3]

Nevertheless it is precisely this economy of life that I am claiming renders Nietzsche an exponent of negativity, where *becoming affirmative equals becoming negativity.* Clearly such a claim needs substantiating and this provokes my second qualification. Since Nietzsche condemns negative forces as life-denying, it may seem strange to call him a philosopher of negativity and it is not a term he ascribes to himself. But negativity is my motif for what Nietzsche variously refers to as Life, nature, chaos, becoming, Dionysus, will to power. Here negativity is the generativity that stands in place of an ontology, where chance and mobility emanate; a restless forming and de-forming that crystallises in the myriad phenomena which are its symptoms or symbols, only to shatter them as it invents itself afresh. To live according to the rhythms of this negativity will then define affirmation for Nietzsche and hence also the terms in which he rejects the west's nihilistic solution to life from Socrates to the *Übermensch*. In terms of the interpretation offered in the last chapter, it shares with dialectical negativity a creative–destructive mode of becoming, as well as a normative imperative to emulate this process, but its modulations are quite different and this, as I will argue, has significant implications for political practice.[4] Indeed it is already apparent that the master/slave relation Nietzsche sketches bears none of the dialectical engagement of Hegel's rendition and in this distinction between two types, politics is either precluded or relegated to a manifestation of the slave's resentment.

It is Nietzsche who sets becoming free from the logical, synthetic march of the dialectic. Negativity is no longer encumbered by the law, either causal or dialectical, but an aleatory engendering whose pulsings are closer to those of the Freudian unconscious. This however obliges Nietzsche to take up the representational wager that the more scientific Freud would eschew and in which Hegel had failed, inciting a dual strategy whose appreciation I take to be crucial for grasping Nietzsche's work and in particular, his sense of negativity. The challenge here is firstly to convey some meaningful impression of this force whose heterogeneity eludes rational, categorical form. How is this movement that obeys no law to be spoken *about*, when available languages, grammar itself, are saturated with metaphysical presuppositions and stabilising ambitions? How is Nietzsche to avoid either meaninglessness or performative contradiction in trying to communicate with we 'last men' who yet live in the ruins of our will to truth? How is he to render negativity sufficiently familiar for us to grasp it, without succumbing to the cunning of reason? But equally, if he succeeds in invoking it with appropriate circumspection, how is he to avoid implying that it is some noumenal Other, the very idea of which he rejects as metaphysical? In short, how is he to avoid the aporias negativity presented to Hegel and Kant? The stakes are high, since only by alerting us to the impossibility of foundations which negativity entails, can Nietzsche help us move beyond nihilism without simply repeating it.

This is the anguish of Zarathustra, who laments that the common people 'do not understand me, I am not the mouth for these ears. Must one first shatter their ears to teach them to hear with their eyes? ... . Or do they believe only those who stammer?' (Z Prologue: 5) It is also Nietzsche's impatience with himself, the 'soul that stammered with difficulty' in *The Birth of Tragedy* when it should have sung.[5] Zarathustra learns to sing, but he (and Nietzsche) must also deploy more discursive strategies since few of us, his audience, can either sing or hear. It is in this context, I will argue, that we find Nietzsche experimenting with a variety of language games, analogies, metaphors, seeking a way to convey will to power without negating it. Here he will often resort to a tactic beloved of theorists of negativity: differentiating it from what it is not (for the time is not yet ripe for moving beyond the oppositional mode). For our part, we should not be seduced into identifying it positively with any of the familiar models Nietzsche deploys (mythology, physics, biology, psychology).

For there is a second approach, interwoven with the first and subversive of it. This concerns not how negativity might be spoken *about*, but how it is *spoken*, performed. Through what styles and gestures, what symbolisms and rhythms, do we express ourselves as Dionysians, or better, how does this lightning express itself through us? This is no longer a question of knowledge or representation, but of performance, of becoming negativity. It is here then that the stylistic experimentation, poetry and vivid imagery, belong; here where, like the tragic chorus, Nietzsche/Zarathustra struggle to speak in Dionysian tongues. Then they affirm nothing extrinsic but are affirmation in action. Thus Zarathustra's 'wise desire', his 'wild wisdom', sends him flying with 'sun-intoxicated rapture' into a future 'which no dream has yet seen, into warmer souths than artists have ever dreamed of, there where gods, dancing, are ashamed of their clothes' and where even poetic vestments are inadequate. Zarathustra is embarrassed that even he must still 'hobble and stutter' like a poet, where all becoming 'seemed to me the dancing of gods and the wantonness of gods, and the world unrestrained and abandoned and fleeing back to itself' (Z III: 12.2). It is in this context that Deleuze comments on Nietzsche's theatrical desire to 'put metaphysics in motion, in action'. Since representation is already mediation (hence Hegel's alleged failure to go beyond 'false movement'),

> it is a question of producing within the work a movement capable of affecting the mind outside of all representation; it is a question of making movement itself a work, without interposition; of substituting direct signs for mediate representations; of inventing vibrations, rotations, whirlings, gravitations, dances or leaps which directly touch the mind.[6]

As I will show, Nietzsche's two approaches to negativity necessarily circle around one another, but it is also important to recognise them as two strategies addressed respectively to herd and free spirits (*Zarathustra: A Book for All and None*). This dual invocation will indeed reappear frequently among adventurers of negativity, since each must finesse the double imperative of demonstration and exemplification. But as I began to suggest in the previous chapter, this is especially difficult in the political field. For if the emulation of its own rhythms is the philosophical, ethical and political goal negativity bestows, how is this to be declared, instantiated, practised, without compromising it? The political remains the most undertheorised dimension of the riddle, not least because its very inertia is an affront to negativity while its injustices and positive accretions of power summon it most urgently. This is the problem with which I will conclude this chapter, since it is by no means evident how will to power or the Dionysian might be cashed out in political terms.

Primordial contradiction

The Birth of Tragedy (1872) is often dismissed as a youthful work whose premises Nietzsche later rejected. While it is true that he subsequently criticised its immature style, unsatisfactory ontology and residual metaphysical optimism, however, it set an agenda that would animate the later works and illuminates their perspective. Indeed Nietzsche was still engaging with this work in 1886 and 1888,[7] insisting on the enduring nature of its themes. In this section I will interpret the Dionysian versus Apollinian, the opposition around which the book is structured, as the forerunner of will to power; or, as I will claim later, as an alternative (mythic) language game in which negativity is articulated although as yet too dualistically.

In 1888 *The Birth of Tragedy* is condemned by Nietzsche as offensively Hegelian (EH, BT section 1) and it is true that it is structured in terms of contradiction and synthesis, later abandoned to a play of differences. However I suggested earlier that Hegel's ambition was to make things themselves speak and that the deduction of categories was designed to emulate their process of appearing. If the idealist ontology undermined such epistemological radicalism, since it was the language of reason things spoke, in an important sense the project is nevertheless one shared by Nietzsche. He does not start with a Hegelian ontology, where Being and consciousness are one, nor does he accept the dualism of things in themselves and phenomena, even though he utilises this Kantian/Schopenhauerian language in 1872 (1886 self-criticism, BT: 6). He does not even want to invoke 'things', which are already constructs. But he does want to hear the very process of generativity, life, expressing itself in a way that eludes merely subjective representation. Like Hegel, he wants us to participate in the appearing, the becoming, of phenomena, but he privileges music rather than reason.

Nietzsche already then appreciates in 1872 that he must avoid epistemological dualism as well as ontological monism. Accordingly, he begins to imagine the figurative structure which Heidegger, Merleau-Ponty and other philosophers of negativity will adopt: of a primal flux, a latency, which itself becomes and takes form, due to its own internal differentiations which play across all dimensions from the material to the ideal. This will be considerably refined as will to power but at this stage it is captured in the formula 'primordial contradiction', where what might have been expressed as a subject–object opposition is now squeezed into a primitive hiatus within nature itself. There is already, and from the start, an incipient tension, a rupturing between universal and particular, chaos and form: specifically, between nature's abundant energies and their differentiation. For the primal soup in its formless excess must manifest itself as something and this requires splittings, separations into particular shapes, no matter how provisional. In the later terminology, this is its will to power, where Nietzsche will still refer to the 'joy in shaping and reshaping' as 'a primeval joy' (WP: 495).

Unlike Hegel's *Geist*, which alienates itself because it is empty, Nietzsche's nature divides because it is too full. Negativity emerges for both thinkers as an internal splitting and opening wherein generativity flourishes. But life does not seek self-knowledge in Nietzsche's case, even if it does require a means of self-expression and thus a means of differentiating its productivities. Its internal fissure is less lack than desire; fecundity not loss; it is generous and affirmative. Nevertheless, while Zarathustra will speak of a gift to distribute (Z Prologue: 1), *The Birth of Tragedy* invokes the loss and suffering this primordial contradiction entails. Nature in the 1872 work is two-fold: a latency or excess and a formative power whose nature is aesthetic. In the later will to power these will fuse as a single upsurge; as the force of openings (will); the temporary moments of closure (power). In *The Birth of Tragedy* they are already very close (such that artistry emanates from nature itself), but they are in contradiction and it is this contradiction that yields both the symbolic problem (how is nature to express itself?) *and* the basis of human and Dionysian suffering.

It is the two sides of the primordial contradiction that the Greek deities Dionysus and Apollo represent. Dionysus, god of ecstatic self-forgetting, of darkness and mysteries, is the 'basic ground of the world'; the dissonance and excess that engender form. It is the Dionysian that 'reveals to us the playful construction and destruction of the individual world as the overflow of a primal delight.' It is the Dionysian that is the 'original artistic power that first calls the whole world of phenomena into existence' (BT: 24, 25). In this sense the Dionysian is always more primary than the Apollinian: nature's very energy and unity. But Dionysus is also the dismembered god, whose rebirth is mythically associated in tragedy with a restored oneness (BT: 10). For nature itself must take form if it is to become and Dionysus duly appears, wearing many masks.

If life suffers its separatings, it also rejoices in the artistic powers they endow. Together they yield the Dionysian–Apollinian opposition. Why call both the primordial excess and a particular art, Dionysian? I think because having opened a gap between life and (self-)presentation, which prevents it from being a sort of Sartrean plenitude (*en-soi*), Nietzsche must at this stage keep that gap as small as possible since he will want to place the blame for its fatal rupturing on Socrates and his rationalist successors. For pre-Socratic Greeks, he insists, this fissure could still be traversed; there remained a bridge leading in both directions. Dionysian art is still virtually one with Dionysian chaos (music as life); the Apollinian is further removed in its images, but it remains nature's art and it moves closer still in the fraternity established with Dionysus in tragedy. It is Socrates who abandons art for reason, turning back on nature to theorise it from outside; closing himself to the instinctual wisdom which speaks to him only in dreams.

The art deities themselves symbolise the deforming and reforming which is life's own aesthetic impulse. Dionysus, god of intoxication and self-

abnegation; Apollo, god of individuation, appearances and 'just boundaries', whose art is expressed in the beautiful illusions of the dreamworld, in
images and figurative forms. Dionysian art (music) is then expressive of the
energetic unity of life and destruction of its specificities; Apollinian art
(sculpture) manifests its individualising moments of provisional closure.
Together they are the vehicles and mythic forms of the two moments of
primordial contradiction, both in art (where they are opposed until briefly,
gloriously, synthesised in Attic tragedy) and in life. But Nietzsche also insists
that it is nature itself that summons these artistic energies; they are not an
imposition of subjective will and the true artist becomes 'the medium
through which the one truly existent subject celebrates his release in appearance.' He 'is at once subject and object' (BT: 5). We humans too, as part of
nature, are both Dionysian and Apollinian, and even when we 'violate'
nature with our illusions we express its Apollinian talent: 'this artistic ability
of man *par excellence* – he has it in common with everything that is. He
himself is after all a piece of reality, truth, nature' (WP: 853: a section
sketching a new preface for BT).

If we, as nature's work, share its Dionysian and Apollinian rhythms, as
individuals we are also formed and destroyed in the great effulgence of
becoming; we too come to be and pass away. In relation to 'that mysterious
ground of our being', we are mere phenomena (BT: 4). The primordial
contradiction is not only deified and aestheticised, but also therefore existen-
tialised. We suffer our mortality but we suffer most when we realise its
purposelessness in the wild fulminations of life; when we recognise that life
has no special plan for us but merely tosses us up in its chaotic pulsings.
Then we glimpse the wisdom of Silenus, who entoned:

> Oh, wretched ephemeral race, children of chance and misery, why
> do you compel me to tell you what it would be most expedient for
> you not to hear? What is best of all is utterly beyond your reach:
> not to be born, not to *be*, to be *nothing*. But the second best for you
> is – to die soon.
>
> (BT: 3)

Not to be born; to die. In a sense this death wish is what the individual
achieves when he is caught up in a Dionysian whirlwind through the god's
festivals or musical arts: a 'blissful ecstasy' that wells up from nature's
'innermost depths', where fusion, harmony, is experienced as self-loss and all
the 'rigid and hostile barriers' of culture are overflowed. The challenge for
art is to manifest this fusion in symbolic form, but the challenge for
humanity is to survive this glance into the abyss and sustain a will to live. In
the Dionysian dithyramb, the

essence of nature is now to be expressed symbolically; we need a new world of symbols; and the entire symbolism of the body is called into play, not the mere symbolism of the lips, face and speech but the whole pantomime of dancing, forcing every member into rhythmic movement. Then the other symbolic powers suddenly press forward, particularly those of music, in rhythms, dynamics, and harmony.

(BT: 2)

Folk songs, lyric poetry, then tragedy itself, struggle to give voice to the cosmic whirl without rendering it a merely counterfeit imposition, but music is its privileged voice. It does not copy phenomena, which are already individualised symbols of life, but is 'an immediate expression of the will itself'. Nietzsche insists that it even represents *what is metaphysical*, the thing in itself' (BT: 16), a claim that cannot subsequently be expressed in these terms, yet which evokes an enduring sense of negativity's performance of that effervescence ('will') which yields, but cannot be a ground for, appearances. The language is confusing because it is inappropriate, and will to power will provide a less equivocal way of conveying the sense in which affirming life means creating (and destroying) as it does, rather than reconciliation with some primal unity (the bad odour of Hegelianism and Schopenhauer (EH, BT section 1)).

In 1872, however, Nietzsche retains the gods and their art as comforts for those unable to confront the raw indifference of nature without succumbing to suicidal nihilism. Merely regressing to the Dionysian cannot resolve the existential problem, since life is already the source of its own splitting. At the 'very climax of joy there sounds a cry of horror or a yearning lamentation for an irretrievable loss.' It is as if nature were herself 'heaving a sigh at her dismemberment into individuals' (BT: 2). To glimpse the Dionysian is to experience both its inherent suffering and its intrinsic meaninglessness and since participants must also return to their own individual mortality, the knowledge threatens to destroy them. The genius of the Greeks was then to produce a metaphysical comfort in their gods and in the tragedy that neither turned its back on Dionysus nor denied life's lacunae. In tragedy, the spectators see via the Apollinian dramatisation the suffering that the tragic hero endures at the hands of fate. But in the Dionysian chanting of the chorus they are summoned to experience for themselves the permanence and power of nature. Thus are they reconciled to the transitoriness and futility of individual lives, in celebrating the exuberance of life itself in its generative powers.

We are really for a brief moment primordial being itself, feeling its raging desire for existence and joy in existence; the struggle, the pain, the destruction of phenomena, now appear necessary to us, in view of the excesses of countless forms of existence which force and push one another into life, in view of the exuberant fertility of the universal will.

(BT: 17)

Art thus plays a dual role. It allows nature to disclose itself authentically, in a way that is appropriate to it (music is its own rhythmic voice in symbolic form), and it reconciles us to our suffering by allowing us to experience life while protected by the veil of aesthetic illusion. Its exemplary form is tragic because this combines the Dionysian and Apollinian. Just like life itself, such art expresses *and is* both sides of the primordial contradiction: both life's resplendence but fissuring and its formative/destructive power. It is the *Übermensch* who will later incarnate this combination: 'he is the lightning, he is this madness!' (Z Prologue: 3) He too is Apollo and Dionysus, creator and creativity, closure and openness, discharge and accumulation, artist and excess, power and will. But he will no longer interpose artistic illusion between himself and life; rather he will affirm becoming by emulating it in its aesthetic effulgence.

Negativity as will to power

In Nietzsche's later work the primordial contradiction is replaced by will to power, a self-sustaining negativity. Now the former dualism is elided in a single force but one that is still internally differentiated, such that the play of its differences is itself generative and the relative intensities of its complex wills engender its forms. These forms are then evaluated by Nietzsche in terms of their life-enhancing or nihilistic tendencies.

My point is thus that will to power, as the mode of becoming, is only a more sophisticated and integral metaphor for the force and form, excess and creative individuation, pulsing opening and closing, that Nietzsche had formerly imagined in a state of contradictory tension. The abundant energies (will) of the cosmos manifest themselves in a continuous process of creating and destroying, forming and de-forming (power), but these two aspects are now inseparable. They are not simply synthesised, but are the very phenomenality of phenomena. In later notes, Nietzsche still refers to the 'world as a work of art that gives birth to itself' (WP: 796). It should therefore come as no surprise that he also returns in the later works to mentioning Dionysus as another term for will to power, only now subsuming Apollo (the individualising moment) within the god.

What nevertheless puzzles Nietzsche's critics is the ontological status of this will to power, which seems to underpin his whole mature philosophy. For if phenomena are its symptoms, must he not be claiming some efficacy for it as a 'real' force and antecedent cause (as phenomena *seem* to be the appearing of essence for Hegel or of noumena for Kant)? Some of his

93

statements, and especially some unpublished notes in *The Will to Power*, do seem to suggest that Nietzsche was either tempted by, or failed to avoid, some such foundational claim, in particular when he flirted with scientific terminology.[8] I nevertheless suggest that we should be cautious in ascribing any such metaphysical status to will to power and that such a reading relies on isolating its discursive presentation from its performance.

This question of will to power's status is important because if it is indeed being offered as *the* efficacious force that drives the cosmos and explains phenomena, it does acquire a metaphysical aura. Then Nietzschean negativity is indeed but a novel ontology whose truth Nietzsche claims to know (despite his insistence that everything is interpretation and perspective) and which merely evinces different rhythms and more mobility than Being. As such, Nietzsche could not claim to have escaped a will to truth and where he does so he would fall, as his critics often allege, into self-contradiction. Moreover by virtue of its representation, will to power would necessarily achieve a certain identity, defined by its own laws or patternings, and it would thereby function as a foundation for explaining or evaluating the phenomena which it engenders. As such its implications would be far less radical than Nietzsche implies and his fidelity to negativity would itself be compromised.

This is a controversy that has existential as well as philosophical significance, since if Nietzsche himself fails to avoid the metaphysics of will to truth then it appears that we are condemned to the nihilism in which it is implicated and that Nietzsche merely reproduces. In order to explain why, it is necessary to recognise the connection he makes between nihilism and negativity. For will to power is itself implicated in a narrative which concerns the history of nihilism. Indeed it will become apparent that negativity and narrative are inextricable in Nietzsche's thinking and as this chapter unfolds, so will three time lines, or fragments, of a genealogy whose sequences might be categorised as the trans-human, the pre-human and the human.

The human, historical part can briefly be summarised as follows. Since realisation of life's indifference turns us against it, rendering us suicidally nihilistic, our will to life (life's will to power in us) invents illusions as comforts which, since Socrates, have involved metaphysical systems. The invention of a 'real', 'true' world beyond shifting appearances provides stability, a foundation for truth and value and a privileged place for humanity, thereby granting meaning to its suffering and compensating it. While such illusion sustains us, unlike tragedy it exacts a high price since we have become weak, sickly and life-denying under its aegis. For metaphysics involves condemnation of the instincts, senses, appearances, denial of life itself, as at best unreliable and deceptive and at worst, as evil. In saying no to life, metaphysics is thus itself nihilistic, although ironically it preserves us even while the asceticism it entails (especially strong in Christianity) mortifies us. It is cure and poison: 'life struggles with death and *against* death, the ascetic ideal is a trick for the *preservation* of life' but it is also 'the *real catastrophe* in the history of the health of European man' (GM III: 13, 21).

However in late modernity this takes a terrifying turn as the will to truth (one mode of will to power: interpretation, creativity, gone awry) that erected metaphysics subverts itself; as its continual confessions and interrogations lead it to scepticism and the realisation that none of its foundations is sustainable. Then a new stage of lethargic, pessimistic nihilism ensues as the disintegration of faith in truth is coupled with the horrors of Silenus's wisdom and a frenetic attempt at erecting new certainties, whose half-life becomes increasingly brief under the piercing gaze of critical reason and doubt. Having killed God we remain like the crowd in the marketplace, unable yet to realise the consequences of our loss or, therefore, to hear Zarathustra/Nietzsche in their songs of affirmation (GS: 125; Z Prologues).

The point of inserting the problematic of will to power within this narrative (and thus of situating negativity within a 'bad' history of the negative) at this stage is to show how futile its lessons would be from Nietzsche's perspective, if it were intended simply as a more adequate explanation of reality. For Nietzsche's own foundation would be subject to the same doubts as all such truth claims, while claiming a spurious validity. As Zarathustra insists: 'I am a railing beside the stream: he who can grasp me, let him grasp me! I am not, however, your crutch' (Z 1 Discourse 6).

None of these considerations definitively excludes the possibility that Nietzsche might have unwittingly and illegitimately ascribed explanatory powers and certainties to will to power (or that the cunning of reason might not be unassailable after all). But by drawing on the notion of a dual strategy I discussed earlier, I will in fact suggest that Nietzsche avoided the pitfalls attributed to him and indeed, set traps for his critics which they disingenuously enter when they accuse him of self-contradiction. For by drawing them into the labyrinth that ultimate truth claims entail, Nietzsche is able to demonstrate *performatively* the impossibility of finding final answers about 'the real'. This is not on the Kantian grounds that reason cannot breach certain limits to access the thing in itself, but because every representation is itself an exemplification of, and caught within, the will to power of which it would speak.

My suggestion for interpreting will to power is that its terminology is merely one of a series of metaphors that Nietzsche experiments with when he deploys his first strategy of trying to communicate the motif of negativity to us nihilists. This entails neither a playing with empty signifiers, nor a search for the perfect means of bringing reality to expression, but denotes a series of strategic engagements within the becoming it articulates. Up to a point, Nietzsche sketches negativity discursively by reference to familiar disciplines, but once we pursue their logic we find ourselves unwittingly succumbing to his second strategy of emulating negativity in its undecidability. In the first case we need to understand negativity sufficiently to come to terms with the death of God and metaphysics; in the second, to practise it as an affirmation of life.

All the various figurative languages Nietzsche deploys accordingly convey a sense of mobility, drawing on familiar notions of efficacy: gods, force and drive, life, will, power (potency). These appear in a variety of appropriate but only perspectival discourses. First, he uses the *mythic motif* of the gods, Dionysus and Apollo, such as we saw in *The Birth of Tragedy*, where they symbolise excess and form; divine and artistic productivity. Subsequently the Dionysian, now inclusive of its Apollinian moments, is privileged as a means of demonstrating negativity through becoming it; through creating/destroying as exuberantly as life does. Thus Nietzsche/Zarathustra passes from the discursive to the performative when Zarathustra 'plunges into becoming'. In the text that bears his name, Nietzsche tells us, his 'concept "dionysian" has … become the *supreme deed*; compared with it all the rest of human activity seems poor and conditional.'

> There is no wisdom, no psychology, no art of speech before Zarathustra: the nearest things, the most everyday things here speak of things unheard of. The aphorism trembling with passion; eloquence become music; lightning-bolts hurled ahead to hitherto undivined futures. The mightiest capacity for metaphor which has hitherto existed is poor and child's play compared with this return of language to the nature of imagery.
>
> (EH Z section 6)

Second, there is the *philosophical language* of the pre-Socratics, where Nietzsche refers to flux, chaos and becoming and declares that he feels 'warmer and more well' in the vicinity of Heraclitus than anywhere else, since the latter could already have taught the doctrine of eternal recurrence (i.e. 'of the unconditional and endlessly repeated circular course of all things') (EH: BT section 3). Third, a *cosmological discourse* draws on modern physics, where Nietzsche speaks of quanta of force and refers to the fluctuations even of the inorganic. Since it is in this particular language game that most of the accusations of, and temptations to, a new metaphysics are played out, this will require our particular attention. Like Freud, Nietzsche also sometimes elides this focus with *economic* metaphors which impart value in terms of energy distribution.

Fourth, there is the deployment of *biological terminology*, where Nietzsche speaks of nature, life, growth. Fifth, *will to power* itself, where Nietzsche invokes certain Schopenhauerian and psychological senses of will because they are familiar, although only to distinguish his own sense sharply from them. The potency of the drives as a sort of life force is also implicit here. These fourth and fifth modes are most conducive to the evaluative criteria Nietzsche insists upon. However a sixth way of thinking also occasionally emerges, where the *political* serves as an analogy and inferences are made to politics from will to power.

These various language games do not represent different stages of Nietzsche's work, nor do they appear in isolation. They are not extrinsic communicative devices imposed on some *a priori* will to power, but broadly equivalent attempts at saying the same thing. Their multiplicity is appropriate in that the rhythms of will to power do circulate through, and produce, the cosmic, the biological, the psychological, the political, and so on, without being defined by them. But the discursive resources these disciplines make available are also so many interpretations, perspectives, whose proliferation is itself an exemplification of will to power.

Yet a certain narrative (the transhuman fragment I mentioned earlier) does cut across these discourses in terms of their referents, which grants them a certain ranking. The inorganic is then spoken of by Nietzsche as a more primitive, because less differentiated and hence less lively, mode of will to power than the organic. Accordingly 'mechanism and matter: both are only expressions of lower stages, the most despiritualized form of an affect (of "will to power")' (WP: 712). The formation of the organic is 'an exception of exceptions' of relative duration particular to our 'astral order' (GS: 109) but it has greater fecundity than the inorganic and it too engenders new modes. 'Consciousness is the last and latest development of the organic' (GS: 11). Although all these orders evince the same rhythms of will to power, there is a sense of its intensification – and weakening – with the evolution of humanity, permitting evaluative criteria. There is no teleology but there is a general economy of more or less lavish expenditure and a generative complexity contingent on a multiplication of difference (all this is brought together in a long note written in 1885 (WP: 1067)). With this evolution and evaluation in mind, I want now to look more specifically at some of Nietzsche's discursive experiments in order to see what he says about will to power and hence negativity.

Cosmology and methodology

Nietzsche was certainly interested in physicists' attempts at explaining the cosmos in terms of mechanics (laws of motion) and dynamics (forces). Both Marx and Freud refer to Newtonian laws of motion in trying to understand economic or psychical laws and this is perhaps unsurprising, given the close association between negativity and movement, despite Newton's homeostatic model. What Marx and Freud feared, however, was the inertia predicted by the second law of thermodynamics and repeated in political economy (the dismal science with its anxiety lest productivity should stagnate) and Freud's death drive. While Nietzsche's eternal return draws on the first law of thermodynamics, regarding the conservation of energy ('This world: a monster of energy, without beginning, without end; a firm, iron magnitude of force that does not grow bigger and smaller, that does not expend itself' (WP: 1067)), he also insists upon an entropic model of ebbs and flows, cycles and becomings, where the connectedness but differentiation of all things is endlessly productive ('my *Dionysian* world of the eternally self-creating, the eternally self-destroying'). In addition, Nietzsche describes will to power in terms of quanta of force of differential intensity. But rather than a Newtonian–Cartesian model of forces and units, will to power is autoporetic, self-(re)generative; forms are not an effect of some external force. And while deploying scientific language to communicate these elusive ideas, Nietzsche is equally interested in exposing the limits of scientific truth.

Newton may have postulated a universal force, gravity, operating between all particles of matter in the universe and manifest in terms of changes in velocity, but he had not actually been able to explain gravity itself. This had clearly bothered him and he seems to have held some rather theological notions regarding a Creator as original cause. As he wrote to the theologian Richard Bentley: 'Gravity must be caused by an agent acting constantly according to certain laws; but whether this agent be material or immaterial, I have left to the consideration of my readers.'[9] In the *Principia* (1687) he declined to speculate on original causes or final ends, but in any case Newton had no difficulty in recognising gravity as a real, efficacious, force, since his observations bore out predictions made on this basis which could be explained mathematically.

For the sceptic, gravity might however look less like a final explanation than, as Nietzsche writes in a different context, 'actually just a fat word in place of a spindly question mark' (GM III: 16). It seems more descriptive than explanatory. In fact this is the kind of disquiet that will to power arouses when we ask about its reality, or the sense of vertigo that negativity incites as merely a play of differences and circulating of effects. But what is meant by real here? That it is empirically observable? That it is fully explained in terms of its antecedent causes? That it is given substance? Kant had tried to halt such impossible questioning by rendering cause and substance transcendental categories, but like Newton he had also found it necessary to invoke some ultimately unknowable cause of phenomena.

From this perspective, Nietzsche could be interpreted as claiming will to power as more real than any other force in terms of its explanatory powers or observational(/introspective) verification. He indeed experimented in his notes along these lines, writing as late as 1888 that 'I require the starting point of "will to power" as the origin of motion. Hence motion may not be conditioned from the outside – not caused – I require beginnings and centers of motion from which the will spreads –' (note added to WP: 551). One can see why the lacunae of the gravitational model of bodies and forces might encourage such a search, in particular to overcome the seemingly bizarre connection (whose origins were probably more alchemical than scientific) that it supposes in action at a distance. To play this particular language game is to think in these terms. But Nietzsche again sees it only as analogical: 'The concept "atom," the distinction between the "seat of a driving force and the force itself," is a sign language derived from our logical–psychical world' (WP: 625). The seat and the force must be amalgamated (as they are in will to power) but they are still only metaphors. Nietzsche comments revealingly that the

> victorious concept 'force,' by means of which our physicists have created God and the world, still needs to be completed: an inner will must be ascribed to it, which I designate as 'will to power,' i.e., as an insatiable will to manifest power; or as the employment and exercise of power as a creative drive, etc. Physicists cannot eradicate 'action at a distance' from their principles; nor can they eradicate a repellant force (or an attracting one). *There is nothing for it: one is obliged to understand all motion, all 'appearances,' all 'laws,' only as symptoms of an inner event and to employ man as an analogy to this end.* In the case of an animal, it is possible to trace all its drives to the will to power; likewise all the functions of organic life to this one source.
>
> (WP: 619, emphasis added; see also WP: 660)

Several points are of interest here. First, scientists have *invented* the world in these terms; they are like theologians in that the latter also invented God as an ultimate explanation and cause and because scientists still think in these terms, i.e. theologically. But if we think in these terms, scientific deductions are anyway incomplete (and incompletable: they cannot explain force itself) and besides, elsewhere Nietzsche has subverted the belief in causality genealogically: 'the psychological necessity for a belief in causality lies in the inconceivability of an event divorced from intent' (WP: 627; see also WP: 664, 667, 689; BGE: 36); cause and effect are 'conventional fictions for the purpose of designation and communication' (BGE: 21). 'The scientists do no better (than the common people who ascribe agency to every occurrence) when they say "force moves, force causes" and the like, – all our science ... still stands exposed to the seduction of language (subject and predicate)' (GM I: 13).

However if he must yet communicate in these metaphysical terms, Nietzsche will exploit science's lack of foundation in its own terms. He will attribute a (self-sustaining) inner force to things, which avoids the problems of infinite regression and substitutes a model of circulating, mutual effects for the causal chain. And he will do so by using the analogy which is most familiar to people precisely because it is the fiction of intentional will that gave rise to beliefs in causality in the first place.[10] 'We cannot think of an attraction divorced from an *intention*. – The will to take possession of a thing or to defend oneself against it and repel it – that, we "understand": that would be an interpretation of which we could make use' (WP: 627). So Nietzsche will use this popular belief to convey his own theory, although he neither himself believes in the will in this sense (as free, volitional, intentional, efficacious, morally responsible) nor that one can really explain the world in any ultimate way.

Thus we again see the first level of Nietzsche's communicative strategy, but it is only strategy and he never believes this scientific language (which is still metaphysics, still will to truth (GM III: 23)) can yield Truth. We might recall a passage from *The Birth Of Tragedy* here, where Nietzsche insisted on the profound metaphysical illusion science holds in believing that 'using the thread of causality' it can 'penetrate the deepest abysses of being'. He predicts that scientists will 'see to their horror how logic coils up at these boundaries (on the periphery of science) and finally bites its own tail' (BT: 15).

Beyond Good and Evil section 36 is nevertheless cited frequently by Nietzsche's critics in support of claims that will to power is granted ontological standing in his work, so it is necessary to look at this section. It commences with a supposition; 'reality' in scare quotes; an experiment and a question. *If* we were to *suppose* that 'nothing else were "given" as real except our world of desires and passions', and we could reach no reality other than that of our 'drives', then would an *experiment* not be permitted: namely, to see whether the world (including that of mechanics) might not be understood on this basis? (Implication: to provide the foundation science cannot.) As Nietzsche goes on, he alludes to the (transhistorical) narrative mentioned earlier: the mechanical world would be as real as our affects here (our loving, hating, fearing, etc), only (because it is inorganic) it remains in a more primitive form, 'in which everything still lies contained in a powerful unity before it undergoes ramifications and developments in the organic process'; 'a *pre-form* of life.'

Now Nietzsche continues with the experiment. 'In the end not only is it permitted to make this experiment; the conscience of *method* demands it. Not to assume several kinds of causality until the experiment of making do with a single one has been pushed to its utmost limit'. But this is the scientist's morality and method, not Nietzsche's. ('It is perhaps just dawning on five or six minds that physics, too, is only an interpretation and exegesis of the world (to suit us, if I may say so!) and *not* a world-explanation' (BGE: 14)). Surely he only parodies it: yes, he too can tread this methodological path – and push it, as he says, 'to the point of nonsense'. For those who believe in causality, this is the route necessary to explain will to power. But it allows Nietzsche to have it both ways. For those who still have a will to truth that privileges scientific method (and *Beyond Good and Evil* opens by acknowledging that the 'will to truth ... will still tempt us to many a venture'

(BGE: 1)), they must recognise Nietzsche's claims about the primacy of will to power as plausible and rigorous in terms of efficient causes, as well as recognising the methodological duty to conduct the experiment. Thus he convinces them within their own language game and within the limits of what it can grasp. *In this context*, will to power does have more explanatory power than the alternatives. But on the other hand, is Nietzsche not also showing the absurdity of this process and the impossibility of its ever disclosing any definitive truth? He invites those who seek the world's 'intelligible character' into the labyrinth where they must accept his hypothesis as valid (along with the paradox that any such claim is only interpretive and all such truths are now rendered relative) according to their own criteria, or acknowledge it as only one interpretation alongside their own. Either way, Nietzsche makes his point and turns the performative contradiction against his critics. There is no bedrock, no Truth to be brought into presence.

This reading, of a doubly-coded text, is reinforced in section 22 when Nietzsche again insists that physicists' laws of nature are only interpretive anthropomorphisms and reveals rather more explicitly the double bind such a will to truth entails. 'Somebody' might

> end by asserting the same about this world as you do, namely, that it has a 'necessary' and 'calculable' course, *not* because laws obtain in it, but because they are absolutely *lacking*, and every power draws its ultimate consequences at every moment. *Supposing that this is only an interpretation – and you will be eager enough to make this objection? well, so much the better.*
>
> (BGE: 22, emphasis added)

This passage both allows Nietzsche to present his sense of will to power quite lucidly and once more to entangle those who cling to the scientist's approach in a web of paradoxes, whose fecundity is demonstrated. As he summarises his tactics elsewhere:

> Each time a beginning which is *intended* to mislead, cool, scientific, even ironic, intentionally foreground, intentionally keeping in suspense. Gradually an increasing disquiet; isolated flashes of lightning; very unpleasant truths becoming audible as a dull rumbling in the distance – until at last a *tempo feroce* is attained in which everything surges forward with tremendous tension.
>
> (EH: GM section)

This can be compared with another place where Nietzsche discusses method, but this time without irony: the genealogical approach he sketches in *The Genealogy of Morality* (GM II: 12). He has shifted to the more analogically persuasive discourse of life, but it can usefully be read back into the cosmology to yield a provisional conclusion. Here Nietzsche seems to take the efficiency of will to power as given: 'everything that occurs in the organic world consists of *overpowering, dominating*'. But this is clearly not meant in a causal sense since the purpose of the passage is to reject either causal or teleological approaches. Will to power is not an origin but interpretation and becoming. Through this process phenomena mutate, sometimes randomly but more often, according to a process of subjugation and resistance (assimilation and rejection; action and reaction). This obeys no overall plan but is simply the play of differences under the aegis of a will to form. It is the (Apollinian) will to take up scattered givens or primitive unities and impose upon them a pattern; to colonise and integrate them; to destroy and reform. Thus returning the above quotations to their context, it becomes evident that theoretical accounts are as much caught up in an interpretive process as the phenomena they interpret. Here,

> anything in existence, having somehow come about, is continually interpreted anew, requisitioned anew, transformed and redirected to a new purpose by a power superior to it; ... everything that occurs in the organic world consists of *overpowering, dominating*, and in their turn, overpowering and dominating consist of re-interpretation, adjustment, in the process of which their former 'meaning' [*Sinn*] and 'purpose' must necessarily be obscured or completely obliterated ... every purpose and use is just a *sign* that the will to power has achieved mastery over something less powerful, and has impressed upon it its own idea [*Sinn*] of a use function; and the whole story of a 'thing', an organ, a tradition can to this extent be a continuous chain of signs, continually revealing new interpretations and adaptations, the causes of which need not be connected even amongst themselves, but rather sometimes just follow and replace one another at random. The 'development' of a thing, a tradition, an organ is ... a succession of more or less profound, more or less mutually independent processes of subjugation exacted on a thing, added to this the resistances encountered every time, the attempted transformations for the purpose of defence and reaction, and the results, too, of successful countermeasures. The form is fluid, the 'meaning' [*Sinn*] even more so ... . It is no different inside any individual organism: every time the whole grows appreciably, the 'meaning' [*Sinn*] of the individual organ shifts ... .'
>
> (GM II: 12)

I have quoted this passage at length because it conveys so well Nietzsche's sense of negativity and of our implication in it. Each change in one part reverberates through the others, affecting them as their overall signature changes and a new dominant patterning is imposed (as in a work of art).

Appearances are *not* the phenomenal manifestation of some ultimate force, as the cosmological language would imply, but will to power is the appearing of appearances in their mutating contingency and significance. In other words, this is Dionysus/Apollo: not the rejected dualism of subject–predicate, doer–deed, cause–effect, but the formative process in its forming; in its internal fulminating. In life, Nietzsche adds in the same passage, we must never overlook its 'highest functionaries': 'the prime importance which the spontaneous, aggressive, expansive, re-interpreting, re-directing and formative powers have.' Whether form crystallises because of an immanent resolution of parts into a provisional unity, or is imposed by some external power that colonises it, remains open in any particular case.

It is this rhythm, this figure of negativity as the *directional* play of differences (to form), that is common across all the different discourses – an equivalence in mythic, aesthetic, cosmic, vital or psychic terms; will to power as 'a forming, shaping and reshaping' (WP: 656). Note that will to power as thus described is not equivalent to simple dissonance. It invokes a non-teleological, acausal fulminating of indifferent forces *and* their congealing in more or less enduring forms. Genealogy is itself an interpretive tracing of the traces of previous formings which, even if they occurred randomly, become invested with power. It will be important to recall this modulation of Nietzschean negativity when will to power is interpreted politically.

I have suggested in this section that Nietzsche uses the language of science strategically but also ironically. In his notes he experiments with its resources for expressing will to power but he neither believes it can convey the latter adequately, nor does he privilege a chaotic cosmos as its grounding, although the latter can be plausibly described in this way since it is indeed a primitive manifestation of will to power.[11] In physicists' terms, negativity then emerges as a circulating of mutual effects in which everything is interconnected. Nehamas suggests that Nietzsche prefigures Saussure here, except that *everything* emerges as structured like a language in terms of the play of difference.[12] But there is also the evolutionary narrative that cuts across Nietzsche's language games, from whose perspective the 'higher' forms of negativity suggest a departure from the monotonous and valueless fluctuations of the cosmos, which has no investment in its forms and their destruction. In other words, power emerges very weakly at this level and it would make no sense to practise a genealogy upon it. It is time then to move on to the next level and a different discourse: that of Life.

'[L]ife itself is will to power' (BGE: 13)

The phrase quoted to introduce this section poses again the question of will to power's status. Is negativity after all reducible to one domain, to life? Certainly Nietzsche seems to privilege life in this context in a number of ways. First, it has discursive familiarity and is thus a useful means for conveying the coming to be and passing away of phenomena (creation/destruction as life/death). Forces are comprehensible as drives; their dynamism as growth (as we saw, Hegel also used this analogy to present the fecundity of dialectics). Although 'the will to accumulate force is special to the phenomena of life', should 'we not be permitted to assume this will as a motive cause in chemistry, too? – and in the cosmic order?' In this sense, the biological language game is privileged as strategy rather than truth. 'Life, as the form of being most familiar to us' (WP: 689). However in appealing to the familiar, it also runs the risk of anthropomorphising the world.

> Let us beware of thinking that the world is a living being ... . How could it grow and multiply? We have some notion of the nature of the organic; and we should not interpret the nature of the exceedingly derivative, late, rare, accidental, that we perceive only on the crust of the earth and make it something essential, universal, and eternal ... . This nauseates me.
>
> (GS III: 109)

Secondly, life is privileged in terms of the narrative reconstructed earlier. It is literally more lively, more productive, than the inorganic register to which physics refers. Because it is more complex and differentiated, it is more fertile in throwing up and moulding new configurations. It is more congenial to the rhythms of becoming, as excess and form, although its emergence was entirely 'accidental'. In short, the organic more powerfully exemplifies and expresses will to power. 'Even the body ... will have to be an incarnate will to power, it will strive to grow, spread, seize, become predominant ... because it is *living* and because life simply *is* will to power' (BGE: 259). Unlike the indifferent spasms and pulsings of the cosmos, its becoming is an overcoming. 'And life itself told me this secret', Zarathustra confides, '"Behold," it said, "I am that *which must overcome itself again and again*"' (Z II, Of Self-Overcoming). Its internal dynamic is in this sense less problematic than the cosmological search for efficient causes.

Finally, it is, after all, life that is of particular interest to Nietzsche. It is here that values are both derived and applied: ascending and descending life, health and sickness. The healthy are those who affirm life, both by exemplifying its artistic vitality ('One must understand the artistic basic phenomenon that is called "life" – the building spirit' (WP: 1046)) and by embracing its sensuality. The sick and nihilistic tendency which the ascetic ideal represents in extreme form, manifests on the other hand

> hatred of the human, and even more of the animalistic, even more of the material, this horror of the senses, of reason itself, this fear of happiness and beauty, this longing to get away from appearance,

NIETZSCHE: NEGATIVITY AS WILL TO POWER

transience, growth, death, wishing, longing itself – all that means ...
an aversion to life, a rebellion against the most fundamental prereq-
uisites of life ... .

(GM III: 28)

It is life, not the inorganic, that contains the rank orders and their
struggle. Although Nietzsche is most interested in the human dimension of
this agonism, he suggests that we understand nature more generally as exemplary of will to power: 'the formula must apply as well to trees and plants as
to animals' (WP: 704).

What is significant in life, then, is the way forms effervesce; grow and
decay. Again, there is no distinction to be made in its will to power, between
its vitality and the forms this takes: life is, once more, the excessive/formative
process itself, whereby parts are drawn into provisional, aesthetic (sensuous)
wholes which themselves expand or disintegrate. Each biological form is but
the residue of previous acts of unification across the spectrum of organic
life, which teems with desires, cells, impulses, organs, organisms, senses,
bodies; a whole multiplicity of shifting unities, each representing a temporary victory for its organising principle, its will to power. What 'every
smallest part of a living organism wants, is an increase of power' (WP: 702).

However the overall style that springs from parts' affinity, stamping them
with an overall sense ('All meaning is will to power' (WP: 590)), while it
might be random, is more likely to result from their colonisation. For in the
hierarchy of rankings, those forces which have achieved greater coherence
and hence power will succeed in integrating external parts and inscribing
their own identity upon them (unless they disintegrate due to their own
complexity). '[L]ife itself is *essentially* appropriation, injury, overpowering of
what is alien and weaker; suppression, hardness, imposition of one's own
forms, incorporation and at least, at its mildest, exploitation' (BGE: 259).
The brutality of this process should not be underestimated: despite its
aesthetic choreography, will to power is often, if not necessarily, a cruel
becoming. The model of a work of art that emerges harmoniously, where
power equals style, should not therefore be overextended in reading
Nietzsche. Nor should the sense in which will to power is merely a play of
differential intensities. If ontologically will to power represents no external
cosmic force, it is nevertheless suffered in particular cases as an unwelcome
power of mastery. For it is not after all just differences that circulate to yield
form, but differences *qua* differentials in power. While life as such has no
overall meaning or purpose, the (unconscious) aim of any particular will to
power will be to impose its significance across its specific field of domination. This is significant for Nietzsche's patterning of negativity. For while it
is invoked as a play of differentiations which throw forms out of chaos, this
play is driven to sustain closures as well as capitalising on life's openness.
This is why it is power as well as will. In tragic cases such power might

disintegrate due to its internal complexity, but it might also impose an unhealthy unity whose reification paralyses further transformation. This will be important when considering its *political* import.

Meanwhile, thinking about life as a repetitive but impersonal process of production and decay challenges us to think beyond the discourses that humanise it. Just as physically no energy is lost but merely changes form, so biologically we can envisage a genetic permutation whose combinations recreate the new from the pre-existent, just as Nietzsche always insists that the individual of great strength is the chance product of a lengthy and contingent reproductive chain. I think Julia Kristeva expresses such ideas well when she writes:

> Compulsed matter, a spasm in the memory of the species that combines or divides itself in order to perpetuate itself, a series of marks with no other signification than the eternal return of the life–death cycle. How do we speak this memory anterior to language, irrepresentable? Heraclitus' flux, Epicurus' atoms, the swirling dust of the Kabbalist, Arab, Indian mystics or the dotted drawings of psychedelics seem to be better metaphors than theories of being, Logos and its laws.[13]

Just as Nietzsche's notes reveal a fascination with post-Newtonian mechanics, too, they also show him engaging with the Darwinian theory of evolution. He takes issue with evolution regarding the survival of the fittest (the noble, healthy, are the most vulnerable; it is the mediocre herd that survives best), while will to power is never simply reactive adaptation or self-preservation since the living thing always strives to become '*more*' (WP: 688). The 'essential thing in the life process is precisely the tremendous shaping, form-creating force working from within which *utilizes* and *exploits* "external circumstances"' (WP: 647). When for example a new organ emerges, it does so thanks to interpretive work that inscribes new boundaries (WP: 641). Evolution is not then teleological, negative or simply random. To endure, expand, integrate; to achieve greater scope and cohesion, is to strengthen power in its collision with other resistant forces as well as its vulnerability to disintegration. Criteria for evaluation thus emerge. 'The standpoint of "value" is the standpoint of conditions of preservation and enhancement for complex forms of relative life-duration within the flux of becoming' (WP: 715).

Man 'is the sick animal' (GM III: 13)

Although will to power has emerged thus far as an anonymous and indifferent play of forces, the terminology itself invites a psychological interpretation. Nietzsche both accepts and resists this. On the one hand this is the most familiar and intuitively accessible sense will to power can have for us and Nietzsche never denies that we do enjoy feelings of, and psychological orientations towards, power. But on the other hand he neither accepts traditional understandings of will (as intentionality emanating from a conscious state, where it is both efficacious *vis-à-vis* consequences and morally responsible), nor can will to power ever be reduced in his work to some rational capacity. In situating the human, and the discourses explicitly associated with it, it will be helpful to return to the narrative that has been surfacing intermittently.

In *Will to Power*, Nietzsche toys with the idea that the human species is merely a temporary expedient in an organic will to power.

> [P]erhaps the entire evolution of the spirit is a question of the body; it is the history of the development of a higher body that emerges into our sensibility. The organic is rising to yet higher levels. Our lust for knowledge of nature is a means through which the body desires to perfect itself ... . In the long run, it is not a question of man at all: he is to be overcome.
>
> (WP: 676)

Or again, more eloquently, '[m]ankind is merely the experimental material, the tremendous surplus of failures: a field of ruins' (WP: 713). In this sense the species has a particular identity, even role, although only temporarily. It is important in this context to distinguish between humankind as such and our ideas about the status of its individual constituents. At this stage I will focus on the former. The species *homo sapiens* might from this perspective be described as part of nature's artistry: a form thrown up accidentally and one which it will subsequently destroy. The species thus enjoys no privilege within any metaphysical plan. However its appearance is fortuitous *vis-à-vis* will to power (even if only humans like Nietzsche can put it this way), in that it is not merely a new configuration of nature's physiological materials (its particular body styles) but also undergoes a unique metamorphosis which does grant it a heightened value in the formative artistry of life's will to power. This reaches its height in artists such as Goethe, where 'the most sensual functions are finally transfigured by a symbol-intoxication of the highest spirituality' (WP: 1051). Where humanity itself becomes bankrupt in the great profusion of life, however, it will in its turn be overcome.

> Man is a rope, fastened between animal and Superman (*Unmensch und Übermensch*) – a rope over an abyss.
>   A dangerous going-across, a dangerous wayfaring, a dangerous looking-back, a dangerous shuddering and staying-still.
>   What is great in man is that he is a bridge and not a goal; what

can be loved in man is that he is a *going-across* and a *going-under* (*Übergang und Untergang*).

(Z Prologue: 4)

Humanity marks a rupture within nature's mute fulminations, an aperture which is both the scene of its suffering and a capacity to create in an intensified way. In other words, while the species remains caught in the circuit of differences it also opens up more distance between them and facilitates their greater complexity. It shifts the general economy of life. For 'higher type' refers precisely to the 'richest and most complex forms' (WP: 684). Moreover, while the cosmos is indifferent to its becoming, a form now appears for which its becoming is not a matter of indifference. Although its nihilism has both hidden this indifference from it and (thereby) stifled its creativity, it might yet acquire for life an unprecedented affirmation.

In *The Genealogy of Morality*, which might be read as equivalent to Hegel's *Phenomenology of Mind* in this regard, Nietzsche fills in the transitional stages between the two narratives I have so far elicited (the enhanced will to power acquired in shifts from the inorganic to the organic – the transhuman – and the human history of nihilism). What links them is the pre-history of the species, where the latter emerges both as a more volatile mode of will to power than the organic as such and as nature's sickness. Nietzsche's history is more ambiguous, more contingent, more fragmented and chronologically diffuse than Hegel's, but in it life's adventures acquire a new intensity once man is constituted as the 'interesting animal' (GM I: 6).

In the book's second essay, Nietzsche takes up the sorts of question Hobbes and other contract theorists should have considered in their more formal deductions of the transition from a state of nature to civil society. What physiological and psychological changes had to be wrought in humans for them to become available for political or moral life? For Nietzsche this is no process of reason but one of chance and cruelty, itself a consequence and exemplification of will to power. Out of the mute instinctual vicissitudes of animality there emerge consciousness, conscience and, most fatally, bad conscience (the sequence is more akin to Freud's chronology, whereby the primary process succumbs to the secondary process; the pleasure principle to reality principle and finally to superego, via a series of separations and repressions, than it is to the 'fantasy' of contractual beginnings) (GM II: 17).

In order to make promises, Nietzsche surmises, the animal man had to acquire memory; a suspending of the natural state of forgetfulness which he associates with a '*robust* health'. Promising requires deferral; responsibility taken in the present for the future; a capacity to think instrumentally and temporally; 'a world of strange new things' interposed between the promise and its redemption. Thus 'man himself really will have to become *reliable, regular, automatic* [*notwendig*] even in his own self-image'; uniform, predictable, fungible. Reflective consciousness, reason, memory, conscience were all preconditions of social order. Since pain is their most powerful cata-lyst, cruelty and sacrifice were their means: 'perhaps there is nothing more terrible and strange in man's pre-history than this technique of *mnemonics*' (GM II: 3). Nietzsche describes the process as a mixture of species' self-development and an imposition by those whose will to power was strongest.

Just as the primordial contradiction in *The Birth of Tragedy* marked a hiatus within nature that engendered both art (individuation of form) and suffering (separation, transience), so the process undergone by the animal man marks a more devastating fissuring that rips nature apart (a prelude, and somewhat analogous, to the rupture blamed on Socrates in the earlier work), introducing a terrible sickness (man himself) but, also, a new realm of possibility (for nature, will to power). Like all nature, humanity is both Dionysus and Apollo. 'In man *creature* and *creator* are united; in man there is material, fragment, excess, clay, dirt, nonsense, chaos; but in man there is also creator, form-giver, hammer hardness, spectator divinity, and seventh day' (BGE: 225). Consciousness – 'that most impoverished and error-prone organ!' – is no match for the intensity of impulse but worse, the rift it opens is hollowed out into a 'torture-chamber' where bad conscience thrives. The instincts, denied and dysfunctional yet still operative once social order is initiated, are turned inwards. This is what Nietzsche calls the '*internalization* of man', the production of his 'soul'. It is this internalisation that forces a spacing, a rupture in nature (analogous to productive labour and its division in Marx) where previously there had only been a thin diaphragm, a sliding of planes.

> The whole inner world, originally stretched thinly as though between two layers of skin, was expanded and extended itself and gained depth, breadth and height in proportion to the degree that the external discharge of man's instincts was *obstructed*.
>
> (GM II: 16)

Note that there is nothing ontologically pre-existent or new here, but merely a novel configuration created through a reversal of energy's direc-tion, whereby life's forces turn back on themselves. Yet this is nothing short of 'a breach, a leap, a compulsion, a fate which nothing could ward off, which occasioned no struggle, not even any *ressentiment*' (GM II: 17). Like all nature, the human animal is a mix of wild, excessive vitality and creative, interpretive talent (will and power), but now they come again into contradic-tion as life and its suppression conflict. Thus 'full of emptiness and torn apart with homesickness for the desert', 'consumed by longing and despair', 'man patiently ripped himself apart'. In this 'puzzling and contradictory' occurrence, 'the whole character of the world changed in an essential way' (GM II: 16). Man is no longer just a product of nature's will to power but

109

also an intensification of its powers; an aperture in which greater distances unleash unprecedented nebulas of creative – and destructive – energy. Thus this middle phase of the narrative Nietzsche tells falls into place and, indeed, it is the pre-condition of his telling it at all. Unlike Hegel's *Phenomenology* this is not however any pre-determined passage to absolute knowledge. Its destiny remains ambiguous: so far it has yielded life-denying sickness, yet it is a 'sickness rather like a pregnancy' (GM II: 19), a malaise that is also productive. For in terms of the economy of life it undoubtedly has great value.

> This secret self-violation, this artist's cruelty, this desire to give form to oneself as a piece of difficult, resisting, suffering matter, to brand it with a will, a critique, a contradiction, a contempt, a 'no', this uncanny, terrible but joyous labour of a soul involuntarily split within itself, ... this whole *active* 'bad conscience' has finally – ... – as true womb of ideal and imaginative events, brought a wealth of novel, disconcerting beauty and affirmation to light ... .
>
> (GM II: 18)

The negative is in this sense a pre-condition of affirmation and repression, suffering, a spur to greatness. Man, 'the great experimenter with himself, the unsatisfied and insatiable ... the still unconquered eternal-futurist who finds no more rest from the pressure of his own strength, so that his future mercilessly digs into the flesh of every present like a spur' (GM III: 13). Nature's anguish, so graphically portrayed in 1872, is now the particular if fertile anguish of the human species. But Nietzsche takes us full circle: it is these self-conscious, guilty beings who, finding the meaninglessness of their suffering unbearable, invent metaphysics and the ascetic ideal that will pit the will to power against itself, where life tries to master life through its destruction: the ultimate negation; a will to nothingness. Paradoxically, it is only in its self-overcoming (as *Übermenschen*), which will involve a renunciation of Truth, of good and evil, even of grammar, that its promise of symbolic profusion will be redeemed: not as a retrospective knowledge of its coming to reason (Hegel) but in its enacting again the Dionysian metabolism of life as negativity.

Is humanity then a privileged species *vis-à-vis* will to power? In one sense Nietzsche is of course at pains to subvert any such metaphysical conceit. But according to the disjointed narrative I have reconstructed, it does have unprecedented powers to practise an intensity of will to power if it can reconfigure itself according to what, using psychoanalytic language, might be called a different libidinal economy. The difficulty lies in understanding how it can both affirm (return to) life in its sensuous heterogeneity *and* sustain its creative symbolic powers. In other words, how might *Übermenschen* effect once more that fraternity of Dionysus and Apollo once achieved in tragedy or, in psychoanalytic terms, how might they regress to the instinctual without losing secondary process capacity and subjective integrity? Although I have argued that will to power is in fact the elision of Dionysus and Apollo, the problem with its historical practising is precisely that they have been culturally severed. The Apollinian has crushed the Dionysian. How, then, is the individual to be understood in this context?

From a discursive point of view, we have seen Nietzsche capitalising on the familiarity of the notion of will as an efficacious force even while he subverts it. Clearly will to power cannot be reduced to the exercise of individual aggression in some Hobbesian sense even though this might be one (rather crude) example of it. Nor, from what I have previously noted, could it be reduced to a psychological intentionality, even if will to power is manifest in this domain as in all others. In examining the actual process of willing, Nietzsche insists that it is, like promising, extremely complex. 'My proposition is: that the will of psychology hitherto is an unjustified generalization, that this will *does not exist at all*' (WP: 692; also 671; 668; GS: 127). It involves a plurality of sensations (regarding, as in physics, forces of attraction and repulsion towards objects) and habitual bodily responses; a 'ruling thought'; affect (the pleasure of command). It does not operate causally, as intention to effect, because the willing and the deed are one (as in the fusion will to power where forms and the formative powers are one). The feeling imparted is the taughtness, the exuberance, of overcoming resistance; of dominating disparate or alien units by assembling them: a politico-aesthetic pleasure. But the self which enjoys the illusion of efficacy is caught up in the same process since its own parts – its underwills, multitudinous and unconscious – are similarly caught in the drama of obedience and command (BGE: 19).

The implication is then that the individual is already a contingent form created by will to power and that it is constituted by many such wills operating between parts in various dimensions. In other words, individual boundaries are diffuse; provisional and porous constructs through which mobile forces move in their forming and de-forming of structures in dominance. This is true of psychic phenomena (where subjects might, in Julia Kristeva's words, be described as 'in-process') and of bodies, whose fragmented parts are also governed by nutritional needs, habits, a certain style (or colonised, disciplined, as Foucault would later explain the exigencies of bio-power). 'The "apparent *inner*" world is governed by just the same forms and procedures as the "outer" world' (WP: 477).

This does not however preclude the configuring of a certain integrity of form, where one force dominates to lend character and style such that an individual emerges under the aegis of a dominant will to power. Such a well-constituted person would then be well positioned to exert their own will to power, provided a relatively open, complex but balanced, self-disciplined unity is achieved rather than a draining and rigid repression (for example one who practises care for the self, such as Foucault ascribes to the ancients,[14] as opposed to Adorno's potentially-fascist authoritarian personalities). This means that where command is strong a certain closure is sustained, in that parts in their complexity are held together, a force is honed, a stylistic (aesthetic rather than moral) discipline imposed. 'The multitude and disintegration of impulses and the lack of any systematic order among them result in a "weak will"; their coordination under a single predominant impulse results in a "strong will"' (WP: 46; see also 842, 1051). Those with weak wills remain merely herd animals who have an identity imposed upon them by others. Just as will to power generally is predicated on, but is always striving to overcome, dissonance, so it is with the individual.

One who achieves this has stylistic integrity like a work of art. But the individual is also like the artist who must continuously work her magic lest those parts freeze into immobility. Only as a work in creation does she exhibit her own creativity, her negativity. Such a self has many masks; it is not transparent but it does have self-knowledge in that it grasps its own organising principle and remains true to it, without denying its multiple subordinate parts. In this lies its uniqueness; its capacity to prescribe its own values for itself and become what it is; to avoid the moral codes of the herd without becoming simply disoriented, nihilistic, psychotic (Z III: 11.2). Its artistry is both mastery (over chaos) and surrender (self-forgetting, unconsciousness). Depending on whether one emphasises the harmonious, ascetic or conflictual aspects of this process, one might speak respectively of an aesthetics, an ethics or a politics of the 'self'.

> *One thing is needful.–* To 'give style' to one's character – a great and rare art! It is practiced by those who survey all the strengths and weaknesses of their nature and then fit them into an artistic plan until every one of them appears as art and reason and even weaknesses delight the eye ... . In the end, when the work is finished, it becomes evident how the constraint of a single taste governed and formed everything large and small ... .
>
> It will be the strong and domineering natures that enjoy their finest gaiety in such constraint and perfection under a law of their own ... .
>
> Conversely, it is the weak characters without power over themselves that *hate* the constraint of style.
>
> (GS: 290)

Nietzsche stresses many times that achieving this artistry – exemplifying negativity, will to power – while it requires a retrieval of life and the body, cannot be merely regression into hedonistic sensualism. It requires self-discipline, austerity, sublimation. Life forces should be neither squandered (on sexual activity especially) nor dammed-up (WP: 815, 816; see also BGE: 188).

It is perhaps helpful in this context to anticipate Freud's notion of sublimation, as a diversion of instinctual forces away from sexual aims and their direction into new ones. Unlike repression, it involves little energy loss but it does court a certain madness alongside creativity. Sublimation

> enables excessively strong excitations arising from particular sources of sexuality to find an outlet and use in other fields, so that a not inconsiderable increase in psychical efficiency results from a disposition which is itself perilous. Here we have one of the origins of artistic activity; and, according to the completeness or incompleteness of the sublimation, a characterological analysis of a highly gifted individual, and in particular of one with an artistic disposition, may reveal a mixture, in every proportion, of efficiency, perversion and neurosis.[15]

In so far as this is classified as a defence mechanism by Freud it would remain too reactive for Nietzsche. But because he does not associate will to power with specifically libidinal energy, its moving from one mode to another does not carry this implication for him. Rather the suggestion is that life's forces can be gathered, focused, targeted: a creative self-mastery which transforms the negative forces of repression, guilt and denial into an affirmative process. As Zarathustra says, 'one must have chaos in one, to give birth to a dancing star' (Z Prologue: 5).

Nietzsche's prescription for a healthy will to power in individuals seems then to be that while consciousness must be demoted and bad conscience eliminated, a certain spirituality must be preserved since this is after all what enriches the will to power over its merely organic fulminations and instils its incredible lightness. Here he associates spirituality with corporeal more than intellectual cognition. He often argues (rather like Freud – and Hobbes –) that consciousness, reason and thinking are merely instrumental for the body (e.g. WP: 674; GS: 354; Z I Discourse 4). In insisting upon the retrieval of the body he writes as if this has epistemological rather than pleasure value. Or rather, because it is part of life, it has an existential sense of it (of its 'darker, fuller, more floating states' (WP: 1050)). 'The body is a great intelligence, a multiplicity with one sense, a war and a peace, a herd and a herdsman. Your little intelligence, my brother, which you call "spirit," is also an instrument of your body, a little instrument and toy of your great intelligence' (Z I Discourse 4; see also BGE: 3).

How can this be understood? Certainly Nietzsche implies that the body has an instinctual sense of its own vital needs, which it exercises as its will to power and of which consciousness remains ignorant (incorporating food, shaping its organs to functional usage, etc). 'It is our needs that interpret the world; our drives and their For and Against' (WP: 481). But through its styles, its gestures, its dancing, the body also organises space, carving it up, re-orienting it; it lives spatially and architecturally; it inscribes the spaces that differentiate and give form to the spatial. Indeed the Dionysian seems to inhabit space rather than time, which is why everything can coexist in one differentiated and interconnected dimension in the cycles of eternal recurrence. Perhaps it is in this negativity beyond time that its deification is finally achieved. Nietzsche sometimes writes indeed as if action, performance, style – rhythmic, gestural rather than linguistic, symbolism – were the only authentic mode of inscribing meaning without doing violence to life. 'Compared with music all communication by words is shameless; words dilute and brutalize; words depersonalize; words make the uncommon common' (WP: 810). Only the body or musical cadence can really 'know' and emulate the fleet and dense fulminations of life in its excess.

It will be interesting to remember this corporeal negativity when considering Merleau-Ponty's phenomenology of perception and Kristeva's semiotic. For a persistent theme in the adventures of negativity is precisely this intimation of a material yet significant rhythm: one which eludes grammatical language and reason, even as it produces them, yet whose invocation and practising can alone revitalise the exhausted tautologies of over-rationalised modern culture. Nietzsche is nevertheless unusual in alluding to the crossing of this threshold into a transorganic region (a state that Kristeva will associate with psychosis). But the *Übermensch* is after all super-human and not constituted as we are (by will turning back on itself to produce bad conscience). Perhaps it remains on the horizon of our imagination as a non-Œdipalised formation.[16] Meanwhile the free spirits, like Nietzsche, who move on the borders of this threshold (in that place where Kant set reason's limits?) remain the consummate sublimators. They practise negativity but still within the symbolic.

Will to power and the political

The preceding discussion of will to power as negativity has been predicated on the claim that it marks a rhythm of productivity rather than an ontology. Its mode of appearing has been identified with the becoming of all phenomena, from the cosmic to the psychological, so it is unsurprising that it can be summoned, albeit rather cryptically, via a variety of discursive experiments relative to these domains (these discourses and domains themselves being exemplars of will to power as it cuts up and stylises the manifold). What has emerged is a generalised process of creation/destruction whose *movement* derives from the play of differences but whose *phenomenality* is also forged through the differential strengths of wills to power in their formative quest. The purpose of Nietzsche's writing here, I suggest, is not primarily philosophical but political in the broadest sense.

That is, he wants to show us the sacrificial nature of sociopolitical order and to allude, if not to liberation or justice, then to a non-repressive order, a perfect nihilism beyond ascetic no-saying. This is not some future utopian state but an exhortation to emulate the rhythms of will to power itself. This is why affirmation equals negativity, while it is this critical intent (coupled with the equation between generativity and difference) that renders Nietzsche's philosophy an adventure in negativity despite its affirmative orientation. Although it has been necessary for him to communicate what this negativity/affirmation entails, it is achieved only when representation gives way to performance.

In this section I am, however, less concerned with this elusive narrative of overcoming, Dionysian performance and eternal return, or with Nietzsche's explicit judgements about the political,[17] than with the significance of the modulations of will to power for an understanding and practising of politics. What analogies and inferences might be drawn from will to power for grasping the political? What lessons might be learnt from Nietzsche's summoning of negativity for the practising of political artistry as a style of collective life?

Nietzsche occasionally uses political analogies as familiar models for explaining will to power, but he also draws inferences for the political from it. For example, he suggests that the 'correct idea' of the subject's unity can be gained not from thinking according to ontological givens like the soul, but in terms of the struggles typical of the state (WP: 492; BGE: 19). Although a regent like the 'soul' seems to be in control and indeed enjoys some dominance, both are dependent on the ruled: those differentiated forces which make the polity, or subject, possible. In the command/obedience relation the regent must therefore undertake 'a fluctuating assessment of the limits of power', including his relative ignorance of individuals' activities and subversions.

I take Nietzsche's point here to be a basically Machiavellian one. No ruler is sufficiently strong to rely on naked power and would be foolish to try. Given the density and reversals of the political, with its multiple wills and shifting formations, the art of command requires flexibility; a strategic reading of the times; in short, the sort of interpretive artistry that Nietzsche associates with will to power and Machiavelli, with *virtù*. A naïve regent is one who believes everything is transparent and controlled, failing to recognise command and obedience as aspects of an on-going struggle in which 'the ruler and his subjects are of the same kind, all feeling, willing, thinking'. Both these claims are underlined elsewhere: '"Obedience" and "commanding" are forms of struggle' (WP: 642). '[I]nterpretation is itself a means of becoming master of something' (WP: 643).

The inference that Nietzsche draws from this analogy regarding the *distribution* of power is also quite Machiavellian in that he commends hierarchy, surmising that the *management* of power, while modelled on artistic prowess, is best exercised by the noble. Explicitly, this takes the form of the aristo-cratic ranking most obviously associated with Nietzschean politics and directly inferred from the idea of a will to power. This inference is however problematic if we look more carefully at the aesthetic process on which it draws.

Nietzsche often writes of political rule as if it were the equivalent of aesthetic activity: simply the formative Apollinian art applied to the chaotic forces of the masses. Thus for Zarathustra 'man is formless material, an ugly stone which requires the sculptor' (EH: Z section 8). This analogy is again utilised in the *Genealogy*, where Nietzsche both likens the founders of polit-ical order to artists and insists on the hierarchical brutality of the process. In reconstructing the origins of the political, he describes how a population was 'shaped' into a 'fixed form' where previously it had been 'unrestrained and shapeless'. The 'raw material' of an emergent people, 'shapeless and shifting', was 'kneaded', '*shaped*', rendered compliant (GM II: 17). One might think benignly of Rousseau's legislator here, but this is for Nietzsche a more primitive process borne precisely by those Rousseau would have excluded from such work. They are the beasts who have not attained mastery over instinct but who are already masterful 'by nature'; who came like a fate to 'create and imprint forms instinctively'; these 'most involun-tary, unconscious artists' governed by an artist's 'terrible egoism' in which the work is its own justification and where something new is imposed, 'in which there is absolutely no room for anything which does not first acquire "meaning" with regard to the whole.' These first political artists are them-selves beyond good and evil, but their imposition of social and political order (a creative destructiveness resonant with possibility and sacrifice) initi-ates the repression that will result in bad conscience. Indeed Nietzsche draws an explicit parallel between the development of bad conscience as an act of brutal artistry of the self on itself and the formative political artistry of these early conquerors. In both cases we see will to power shaping scattered forces into new wholes, where 'the essence of life, its *will to power*' lies in 'the spontaneous, aggressive, expansive, re-interpreting, re-directing and forma-tive powers' (GM II: 12).

Nietzsche reiterates this scrap of genealogy in *Beyond Good and Evil* (section 257), where he explains these founding nobles' victory in terms of their 'unbroken strength of will and lust for power', their integrity as yet undissipated by conscience. But he also insists on the enduring value of the hierarchy they introduced.

> Every enhancement of the type "man" has so far been the work of
> an aristocratic society – and will be so again and again – a society
> that belongs in the long ladder of an order of rank and differences
> in value between man and man, and that needs slavery in some
> sense or other. Without that *pathos of distance* which grows out of

ingrained difference between strata – when the ruling class constantly looks afar ... keeping down and keeping at a distance – that other, more mysterious pathos could not have grown up either – the craving for an ever new widening of distances within the soul itself, the development of ever higher, rarer, more remote, further-stretching, more comprehensive states – in brief, simply the enhancement of the type "man," the continual "self-overcoming of man" ... .

(BGE: 257)

In response to this influential statement I would like to suggest both that it is inconsistent with the more aesthetic choreography of will to power described elsewhere and that critics who push it in this direction often go too far in counteracting the more hierarchical, even Hobbesian, elements of Nietzsche's thinking.

In the first case one might ask what it is that Nietzsche values in the quote above: the ranking or the difference. True, his idea of artistry suggests the ruler who moulds his human clay while it is the repression he demands which permits an intensified state of existence. But if we move beyond this simple analogy, might will to power not operate as the creative effervescence immanent to society in its own self-overcoming? For the difficulty in eliding will to power with the founder artist analogy is that in will to power force and form are one, a single appearing, whereas in the political case Nietzsche has separated them such that one particular force (the master rulers) is hypostatised as active and the other, the mass, is rendered merely inert; a passive material lacking formative powers of its own. There is none of the strategic struggle alluded to above between regent and ruled (an agonism praised elsewhere as imparting pleasure in the face of resistance) nor any hint of collective life as a self-generative process. Nietzsche's central criticism of the modern state and its ideologies is indeed that its egalitarian policies are levelling; that it produces conformist herd animals who are all the same. They thus lack generative vitality because of a failure to sustain the spaces and differentiations that facilitate becoming, negativity.

But might a *diverse* population of political equals not forge an identity out of their multiplicity, much as the great individual does who acquires style without disowning its constituent parts? Is this not after all the sort of politics that Nietzsche tended to idealise among the ancient Greeks? Note that in the quotation above it is difference and distance that are important, but might these not be sustained horizontally instead of vertically within a non-homogeneous population? It is this model of aesthetic becoming that has encouraged some recent critics to find in Nietzsche a precursor of a postmodern or discursive politics of difference.[18] For the aesthetic rhythms of becoming that he calls will to power are surely as conducive to radical democracy as to aristocratic ranking inasmuch as forms cohere through

self-overcoming and self-mastery as well as through colonisation and discipline. While Nietzsche writes that 'perfecting [mankind] consists in the
production of the most powerful individuals, who will use the great mass of
people as their tools (and indeed the most intelligent and pliable tools)', he
also associates such perfecting with 'greater complexity' (WP: 660).

I have claimed in this chapter that will to power is an elision of two
moments which Nietzsche had originally separated: *will* as the force of
openings, *power* as the creative, formative moments of provisional closure.
Merged as will to power, they suggest a single upsurge and one which seems
appropriately to be defined in aesthetic terms. Aesthetic here carries connotations of sensuousness as well as the formation of wholes whose unity
emanates from their style rather than being imposed by logic, causality or
coercion (in Kantian terms, lawfulness without law). The very idea of style is
that it is not something fixed, merely formal or limited to a specific space; up
to a point it is open to extemporisation, experimentation and an extension
of its scope whereby it incorporates and marks new things. In other words it
is a concept that describes very well the work of the artist and the creative
fluidity of will to power.

Yet this aesthetic model, with its consensual and harmonious connotations, surely cannot imply that Nietzsche would have endorsed the sort of
tame liberal democratic/postmodern pluralism found in modern western
states. Nor should we ignore the processes of becoming described in the
Genealogy: where both random mutations *and* acts of subjugation are at
work. If a political choreography is to be elicited from will to power it
follows that politics is about struggle; that practising negativity is inevitably
destructive as well as creative and that no social order in a universe where
negativity plays is immune to disintegration or destined for consensus. As
Tracy Strong has recently summarised this political lesson: 'Politics requires
something of the Dionysian to be politics. Those who want a politics
without the Dionysian would then not really want politics, but only the security of a story with an ethical ending.'[19] Contemporary liberalisms,
Nietzsche might have observed, are more about will than power.

Yet beyond this general understanding of political life, does Nietzsche's
philosophy not lack any transformative strategy or account of collective
acts? And does this not identify precisely the limits of his *political* vision? Is
the affirmation of the eternal return not rather an existential solution? It
may be critically resonant in conveying the decadence of modernity, but
does it not remain politically inefficacious in changing it? This is not necessarily a devastating criticism of Nietzsche, in that he does not present
himself as a political radical, but it does suggest that if we want to draw
political relevance from his sense of negativity then we should be wary of
accepting his own inferences or moving too rapidly from an interpretation of
will to power to conclusions about the political distribution of power.

As I argued earlier, the political has its own tempo and rhythms of becoming so the challenge for political theorists and actors is to grasp how more general processes of negativity are to be understood and practised in this domain of collective life. Merely analogical inferences are quite insufficient. In Nietzsche's case, the swift and evanescent mobilities of creation–destruction that an existential-aesthetic Dionysianism suggests seem ill-suited to the turgid and conflictual realm of the political, where the inertia of institutions and shared practices is reinforced in the interests of privilege and stubborn social stratifications are monotonously reproduced. It is not then obvious how the aesthetic tempo of will and power, openness and closure, might operate politically in a way that does justice to political power. In particular, while will to power yields a vision of Dionysian openness in the face of moral dogmatism and psychopolitical reification, Nietzsche's depiction of moments of closure (of power) as provisional and fluid artistic creations is much too thin to yield any adequate analysis of political context. In Machiavellian terms one might argue that it encourages surrender to *fortuna* without advertising *virtú*.

I will explore these implications further in a dialectical context in the next two chapters, but I will conclude by pursuing them briefly through a figure whose genealogical commitments are closer to Nietzsche's own. In Foucault's work, power is described in terms of a generativity whose modulations are very similar to those of will to power. In this sense he espouses rhythms of negativity that are more typical of poststructuralism than dialectics. However he does not simply evoke flux, heterogeneity and deferral; Foucault also focuses on the positive forms and congealings that power constitutes. Thus the flows and mobilities he insists upon *methodologically* in analysing power are coupled with a recognition of its actual congealing, such that the network of force relations it inscribes is also structured by more enduring clots and institutions that incite resistance. Again, it is important to recall that for Nietzsche the self-generativity of will to power involves not just growth but also subjugation. Foucault then recognises that this throws us into the political while better understanding politics as an index of (will to) power. What he offers is not an escape from the decadence of modern politics but a way of understanding and engaging its internal choreography.

Just as Nietzsche sets negativity free from any dialectical or causal law, so Foucault wants to set power free from the juridical understanding that since Hobbes has presented it in a positivist sense regarding its legitimacy, its monopoly of coercion, its centralisation and authority to enforce the law. Instead he exhorts us methodologically to approach a power whose fluid processes are those of negativity; to replace 'the privilege of sovereignty with the analysis of a multiple and mobile field of force relations'.[20] Power is now to be grasped as 'the multiplicity of force relations immanent in the sphere in which they operate and which constitute their own organisation; as the process which, through ceaseless struggles and confrontations, transforms, strengthens, or reverses them'. It is the name for 'a complex strategical situation' where a 'network of power relations' forms a 'dense web'. It is not the prince or the noble/artist who deciphers its vectors and imposes a form, but the internal dynamic of these multiplicitous relations and micropowers that engenders a field in which strategies and resistances are as variable and dispersed as power itself. Like will to power none of these mobilities has any specific ontological anchor, but power and its effects are continuously incited and, in turn, endlessly productive. There are 'mobile and transitory points of resistance' that fracture unities and traverse identities, bringing about regroupings and disintegrations.[21]

Methodologically, then, Foucault presents himself as an exponent of negativity and bids us grasp the sociopolitical domain in this manner. At the same time, however, he recognises that the political is not just an endless circulation of power in a featureless landscape because, as in will to power's genealogy, banal techniques or random events sometimes become unintentionally generalised across a field (as in panopticism or confession) or are colonised by institutional powers. Thus 'the manifold relations of force' are 'the basis for wide-ranging effects of cleavage that run through the social body as a whole'. The effects of power are a 'general design' or 'institutional crystallization' embodied in various 'social hegemonies'. While power circulates through multiple techniques and strategies, then, there are always attempts to centralise it; to 'arrest' its movement and instantiate a 'Power' that is 'permanent, repetitious, inert and self-reproducing'. Both methodologically and practically, power tends towards positive form.

In fact Foucault distinguishes between the sort of mobile power he describes, where it plays freely in an agonistic and 'very complex field', and domination where 'stable mechanisms replace the free play of antagonistic reactions'. Here relations of power become fixed and hegemonic, 'perpetually asymmetrical'; 'firmly set and congealed'; 'impassive and invariable'. A 'massive and universalizing form, at the level of the whole social body' then appears.[22] Foucault especially associates this totalising process with the modern state[23] but stresses that domination need not necessarily take this narrowly political form (he cites eighteenth-century patriarchy as an example).

Foucault thus emphasises the inertia and blockages which are power's effects alongside his methodological insistence on its productivity. Like Nietzsche he gives this negativity a critical dimension in that he calls upon us to re-open the political field for strategic games and reversible power relations wherever reifications and domination occur. 'On the critical side ... philosophy is precisely the challenging of all phenomena of domination at whatever level or under whatever form they present themselves.'[24] 'I would say that the analysis, elaboration, and bringing into question of power relations and the "agonism" between power relations and the intransitivity of freedom is a permanent political task in all social existence.'[25] Not only must the negativity of power be theoretically recognised, however, but it must also be practised. In this context Foucault distinguishes between liberation (an assault on the closed totality of domination in order to re-open the force field of power relations) and the unspecifiable 'practices of liberty' whose experiments it accommodates.

It surely follows that actors must read their times well – they must exercise *virtú* – in order to discern their possibilities and degree of closure (under domination, Foucault insists, the problem is to ascertain precisely where resistance should organise and its tactics[26]). The ludic metaphor of strategic games does not perhaps sit comfortably with the mechanistic one of a field of forces, but they both convey a sense of dynamism tempered by rules and blocks. If it is methodologically unacceptable to treat institutions as autonomous causes of history or its telos, it is not illegitimate to track their discontinuous yet relatively enduring forms genealogically in order to challenge them. Moreover strategy games cannot be enjoined via simply gratuitous moves but must take into account the trajectory and momentum in whose context interventions are made. In particular it is important to know whether one is playing a game of strategy or confronting a system of domination.

Because he breaks up the force field of power with clottings and institutional blocks, and defines politics as acting strategically there, Foucault accordingly shows how negativity is always an entwining of positive and negating forces. In this sense his analysis has some affinity with dialectics. The difference between (classical) dialectical and genealogical interpretation is that the latter recognises the contingent and reversible nature of forms, in which every interpretation is caught up in the power relations it describes and there is no presumption of identity between the real and its conceptualisation; no privileging of a particular stratification or agency, nor any telos imagined beyond power. There is no presumption of a truth beneath appearances but it is sensible for oppositional political actors to practise some hermeneutical art if their interventions are to be strategic and efficacious.

Foucault did not himself pursue this sort of analysis very far, perhaps because it would be inappropriate to generalise too far in an agonistic situation. Instead he wrote about the aesthetics of the self in a field newly opened by the collapse of two millennia of Christianity. I suggest nevertheless that the sort of political practices his work implies are closer to those pursued by negative dialectics than is usually acknowledged and that this brings out the latter's implicit affinity with Nietzschean genealogy, too. It is these practices of negative dialectics that will be explored in the next two chapters.

4

NEGATIVITY AS INVISIBILITY
Merleau-Ponty's dialectical adventures

The following two chapters will focus on dialectical attempts at rethinking and practising negativity in light of the criticisms and possibilities already discussed.[1] Merleau-Ponty and Adorno, who were almost exact contemporaries, were both eager to rescue dialectics as a critical enterprise liberated from rationalism and positivism. They interpreted this challenge in terms of further exploring negativity. In some ways their discourses already prefigure poststructuralism. Negativity emerges in their work as ineliminable difference or non-identity, its generativity witnessed in the creation and destruction of positive forms. They anticipate the distaste for totality and teleology, absolute knowledge or the end of history, with which dialectics would be dismissed by their successors. Like them, they refer to pluralities and multiple tensions rather than using a more binary language of contradiction and negation. But Merleau-Ponty and Adorno also remained materialists who felt compelled to approach the negative from the perspective of meaning in history and a radical politics oriented to broadly humanist concerns. If positive appearances of power and knowledge now emerged contingently, without guarantees and menaced by ambiguity and dissonance, they still called for both critical interpretation and the sort of changes that could only be wrought by material forces which had somehow to be identified within the reified totality of late modernity.

The existential phenomenologist and the critical theorist can each then be situated at that crucial juncture where negativity was becoming associated with a wilder process and an anti-rationalism which distanced it from its Hegelian and Marxian formulations, while its importance for an emancipatory political project and rationality was yet (albeit with increasing difficulty) retained. For both of them, positive and negative – sense and non-sense, visible and invisible, identity and non-identity – are inseparably interwoven; interwoven indeed with an intimacy that draws on Nietzsche and Heidegger in addition to Hegel and Marx. Merleau-Ponty explored this 'chiasm' primarily through ontology and Adorno, through epistemology. But they both tried to reveal the experiential and political significance of the negativity they discerned, criticising the structures of late modern collective life from its perspective while associating recognition of negativity's unassailability with an exemplary style of coming to (philosophical and concrete) meaning. Like Nietzsche, they felt compelled to operate a dual strategy here: each struggles to communicate a sense of negativity via the inadequate resources of the philosophical language they inherit, while attempting to renew the philosophical project by practising the 'hyper', or negative, dialectics this would call for.

While there are many similarities between Merleau-Ponty and Adorno, a difference in tone is nevertheless evident. Both locate themselves in that space where being and meaning, subject and object, appear (and disappear) as distinct yet co-dependent; where negativity is the production and ruin of all identity. But while Adorno's inclination is to emphasise the fragmentation and heterogeneity that subvert the positive as full presence, Merleau-Ponty is more concerned with those moments when forms cohere and with the incipient rationality their cohesion promises. This should not, however, overshadow their shared judgement that modernity has succumbed to a rationalism they associate with violence, domination and closure; with reified social and economic powers defined precisely by their suppression and denial of the negative. The irony was that both devoted their philosophical studies to disclosing the ineradicability of negativity, in order to subvert the foundations of this rationalism, while they each lament in their respective critiques of late modernity that it has been (virtually) eliminated in practice.

Merleau-Ponty's thinking occupies a pivotal position within the discursive history of negativity. Committed to phenomenology, he tried to rescue it from the idealism associated with Husserl. An existentialist, he nevertheless rejected the Cartesian/Kantian dualism of Sartre's *Being and Nothingness* (where consciousness, *pour-soi*, is the negativity that imposes meaning on the positive in-itself, *en-soi*). Like the young Marx, he situated existence in that dialectical space where significance and sensibility, subject and object, meet. Indeed his own Marxism was methodologically indistinguishable from what he variously pursued under the titles of phenomenology and existentialism, or as the hybrid 'Weberian Marxism' and 'Machiavellian Marxism', all of which were defined as dialectical practices. If his explicit political allegiance shifted from an avowedly Marxist one to a qualified support for parliamentary democracy and the non-Communist Left, the sort of political style he was advocating remained broadly unchanged: a dialectical, intersubjective process predicated on values of coexistence and exemplified in a practising of negativity.

Merleau-Ponty's project can then be identified as a sustained adventuring in dialectics and in this sense his aim was always one of exploring negativity. However this exploration did inspire a bout of self-criticism during the early 1950s, directed at his earlier political and philosophical positions. The result was a new terminology and a deepening of the phenomenological exploration of the primordial, manifest in the increasing importance of Heideggerian and structuralist anti-humanisms. The former's influence is apparent in the later ontology, where negativity, dialectics and Being ('Flesh') now appear as more or less synonymous and are presented through a new language of hinges, joints and folds, silence and invisibility, that anticipates Derridean *différance* and Deleuzean differenciation.[2]

At the same time (according to Foucault), it was Merleau-Ponty who was introducing Saussurean structural linguistics into French philosophy and it would play a significant, if somewhat idiosyncratic, role in his own thinking about negativity. Some critics indeed interpret the final writings as more structuralist than phenomenological.[3] Yet Merleau-Ponty's understanding of structure remained more dialectical than structuralist and his sense of negativity, more akin to poststructuralism than structuralism. This kinship must anyway be qualified by insisting once more on his enduring concern with a philosophy of history and with a form of reason which would be manifest in concrete socioeconomic structures as well as in the political processes of collective life. In this sense his Hegelian and Marxian heritage remained extant and it is this attempt at holding onto and rethinking the relationship between negativity and politics (a relationship already become tenuous in Nietzsche's writing, I suggested, and as yet poorly developed by his poststructuralist successors) that encourages me to privilege his work in the current study.

Rationalism and dialectic: the problematic of the negative

Merleau-Ponty's critique of rationalism is aimed at all those philosophical and political forms which are grounded in a belief that, through their reason, subjects can achieve complete knowledge and control of the world. Like Adorno, he presents such rationalism as internally allied with violence and as endemic in late modernity. He begins by targeting ontologies predicated on the severance of subject and object (which he traces back to Descartes) and challenges the epistemologies they engender, whether idealist or realist. These were obliged to reconnect the consciousness and matter they misconceived and dirempted, with theories of knowledge that presented truth as a mirror of nature: either because subjects constitute the world or because knowledge correctly reflects it (Ph.P: 28, 41; AD: 210; IP: 52; S: 147; VI: 103). Failing to question or engage with the real, such knowledge has no means of verifying itself or of bridging the gap between reality and its representation, so that truth remains vulnerable to dogmatism or scepticism. We already found Kant worrying about this, in chapter 1, but saw how Merleau-Ponty implicated his own Copernican Revolution within it. Similarly in politics, action which fails to situate itself within a dense but contingent historical situation must find itself continually deflected by forces it can neither understand nor engage. It, too, is condemned to impotence or violence, even if its values are humane. Thus Merleau-Ponty levelled an equivalent attack on epistemology and on what he referred to as a politics of understanding and a politics of reason.

In its Kantian, liberal-democratic forms, a politics of understanding was charged with ignoring the density and adversity of history; with perceiving it as an empty terrain on which subjects' moral values might be simply imposed with sufficient goodwill and consensus. The 'weakness of democratic thinking is that it is less political than moral, since it poses no problem of social structure and considers the conditions for the exercise of justice to be given with humanity' (SNS: 103). A politics of understanding denied itself the engagement with social structures that would allow it either to comprehend and evaluate their existential significance, or the means to intervene efficaciously in changing them. For the

> value of a society is the value it places upon man's relation to man. It is not just a question of knowing what the liberals have in mind but what in reality is done by the liberal state within and beyond its frontiers ... . To understand and judge a society, one has to penetrate its basic structure to the human bond upon which it is built.
>
> (HT: xiv)

Liberalism effectively condones the violence of its economic arrangements (colonialism, war, exploitation, poverty) while condemning all oppositional violence as immoral. It represses the truth of political life since, inherently Cartesian/Kantian, it fails to recognise the internal connection between ideas and their material situation and thus denies itself the means to instantiate its values.[4] 'The curse of politics is precisely that it must translate values into the order of facts ... . A policy cannot therefore be grounded in principle, it must also comprehend the facts of the situation.' Since we cannot know the future we may only, after carefully reading the situation, 'push it in our own direction.' Politics is not then about acts of will; like freedom, reason 'has to be made in a world not predestined for it' (HT: xlii).

Penetrating the 'basic', existential structure of things was precisely the task Merleau-Ponty would set phenomenology; navigating within a contingent but meaningful history was just the process he attributed to praxis. Since both are conceived by him as dialectical, this is clearly the solution being offered simultaneously for philosophical and political rationalism. When however Merleau-Ponty also condemned a politics of reason, he was referring to the sort of dogmatic reading of history that dialectics had hardened into after, or even with, Marx.

For the problem with dialectics was that it had itself degenerated into rationalism and Merleau-Ponty came to suspect that the problem did not lie solely with Marx's successors (in *Adventures of the Dialectic* he traces its oscillation between subjectivist and objectivist aberrations from the young

Marx, through Lukács, Lenin and Trotsky, to Sartre). In both its Hegelian and Marxian forms, he realised, dialectics already entailed rationalist assumptions that made fidelity to the negative impossible and subverted the existentialist interpretations he had originally proffered.

Such concerns lay at the heart of a certain line of criticism I discussed in chapter 2 where, despite an account of subject–object reciprocity, both Hegel and Marx were accused in their mature writings of presenting that process from the positivist/idealist perspective of the omniscient and disengaged knower. But Merleau-Ponty came increasingly to believe that this problem derived from an insufficiently dialectical ontology, whose dualism was only replicated in the subsequent failure to link non-philosophy and philosophy, existence and thought, in a dialectical method. He concluded that the later Marx's rationalism was actually a consequence of flaws in the earlier, and apparently more consistently negative, works, where it arose from an unresolved tension in his understanding of nature. For while, on the one hand, nature was the medium of negation and self-transcendence (and quite amenable to Merleau-Ponty's Heideggerian gloss: there is 'a single Being where negativity works' (PNP: 101)), on the other, nature defined a positive and material ontology that suggested an ideal equilibrium of non-alienated life (TL: 63ff). In this latter sense history was always alien to some naturalised (human) essence which served it as a goal of reconciliation.

> In Marx at the time of the 1844 Manuscripts, alongside a conception of history as "man's act of birth" and as negativity ... , we found a naturalist philosophy which localizes the dialectic in the preparatory phase of human "prehistory" and assumes as its horizon, beyond communism, as the "negation of the negation", the wholly positive being which is the resolution of the enigma of history.
>
> (TL: 58f; cf. PNP: 95)

It was then from the perspective of this ideal that the critique of capitalism was undertaken, robbing Marx's inquiry of its openness by imposing a preconceived meaning on events and granting to the proletariat an ontological privilege as idealised negativity.[5] Reading history accordingly became a matter of discerning its underlying truth, rather than a dialectical attempt at eliciting provisional meanings from its ambiguous and contingent lines of force (PNP: 84ff; AD: 62, 71). If under Communism the dialectic had become ideological justification and a positivism of correct economic structure, it was no use simply returning to Hegel and Marx. Dialectics had itself to be reconsidered, beginning with its ontology:

> what was impossible for modern dialectical philosophies, because the dialectic which they contained remained bound by a predialec-

tical ontology, would become possible in an ontology which reveals in being itself an overlap or movement.

(TL: 91)

When Merleau-Ponty came to criticise his own early ontological studies for remaining too Cartesian (they still retained concepts of consciousness and mind and were insufficiently sensitive to the role of language (VI: 171)), the motivation sprang at least in part from his disillusionment with Marxism and his determination to present a genuinely dialectical ontology as a basis for rethinking the political.

> Our state of non-philosophy – Never has the crisis been so radical –
> The dialectical 'solutions' = either the 'bad dialectic' that identi-
> fies the opposites, which is non-philosophy – or the 'embalmed'
> dialectic, which is no longer dialectical. End of philosophy or
> rebirth?
> Necessity of a return to ontology –
>
> (VI: 165)

The challenge here was simultaneously to describe a primordial, pre-dualist relationship between meaning and matter (conceived from the start as a phenomenological exploration of the lifeworld (*Lebenswelt*)) and to present this account without severing it from the mute processes of which it spoke. Merleau-Ponty listed three areas of concern after the quotation above: nature, subject–object and intersubjectivity (i.e. questions that related to the three tiers of the dialectic as Kojève had analysed it).

At the heart of this challenge lies precisely the one identified in the previous chapter: how could negativity be recognised and its significance communicated, without thereby rendering it positive and ideal? In criticising Sartre's pursuit of the negative, Merleau-Ponty recognises the problem explicitly:

> There is a trap inherent in the thought of the negative: if we say
> that it is, we destroy its negativity; but if we maintain strictly that it
> is not, we still elevate it to a sort of positivity, we confer upon it a
> sort of being, since through and through and absolutely it is
> *nothing*. The negative becomes a sort of quality precisely because
> one fixes it in its power of refusal and evasion. A negativist thought
> is identical to a positivist thought, and in this reversal remains the
> same in that, whether considering the void of nothingness or the
> absolute fullness of being, it in every case ignores density, depth, the
> plurality of planes, the background worlds.
>
> (VI: 67f)

This is precisely the power of Hegelianism, always to draw its opponents back into the circuit of identity. It is also the aporia of the dialectic in that once its logic is identified – whence it becomes 'motto' not 'epithet'; a 'power of Being' and 'explicative principle' (VI: 93) – it is rationalised and reified. Its negativity is hypostatised as a dead formula once defined and its openness foreclosed once it is identified with any particular agency or goal. The

> dialectic is unstable ... it is even essentially and by definition unstable, so that it has never been able to formulate itself into theses without denaturing itself, and because if one wishes to maintain its spirit it is perhaps necessary to not even name it.
>
> (VI: 92)

Yet without some grasp of the negative and its significance, no political lessons can be learnt. As the working notes to *The Visible and the Invisible* insist, hesitation in naming dialectics 'is not for the profit of a *Grund* of which one could not *say* anything. The failure of the thesis, its (dialectical) reversal discloses the *Source of theses*, the physico-historical *Lebenswelt*, to which we have to return'. The challenge was to avoid an opposition between discursive and pre-discursive without denying the difference between the conceptual and the perceptual. 'The problem is to have a conception of the negative that does not transform nature, man and history, into abstractions, a conception of the negative which is their very fabric' (PNP: 100f).

Having established the problematic of negativity and its relationship to dialectics and politics in Merleau-Ponty's thinking, it is now necessary to examine its emergence there, beginning with the phenomenological return to the lifeworld whose aim was, from the start, to describe a non-dualist ontology in a non-idealist way.

Nature: a dialectical ontology

In returning to the lifeworld Merleau-Ponty's primary question concerns, in effect, the ontology of negativity. The challenge is to find discontinuities, difference, within the density of the objective world so that it is not locked in self-identical givenness but already has within it an indeterminacy and mobility, a possibility of appearing and changing. This was what was lacking in Kantian noumena or phenomena, with the result that all constitutive activity had been placed on the side of the subject. Merleau-Ponty begins instead with a primordial difference, or spacing, whereby sense is there from the start (the French *sens* better captures the twin ideas of meaning and direction). Pre-reflective and pre-linguistic, this rudimentary meaning is existential, opened up by the incursions of the body and significant for it.

The phenomenal body and the flesh of the world

Merleau-Ponty's main works on ontology are his early *Phenomenology of Perception* (1945) and the final (incomplete and posthumously published) *The Visible and the Invisible* (written 1959–61). In his first book, *The Structure of Behaviour* (1942), he had criticised stimulus–response models of animal behaviour by arguing that they failed to appreciate the way such behaviour was already situated within a meaningful environment. Rather than just responding to external stimuli, organisms cast an 'intentional arc' around themselves which structures their milieu according to biological needs and tasks. 'Already the mere presence of a living being transforms the physical world, bringing to view here "food", there a "hiding place", and giving to "stimuli" a sense that they had not hitherto possessed' (Ph.P: 189; SB: 151). There is an 'embodied dialectic' (SB: 161), so even at this material level the world is never (in Sartre's words) a 'solid', 'self-identical' 'full positivity' that can 'encompass no negation', but a meaningful situation structured by a practical engagement.[6] 'The relations of the organic individual and its milieu are truly dialectical relations ... and this dialectic brings about the appearance of new relations' (SB: 148).

The body acts here less as a lack, or negating power, than as an interrogative opening: 'an attitude directed towards a certain existing or possible task' which is experienced 'only in the form of a vague feeling of uneasiness'. Everything comes to pass 'as though the visible body remained incomplete, gaping open' (Ph.P: 17f; VI: 147). In the language of the previous chapter, one might present this as a corporeal will to power which explains how a certain non-cognitive knowing already brings form to the sensible world. Although Merleau-Ponty calls the relation dialectical, since he thinks in terms of a reciprocity between, and mutual production of, subject and object, the gap between the latter dyad's primordial representatives remains very small, reversible, and filled with the material density of the visible world, so they are not really distinct at all (it is reflection that subsequently makes the division). He is not claiming (*pace* Kant) that he has managed to access some intrinsically meaningful thing in-itself, but the lacunae and interrogations of the body do introduce a spacing whereby sense emerges prior to reason, albeit in a provisional, corporeal and ambiguous way.

The lived body is able to (re)structure its environment because it is a dynamic, not completed, unity; an open synthesis that continually reorganises itself in order to respond to its milieu in the more structured manner that will enable it to pose more complex questions, thereby engendering a more significant environment to which it will again adapt. Sense emerges because it is able to differentiate and integrate pre-existing parts of its milieu into richer structures which were previously but latent possibilities. Yet these only arise due to a questioning that is contextual, circumscribed by the inertia of accumulated habits and by what can at each stage be a meaningful answer for it. How does the body practise this 'silent knowing'? Not by distancing itself from the world, but by existing as it does: it can 'apprehend by coexistence, laterally, by the *style*' (VI: 178, 188). 'Things have an internal equivalence in me; they arouse in me a carnal formula of their presence' (PP: 164). The world is no pre-written script simply awaiting its decoding, but neither is it just an assembly of disconnected parts. In the body–world system there is a dialectic of discovery and creativity, whereby nature's potential is given (provisional and contingent) form. 'To experience a structure is not to receive it into oneself passively: it is to live it, to take it up, assume it and discover its immanent significance' (Ph.P: 258). That immanent significance is the thing's existential style, its manner of being-in-the-world (in this sense the body already practises a phenomenological art and phenomenology will be modelled on its Apollinian talent).

The difference that fissures the world and allows it thus to appear is lodged within the body itself. Although it is coextensive with the world, the body is a special kind of flesh because it is internally nourished by an irresolvable non-coincidence: it touches and is touched, sees and is seen. It is self-reflexive and if its two moments are never in opposition (there is a 'solid, unshakeable' hinge between them (VI: 148)), yet neither can it bring these two moments into perfect correspondence. These 'experiences never exactly overlap' because there is a 'shift' or 'spread' (*écart*) between them. In other words, ontological dualism has been narrowed to the point where it is no longer a gulf between subject and object, but a divergence within the body itself, a fold rather than a void. It is then this disjunction that facilitates a transcendence of the given which is not rupture and a sense of the world which is not identity. Here plays a negativity that has no innate qualities and which avoids even the paradox of 'being' nothing, since it is filled with all the lively density of the flesh.

> ... *reversibility* is not an actual *identity* of the touching and the touched. It is their identity by principle (always abortive) – Yet it is not ideality, for the body is not simply a *de facto* visible among the visibles, it is visible-seeing, or look. In other words, the fabric of possibilities that closes the exterior visible in upon the seeing body maintains between them a certain *divergence* (*écart*). But this divergence is not a *void*, it is filled precisely by the flesh as the place of emergence of a vision, a passivity that bears an activity – and so also the divergence between the exterior visible and the body which forms the upholstering (*capitonnage*) of the world.
>
> (VI: 272)[7]

Negativity is not introduced then through any mysterious accession of being to consciousness, but via a segregation, a chiasm, of within and without. Merleau-Ponty tries to capture this integrated dyad that is the body with terms like 'exemplar sensible', 'sensible sentient'; 'two-dimensional being'; 'subject–object'; 'obverse and ... reverse'; two halves of an orange'; 'two vortexes', sometimes concentric and sometimes decentred. The 'negative, nothingness, is the doubled-up, the two leaves of my body, the inside and the outside articulated over one another – Nothingness is rather the difference between the identicals' (S: 166; PP: 163ff; VI: 133, 137, 138, 263). The profusion of metaphors demonstrates the difficulty of invoking this radically non-Cartesian body which is reducible to neither material nor spiritual substance.

This account of the body could not on its own yield the sought-for dialectical ontology, however, if it simply imposed meaning on nature through a sort of materialist Kantianism. The body must be different from its environment since it marks the possibility of its reflexiveness and its internal fissuring allows for this, but it does not constitute it; it is only a spacing within a single ontological element where 'the world is made of the same stuff as the body' (PP: 163). The mature Merleau-Ponty calls this stuff, 'flesh' (*chair*).

> The flesh of the world is not *self-sensing* (*se sentir*) as is my flesh – It is sensible not sentient ... . I call it flesh, nonetheless – in order to say that it is a *pregnancy* of possibles – that it is therefore absolutely not an object –
>
> (VI: 250)

Flesh is the general element that is neither mind nor matter; Being which begins to strain the very language of dialectics in so far as the latter is defined as negation of, or solution to, the problematic posed by ontological dualism.

> We must not think of flesh starting from substances, from body and spirit – for then it would be the union of contradictories – but we must think of it ... as an element, as the concrete emblem of a general manner of being.
>
> (VI: 147)

Even so, Merleau-Ponty continues to think about this Being in dialectical terms: 'this interiorly worked-over mass, has no name in any philosophy' but is a 'dialectical absolute', the 'formative medium of the object and the subject' (VI: 147); a wild Being that is not opaque but dimensional, styled. Like will to power, its becoming is not mediated by negativity and it is not the effect of an efficacious force external to it; it *is* negativity in its generativity. Matter is '"pregnant" with its form' (or later, 'the visible is pregnant with the invisible'), where pregnancy is defined as the 'power to break forth, productivity, fecundity' and 'the form that has arrived at itself, that poses itself by its own means' (Ph.P: 291; PP: 12, 15; VI: 208, 216). Being is 'the very movement of the content', 'auto-constitution' (VI: 93), and the dialectic, similarly, is this 'perpetual genesis' on plural levels (AD: 204). In so far as this flesh is understood as an intertwining of positive and negative (identity and difference), Merleau-Ponty speaks of the visible and the invisible. To appreciate this relationship it is necessary to understand the perceptual paradigm that yields the visual metaphor of negativity as invisibility.

Perception and the visual field

In the lifeworld it is not thought or labour, but perception that is privileged by Merleau-Ponty as the 'archetype of the originating encounter' (VI: 158).[8] Idealised levels of significance originate here and they will also continue to bear the contingency and ambiguity of this primordial dialectic. Moreover the process of perceptual coming-to-meaning that Merleau-Ponty describes will serve as his model for understanding all those more cultural activities – such as painting, language and politics – that inscribe significance in the world and as such, it will carry certain lessons and caveats for those more symbolic practices.

Like the body, perception is a site of negativity because it relies on an irreducible differentiation. Its very possibility rests upon a distinction between figure and ground. This separation (*écart*) introduces nothing new into the visible (it brings merely a divergence), but it does allow its structuring as something is extricated for attention yet gains its sense only in relation to the ground it is not. 'To be conscious = to have a figure on ground – one cannot go back any further' (VI: 191). Such differentiation yields perceptual significance through a '*natural* negativity, a first institution, always already there' (VI: 216). Or again, 'the figure–ground distinction introduces a third term between the "subject" and the "object." It is *that separation (écart)* first of all that is the perceptual *meaning*' (VI: 197). Which figures are distinguished will be entirely contingent, while their bringing into focus will remain an ongoing process of interpreting ambiguities. Moreover, the depth and perspective that permit visual clarity belong to neither seer nor seen, but unfold where they meet. In principle there can be no bird's eye view because the look is situated: things can neither be inspected 'without gaps', nor seen 'all naked' (VI: 131, 177). There are only profiles inviting further exploration; a relief where one thing moves into focus at the expense of another. As in all structures of significance, perceptual sense thus remains contingent and contextual; provisional, ambiguous, open. It does not faithfully represent a visible world 'out there', but opens up dimensions, patterns, a system of equivalences; it 'already stylizes' because it differentiates and forms. Since mind will remain irremediably incarnate, it will never escape perception's negativities in enacting this formative 'violence'.

... we shape in the manifold of things certain hollows, certain fissures – and we do this the moment we are alive – to bring into the world that which is strangest to it: *a meaning*, an incitement ... . Style exists (and hence signification) as soon as there are figures and backgrounds, a norm and a deviation, a top and a bottom, that is, as soon as certain elements of the world assume the value of dimensions to which subsequently all the rest relate ... .

(PW: 61)

If the negativity inherent in the figure–ground dyad denies perfect visibility it is also the very possibility of vision, since it opens the space wherein the perceptual encounter between gaze and things flourishes. Like the flesh, this is understood by Merleau-Ponty as a dialectical, intimate and reversible field wherein meaning appears. The visual field is criss-crossed by lines of force which 'breathe into it a secret and magic life by exerting here and there forces of distortion, contraction and expansion' (Ph.P: 48f). It is these lines of force that will later be designated the invisible. Although perceptual significance is therefore 'for-us', as embodied perceivers, Merleau-Ponty is eager to avoid presenting this in terms of seer-versus-seen. It is, he insists, impossible to identify any constitutive agency: 'the things attract my look, my gaze caresses the things, it espouses their contours and their reliefs, between it and them we catch sight of a complicity' (VI: 76). If it is the body that provides 'the hollow whence a vision will come', the seer is part of the visible and feels that 'he is the sensible coming to itself' (VI: 147, 114).

Again, it is as if Merleau-Ponty were struggling to present a Nietzschean/Heideggerian negativity, as generativity, in dialectical terms. The spacing wherein lies its fecundity signals reciprocity and difference, not synthesis and opposition, and the creative–destructive rhythms of will to power are more evident in the descriptions of perception than the orderly logic of synthesis described by Hegel ('perception as a unity disintegrates and reforms ceaselessly' (Ph.P: 38)). But this process remains explicitly a *negativity* for Merleau-Ponty, despite its productivity, because it negates any positive, plenitudinous being in-itself. Moreover, the dialectical heritage is apparent in his concentration on perception as a *formative* process. If the forms, or structures, that appear remain ambiguous and never achieve stable identity, he does not describe a visible field so mobile that meaning is endlessly deferred or just randomly engendered. Positive structures also acquire a certain inertia and their temporality imposes a certain logic on their transmutation. For figure and ground are not simply differentiated; together they comprise a *Gestalt* (form). This is an enduring trope throughout Merleau-Ponty's thinking, indicating precisely that cohesion of sense and sensibility, positive and negative, unity and diversity, that he struggles to convey. When I referred in chapter 2 to a way of interpreting Hegel's dialectical unities aesthetically, this mode of becoming is also inherent in

Merleau-Ponty's conception and it is this that allows him to sustain a dialectical faith in a becoming-of-reason despite the contingency of any particular *Gestalt*.[9]

In the *Gestalt* the whole is, like a work of art, more than the sum of its parts although it is nothing without them. Parts 'magnetize' each other according to a shared but entirely contingent affinity, whereupon they together evince a recognisable style; a pre-conceptual meaning that is derived aesthetically rather than logically. For Merleau-Ponty this style is existential and grasped pre-cognitively, all at once, so while it outruns the empirical (Cartesian matter as *partes extra partes*) it is not constituted by any synthesising reflection. Existence is in fact defined by him as just this 'dialectic of form and content', a 'perpetual re-ordering of fact and hazard by a reason non-existent before and without those circumstances' (Ph.P: 127). In *Gestalten* facts emerge steeped in a generality that renders them meaningful, while meaning originates in the relation between situated parts. The empirical and the ideal are inextricable and Being – flesh – is precisely this chiasm of ideality and facticity (VI: 114ff).

> There is a strict ideality in experiences that are experiences of the flesh: the moments of the sonata, the fragments of the luminous field, adhere to one another with a cohesion without concept, which is the same type as the cohesion of the parts of my body with the world … . We will therefore have to recognize an ideality that is not alien to the flesh, that gives it its axes, its depth, its dimensions.
>
> (VI: 152)

Gestalten are then experienced as styles of existence and it is through them that the body 'knows' the world or that individuals first 'know' their society or language, responding appropriately to their requirements without needing to conceptualise them. Such forms are open because (as with will to power) their overall sense is altered if the relationship between parts changes, or perhaps a new factor accidentally intrudes to shift the physiognomy of the whole. Yet they sustain a structuring of the world and grant it a latent rationality and existential meaning. It is this mode of stylising that also marks the way painting, language or politics operate when they re-form the latency of the given into a new order of signification and it is on this basis that political unities must be judged.

In his later work Merleau-Ponty sometimes conveyed this process using the language of structural linguistics. Rather than shifting from a perceptual to a linguistic paradigm, however, he tended to interpret Saussure from the perspective of perception and to understand linguistic structures existentially, dialectically and in terms of *Gestalten*.[10] Now the latter are characterised as a 'principle of distribution', a 'diacritical, oppositional, relative system' (VI: 206), where diacritical systems are those whose meaning lies not positively, in isolated and self-identical parts, but in a negative relation between them where each part gains its sense from not being its others. In chapter 2 I associated Derrida with this negativity, where *différance* was also conveyed in terms of Saussurean linguistics. Rather than emphasising the contradiction and reconciliation which negation entailed for Hegel, Merleau-Ponty, like poststructuralists, emphasises the plural and open-ended relations between multiple parts. Yet again, his emphasis is less on negativity as pure process and deferral than on the provisional meaning difference allows. It is notable that when he explains Saussure's diacritical theory of signs, where 'the terms of language are engendered only by the differences which appear among them', he adds that the unity Saussure 'is talking about is a unity of coexistence, like that of the sections of an arch which shoulder one another' (S: 39; PW: 103). (Extrapolating here, it might be argued that this is why Merleau-Ponty's politics will continue to echo a project of intersubjective community rather than emphasising irreconcilable diversity.) Language is not anyway for Merleau-Ponty the source of all meaning, but one (albeit privileged) mode of bringing to expression the inexhaustible lifeworld of which it is part. Saussurean difference is only another way of expressing the negativity already elicited in corporeality, figure–ground and *Gestalten*.

When the last writings refer to the visible and the invisible, it is again this indestructible relation between fact and idea that is intended. The new terminology marked a deepening of Merleau-Ponty's attempt at avoiding dualism in conveying negativity. The invisible, like *différance*, is the condition of the visible's appearing and is always implicit within it. 'Sensible being is not only things but also everything sketched out there, even virtually, everything which leaves its trace there, everything which figures there, even as divergence and a certain absence' (S: 172). The invisible is the inner framework of the positive, its hidden depth and skeleton, which allows things to unfold over time with an indefinite legacy trailing them and calling for further exploration. It is not negation of the visible, but an *'other dimensionality'*, a 'negation–reference', 'separation' (VI: 236, 257f). It is what sustains each meaning in its ambiguity and openness but also that which sustains specific meanings according to a syntax of the lifeworld. Merleau-Ponty speaks of the invisible as style or unconscious (VI: 180): the in(de)terminable threads of association which link parts into a significance lived rather than known, a 'negativity which is not nothing' (VI: 151). Each visible gains its sense from these invisible relations, these lines of force, that expand as the more sublime reaches of symbolic structuring emerge. Residues from the past, values and desires for the future, associations, dreams, imagination, myths, all intervene to give every significance a rich and inexhaustible meaning although not one that is immune to interpretation. There remains a dialectical sense in which every appearance is to be grasped in the context of the web of connections that subtend it.

To conclude, the dialectical ontology is described by Merleau-Ponty in terms of a Being that is an architecture of tiers and levels linked through an intertwining and reversibility. It is visible and invisible, sense and nonsense, positive and negative. As for Heidegger, Being is a verb not a noun, a generativity operative 'before the cleavage operated by reflection, about it, on its horizon, not outside of us and not in us, but there where the two moments cross, there where "there is" something' (VI: 95). It is total in so far as everything is ultimately linked through chains of significance and it is the world onto which each partial meaning opens, but Being remains a latency to be created. In creating it, we disclose/engender Being so that reflection, like more corporeal levels of significance, manifests the formative process with its negativities. If the invisible, negativity, is that which sustains meaning then it is no more foundational than Derrida's *différance* or Kristeva's semiotic. As Merleau-Ponty concludes, it 'would be naive to seek solidarity in a heaven of ideas or in a *ground* (*fond*) of meaning – it is neither above nor beneath the appearances, but at their joints, it is the tie that secretly connects an experience to its variants' (VI: 116).

Subject–object: subjectivity, philosophy and language

The flesh, with its visible/invisible effulgence, had yielded Merleau-Ponty at least a sketch of the dialectical ontology he was seeking. In place of Marx's dangerously idealised nature, he had described a lifeworld where negativity is endemic in positive forms yet devoid of metaphysical substance and immune to conceptual identification. However there remained a further level of the dualist problem in that the dialectics of existence was still being reflected upon. How was this negativity then to be thematised without rendering it positive? Hegel and Marx had grappled with this problem of the relation between philosophy and non-philosophy but had failed to resolve it. This is the dilemma signalled in Merleau-Ponty's brief agenda in the 'working notes' as 'subject–object'. The challenge was to inscribe and practise negativity at the level of thought while showing how thinking is continuous with the pre-thetic processes typical of the *Lebenswelt*.

A phenomenology of mind

Although Merleau-Ponty's main concern in this context was with philosophy, the question of the genesis and status of thinking as such was posed by his rejection of ontological dualism. If nature were not inert objectivity, what was the standing of the epistemological subject, the Cartesian *cogito*? The earlier writings tend to present the phenomenon of consciousness, or mind, as a merely evolutionary appearing continuous with the perceptual process, where it represents not an ontological given but a higher level of signification. Mind 'is not a new sort of being but a new form of unity' (SB:

181). If the body's inscription of perceptual sense in its milieu already manifests a rudimentary consciousness, this is enhanced with increasing complexity until sense acquires symbolic form and signification comes into its own. If lived significance ('brute mind') is from the beginning inherent in the silence of the lifeworld, where it is supported by a generalised and non-reflexive 'tacit cogito' (Ph.P: 402ff), thought is but a second, figurative, meaning of vision, a 'sublimation of the flesh' in its reversible form/content effervescence (S: 181; VI: 145). As such, ideal meaning always bears the ambiguity, contingency and opacity of existence and is anchored there by its irreducible invisible supports.

In his later more anti-humanist work, however, Merleau-Ponty clearly felt that even this decentred and embodied subjectivity remained too Cartesian and a more radical way of de-ontologising it is proposed. 'Replace the notions of concept, idea, mind, representation' with '*dimensions*, articulation, level, hinges, pivots, configuration' (VI: 224). This was what the new emphasis on the flesh, with its integral negativity, was to achieve: a self-constituting field that robbed subjectivity of its meaning-bestowing functions without eliminating meaning itself.

> All the positive bric-a-brac of "concepts," "judgments," "relations"
> is eliminated, and the mind quiet as water in the fissure of Being –
> We must not look for spiritual things, there are only structures of
> the void –
>
> (VI: 235)

But what is the status of Merleau-Ponty's own philosophy when it reflects on Being and how is it to avoid the proscription on naming and identifying negativity? The solution he pursued here was a philosophy that would be one tier of Being expressing itself, but in this case it would have to practise the latter's own negativity. This is the circularity sometimes glimpsed in Hegel yet it remains impossible adequately to convey it in the linear syntax available to thought.

Perception, thinking, are 'structured as a language'

One reason Merleau-Ponty became critical of his early work was its insufficient attention to the role of language. A note in *The Visible and the Invisible* reveals his continued anxiety lest the passage from perceptual to ideal sense should reintroduce dualism (VI: 176). Although it was Saussurean linguistics that now allowed him to finesse the problem more satisfactorily, it should nonetheless be borne in mind that Merleau-Ponty's Saussure was not quite the one of structuralism or poststructuralism.

In the former case, as indicated already, he understood the relation between linguistic structures (*langue*) and the subjective will to expression captured in speech (*parole*), dialectically. If the systemic logic of syntactical rules constrains freedom to express, in *parole* the speaking subject may improvise on and even transmute the more sedimented *langue* which is only the anonymous outcome of repeated intersubjective speech acts that are motivated by a will to signify more richly. In the latter case, he insisted that language expresses existential meanings and is not therefore wholly self-referential despite its diacritical structure. If meaning is deferred along a chain of signifiers, the intervals between words are also patterned stylistically, thereby bearing their own, existential, significance ('blank, but full of meaning, vibrating with lines of force, as dense as marble' (PW: 89)).

Crucial to Merleau-Ponty's understanding of language here is a distinction between its manifest and latent meanings. It retains a non-verbal significance, a way of ordering, of stylising, the world, which is lived rather than known. It is able to convey by this style more than it can explicitly say. It has its own flesh since like music or painting it can 'sustain a sense by virtue of its own arrangement, catch a meaning in its own mesh' (VI: 153).

> Each language has its own way of expressing different relationships, like time and space. For example, the structure of Greek will indicate an 'architectonic time' appropriate to the Greeks. Even the manner of distributing the accents, the flections, and even the use of the article are expressive of a world view (*une vue du monde*).
>
> (CAL: 75f)

Its meaning is excessive and, if it tries to articulate a primordial register that outruns it, it also outruns itself as its own meanings leak back into that wild region of mute and invisible negativity that over-determines them. This is why a perfect, transparent language or perfect representation are impossible. But on the other hand, because Being and speech comprise a single text where meaning and existence proliferate, language is both part of the upsurge of Being and, like the body, a privileged part that enjoys a certain reflexiveness. In speaking about Being it is also Being speaking itself: 'language realizes, by breaking the silence what the silence wished and did not obtain' (VI: 176). Once the philosopher understands this, she should abandon fantasies of grounding the world from outside and accept the wager of 'making the things themselves speak' (a project, we might recall, that Adorno had attributed to Hegel) (VI: 125). The philosopher

> knows better than anyone that what is lived is lived-spoken, that, born at this depth, language is not a mask over Being, but – if one knows how to grasp it with all its roots and all its foliation – the most valuable witness to Being, that it does not interrupt an immediation that would be perfect without it, that the vision itself, the thought itself, are, as has been said, "structured as a language," are

articulation before the letter, apparition of something where there was nothing or something else ... . [P]hilosophy is an operative language, that language that can be known only from within, through its exercise, is open upon things, called forth by the voices of silence, and continues an effort of articulation which is the Being of every being.

(VI: 126f)

As such, language both strives to represent the lifeworld and, in doing so, exemplifies its mute rhythms on a symbolic level. In turning back on itself, it re-enters the labyrinth of disclosure and creativity, reflection and emulation, but on a more reflexive level. This allows Merleau-Ponty to gesture towards a dissolution of the philosophy/non-philosophy problem, but only for the philosopher who appreciates negativity and speaks the 'operative language' he associates with phenomenology. Such thinking must itself be part of a dialectical upsurge and not a 'high-altitude' reflection upon it.

Phenomenology and hyperdialectics

What phenomenology comprehends in the lifeworld is not some analytical chaos, but the existential forms that ferment there. Accordingly

to 'understand' is to take in the total intention ... the unique mode of existing expressed in the properties of the pebble, the glass or the piece of wax, in all the events of the revolution ... . It is a matter, in the case of each civilization, of finding the Idea in the Hegelian sense, that is, not a law of the physico-mathematical type, discoverable by objective thought, but that formula which sums up some unique manner of behaviour towards others, towards Nature, time and death: a certain way of patterning the world ... .

(Ph.P: xviii)

In articulating these ambiguous *Gestalten* (which would apply to linguistic as much as to political régimes), phenomenology discloses the structures of existence and can then turn back upon them reflectively. This will be most significant for political life. But whether politically or philosophically, it must recognise that its own structurings obey the same logic of appearing and thus interrogate itself. This is what renders it dialectical.

Merleau-Ponty had begun to think about phenomenology in this way when he presented it as existentialist philosophy in the preface to the *Phenomenology of Perception*. In returning to the things themselves, Husserl's project could not, he points out, mean returning to the Newtonian world of objects since physics is already a second-order sign language. The lifeworld is prior to such thematisation, but re-turning to it cannot entail some impossible project of faithful representation (as Kant had demonstrated). In articulating things we change them; 'the sensible is indiscoverable' (PW: 107) and in expressing it we always therefore loop back into a dialectic. Negatively, phenomenology encourages us to suspend our taken-for-granted senses of the *Lebenswelt* in order to approach it with a sense of wonder and contingency. But in this (in principle ceaseless) interrogation of existence, it also brings it to expression. Theory no more constitutes or passively reflects reality than does consciousness; rather they express a physiognomy that is already ambiguously lived and in doing so they also participate in the formative process, so that in interrogating themselves they are further reflecting on that process itself.

> The phenomenological world is not the bringing to explicit expression of a pre-existing being, but the laying down of being. Philosophy is not the reflection of a pre-existing truth, but, like art, the act of bringing truth into being.
>
> (Ph.P: xx)

Like the writer or painter, the phenomenologist shows the 'same will to seize the meaning of the world or of history as that meaning comes into being' (Ph.P: xxi). Like perception or politics, philosophy stylises the world in disclosing it. Like the body or language, it is self-reflexive and in recognising its own status it understands its own limits as well as the way meaning appears. Once philosophy grasps Being's negativity, it thus recognises the requirement explicitly to *emulate* it (in a move analogous to Nietzsche's Dionysian, whose grasping the logic of will to power means an exhortation to participate in it).

The phenomenologist practises this negativity in the twin senses of its contingent generativity and its dialectics (there must be a constant back and forth between 'subject' and 'object'; a 'dialogue' between the different levels of Being). In this sense thought replicates the form/content relation of the *Gestalt*, the visible/invisible intertwining of their 'chiasm'. Because philosophy is situated, it must put itself into question through 'infinite meditation', always recognising that it bears its own shadow and trails its invisibles (Hegel's failure); that the philosopher is a 'perpetual beginner'. It must recognise philosophy itself as an existential choice, forgoing a foundation in transcendental subjectivity and recognising 'its own dependence on an unreflective life' which denies it solid grounding. This is why a 'phenomenology of phenomenology' is also necessary (Ph.P: 365; S: 178). When Merleau-Ponty describes dialectics, he does so in equivalent terms. 'Being neither an outside witness nor a pure agent, it is implicated in the movement and does not view it from above.' It is a way of 'deciphering the being with which we are in contact' and as such, it 'excludes all *extrapolation*'. It is 'autocritical' (VI: 90–3).

It should now be apparent why Merleau-Ponty was so insistent that negativity and dialectics could not be named; why they 'can count only as what has neither name, nor repose, nor nature' (VI: 88). Dialectics can have nothing to do with the triadic formula of its 'embalmed' Hegelian version: 'the inertia of the content never permits the defining of one term as positive, another as negative, and still less a third as absolute suppression of the negative by itself.' What Merleau-Ponty refers to as a 'good' or 'hyper'dialectic is one which, like phenomenology, always criticises and surpasses itself as statement. It recognises the ambiguity and plurality of relationships and that Being exhibits no positive syntheses but only 'bound wholes where signification never is except in tendency'. Yet it remains dialectical – and this is again why it yields a politics – because it still recognises the spaces and differences of Being as making possible a formative process, a sedimentation that yields meaning and even progress. Even in his last writings, Merleau-Ponty argues that this good dialectic avoids scepticism or relativism because it does not reject a 'surpassing that reassembles' but only its equation with a 'new positive, a new position' (VI: 94). It interprets this appearing but recognises itself as implicated in the process.

Ideally, then, once the philosopher appreciates what Merleau-Ponty conveys about the ontology of negativity, she would move on to the challenge of practising the interpretations and engagements it calls for as an exemplary, dialectical, method. Similarly, once the political has been rethought in terms of negativity then the sort of engagement it summons remains to be practised at the more concrete and intersubjective level of collective life.

Intersubjectivity: history and politics

The lifeworld is not just an anonymous or archaic field of existence but also a milieu of coexistence, continuously reproduced ('not pure being', but the sense which is revealed where my own experiences and those of others 'intersect and engage each other's like gears' (Ph.P: xx)). This is why the ontological descriptions are interwoven with questions about history and politics and why intersubjectivity appeared as a third tier on Merleau-Ponty's dialectical agenda.

In the previous chapter I suggested that a major difficulty in eliciting a politics from will to power lay in Nietzsche's privileging of negativity's aesthetic rhythm and his accompanying reluctance to recognise the slower tempo evinced by the political. Although the choreography of appearing in Merleau-Ponty's work also favours an aesthetic sense of how difference engenders provisional forms, he recognised that the political is especially beset by inertia and cannot possibly emulate the mobile reversals or swift pace of a more Dionysian creation/destruction. For there is a density to the political, where the necessity for shared practices and institutions, together with the inevitable sedimentation of accepted ideas, means that freedom is limited and the effulgence of Being is more leaden than elsewhere. If negativity is ineliminable, political regimes nevertheless try to suppress it, while the clumsy acts of negation they incite have enduring and fatal consequences. In the political domain, meaning and the process of its emergence are thus weighed down with power. When the social field is inscribed with political significance, lived structures take concrete form and give beneficiaries an interest in defending them against change. There is a tendency for the (re-)structuring of the social world to be violently blocked or imposed and in this sense politics is quite different from language. For in coexistence, the spacings that engender and transform positive forms mean encroachment as well as enrichment, terror as well as humanism. On the basis of phenomenology's understanding of how meaning appears and an irresistible negativity plays, can a more humanistic mode of politics be discerned?

Humanism and coexistence

Given recent antipathy towards humanism and the complexity of Merleau-Ponty's own position here, it is important to be aware of the role it played in his politics and the sense in which he used the term. The dialectical ontology had decentred the epistemological subject and transferred its constitutive capacities to a fulmination internal to Being. In this context the late writings are explicit that '[h]umanism must also involve a kind of anti-humanism' and that this is connected with the more Heideggerian ontology where 'Being and man belong to one another without the possibility of thinking their relationship only from man's point of view' (PNP: 46). Indeed if the ideas of a pre-reflective lifeworld and an incarnate consciousness are understood rigorously, this anti-anthropomorphism is surely implicit, if unrealised, from the start. The final note of *The Visible and the Invisible* restates a project whereby the visible, nature and Logos 'must be presented without any compromise with *humanism*' (or naturalism or theology); against the Marx of 1844, the '*visible* has to be described as something that is realized through man, but which is nowise anthropology' (VI: 274).

Like Nietzsche's sick animals or Heidegger's *Dasein*, Merleau-Ponty's humanity is thus displaced from the foundations of meaning yet it is credited with a heightened capacity for its disclosure. It is not a space (hole, lack) wherein meaning appears, but an active and creative spacing (*écart*) that begins as soon as bodies inhabit the natural world. (It is important to avoid any theological suggestion here that Being – God, *Geist* – teleologically creates the means of its self-expression.) This process is exemplified in activities like painting or writing, where Being reveals itself resplendently through the formative violence and interrogative talent of the artist (Nietzsche's Goethe; Merleau-Ponty's Cézanne).

But Merleau-Ponty is also aware that such artistry does not create freely or autonomously: its embodied protagonists inhabit a socioeconomic life-world which circumscribes their opportunities and horizons. The challenge posed by the late writings (one arguably still unmet by contemporary polit-ical philosophy) would have been to *combine the anti-humanist ontology with a sensitivity to collective, political, life*, where subjects themselves are formed and destroyed. In this context dialectics meant an understanding of the interweaving of agency and structure, one which neither eliminated the former nor relied on an exaggerated faith in its freedom. For a politics without subjects would be a strange undertaking, even if consciousness or identity do slide imperceptibly into the negativities of corporeal and inter-subjective life. Merleau-Ponty's work indeed reveals both sensitivity to the sort of moral choices politics sometimes poses and keeps a space for the political virtuosity of exceptional leaders. The challenge would be to grasp how Being's effulgence plays itself through them.

His political theory also involved a recognition that while dialectical engagement in history requires appreciation of its contingency (and humanism 'begins by becoming aware of contingency' (S: 241)), it still requires some criterion by which to evaluate progress and justify its own critical intervention. This is what humanism normatively offered. Now obviously this humanism could not for Merleau-Ponty be grounded in an ontological subject, since this was just what the phenomenology of percep-tion had challenged. Like Foucault, he rejected any humanism predicated on a fixed and ideal definition of 'Man'.[11] The criticisms of rationalist poli-tics reveal his suspicion, too, of the sort of teleological humanism Lévi-Strauss was attacking Sartre for during the summer of 1961 and which Lyotard has more recently associated with modernity's grand narra-tives.[12] Humanism is not then an absolute value for Merleau-Ponty, yet it does have a certain universality that he elicits from the description of the *Lebenswelt*.

In exploring the lifeworld, Merleau-Ponty describes an 'operative ratio-nality' whereby embodied interrogations structure the world and engender forms which, although provisional and contingent, are more valuable in so far as they become more complex yet unified (we might recall that a similar configuration marked Nietzsche's higher beings). 'To say that there exists rationality is to say that perspectives blend, perceptions confirm each other, a meaning emerges' (Ph.P: xix). This lived reason yields a model for inter-subjectivity. Because perfect and complete vision is in principle unattainable, there is a motivation always to go beyond any provisional resolution and also to negate habits or sedimentations that close the perceptual field to further exploration (to 'cross them out' as false). There is accordingly an adaptational impetus towards more broadly-structured environments, supported by the temporal continuity of question and answer, and a nega-tive logic that eliminates 'irrational', entropic or closed forms. Normal organic functioning is described as a process of integration; regression or pathology as 'change to a less differentiated and more primitive structure' (Ph.P: 5,10,127).

By extension (and analogy): as organisms grow by constructing and adapting to a more abundantly-structured, more 'rational', environment, so different cultures also represent diverse solutions to a single problem and can therefore be evaluated or learned from according to a general criterion. The social is mobilised 'by the *common situation* of men, their will to co-exist and to recognise one another' (CAL: 101f). There are 'certain effective problems present at the core of history', which revolve around questions of coexistence (SNS 105). The more perspectives are integrated in a structured yet open unity, the richer the opportunities for negotiating coexistence and the more rational its collective processes. A humanist politics would accord-ingly mean a process of opening up the social field, enriching opportunities for coexistence and communication (for subject–object and intersubjective exchanges), just as 'higher' corporeal structurings facilitate more sophisti-cated questions and answers to thereby enrich the flesh and its potential for further disclosure/creation.

Inversely, once the political field becomes closed, opportunities for responding to history's adversity atrophy. This was precisely the problem with rationalist regimes. They fail to appreciate that all solutions are provi-sional and contextual; that where reason does appear, it is always menaced. They reify allegedly rational solutions rather than practising rationality as a hazardous process of engendering more unified/complex collective institu-tions. They adopt inappropriate orientations of mastery rather than interrogation and accordingly find themselves either condoning or exercising violence in their efforts to impose meaning without historical support.

What is required is thus an understanding of the relationship between values and structures, intentions and consequences, in order to appreciate how meaning appears in an intersubjective world where it is always possible but never guaranteed. A dialectical politics would be humanist in this sense of broadening the scope of coexistence as an ongoing process, and rational in the sense of emulating a more primordial negativity whereby integrated yet diverse forms unfold. The humanist 'arouses us to what is problematic in our own existence and in that of the world, to such a point that we shall never be cured of searching for a solution' (IP: 44). As such humanism is the political equivalent of phenomenology in accommodating an appreciation of negativity.

Towards a philosophy of history

In order to flesh out this humanist politics, Merleau-Ponty needed to consider the nature of history and, on this basis, to elicit an exemplary historicity. Dialectics required that history be understood as a meaningful yet contingent process, one neither teleological nor simply random or discontinuous. If history were not cunningly synthesising all its lessons, it did evince a certain tendency to progress towards 'a life which is not unlivable for the greatest number' (S: 131; cf. Ph.P: xix, HT: xxxv).

Like perception, history advances by throwing up (co)existential *Gestalten* which are lived rather than known. As individuals together undertake their daily activities, shared responses to similar situations congeal over time (according to a 'sort of historical imagination', an 'elective affinity') to yield institutions which then operate as constraints as well as opportunities. These lend societies their identity and imperious logic, which Merleau-Ponty describes as history's 'dimensions'. It is these existential styles that the phenomenologist describes. They are

> typical ways of treating natural being, or responding to others and to death. They appear at the point where man and the givens of nature or of the past meet, arising as symbolic matrices which have no pre-existence and which can, for a longer or a shorter time, influence history itself and then disappear, not by external forces but through an internal disintegration or because one of their secondary elements becomes predominant and changes their nature.
>
> (AD: 16f)

Like languages, social institutions constitute open diacritical systems which emerge and transmute over time, yielding horizons within which problems are addressed yet being open to shifts as contingencies mount; coordinating actors who pre-cognitively grasp what is required of them and live their culture's imperatives without being able (unequivocally) to articulate them (SNS: 111). Because they are assaulted by chance events and their own lacunae, these systems never remain static. Their openness, and hence the freedom they allow, is variable, but if they become too closed the effort of enduring distorts their overall sense. If there are no final or correct solutions to coexistence, there is a continual negative assault which destabilises every provisional equilibrium. This (co)existential imperative will be redefined at every turn since problems are themselves contextual rather than deficiencies regarding a human essence. Negations are always situated and specific and do not rely on some adequate theory of the totality. Merleau-Ponty suggests that judgement will be delivered historically, through the negation of 'false' (closed, dehumanising) systems. This is not because they offend against a higher historical purpose but due to a shared, experiential sense of their limitations, which may or may not come to theoretical reflection.

> If certain regimes disappear, it is because they are incapable of resolving the problems of the time and the intersubjective force of the moment. That which we call the logic of history is a process of

elimination by which only the systems which are capable of taking the situation into account subsist. History is not a hidden god which acts in our place and to which we must submit. Men make their history as they make their language.

(CAL: 102)

Although historical structures retain a high degree of adversity and anonymity, since they emerge in an 'interworld' where multiple acts coalesce, they are responsive to mass disaffection precisely because they are intersubjective.

The crucial question was nevertheless whether, in light of the recognition of this negative logic and the more general negativity of all appearing, history might be negotiated more humanistically. It is in this context that Merleau-Ponty commends the history of language, and its Saussurean understanding, as exemplary (IP: 55; PW: 23). For if linguistic forms also transmute according to a negative logic, they negotiate this in a less violent way, yielding an alternative model of historicity to that evinced by politics. The latter, then, eliminates false or irrational (closed, non-fecund) forms by trial and error or denial. It practises a 'chronic' historicity, caught in a 'mortal circle' of inertia and revolt (S: 79), where the reification of positive forms incites their negation. Language, on the other hand, follows a more dialectical path. It seeks neither to venerate nor destroy its past, but sustains its continuity through a gradual progress which involves a reflexive openness both to the lessons of its traditions and to the potential for innovation. The 'past of language is not just a dominated past but also an understood past' (PW: 101, 105). It turns back on itself to criticise and articulate its stylistic inventions and in so doing leads their meaning into the future, while reinscribing them through its very acts. It is precisely this continuity of meaning across temporal zones, where reflection weaves in and out of its own development to integrate and re-orient itself, that Merleau-Ponty discerns in language *and* presents as a 'good' dialectic:

> [T]he Hegelian dialectic is what we call the phenomenon of expression, which gathers itself step by step and launches itself again through the mystery of rationality. We would undoubtedly recover the true sense of the concept of history if we acquired the habit of modelling it on the example of the arts and language.
>
> (PW: 85)

What distinguishes language from other mute forms of expression is precisely that 'it is not content to draw lines, vectors, a "coherent deformation," or tacit meaning on the surface of the world' (PW: 104). It aims to speak. But at the same time, it accepts that its significations remain open and provisional; that there is no end to its history or complete representational system (since even language 'cannot escape the limits that define sensible expression. It only carries them further' (PW: 111)).

This is distinguished from the 'chronic' historicity more typical of politics, where there is an urge to total power or negation, 'forgetfulness rather than memory', a neurotic ignorance of a past it is thus doomed to repeat (PW: 72). A dialectical historicity here would mean a continual attempt at turning back reflectively on the past to assimilate its lessons for the future, reinvigorating valuable parts within a new synthesis which institutes a more integrated response to the problem of coexistence. As such, dialectics is not history's law of motion, nor a correct method for reading off its truth, but '*a movement which creates its own course and returns to itself* – and thus a movement with no other guide than its own initiative that nevertheless does not escape outside itself but cuts across its own path and confirms itself from cycle to cycle' (PW: 85). Errors carry weight in history in so far as they are understood. Such is the passage from rationalism to reason, where the past (like the lifeworld) is not dead but an open field for interpretation:

> granting all the periods of stagnation and retreat, human relations are able to grow, to change their avatars into lessons, to pick out the truth of their past in the present, to eliminate certain mysteries which render them opaque and thereby make themselves more translucent.
>
> (PP: 9)

Merleau-Ponty insists that this is not a dogmatic rationalism but a methodological one; by penetrating (as the phenomenologist does) to the intentional cores of other historical and cultural resolutions, it is able to grasp their inner meaning since across the wild regions of the lifeworld, they are only variations of a universal existence. Here, reason is neither guaranteed nor some ideal to be achieved, but something which is precariously and intersubjectively forged, through the bringing together of perspectives into provisional agreement. It thus proceeds through communication, questioning and self-critique. It is then this politics that Merleau-Ponty terms humanist: not because it sees history as the vehicle for satisfying some human essence and politics as a means to this end, but precisely because its style, its practices and its existential choices minimise the violence inherent in collective life while emulating an exemplary mode in which its rationality unfolds. It is precisely because our history always outruns our capacity fully to understand or control it that a humanist, dialectical means is required.

Negativity as praxis

It is this means that is defined, politically, as praxis. Just as the organism questions its milieu in order to structure it more richly, while operating within its constraints, so for Merleau-Ponty actors need to interrogate historical structures because their inertia and sedimented power relations circumscribe as well as prompt possible responses. The structures they engage are, after all, only the congealed results of intersubjective acts so, if they are not fully comprehensible or controllable, neither are they completely alien. In all these ways praxis resembles language, with its dialectic between *parole* and *langue*.

Praxis combines the methodological resources of phenomenology and an action that intervenes materially. Like phenomenology, it means criticising and evaluating the (co)existential dimension that gives each culture its recognisable style; interpreting its vectors (which include the lived orientations and small negations or innovations that push it in one direction rather than another); articulating events in such a way that theory resonates with the lived sense of those whose everyday acts make history. As such, a creative and astute interpretation might push this dense, unruly edifice in a progressive direction by galvanising the masses but without claiming to realise some underlying truth. Theory cannot claim to be translating an unequivocal, objective condition, but nor is it a gratuitous imposition of meaning. Merleau-Ponty is not claiming (like Lukács) any subject–object identity that privileged agents enjoy (such as the proletariat). But he does suggest, in the earlier works especially, that political sense can be forged through a reciprocity between theorists and actors, where lived and reflected significance evolves dialectically. While this process is intersubjective, since interpretation emerges out of communication, it is also, crucially, supplemented by a subject–object dialectic whereby history in all its density is read. Without this dimension, material life and the existential dimensions of value could not be criticised or effectively challenged. Praxis is then, like *Gestalten* or the flesh, an interweaving and reversability of the ideal and material. As such it involves active, not merely contemplative, reason. In transcending the subject–object dichotomy of epistemology, it brings concrete reason into the world.

Although the social field is inscribed with negativities (invisibility, adversity, contingency, ambiguity, etc.) it is not devoid of meaning nor, therefore, immune to a hermeneutics. There is no truth hidden beneath appearances, no totality that makes sense of all appearances according to a single logic. But the invisible threads and traces of the real do nevertheless support positive, albeit equivocal and provisional, forms, whose overall style and orientation can yet be elicited as a guide to action. In the earlier writings, especially, it is Marxism that is credited with offering 'a *perception of history* that would continuously clarify the lines and vectors of the present', its immanent rationality, so that action is not blind (HT: 98, 117f; TL: 101). It is the phenomenological reading of history's dimensions that allows them to be compared and assessed against a common measure of coexistence, while ensuring that ideas are judged in the context of their material supports, and a Marxist method is again credited with having 'learned to confront ideas with the social functions they articulate, to compare our perspective with others' (HT: 177). Later, Merleau-Ponty attributes this 'philosophy that questioned history' to a Weberian Marxism and even, to a 'heroic' liberalism which 'lets even what contests it enter its universe' (AD: 29, 226; TL: 34). This process means a 'permanent questioning' that avoids dogmatism or scepticism (i.e. ideological closure or mere relativism). In short, this is a politics of interrogation, not of identity or Truth.

Praxis is then the political dimension of the hyperdialectic and represents a 'good' historicity. Neither a politics of understanding nor of reason, it replaces rationalism with a rational process whereby both the real and its interpretation are permanently reassessed. In effect praxis replicates the reflexiveness and reversibility of the body, only on a higher level of the lived–thought. 'The profound philosophical meaning of the notion of praxis is to place us in an order which is not that of knowledge but rather of communication, exchange, and association' (AD: 50). Here the present is worked on by criticism, so while experience is articulated, its creative/critical interpretation is itself reassessed in light of future changes. Dialectics is described as a 'learning journey', since it acknowledges and engages in the contingency of history. It is 'capable of reaching truth because it envisages without restriction the plurality of the relationships and what has been called ambiguity' (TL: 57; VI: 94).

I anticipated something of this in chapter 2, in offering a possible Marxian politics, but for Merleau-Ponty the connection between praxis and the proletariat must remain entirely contingent. Praxis is not instrumental rationalism but humanism in practice; it 'has no *goal*; rather it is a "manner"' (PNP: 93). It could be described as the practice of a humanist *Gestalt*, or as the politics appropriate to, because it practises, negativity. In principle there seems no reason why any group that aspires to change the course of events, for example women, should not practise this dialectical politics. Although its effect would be to defuse conflict before it arises, the logic of negativity is such that where this fails, more militant negations will be incited. Merleau-Ponty acknowledges that political acts inevitably remain risky and violent. But unlike for example Derrida, he would not therefore defer action; he recognises that in politics decisions must be made and that acts are often definitive (to deny them would effectively replicate the quietism of neo-Kantian liberalism and ignore the fact that politics *is* violence). He welcomes the audacity of those acts which operate a temporary closure, but only if they re-open the political field. While negativity ideally means a smooth imbrication of positive and negative, the nature of the political is such that more definitive negations can never be ruled out. But exemplary political acts are above all fecund: their perpetrators grasp their times according to their vectors and intersubjective significance, then extemporise and lead the people with them; in Machiavellian terms, such actors demonstrate an 'unremitting virtú' (S: 35).

Merleau-Ponty's critics sometimes complain that this politics is simply derived from an analogy with the ontology. But my suggestion here has been that it is, rather, the politics which he perceived as most conducive to the lessons the ontology offered. For as I argued earlier, the dialectical ontology was motivated by political concerns and the style of politics sketched above seems most compatible with the rhythms and lessons of negativity described there. As with the ontology, however, the important thing would have been the practising, not the naming, of this politics. In one sense, Merleau-Ponty's own writings exemplify this: his interrogations of the Cold War antagonists, the Algerian situation, postwar French politics, etc., undertaken in the press as well as in books, is testimony to an ongoing critical engagement. Yet the thrust of his work is to suggest that negativity in politics cannot be reduced to interventions by the critical philosopher, since it also requires more material, concrete engagements that reconfigure the lived in more than a merely ideal way.

More generally, then, there remained the difficult question of how a politics of negativity might be institutionalised. If negativity could not be named philosophically, without identifying it and rendering it positive, an analogous problem besets it politically. No positive institution can *be* the negative in power (AD: 89f), yet humanism required that negativity should not be left outside the system as an intermittently negating force within a chronic history (for example, the sort of unpredictable provocation, or resistance, that would later be associated with postmodern politics). Political theory invites us to consider how best to organise the structures of collective life and not simply to await their subversion. To emulate negativity humanistically, politics must then become a practising of the formative/destructive process as an ongoing dialectic which avoids chronic moments of contradiction. It is precisely the confrontation between positive power and its negation that is to be avoided. This is consonant with the later writings: in moving from dialectical contradiction to the effulgence of Being, they equate negativity with a creative/destructive process which I described as redolent of Nietzsche's will to power but more attuned to the slower tempo of its political choreography. A politics that emulates this negativity must then accommodate the creative, as well as destructive, moments of becoming and this suggests that in the more inertial context of collective life, some institutionalised means of imaginatively expanding opportunities for coexistence need to be instantiated. Merleau-Ponty did not, however, live to tackle this problem (which today goes under the broad title of 'democratisation'). He lamented the loss of political imagination that he saw besetting France during the 1950s (S: 348, AD: 22) and cautiously suggested that Parliament remained the only known institution where some opposition and truth are accommodated (AD: 226), but this does not take us very far. While he bequeaths us considerable insight into the nature of the political, and sketches an exemplary style for its practising in light of an appreciation of negativity, the question of how this praxis is to be undertaken, and by whom, remains unresolved.

Subject–subject and subject–object dialectics: Merleau-Ponty and Habermas

With this problematic in mind, it will be instructive to end this chapter by comparing Merleau-Ponty with Habermas, although obviously there is space to do so only very sketchily.[13] The attraction of the comparison is that Habermas is also concerned with political practices that are critical and emancipatory and he has adumbrated them in a more contemporary context. Moreover, there is a *prima facie* overlapping of vocabularies: both speak in terms of a lifeworld and intersubjectivity; both are critical of instrumental reason while aspiring to renew a process of reasoned politics. Habermasian communicative action, deliberative democracy and the restoration of a public sphere seem a possible incarnation for praxis as Merleau-Ponty conceived it. Thomas McCarthy's recent summary of a Habermasian politics emphasises the sense in which it is congenial to negativity:

> democratic institutions should be understood as 'projects' that are always incomplete, and subject to the ongoing exercise of political autonomy, as shifting historical circumstances demand. Because public discourse is ineluctably open and reflexive, our understanding of the principles of justice must remain so as well.[14]

I want nevertheless to highlight the differences between their respective projects here, since these will allow me to show the senses in which Merleau-Ponty's thought remained more imbued with negativity (and thus ultimately closer to Adorno than Habermas).

During his attack on poststructuralism as a post-Nietzschean irrationalism, Habermas criticises Merleau-Ponty in passing. Like other critical discourses of counter-Enlightenment other than his own, Merleau-Ponty's is dismissed as a praxis philosophy that was grounded in subjectivity. According to Habermas, he thus remained caught in the same aporias as other exponents of this Cartesian–Kantian tradition with its irresolvable oscillation between subject and object, subject and other. Unlike his own intersubjective premises, which are derived from the communicative possibilities of language, Merleau-Ponty's philosophy was still mired, Habermas argues, in an anachronistic subject–object paradigm.[15] He objects to the latter because he thinks its epistemological focus on propositional truth is too restrictive for the intersubjective domain where normative questions are at stake and a different kind of reasoning is appropriate. Communicative action is then an intersubjective, discursive process whereby individuals bring their diverse perspectives together but strive for consensus through accepting the rational force of the better argument. Such a possibility is underwritten by an ideal of undistorted communication.

In so far as this process is construed as a creative blending of perspectives via self-critical exchanges, then it seems feasible to imagine its attractiveness for Merleau-Ponty and Habermas's dismissal of him as a convert to inter-subjectivity seems rather overstated. For, as we saw, Merleau-Ponty decentred the subject as bestower of meaning and even the early descriptions of an incarnate cogito always presented individuals as products of a coexistential lifeworld where meaning appears at the intersection of myriad acts. As he had written of existentialism early on: '*For the first time since Hegel, militant philosophy is reflecting not on subjectivity but on intersubjectivity*' (SNS: 134).

I think, nevertheless, that Merleau-Ponty would have been reluctant to be wholly exonerated of Habermas's charges, since it is central to his politics that any subject–subject dialectic must be integrated with a subject–object one. To the extent that embodied subjects are themselves understood in such terms, the gap which differentiates the body and yields its reflexiveness is marked by fecundity rather than aporia. But more importantly it is this very negativity, which prevents the subjective or the intersubjective from becoming transparent to or identical with itself, that subverts any possibility of ideal speech or consensus – illusions which Merleau-Ponty would surely have found dangerously rationalistic since they idealise a foreclosure of the interrogative process which he presents as in principle interminable. If the differences between Habermasian interlocutors (who after all remain subjects and merely gather for debate) are interpreted as a negativity, then this remains a very thin version and one which it is the very purpose of their discourse to transcend.

Because of his criticisms of neo-Kantian liberalism, with its uncritical, moralising philosophy of 'clean hands', and his premise that history is violence, Merleau-Ponty is sceptical that politics can become such a rational, reflective process. Because coexistence means encroachment as well as enrichment, politics remains allied with violence; if its violence can be minimised by its being undertaken dialectically, it can never become wholly rational. For 'the social is ... intersubjectivity, a living relationship and tension among individuals' (SNS: 90). If values are to be realised, difficult strategic questions have to be addressed and choices made. 'Political action is of its nature impure, because it is action of one person upon another and because it is collective action' (HT: xxxii). As such, politics remains both adverse and only amenable, at best, to the sort of hazardous praxis described above. Merleau-Ponty insists that, like the flesh, the political remains a dense, heterogeneous element, which we can engage but on which we try to impose definitive ordering at our peril.

If (western) modernity perceives itself as historically superior, then

Merleau-Ponty reminds us (as he had Hegel) that its rationality reflects its own existential choice of approaching the world through knowledge and action; a choice it must in turn interrogate critically and recognise as provisional. At the same time, and like all social forms, it inevitably reproduces and is produced by negativities. While Merleau-Ponty shares with Habermas the view that nothing in the *Lebenswelt* is in principle immune to problematisation and thematisation, he is then rather closer to poststructuralism in emphasising the limits of this process and the extent to which the excesses and opacities, the negativities, of the lived always outrun any particular reflection. This is why reason in politics must always be exercised dialectically.

At an *intersubjective* level, Merleau-Ponty begins with the inevitably contextual nature of all perspectives. This does not mean they are simply conflictual wills to power or that meaning disintegrates into a play of difference. Communication between diverse perspectives is facilitated by their opening on one lifeworld[16] and it is desirable because it infuses the complexity unities need to remain fertile and open. This was after all the logic of an operative rationality and, through communication, we would expect new, richer ways of structuring the social world to be forged (in this sense Merleau-Ponty is closer to Habermas than to postmodern emphases on transgression and incommensurability). 'Rationality, or the agreement of minds, does not require that we all reach the same idea by the same road, or even that significations be enclosed in definitions. It requires only that every experience contain points of catch for all others and that "ideas" have a configuration' (PW: 143). But there is no possibility, even if it were desirable, of achieving ideal speech or consensus, here, since every position is charged with negativity; each is like a visible subtended by its invisibles. There 'is no guarantee that the relationship between men does not inevitably involve magical and oneiric components' (VI: 24). Moreover, because communication is existential as well as linguistic, it incorporates the excessive, gestural dimensions of the lived (which is even the case with language itself). It cannot be purged of these as if they were distortions since they yield the very possibility of communication. Political thinking, for example, is the elucidation of a historical perception wherein 'all our understandings, all our experiences, and all our values simultaneously come into play – and of which our theses are only the schematic formulation' (PW: 112). So while intersubjective communication is undoubtedly enriching and an index of a humanist politics for Merleau-Ponty, it remains also a scene of difference and violence, where every unity remains provisional and internally differentiated. An exemplary intersubjectivity can only then be an ongoing process; one oriented less towards agreement than towards a creative process of etching provisional meanings in an ambiguous social field where it remains part of a broader genesis. In politics it is not a question of the force of the better argument establishing validity claims, as Habermas suggests, but of a process of interrogation and verification, where irrelevant or infertile options fail to galvanise the necessary support and are accordingly 'crossed out' as false, irrational. In other words, resolutions remain *political* and riven with power, while the negotiations that take place in the public sphere would also need supplementing with a phenomenology of how diverse meanings proliferate.

Moreover, although the appearing of reason is identified by Merleau-Ponty as a meeting of perspectives motivated towards complex synthesis, thereby suggesting an intersubjective process, it is crucial to his political radicalism that he does *not* abandon the *subject–object relation* to it. For although this latter relationship had to be rethought more dialectically, dialectics itself requires an ongoing interrogation of the historical, material domain in which intersubjectivity operates and which cannot be reduced to it since it exerts its own weight. In other words, a tendency among almost all contemporary political theorists, to situate politics on a solely dialogical or analytical level, is resisted by Merleau-Ponty. He is able to do so because, unlike Habermas, he does not ground intersubjectivity in language and its potential for communicative action, but in perception. This makes his thinking more resistant to the sort of rationalism of which Habermas is often accused, since the perceptual paradigm is again irremediably riven by negativity: the difference, contingency and ambiguity inherent in all forms renders them immune to consensual resolution.

Questions of power and politics, although they are undoubtedly negotiated intersubjectively, cannot then be reduced to discursive operations. They must *also* be addressed through an engagement with history that interprets its existential dimensions, reads its trajectories and opportunities, in order to direct efficacious, material interventions. For Merleau-Ponty meaning is not reducible to linguistic exchanges and if there is no objective truth to be excavated, there is an existential inertia where interpretation is distinct from the force of the better argument. It is the subject–object dialectic that sustains criticism and negation of closed, violent structures, while orienting political acts within a field where only limited freedom exists. In this sense Habermas is quite right that Merleau-Ponty does remain a praxis philosopher. For any progressive politics needs to be anchored in a reading of historical opportunities as they unfold (a problem manifest in Habermas's juxtaposition of communicative action and the 'steering media' of money and power, where the former seems incapable effectively of engaging with, or challenging its colonisation by, the latter). Sometimes negations more militant than discourse may be required to re-open the social field: Merleau-Ponty cites strikes, harassment by the political opposition, and refuses even to rule out a revolutionary option. He recognises that more militant actions may be needed when structures become too immobile, but praxis is never blind action any more than it is the strategic instrumentalism Habermas associates with the subject–object paradigm. It is an engaged politics which is concerned not only with idealised democratic processes but also, with how those processes are to be instantiated within hierarchical and rationalistic cultures.

The importance of Merleau-Ponty's political philosophy in the contemporary context is, I think, the way he combines an account of an unassailable negativity with attention to the peculiarities of collective life. His own concern was generally to emphasise the contingency and provisionality of all forms, in opposition to Marxist dogmatism and liberal intransigence. For us, his importance resides in the insistence on the density and adversity of political life, as a counterweight both to a continuing neo-Kantian, liberal democratic formalism and to a Nietzschean poststructuralism which lacks the resources for associating the fleet and heterogeneous plays of difference with the closures and inertia of the political. It is because the rhythms of negativity he describes vary across different tiers of Being, so that they evince specificity in combining positive and negative, and because their choreography combines an excessive, Nietzschean generativity with a more Hegelian synthesising process, that he can offer a critique of unduly positivist *or* negativist political thought or action.

5

SUBJECT–OBJECT RELATIONS AGAIN

Identity, non-identity and negative dialectics

In the previous chapter I discussed Merleau-Ponty's pursuit of a dialectics faithful to negativity and his insistence that negativity is to be understood/practised as dialectics. I will explore a similar project in this chapter, through the work of Adorno.[1] Both struggled to theorise in ways that *exemplified* dialectics at work, so when Merleau-Ponty writes that fidelity to the dialectic means 'it is perhaps necessary to not even name it',[2] Adorno agrees that 'there is no definition that fits it' (H:TS: 9). In part, their task was to force philosophy to include recognition of its own involvement in the processes of which it spoke: when Merleau-Ponty describes phenomenology as 'the ambition to make reflection emulate the unreflective life of consciousness',[3] he is echoed by Adorno's assertion that at a 'distance, dialectics might be characterized as the elevation to self-consciousness of the effort to be saturated with dialectics' (ND: 29). Both are fascinated by Husserl's aim of returning to things themselves, as reflected in Merleau-Ponty's descriptions of the lifeworld and Adorno's insistence on the 'primacy of the object', but each rejects Husserl's idealism and defines himself as a materialist who recognises the paradoxical nature of the phenomenological quest.

There is however some difference of tone, anticipated in the previous chapter, between Merleau-Ponty's phenomenological emphasis on an appearing of reason and Adorno's almost deconstructionist insistence on its aporias. Merleau-Ponty was inclined to extend Hegel's assertion of an ontological continuity between thought and being in a Heideggerian direction, whereby negativity marks the internal generativity of one Being (Flesh) rendered dynamic by its spacings and differences. In its rhythms of becoming he emphasised its formative impetus towards rational, if contingent and ambiguous, unities. While this rhythm exhibited various tempos, an important element of his argument was that such negativity should be exemplified in a political praxis whereby rational forms of coexistence would unfold continuously over time. Adorno, in contrast, frames his thinking in an epistemological terminology of subjects and objects. Despite understanding their relationship in a thoroughly dialectical way, his emphasis is on the dissonance and non-identity, as well as the almost indecipherably complex and mobile relationships, between the two terms. As such, the choreography of negativity he discerns comes rather closer to a Nietzschean (and poststructuralist) emphasis on heterogeneity, even while he struggles to hold onto a project of determinate negation, immanent critique and emancipation/reconciliation.

An objective of this chapter will be to convey the way Adorno practised this negativity in his philosophical writing, which has a much more negativist feel to it than Merleau-Ponty's elegant prose. My strategy in trying to communicate this practice, without myself reifying it, will be to circle through some of Adorno's essays, locating the complex dialectical levels that are repeated, varied and syncopated there. The most significant text regarding negativity is *Negative Dialectics*, but I will show that it is prefigured throughout Adorno's *œuvre*.[4]

One reason for Adorno's Kantian enframing of negativity in terms of subject–object relations is that he believes the critical philosophy recognised a lesson crucial to negativity when it insisted on the impossibility of knowing things in themselves. As such, it refused Hegel's belief that all otherness could be resolved into identity through rational comprehension. Adorno does not however understand the Kantian caveat in terms of any off-limits, noumenal alterity. He rejects Kant's distinction between 'the transcendental thing in itself and the constituted object' as his 'most questionable theorem' (S&O: 507; H:TS: 8, 64). He is sympathetic to the phenomenological projects of both Hegel and Husserl inasmuch as they presented philosophy as an attempt at articulating its other. In

> philosophy we literally seek to immerse ourselves in things that are heterogeneous to it, without placing those things in prefabricated categories. We want to adhere as closely to the heterogeneous as the programs of phenomenology and of Simmel tried in vain to do; our aim is total self-relinquishment.
>
> (ND: 13)

But he denies that objects can in principle be brought into full presence, or appear without remainder, to the rational subject. He is therefore profoundly critical of Kant for negating the non-identity of subject and object at the level of understanding, where he espoused a correspondence theory of truth. Yet if there remains an ineluctable difference between (phenomenal) objects and concepts, there is also a complicated reciprocity between them. It is in this dialectical space that identity and non-identity irreducibly flourish and it is here that the drama of negativity is played out for Adorno.[5] There is always an excess, difference, that refuses unification and idealisation even while it invites understanding.

Materialism and epistemology: the project of a critical theory

Before embarking on this exploration of Adorno's philosophy, I want first to offer some more general comments about subject–object relations in the context of critical theory. In particular, I want to show why this apparently epistemological relationship also has profound political implications. Critical theory was inspired by the Marxist idea that it should interpret the world in order to change it. Horkheimer had put the matter bluntly: 'the theory never aims simply at an increase of knowledge as such. Its goal is man's emancipation from slavery.'[6] Methodologically it must combine philosophical reflection with sociological enquiry, consonant with the dialectical insistence that conceptual and material developments are interwoven. If the critical theorists rejected mere empiricism as insufficiently critical of either itself or its data, they were equally aware that purely abstract thinking was unable to engage with real developments. Moreover, since social formations were seen as complex totalities in which economic, political, psychological and cultural forms broadly correspond, it would be necessary to proceed in an interdisciplinary way in order to explore the connections between these various dimensions. True to these imperatives, the first generation of the Frankfurt School did not perceive subject–object relations simply in epistemological terms, but also saw them involving complex structural and existential dimensions that called for analysis and critique. At the forefront of their work there remained a stark, combative opposition: negative thinking means a rejection of uncritical, positivist thought *and* a negation of reified, positive social forms.

Although epistemology appears merely to present a formal distinction between knowing subject and object known, it is charged by the critical theorists with reflecting and reinforcing a more general physiognomy of power relations whereby the subject (culminating in bourgeois man) dominates its objects. Where subjective representations allegedly mirror the objective world and truly reflect it, this is identified with a broader cultural orientation wherein uncertainty, heterogeneity, alterity and contingency are perceived as undesirable lacunae associated with error, even evil, and marked as targets for conquest. Suppressing this negativity becomes a political as well as an intellectual imperative once instability and adversity are associated with opposition and diversity.[7] Political theory colludes in this practice inasmuch as (from Hobbes to Rawls) it presents the political as a formalised set of universal procedures used to impose social order, rather than as an irresolvably conflictual, strategic process of collective life (in a more Machiavellian–Foucaultian sense). Like other philosophers of negativity, the critical theorists both opposed the negative to rationalism and identified the latter with a general ethos of domination plus a penchant for authoritarianism, which are inscribed in the material and psycho-cultural practices of modernity.[8] Bureaucracy, capitalism and philosophy conspire to treat subjects themselves as objects (objects of administration; commodities whose labour power is bought and sold; objects of knowledge). As subjects become objects, they are thus subjected to the very instrumentalism that subjectivist epistemologies imply and to which Kant had objected in his *Second Critique*. Marcuse expresses the problem succinctly. 'This is the pure form of servitude: to exist as an instrument, as a thing.'[9]

When critical theorists spoke of objects, however, they did not generally mean the Kantian object. Kant's phenomena were the dead material objects of natural science, related according to determinist laws of motion and constituted according to the space–time and categorical forms of intuition and understanding. As such they lacked any internal dynamism, meaning or potential; in so far as empirical subjects inhabited this realm of experience, they were implicated in its unfreedom. Although this was not necessarily the way things in themselves worked, Kant had argued that we must operate 'as if' Newtonian science were true since the very possibility of knowledge depended upon the order and stability it described.

While the critical theorists agreed that physics is a language imposed on things, they also insisted on its historicity. Appearing at the threshold of modernity, science manifests, like Kantian idealism itself, a particular configuration of subject–object relations calling for critical scrutiny. Scientific discourse helps to constitute subjects and objects as well as their relationship; its modern hegemony occludes its own particularity and thus the possibility of alternative relations. If, moreover, subject–object relations change over time, this is in part because objects are not simply given as inert, natural things, but are constantly worked over and (re)produced historically: by art and architecture, productive and domestic labour, etc. As such they are not alien stuff on which we impose hypothetical formulae, but phenomena imbued with (inter)subjective purposes and therefore amenable to interpretation. In other words, any object we experience is already a subject–object amalgam, which is why we can have access to it without claiming an impossible noumenal intelligence. As Horkheimer writes, the 'world which is given to the individual and which he must accept and take into account is, in its present and continuing form, a product of the activity of society as a whole.'[10] The porous and intricate object is thus heavily overdetermined. It cannot be subsumed without remainder under concepts, once the recalcitrant materiality of things and the heterogeneity of their historical accretion is acknowledged.

From a Marxist perspective the most important subject–object relation involves biological need, labour, production. Natural things become formed, during the course of history, into use values and under capitalism, into commodities, exchange values. As such, objects become woven into a reified economic system that rules with the unassailable force once ascribed to nature. The critical theorists' condemnation of the impoverished subject–object relation that results was already anticipated by Marx when he wrote that private property 'has made us so stupid and one-sided that an object is only *ours* when we have it, when it exists for us as capital or when we directly possess, eat, drink, wear, inhabit it etc., in short, when we *use* it.'[11]

Such experiences are nevertheless hermeneutically resonant. The critical theorist approaches objects as artifacts: repositories of stored-up labour performed under particular sociotechnical conditions; commodities that must seduce buyers by advertising themselves as solutions to their wants. Inscribed with material practices and power relations, invested with hopes and dreams, they invite interpretation. In bearing their convoluted messages they also become ciphers of the past: repositories of repressed memories and of the complex historical mediations that produced them. In reading them, their internal complexity, as well as their inscription in the weblike connections of the social totality, must all be retained. Despite the proscription on identity thinking, there is equally a taboo on fetishising any ideal of immediacy or of the isolated object.

The sort of critical analysis this inspired is exemplified in a passage from *Minima Moralia*, where Adorno reminds us that a dynamic subjectivity can only be understood in the context of its changing object relations. 'The new human type cannot be properly understood without awareness of what he is continuously exposed to from the world of things about him, even in his most secret innervations' (MM: 40). In something as seemingly banal as the replacement of casement windows by sliding frames, he discerns a behavioural shift from opening to shoving indicative of a technology that brutalises gestures and everyday practices, resulting in a 'withering of experience'. For 'things, under the law of pure functionality, assume a form that limits contact with them to mere operation, and tolerates no surplus' of free conduct or 'autonomy of things' unexhausted by action. The totality can be read synecdochally from its parts.

If the only objects we can know or experience are already endowed with subjectivity, the incarnate subject is also an object. It is a part of nature although equally historical. Marxism relies on the premise that sensuous subjects are produced through the process of satisfying material need. Freud agrees, but it is psychoanalysis that takes this objectivity to the heart of the subject when it reveals the ego/I emerging precariously from an id/it and governed by unconscious motivations which arise not from reason, but from instinctual wishes anchored in the body. For Freud the subject–object split occurs developmentally as the ego separates itself from the world of objects ('The antithesis between subjective and objective does not exist from the first'[12]). The boundaries between inside and outside, phantasy and perception, self and other, always remain dynamic and somewhat hazardous. Pathology and regression, as well as reason and desire, render the space between subject and object psychically dynamic since the ego is 'not sharply separated from the id'.[13] Instinct and judgement cannot be definitively distinguished in mental functioning, where the unruly logic of the (unconscious) primary process always threatens to irrupt into the calm waters of reason.

The subject's identity remains unstable not only because it evolves through precarious separations from its objects, but also because it is constituted by them through its object identifications (a claim on which Adorno would draw in explaining the appeal of Fascist leadership and propaganda[14]). It introjects the loved object; identifies with it; becomes like it or is repelled by it. At the same time, its objects are never regarded in a merely utilitarian or instrumental way. If at first, according to Freud, all presentations are of real objects, memory traces allow absent objects to be fantasised. Reality testing is motivated by a search for *lost* objects which once brought real satisfaction. It is thus driven by desire and its objects are not just perceptual things, but objects of gratification. 'On our hypothesis, perception is not a purely passive process.'[15] If judgement belongs to the secondary process, its motivation is not ultimately truth but (un)pleasure; not precise epistemic correspondence but satisfaction. It belongs to a libidinal as well as a veridical or political economy. The object in Freud's analysis is not then the inert one of science, passive intuition or active judgement, but the object of desire. 'The object [Objekt] of an instinct is the thing in regard to which or through which the instinct is able to achieve its aim.'[16] Such objects (often other subjects or their body parts) thus retain their instinctual resonance; they hum with memory traces and pulse with erotic significance. Objects play subjects like broken or marvellous instruments. While not all objects are invested with this libidinal vibrancy, the apparently rational world is mapped according to a shifting cartography of desire whose associations shift with the bizarre logic of the primary process. As Fredric Jameson puts it, 'unbeknownst to us, the objects around us lead lives of their own in our unconscious fantasies, where, vibrant with mana or taboo, with symbolic fascination or repulsion, they stand as the words or hieroglyphs of the immense rebus of desire.[17]

These psychic mediations are also taken into consideration by the critical theorists. Because individual patterns of desire evolve through the Œdipal dramatics of the family, and the historically-changing family mediates between society and individual,[18] this fantastic dimension is also entwined with everyday objects and the social formation. Fantasies also become lodged in the collective experience of objects through art. Art plays a special role in Adorno's thinking precisely because it is here that subject and object seem to be reconciled in a dialectic between rational and instinctual, formal and sensuous, general and particular. This is why art's commodification, and the loss of aura which mechanical reproduction and cooptation into the culture industry bring, mark an especially tragic twist in late modernity's subject–object relations. If exchange relations entail reification in the sphere of production, they also flatten out the unconscious and aesthetic dimensions of things, suppressing their radiance as well as the critical-exemplary role of art. 'The liberation which amusement promises is freedom from thought and from negation', where to 'be pleased is to say Yes' (DofE: 144). Re-enchanting the object and re-sensualising the subject are vital aspects of any emancipatory politics.

The preceding account describes the dense terrain on which critical theory located itself in exploring the dialectical space of subject–object relations. I have tried, by drawing attention to the reversals, overdeterminations and interweavings that play there, to show that far more than merely epistemological questions are at stake. While the non-identity of subjects and objects would pose significant philosophical challenges for Adorno, the historical, lived relations between them also called for critical interpretation and lent his philosophy a political dimension irreducible to the dynamics of intersubjectivity alone. Methodologically, in fact, Adorno's assault on Kant's separation between classification and experience would make the severance of epistemological and political themes impossible. This is already apparent in the 'fragments' Adorno and Horkheimer collected under the title *Dialectic of Enlightenment*.

Dialectic of enlightenment

First published in 1947, this work can suggestively be compared with Hegel's *Phenomenology*, or with *The German Ideology*, as a dialectical account of unfolding relations between subject and object (rendered here as 'man' and history). However its discontinuous narrative and overall pessimism are more reminiscent of Nietzsche's *Genealogy*. For this is no teleology whereby objectivity becomes subjective, but a schematic account of how subjectivity emerged only to sink back into object status. The 'submission of everything natural to the autocratic subject finally culminates in the mastery of the blindly objective and natural' (DofE: xvi). If negativity's historical dynamism ceases this is not because all contradictions have been resolved, but because modernity is a false unity (a static yet antagonistic totality).

The book's title must nevertheless be taken seriously, since Horkheimer and Adorno insist that the history of reason is genuinely dialectical. If modernity finds itself subjected in the same way to the blind forces of fate as primitive humanity, this is because domination is inherent in the very logic of enlightenment. Like Nietzsche's genealogical tracing of a fecund yet sacrificial subjectivity which succumbs in modernity to the nihilism inherent in its own birth, Horkheimer and Adorno track the reversals of subjectivity's psychological and material evolution. Yet the process remains dialectical rather than simply nihilistic, since the emancipatory impulse that drove enlightenment remains lodged there as a possibility of freedom. 'We are wholly convinced', they would insist in their 1969 Preface, 'that social freedom is inseparable from enlightened thought' (DofE: xiii).[19] The alternative to a hegemonic instrumental reason is dialectical reasoning, such as Adorno will practise under the title of negative dialectics.[20]

There is in addition an elusive yet persistent invocation of some almost-extinct memory of an alternative subject–object relation associated with magic, art and the pleasure principle. 'The work of art still has something in common with enchantment' and the authors refer to their task as 'the redemption of the hopes of the past' (DofE: 19, xv). But this is no more an appeal to irrationalism or archaism than it is to some future utopian redemption. Again, it is reason itself that must practise the non-hierarchical subject–object relations yet glimpsed in the detritus of history. For even in its profane versions, Adorno will insist, most thinking (and *a fortiori* his own) retains a mimetic element: 'there survives a groping for that concordance which the magical delusion used to place beyond doubt' (ND: 45). The whole appears within the particular here and there is no sign–image split, no domination of the object. If intuition endures as an archaic rudiment of mimetic reaction, it still 'holds a promise beyond the ossified present' (ND: 8).

Although regression to magic offers no emancipation, the authors do then invoke it as a counterfactual to its instrumentalist successor. 'The world of magic retained distinctions whose traces have disappeared even in linguistic form' (DofE: 9). It recognised the multiplicity of things and interacted with them mimetically, rather than subordinating them to representation. 'Animism spiritualized the object, whereas industrialism objectifies the spirits of men' (DofE: 28). Thereafter, this knowledge which 'really concerned the object' would be tabooed. Emancipation must somehow revitalise the object without fetishising it, but magic reminds us of a moment when the relation between subject and object yet evinced a certain fantastic, irreducible shimmering and reciprocity.

Similarly, regarding inner nature, there is no suggestion that liberation requires the end of repression. All happiness, the authors remind us, is social and dependent on renunciation. For on a purely instinctual level, pleasure is merely 'appeasement of need' (DofE: 105). But following Freud it is implied that liberation does require repression's reduction: psychically, too, a more vibrant subject–object (conscious–unconscious) relation must be attained. Following Nietzsche, Horkheimer and Adorno acknowledge that

[m]en had to do fearful things to themselves before the self, the identical, purposive, and virile man of nature, was formed, and something of that occurs in every childhood. The strain of holding the I together adheres to the I in all stages; and the temptation to lose it has always been there with the blind determination to maintain it.

(DofE: 33)

There is always a deathly temptation to self-loss (hence the allegory of Odysseus and the Sirens), since self-preservation entails self-alienation. The material and psychic histories of subject and object are thus interwoven, while ontogenesis recapitulates phylogenesis. The domination of external and internal nature necessarily proceeds as a single process.

This interweaving is evident in the drive for (a rather Hobbesian) self-preservation that motivates enlightenment (*qua* 'the progressive technical domination of nature' (CIR: 92)). The dual imperatives of satisfying material need and assuaging psychic terror in face of nature's alien forms are pursued through strategies of control. Enlightenment begins with magic and myth, only later yielding idealist philosophy and science. 'Nothing at all may remain outside, because the mere idea of outsidedness is the very source of fear' (DofE: 16). Nietzsche had advanced a similar claim.

> In the inner psychic economy of the primitive man, fear of evil predominates. What is evil? Three things: chance, the uncertain, the sudden ... . Now the whole history of culture represents a diminution of this fear ... . For culture means learning to think causally, to forestall, to believe in necessity.[21]

Elsewhere Adorno would explain that self-preservation entails predatory acts, goaded on by a rage against their victim. Idealism merely sublimates this fury into the inferiority of the not-I, nature, '*l'autrui*', in order to rationalise its epistemological devouring. 'The system is the belly turned mind, and rage is the mark of each and every idealism' (ND: 22f). (He would also build on Freud's *Group Psychology* to explain how authoritarian groups unify by turning this rage on outsiders, their others (FTFP).)

Together with fear, scarcity drives the species to attempt nature's material domination. Again, technology and commodification are to leave no residue that cannot be made useful or realise profit. Marx had noted that the first significant division of labour arose between mental and manual forms, which saw the emergence of a priestly class. Horkheimer and Adorno similarly recognise that the subject–object split which the sacred instantiates has a material equivalent: it translates into hierarchical social relations. By enslaving others, the master obliges them to mediate objects on his behalf. 'The distance between subject and object, a presupposition of abstraction, is grounded in the distance from the thing itself which the master achieved through the mastered' (DofE: 12). Modes of production, class relations and psycho-cultural forms follow a similar historical trajectory; at each stage, subject–object relations correspond across different spheres.

It is important to keep in mind here a distinction between the Enlightenment, whose project was to free the mind from superstition by subjecting nature to rational knowledge and instrumental control, and the process of enlightenment which is more or less synonymous with history as such. It is the former which typifies modernity and its self-conscious project of mastery, but this is only the apogee of the more enduring logic of self-preservation. Eventually processes of enlightenment culminate in the Enlightenment, where nature is reduced to *res extensa* in order to be known, mathematicised, manipulated. Alterity and heterogeneity, scarcity and disorder, are its targets. Disenchanted objects thus lose the generativity that myth and magic had ascribed them. 'From now on, matter would at last be mastered without any illusion of ruling or inherent powers, of hidden qualities' (DofE: 6). (Although, as Marx's account of commodity fetishism shows, the commodity in fact reassumes something of this magical status.) Ironically the active subject of scientific method and idealist philosophy suffers an equivalent sclerosis since, trapped within its own tautologies, it finds only its own sterile categories reflected back to it. It 'recognizes nothing new, since it always merely recalls what reason has always deposited in the object' (DofE: 26).

Under the Newtonian–Cartesian regime, the ritualised thinking of mathematics renders thinkers as machine-like as the machines it facilitates. Formal logic, mathematics, become the schema of the world's calculability. In this mechanistic world, actors become defined as things which play out their objective roles in the social mechanism in a merely functional way. Indeed this is the material truth of capitalism, where workers are reduced to equivalent, fungible commodities, objects of the fully-administered life, 'mere species beings, exactly like one another' (DofE: 36). Even the apparently powerful capitalist is in thrall to the forces he constantly reproduces. *Dialectic of Enlightenment* is a history of alienation and reification, in which the objective forces that subjects create take on a terrifying life of their own and eventually swallow them up, reproducing them in their own form and acquiring the unassailability once ascribed to fate.

Horkheimer and Adorno make much of the dialectical correspondences that structure modernity's various subject–object relations and mark them with the totalising stamp of equivalence. The latter motif acts as a 'key' for interpreting the totality. Qualitative difference is surrendered to the rigour of quantity, allowing a mythic repetition of the same: Enlightenment 'excises the incommensurable' (DofE: 12). Non-identity, particularity, are translated into abstractions and measured; the dissimilar becomes comparable. 'The multiplicity of forms is reduced to position and arrangement.' There is 'universal interchangeability' (DofE: 10). Subjects' own fungibility within bureaucracy and the market renders them equivalent to the natural objects that science reduces to identical atoms; all become indifferent units of numerical, manipulable, exchangeable stuff. 'The same equations dominate bourgeois justice and commodity exchange' (DofE: 3). Subjects' atomisation is further achieved by the levelling effects of mass culture, whose own products are equally standardised and commodified, and by changes in the family whereby individuals are increasingly socialised by outside forces which breed conformity rather than the rebellious egos of the patriarchal family. The positivist turn in philosophy, like empiricism in science, merely replicates and uncritically celebrates the given. It reduces substantive questions to language, in a world where language is itself reduced to a ritualistic repetition of empty signifiers cast adrift from their referents (DofE: 17f). Concepts become formulae, cowering before the facts and fearful of the particularity that might escape them to disrupt the reign of the ever-identical.

When capitalism, bureaucracy and positivism (i.e. modern rationalism) equally objectify subjects within the technical process, history comes full circle: thinking is objectified, as it was in myth, where objects were imitated and thought was repetition and ritual. The new is only more of the same; as in myth, the eternally the same is a fate to be feared and obeyed, whether it is the hidden hand of the market, the facts which are alone tolerated by knowledge, the determinist laws of motion described by science, or the unassailable power of the totalitarian state. 'Enlightenment is mythic fear turned radical' (DofE: 16). Although nature under late capitalism has been made over by the species and thoroughly dominated, fear of mass destruction by an uncontrollable world is as acute as that original fear of nature which set the process of enlightenment in motion. There is both a terrifying return of the repressed, where Fascism harnesses the death drive to its own rationalisation programme, and the reproduction of social constructs – second nature – as fate. Mythic time, eternal return, replaces historical progress. The deification of the positive rules out negative thinking as metaphysical, obscure and irrational. In science, as in myth, 'the everlastingness of the factual is confirmed' (DofE: 27; cf. ND: 56).

> Men have always had to choose between their subjection to nature or the subjection of nature to the self. With the extension of the bourgeois commodity economy, the dark horizon of myth is illumined by the sun of calculating reason, beneath whose cold rays the seed of a new barbarism grows to fruition.
>
> (DofE: 32)

This closure is both sustained and exemplified by the culture industry. Horkheimer and Adorno refer here to the 'rhythm of the iron system', 'the false identity of the general and particular' and the 'circle of manipulation and retroactive need in which the unity of the system grows ever stronger' (DofE: 120, 121). Where Kant had granted a constitutive role to the subject, the culture industry takes over the schematising function of the imagination. It has 'deciphered the secret' of the soul's mechanism and its producers now schematise on consumers' behalf, reducing them to passive recipients while bringing culture into the sphere of administration (DofE: 124f, 127, 131). Unlike in authentic art, negativity is thus negated: there remains no dialectical ferment between audience and product and within cultural products themselves, there is neither fecund opposition nor fertile connection, hence no stimulus to imaginative engagement or spontaneity. Instead of testing style against 'refractory material' to unleash an aesthetic vitality, where the formative process invites recipients themselves to re-form convention, a pre-arranged and formulaic harmony reigns. In short culture, like knowledge, becomes repetition because difference and creativity are suppressed. Like myth, propaganda and advertising, it is reduced to slogans and operates ideologically in reproducing the status quo.

Dialectic of Enlightenment thus traces the suppression of negativity across all aspects of the social formation. The authors' very recent experiences of Nazism inevitably coloured their bleak diagnosis. But they would go on to recognise more similarity than difference between Fascist, Soviet state capitalist and New Deal liberal-democratic totalitarianisms, where prejudice and mass culture in the latter would be (statistically, psychoanalytically) recognised as bearing many of the marks of fascist propaganda and where the onward march of commodification and administration suggested no emancipatory alternative. But do Horkheimer and Adorno themselves manage to sustain a creative tension – a critical distance, a movement of negativity – between the closed totality they describe and their own philosophy, or does their account itself lapse into dogmatic and positivist description?

Certainly, there are few of the methodological reflections and stylistic nuances here that mark Adorno's own work. But there is in the critical presentation of late modernity's lacks and losses a negative moment. There are also some almost magical invocations of an awakening; of people coming to their senses as from a bad dream, with a spontaneity that is more typical of Horkheimer's early work.[22] And there are occasional allusions to practices not yet quite assimilated to the logic of the whole. Thus the 'culture industry does retain a trace of something better in those features which bring it close to the circus' – in the 'nonsensical skill of riders, acrobats and clowns'; in the 'refuges of mindless artistry which represent what is human as opposed to the social mechanism' – although even these are fast disappearing and remain anyway unmediated and apolitical (DofE: 143).

Did Horkheimer and Adorno then envisage any different aesthetic, philosophical and *political* form emerging from this structure of domination? In order to broach this question it is necessary to look more carefully at the way Adorno tried elsewhere to adumbrate and practise the exemplary dialectical relation between subject and object that I have merely alluded to thus far and which the 1947 work summons. For I will contend that it is dialectical reasoning which itself figures instrumental reason's other and instantiates Adorno's sense of negativity. It is only by entering into the mediations of subject and object, such as the authors attempt and recollect here and which Adorno will increasingly experiment with as negative dialectics, that reason might avoid its positivist fate to regain an active, critical role where subjects neither become like nor dominate objects. 'The task of cognition does not consist in mere apprehension, classification, and calculation, but in the determinate negation of each im-mediacy' (DofE: 27).

Adorno's 'Subject and Object'

One of Adorno's last essays, 'Subject and Object' (1969), reintroduces some of *Dialectic of Enlightenment*'s key themes but from a more explicitly epistemological perspective. The complicities between dualist theories of knowledge and social reification are again insisted upon, but the consequences of a dialectical understanding of subject–object relations, and the significance of this dialectics for philosophical practice, are now more evident. The essay is extremely dense since it works on a number of levels, consonant with the epistemic negativity it negotiates. If it constantly deconstructs every formula of subject and object, it nevertheless tracks back through their mediations to show the lingering significance of each partial formulation. The major argument of the essay can be adequately conveyed, however, via two short quotes. 'The only way to make out objectivity is to reflect, at each historic and each cognitive step, on what is then presented as subject and object, as well as on the mediations' (S&O: 506). 'The difference between subject and object cuts through both the subject and the object. It can no more be absolutized than it can be put out of mind' (S&O: 508).

Reiterating Merleau-Ponty's dialectical disquiet, cited in chapter 1, Adorno condemns Kantian idealism both for reifying the inert object of knowledge and its transcendental counterpart and for precluding any process whereby subjects might engage with objects of experience to verify and develop their understanding. 'The test of the object's primacy is its qualitative alteration of opinions' (S&O: 503). Only through this interaction can objectivity really be approached. *Contra* Kant, Adorno also explores the shifting historical imbrications of modes of classification and social experience.

On a second level, it is not however acceptable for the dialectical philosopher to define and identify a subject–object dialectic from outside, since this would itself be complicitous in an act of mastery and insufficiently attentive to its own reflective intervention. Adorno accordingly reveals a constellation of irreducible relations whose complexity is in turn inscribed in the rather aesthetic structure of his own discourse. The essay's message is thereby communicated on two levels, discursively and stylistically; it is both communicative and mimetic. To complicate matters further, this strategy cuts across another which is more politically motivated. On the one hand, the subject–object opposition that is epistemologically flawed does capture a truth of modern experience which the critical thinker must clarify. On the other, the stylistic practising of negativity invokes a dialectical alternative of reconciliation, the latter itself modelled on that imbrication of non-identity and reciprocity which modernity suppresses. There is, then, an immanent critique of the reified totality *which is at the same time* a demonstration of its overcoming. *The essay is both an act of negation and a practising of negativity*, its critical and utopian moments inseparable.

This complicated strategy is exemplified in Adorno's critique of Kant. Kant was ontologically mistaken in severing subject and object to begin with. But since he also ended up identifying them through the subject's reason, his philosophy was flawed on two counts. In another sense, however, Kantian idealism conveys a historical truth of subject–object relations, which really have been both dichotomised and resolved into subjective mastery. 'The separation of subject and object is both real and illusory' (S&O: 499). Nor is this an innocent coincidence, since idealism also works ideologically. It both insists on the unassailability of this oppositional and hierarchical relation and compensates the empirical subject, objectified in the totally-administered society, by insisting upon its transcendental power over objects. It peddles the illusion that subjects are free and in control, yet it also subverts that illusion because the transcendental subject is as limited and imprisoned in its formal, uncreative powers as it is in the real world of Newtonian nature and capitalist relations. 'The categorial capacity of individual consciousness repeats the real captivity of every individual' (S&O: 505). While commodity fetishism reduces social relations and historical objects to reified exchanges between things, Kant rendered objects timeless under the immutable forms of transcendental consciousness. In this sense idealism is a cipher of reality. 'What shows up faithfully in the doctrine of the transcendental subject is the priority of the relations – abstractly rational ones, detached from the human individuals and their relationships – that have their model in exchange' (S&O: 501). In condemning these sterile dualisms, Adorno reveals the multiplicitous relations that actually sustain them.

If he criticises idealism for its subjectivism, he is however no more inclined to promote the object itself, which would be equally undialectical. This is important since his sympathy for 'the primacy of the object' might appear to support such a view. There are however two main objections to any such subterfuge. The first is, again, epistemological. Scientific reductionism itself claims to prioritise the object, and to claim objectivity for itself once is subtracts all residues of subjectivity from its knowledge. Adorno is predictably scathing about such claims, pointing out that they are already thoroughly subjective. Like Merleau-Ponty, he recognises idealism and realism as but two sides of one subjectivist coin.

The second objection harks back to a caveat Adorno had already delivered in *Dialectic of Enlightenment*. Just as he had argued there that returning to unmediated nature would mean succumbing to pre-reflective fatalism, so he now warns against any romanticised fantasy of 'a temporal or extratemporal

original state of happy identity' between subject and object. 'The undifferentiated state before the subject's formation was the dread of the blind web of
nature, of myth'. Elimination of subjectivity would mean 'regression to
barbarism' (S&O: 499). Adorno is not then seeking any 'trustful bondage to
the outside world'; his reference to its 'total social tutelage' perhaps alludes
to the pre-critical subordination to authority that Kant had himself
condemned as antithetical to the spirit of enlightenment.

When Adorno refers to the primacy of the object as a second Copernican
revolution, he is not then alluding to some mysterious meaning or secret life
intrinsic to things in themselves (the target of Kant's first Copernican revolution), but to the dialectical object whose mediations already inscribe it
with subjectivity and which are the very condition of its objectivity.[23] 'If one
wants to reach the object … , its subjective attributes or qualities are not to
be eliminated, for precisely this would run counter to the primacy of the
object' (S&O: 502). He is therefore less ambiguous when he refers to the
'object's dialectical primacy'. 'Strictly speaking, primacy of the object would
mean that there is no object as the subject's abstract opposite.' But equally,
there 'is no subject as such': neither makes sense without its other (S&O:
508).

Adorno is determined to avoid any reified sense of subjectivity. He does
not identify it with any ontological, ahistorical spiritual substance, but cites
it as the mere possibility (the 'How') of mediation. In this sense he is as wary
of humanist definitions of a privileged species of 'Man' as Merleau-Ponty
(AP: 132). The 'epistemological I', itself modelled on the permanence of the
self-identical object, is similarly challenged. Adorno signifies subjectivity
merely as an ineradicable 'element' (a formal condition of the possibility of
experience or knowledge) whose own historical mediations in theory and
practice require tracing (as they were in 1947). But it is never his intention to
eliminate subjectivity as such, since this would substitute for dialectics a
fantasy of pure objectivity or structure, a loss of negativity. As he defines his
task in *Negative Dialectics*, it is to 'use the strength of the subject to break
through the fallacy of constitutive subjectivity', since subjectivity facilitates
critique as well as mastery. Adorno's view of the subject is similar, if politically antithetical, to Foucault's here. Both present it as a historical construct
although Adorno identifies that construct's self-emancipatory potential and
decries its suppression, while Foucault notes its implication in circuits of
disciplinary power and welcomes its imminent demise (although even here
one should distinguish between its epistemological erasure and the aesthetic
re-creation of the self Foucault gestures towards in his later work). This is
why Adorno's remains an immanent, politicised critique; one that laments
(like Habermas's later summoning of the public sphere) the loss of that
autonomous, critical spirit born in the early bourgeois and itself 'the precondition for a democratic society which needs adults who have come of age in
order to sustain itself and develop' (CIR: 92).

There remains nevertheless a formal and irreducible asymmetry between subject and object since subjectivity is intentional: without an object to intend, consciousness would be empty and it thus depends on the object. But on the other hand, without its determinate negations the object would be nothing. 'After elimination of the subjective moment, the object would come diffusely apart like the fleeting stirrings and instants of subjective life' (S&O: 509). Identity and difference are co-terminous. As Adorno puts it in *Negative Dialectics*, what is 'waiting in the objects themselves needs such intervention to come to speak.' Thinking 'heeds a potential that waits in the object' (ND: 29, 19). It is however the empirical, not the transcendental, subject that is co-constitutive here, and so its form-giving role is socially-mediated, both in terms of the specific schemata it applies and regarding its very relationship to the object. Adorno wants to avoid the alternatives of locating a dialectical method in the subject, or an ontology of negativity in the material domain; instead, rather like Merleau-Ponty, he wants to sustain a dialectical *frisson* in what the latter called the 'interworld'.

This then raises the question of an alternative subject–object relation where knowledge and experience might be structured differently. I have already argued that although Adorno speaks of reconciliation in this context, he should not be read as intending any utopian identity, either as a regression to undifferentiated origins or as transcendence towards some unimaginable noumenal *telos*. This reminder is important in light of Habermas's attribution to his predecessor of an undialectical, even messianic, fantasy of redemption. Adorno failed to identify reconciliation with communicative action, Habermas charges, because it 'would not entail the demand that nature open up its eyes, that in the condition of reconcilia-tion we talk with animals, plants, and rocks.'[24]

I will come back to the question of whether Adorno could have accepted Habermas's intersubjective resolution, but there is no indication that he aspired to the sort of facile resurrection of nature that Habermas describes here. In the epistemological frame of 'Subject and Object', it is their very non-identity which is to be preserved (S&O: 499). If there is 'communica-tion' between them, it is of the sort practised here and elsewhere defined as negative dialectics. Its way of engaging in an immanent critique of the present, I have argued, *demonstrates* a process of dialectical reconciliation (but not unification) without projecting it onto reason's Other. Indeed it is this practice that I have implicitly credited with exploring negativity while avoiding the charges of performative contradiction that such adventurers always court and which Habermas in particular has consistently levelled against Adorno.[25] To engage in this practice, which is also exhibited by, but *not* reducible to, art, it is necessary to suspend the conceptual, constitutive, mastering orientation endemic to material and philosophical modernity and to 'relax the cognitive subject until it truly fades into the object to which it is akin, on the strength of its own objective being' (S&O: 506). Adorno goes on:

> approaching knowledge of the object is the act in which the subject rends the veil it is weaving around the object. It can do this only where, fearlessly passive, it entrusts itself to its own experience. In places where subjective reason scents subjective contingency, the primacy of the object is shimmering through – whatever in the object is not a subjective admixture. The subject is the object's agent, and not its constituent … .
>
> (S&O: 506)

This can only be achieved by, and is indeed practised in the course of, a critical exploration of those mediations which subtend the object and subvert its apparent stasis.

Having insisted on the negativity of Adorno's thinking here, there are nevertheless two problematic areas remaining. The first concerns the difficulty of translating his exemplary philosophical reconciliation into any political equivalent. Clearly Adorno recognised this imperative, since he writes that 'even epistemologically, the relation of subject and object would lie in the realization of peace among men as well as between men and their Other. Peace is the state of distinctiveness without domination, with the distinct participating in each other' (S&O: 500). But as Martin Jay points out, while remaining 'fearlessly passive' epistemologically may mark a laudable defence against conceptual imperialism, it is 'hardly a formula for political activism.'[26] I will return to this. The other lacuna concerns the cryptic nature of Adorno's methodological exhortations themselves: what might an orientation of 'fearless passivity' entail? I suggest that some light may be shed by turning to a much earlier essay, the 1931 inaugural lecture where Adorno's ideas in their less mature state are revealing in their will to present an explicit programme for a critical philosophy.

'The Actuality of Philosophy'

The title of Adorno's lecture suggests an ironic gesture towards Hegel but it also raises serious questions about the continuing viability of the philosophical project itself. In Hegelian terms, the actualisation of philosophy had meant its realisation in Absolute Knowledge, whereby thought and reality would coincide. While Adorno wants to expose as illusory any claim that thought has sufficient power to grasp 'the real' in its totality, he also suggests that this is specifically precluded by the modernity Hegel saw as its pre-condition.

No justifying reason could rediscover itself in a reality whose order and form suppresses every claim to reason; only polemically does reason present itself to the knower as total reality, while only in traces and ruins is it prepared to hope that it will ever come across correct and just reality. Philosophy which presents reality as such today only veils reality and eternalizes its present condition.

(AP: 120)

Most of the lecture proceeds with an immanent critique of philosophy, although its primary target is the Heideggerian ontology which Adorno perceives as an apolitical and doomed attempt at restoring philosophy's lost metaphysical grandeur. Instead, he insists, 'one of the first and most actual tasks would appear to be the radical criticism of the ruling philosophic thinking.' Denying anticipated charges of unfruitful negativity, he argues that the dissolution of traditional philosophical problems is a dialectical way of proceeding, since to criticise philosophy is also to criticise the real and vice versa. For how could reason find itself reflected in an irrational totality? What is of particular interest in this youthful piece is Adorno's exploration of the interpretive philosophy he hopes will succeed the demise of its metaphysical predecessor: an approach which might after all actualise philosophy by re-engaging it in the material realm where reason, freedom and justice must be concretely realised. As such, philosophy is inherently political.

Adorno was strongly influenced at this stage by Benjamin's *Trauerspiel* study.[27] This influence has been well documented elsewhere[28], but a few points are germane here because of Benjamin's attempts at presenting subject–object relations in a radically un-Kantian way. Benjamin was himself influenced by Surrealism, with its projects of winning the 'energies of intoxication' for the revolution and of bringing, through art, 'the immense forces of "atmosphere" concealed in … things to the point of explosion.'[29] While recognising their lack of dialectical analysis, he sympathised with the surrealists' aim of re-enchanting objects and smashing their bourgeois encoding. By presenting his own work as a montage of images, he too wanted to invoke an experience different from that of reified commodity production. Like Adorno, Benjamin associated this task philosophically with challenging the monotonous space–time continuum and fixed categories that Kant had presented as the *a prioris* of experience, and thus with introducing contingency through injection of discontinuity and hiatus into Kantian subject–object relations (and into the capitalist world that instantiates them). Focusing on the excess and resistance of objects to reification, and on chance rather than causality, his own writing replicated the fluid world he invoked.[30] It is a Benjaminian idea of dialectical images, or constellations, that finds its way into Adorno's thinking here, together with its proposition that if philosophy is to decipher the world it must replicate its fragmented, dissonant structure in its own form.

Adorno accordingly emphasises both the non-identity of subject and object and the elusive nature of the 'correct and just' reality wherein reason might discover itself. Faithful to the dialectical imperative that reality needs (re)constructing according to its internal mediations, he nevertheless denies any sense in which there lies a true totality beneath appearances, with the world a pre-written script merely awaiting revelation. Dialectics rather means an ongoing, hazardous tracing of connections and contradictions; an eliciting of vestiges of reason from the detritus of history and a simultaneous deconstruction of the irrational totality. 'For the mind (*Geist*) is indeed not capable of producing or grasping the totality of the real, but it may be possible to penetrate the detail, to explode in miniature the mass of merely existing reality' (AP: 133).

Although it is scientific positivism that is charged with liquidating philosophy, Adorno appeals to science in two ways. First he acknowledges that empirical data, especially that generated by sociology, is essential to dialectical thought as it provides it with the factual bric-à-brac of experience which any concrete philosophy must analyse. But second, he uses the opposition between (negative) philosophy and (positivist) science to explain the distinctiveness of the former. The key difference between them is that while science researches, philosophy interprets. It is interpretation whose subject–object relation anticipates what will later be figured as reconciliation and practised as negative dialectics.

The history of philosophy as Adorno presents it is continuous only in the sense that its task has always been to make sense of a recalcitrant and fragmented reality. Its myriad strands must all be kept in play, since philosophy cannot 'do without the least thread which earlier times have spun', but it must also 'always begin anew' in attempting to turn these ciphers into text. Such attempts are likened to riddle solving. If philosophy advances truth claims, it must 'proceed without ever possessing a sure key to interpretation; nothing more is given to it than fleeting, disappearing traces within the riddle figures of that which exists and their astonishing entwinings' (AP: 126).

The riddle does not offer a solution to an answer it merely hides, but is a configuration in which question and answer are interwoven in the moment of its snapping into relief. Riddle solving means 'to light up the riddle-*Gestalt* like lightning and to negate it (*aufzuheben*), not to persist behind the riddle and imitate it.' It lights up a meaning only 'suddenly and temporarily' and 'consumes it' at the same time (AP: 127). Riddle solving does not therefore seek a hidden law, nor try to sustain any reified conceptual order. But equally, riddle solving is dialectical inasmuch as it is not content merely to deconstruct and lay bare the 'refuse of the physical world'. Even if only briefly and provisionally, it seeks to illuminate a certain patterning within shifting relationships and connections. Just as riddle solving brings the singular and dispersed elements of a question into a temporary grouping just long enough for it to achieve closure as a figure, so philosophy brings scientific data into 'changing constellations' or 'trial combinations'. Its task is to interpret 'unintentional reality' by constructing 'figures or images' out of its elements, juxtaposing and reconfiguring its smallest elements.

In doing so, interpretive philosophy constructs 'keys' before which reality 'springs open': keys which are neither too large (as in idealism's grand narratives) nor too small (as in sociological nominalism). It is however important that these keys are in no sense taken as fixed concepts or laws of the real. 'In regard to the manipulation of conceptual material by philosophy, I speak purposely of grouping and trial arrangement, of constellation and construction. The historical images ... are not simply self-given.' They thus remain provisional constructs whose legitimacy is only upheld where reality crystallises conclusively about them. As Adorno would remind Benjamin, 'dialectical images are as models not social products, but objective constellations in which "the social" situation represents itself' (AtoB: 115f). Eschewing claims to articulate an inner language of objects or to mirror reality, they act as 'magnetic centres' of objectivity; models whose pattern reality will verify if they are correctly imprinted (Adorno found Marxian and Freudian 'keys' especially fecund here). Later he would associate these keys with Weber's ideal types: concepts of gradual composition which, although they are subjective creations, are legible as a 'sign of objectivity' and which literally unlock it.

> As a constellation, theoretical thought circles the concept it would like to unseal, hoping that it may fly open like the lock of a well-guarded safe-deposit box: in response, not to a single key or a single number, but to a combination of numbers.
>
> (ND: 163)

With the suggestion that philosophy should be producing constellations rather than conceptual classification, Adorno is describing a dialectical reasoning that endeavours to do justice to the heterogeneity of objects without abandoning philosophy to merely empirical description, poetry or collage. Thus phenomena are to be deconstructed, revealing the internal dissonance and antagonisms, the non-identity, which their given appearance occludes. In demystifying the reified totality, philosophy hopes to incite its practical negation. But it cannot rest content merely with laying out the wares of the sensuous manifold (any ontologising of negativity as an underlying chaos is itself a subjective act; one which downgrades the world for the sake of its spiritual domination (AE: 18)). 'A thinking whose course made us incapable of definition, unable even for moments to have a succinct language represent the thing, would be as sterile, probably, as a thinking gorged with verbal definitions' (ND: 165). Reason must also therefore reconstitute the internal lines of force, the inner logic of connections and contradictions that grant to objects their liveliness and potential to change. It is accordingly negative in a twofold sense: in negating identity and in disclosing the unrealised possibilities of the existent. In Merleau-Ponty's terminology, it articulates the invisibility that subtends and lines each visible to render it meaningful within a provisional *Gestalt* (and Merleau-Ponty also appeals to Weber's methodology of ideal types and 'historical imagination'[31]). Constellations are then the experimental, but not gratuitous, figures that emerge in non-identity thinking.

Constellations are not reductive but themselves reside in an array of concepts, whose patterning conveys the complexity of things. It is this mimetic aspect that overcomes the subject–object opposition inherent in traditional epistemology: philosophy, like reality, exhibits both, since in its mimetic aspect it replicates the figurative yet mobile nature of the object world it represents. This is where it breaks with classic dialectics. As Susan Buck-Morss explains, 'the procedure was one of mimetic representation rather than synthesis.'[32] Philosophy's historical images are hieroglyphs of the connectedness/dissonance, ideality/materiality of the real, where each object is itself a cipher of the social totality. Constellations are not then a bridge between subject and object, but a site of their affinity. Adorno would return to this in *Negative Dialectics*, where he would offer constellations as the unifying moment which survives without the transcending aspect of the negation of the negation. Here there is no *aufhebung/relève*, nor conceptual progress towards identity, but a conceptual patterning (like a constellation of stars or a musical composition) which, like language, signifies by a relation between terms while remaining centred on the object signified. Concepts, like their objects, are therefore contextualised, overdetermined, figurative of non-identity even while they identify (ND: 162–6). As Adorno writes elsewhere:

> Constellation is not system. Everything does not become resolved, everything does not come out even; rather, one moment sheds light on the other, and the figures that the individual moments form together are specific signs and a legible script.
>
> (H:TS: 109)

Such is thinking's aesthetic dimension. It is then no coincidence that in his *Aesthetic Theory* Adorno explains that art 'is related to its other as is a magnet to a field of iron filings.' In

> art works, the criterion of success is twofold: whether they succeed in integrating thematic strata and details into their immanent form and in this interpretation at the same time maintain what resists it and the fissures that occur in the process of integration.
>
> (AT: 7)

The discussion of constellations then fleshes out the sense in which Adorno would later refer to reconciled subject–object relations in terms of the 'primacy of the object' and the subject's 'fearless passivity'. Thinking meets the real half-way since this is not a quest of discovery or mastery but an experimental in(ter)vention, where the diversity of parts as well as the pattern of their relations is sustained and

> the *organon* of this *ars inveniendi* is fantasy. An exact fantasy; fantasy which abides strictly within the material which the sciences present to it, and reaches beyond them only in the smallest aspects of their arrangement: aspects, granted, which fantasy itself must originally generate.
>
> (AP: 131)

In *Negative Dialectics* Adorno will interpret this dual capacity of reason for fantasy and precision in Freudian terms. A double mode of conduct is facilitated by the psyche's conscious/unconscious processes: that of critical reason (where the judgement and inference typical of the secondary process occur) and 'a free, unbound one like a stepping out of dialectics' which itself recalls thought's (unconscious) outside. As such, the 'unregimented thought has an elective affinity to dialectics' when it yields exact fantasy. Philosophical language combines cogency and play, expression and rigour (ND: 15, 18). It thereby expresses the identity/non-identity, ego/id structure of a subjectivity which is, in Kristeva's terms, in-process.

In light of more recent postmodern aporias, Adorno's remains a very contemporary quest but, like Merleau-Ponty's, his dialectical resolution keeps hold of the political in that it is deconstructive for explicitly critical and emancipatory reasons. It dialectically sustains both the excessive and heterogeneous and a possibility of critical agency in the pursuit of form. It both tears apart the apparent solidity of the positive to reveal the connections and disjunctions of the social world, and it re-configures the more enduring structures and antagonisms of power which are to be subjected to critical analysis and transformation. It locates pressures and resistances in objective life and does not reduce negativity to the rhythmic play of signifying or discursive process.

Nevertheless, the fleet and evanescent constellations inspired by Benjamin perhaps look a little light in the context of domination. Adorno's admission that his approach amounts to 'an aesthetic picture game' has inspired some critics to worry that the 'exact' fantasy may be merely fantastic and Adorno seems later to have felt it granted too much to intuition. After the 1930s his emphasis on momentary illuminations would yield to a more painstaking tracing of theoretical linkages. But whatever the tempo of the real/thought, what he is attempting is to tread a precarious path between a process of verification (where the real conforms with or refutes the patterns elicited) and a recognition that there are no foundational, objective guarantees of truth; a route which avoids relativism or absolutism, scepticism or dogmatism, nihilism or utopianism; one that makes sense of the real without imposing subjective categories upon it. As Adorno would write in *Negative Dialectics*,

> [t]he open thought has no protection against the risk of decline into randomness; nothing assures it of a saturation with the matter that will suffice to surmount that risk. But the consistency of its performances, the density of its texture, helps the thought to hit the mark.
>
> (ND: 35)

There are affinities here between Adorno's idea of constellations and Merleau-Ponty's *Gestalten* (the latter even occasionally uses the term constellations himself[33]), both of which indicate attempts at emulating in thought, the shifting relation between parts and whole, materiality and meaning, that are associated with objectivity as such. However Adorno's ideal forms seem more precarious and he is less inclined to recognise the whole as more than the sum of its parts. His emphasis is more on the non-identity and dissonance that thinking must avoid crushing. Compare, for example, his contention that the 'text which philosophy has to read is incomplete, contradictory and fragmentary, and much of it may be delivered up to blind demons' (AP: 126) with Merleau-Ponty's phenomenological programme of grasping the 'unique core of existential meaning' that shines through the object's diverse perspectives, where understanding means 'to take in the total intention.'[34] Contradictory and fragmentary is not, finally, the same as ambiguous and provisional, although both are indices of negativity.

It is important nevertheless to emphasise Adorno's insistence that his method is *dialectical*. This comes across clearly in his responses to drafts of Benjamin's early work which were conveyed in a series of letters written only four or five years after the inaugural lecture. Adorno complains that despite the brilliance of Benjamin's presentation of the ruins of history, his objects lack 'historical exactitude' and 'mediation'; there is a tendency to juxtapose them without interpretation, where these traces rather needed 'dialecticizing by theory' (AtoB: 117, 119, 128; ND: 19). By this Adorno means a historical materialist explanation of phenomena in terms of general social and economic tendencies. Benjamin's connections remain too inferential, immediate, even mystical, imputing

> to phenomena precisely that kind of spontaneity, palpability and density which they have lost in capitalism. In this sort of immediate ... materialism, there is a profoundly romantic element ... . The 'mediation' which I miss ... is nothing other than the theory which your study omits. The omission of the theory ... deprives the

phenomena, which are experienced only subjectively, of their real historico-philosophical weight.

(AtoB: 129)

Adorno goes on to warn against a 'wide-eyed presentation of mere facts' that locates Benjamin's *Arcades* study 'at the crossroads of magic and positivism'. Despite his own fascination with the singular objects of everyday life, they must be recognised as indices of the total social process that has produced them and which can again be read there. Because Benjamin's constellations lack historical rigour, he allegedly succumbs to a romantic view of change: Adorno warns against an 'anarchistic romanticism of blind confidence in the spontaneous power of the proletariat' (AtoB: 117, 123).

It should then come as no surprise that Adorno notes his own method's 'astounding and strange affinity' with (historical) materialism, which imparts the necessary rigour. Such interpretation 'of the unintentional through a juxtaposition of the analytically isolated elements and illumination of the real by the power of such interpretation is the program of every authentically materialist knowledge' (AP: 127). He insists that constructed constellations are not just thought experiments, but also incite practical negations.

The interpretation of a given reality and its abolition are connected to each other ... [because] out of the construction of a configuration of reality the demand for its real change always follows promptly. The change-causing gesture of the riddle process – not its mere resolution as such – provides the image of resolutions to which material praxis alone has access. Materialism has named this relationship ... : dialectic. Only dialectically, it seems to me, is philosophic interpretation possible.

(AP: 129)

Unfortunately Adorno does not elaborate on this sense of praxis here. But philosophical reason clearly reaches its limits where it encounters an irrational reality: at the limits of thinking, material action must intervene. Thus philosophy 'will stop where irreducible reality breaks in upon it'; a break which occurs 'concrete-historically' (AP: 132). But since he rejected any romantic conjuring of revolutionary agency, and his own mediations pointed to no material force which would change the real, Adorno was already anticipating the political impasse critics associate with his work. Rather than placing unwarranted faith in some non-existent revolutionary force or in a merely ideal solution, he would translate praxis into a process of immanent critique that was itself a model of subject–object reconciliation. This negative dialectics could only however evolve via a more detailed engagement with Hegel, since it 'goes beyond, and to the point of breaking with, the dialectics of Hegel' (ND: 34).

From Hegelian dialectics to negative dialectics

Between 1956 and 1963 Adorno composed three studies on Hegel which were collectively described as preparation for 'a revised conception of the dialectic' (H:TS: xxxvi). Although he concedes that Hegel eventually succumbed to the positivity of the Absolute and the primacy of the subject, it is his negativity that is emphasised in these generally sympathetic *Studies*. In *Negative Dialectics* Adorno's judgement of his predecessor is much harsher, since he must distinguish his own negativity and rid dialectics of its positivist residue.

For Adorno here (unlike his poststructuralist successors), the dialectic is not irredeemably infected with *positivity* although it does exhibit a laudably *affirmative* (utopian) moment in Hegel's aspiration to a reconciled whole. The Hegelian totality, inasmuch as it keeps faith with dialectics, is defined in resolutely negative, non-totalitarian terms. Rather than a triumph of identity and closure culminating in a harmonious *telos*, Adorno insists that the whole is no more than the quintessence of partial moments which generate one another, their internal connections relying less on unbroken transition than on 'sudden change' and 'rupture' (H:TS: 4–5). It is of course this complex whole/parts, identity/non-identity effervescence that Adorno himself associates with a dialectical reasoning which struggles to articulate and emulate the process of which it speaks, and it is such a project that he credits Hegel with here (although its discontinuities sometimes look more genealogical than dialectical).

Even where Hegel appears to transcend dialectics Adorno argues that this, like Kant's dualist thinking, has its historical truth. For although reality has not actually acquired the rationality Hegel ascribed to modernity, the latter has become just the systemic totality indicated by the Absolute, albeit an irrational and antagonistic one. It has not reconciled subject–object relations but it has suppressed the negativity that would engender further change. In the 'radically societalized society', spirit does indeed experience the 'remorseless consolidation of all partial moments and acts of civil society into a whole', 'the totality of the negative', i.e. of the untrue. The Absolute that might master everything finds its mirror image in a society unified under domination (H:TS: 87).[35] But, unlike Marx, Hegel failed to envisage even an ideal resolution to bourgeois contradictions and in this sense, he was obliged to 'maintain the affirmative' (H:TS: 80). In this sense Hegel is untrue philosophically but his work can be interpreted as a cipher of sociological truth.

> In all its particular moments Hegel's philosophy is intended to be negative; but if, contrary to his intentions, it becomes negative as a whole as well, it thereby acknowledges the negativity of its object. In that ultimately the nonidentity of subject and object, concept

and thing, idea and society, emerges, unpacifiable, in his philosophy; in that it ultimately disintegrates into absolute negativity, it also redeems its promise and truly becomes identical with its ensnared subject matter.

(H:TS: 31–2)

The plethora of positive and affirmative oppositions that defines the negative here results in a constellation of senses. In an antagonistic society (pejoratively negative because untrue, unjust, irrational, in relation to its own potential to be otherwise), only negative experiences are justifiable: experiences of what is not (yet). Such negativity does not however mean nihilistic despair, but a critical *and* affirmative orientation towards possibilities discerned via immanent (as opposed to abstract) negation and caught in philosophy's speculative moment. But if it has an affirmative, even utopian, aspect, critical reason must remain negative in its anti-positivism. It sets static elements in motion and undermines every position. The non-identity of thought and experience indeed ensures Hegel's critical distance from reality, where facts worked over in thought are presented as other than they are or claim to be and are thus disclosed in their own negativity. That is, each fact is shown to depend on a series of relationships and oppositions; each depends on what it is not and is caught in the flux of its own incompletion.

The very act of (dialectical) thinking thereby sustains a negative moment *vis-à-vis* the positive: the distance from objects that condemns it also saves it from simply applauding the given. Unlike understanding, such thought is 'an act of negation, of resistance', and against the totality that would crush all critical appraisal the 'effort implied in the concept of thought itself, as the counter-part of passive contemplation, is negative already – a revolt against being importuned to bow to every immediate thing' (ND: 19). If on the one hand reason remains inadequate to the particularity of which it speaks, then, each particular is also inadequate to its concept. This is why the critiques of philosophy and of experience go hand in hand. It is in this force field that dialectics is practised as 'the unswerving effort to conjoin reason's critical consciousness of itself and the critical experience of objects' (H:TS: 9f). It is precisely because knowledge always recognises its own internal limitations *vis-à-vis* experience that it is driven to criticise itself and reality; to seek more adequate knowledge and radical change.

In the third Study, the paradoxes of negative thinking that Adorno must himself negotiate are explicitly tackled. Hegel's aim, Adorno contends, was to compel his material to speak. This is where an orientation of passive surrender and spontaneous receptivity is appropriate (H:TS: 7). Yet the very nature of becoming's complex, dynamic parts/whole relation defies literary presentation. The challenge is to find an expression that would 'fit the matter expressed precisely', where that matter lacks the firm outlines philosophy trades on in its will to identification. It is the challenge Adorno had begun to address methodologically in his inaugural lecture. In articulating the heterogeneous nature of its objects, philosophy must not regress to a formless poetics but is obliged to recognise the formative moments of becoming which allow it to speak with distinctness, if not clarity. The conundrum is now located (and resolved), in a rather Nietzschean way, within (philosophical) language itself.

The problem here is that language is by nature identitarian: 'language and the process of reification are interlocked. The very form of the copula, "is," pursues the aim of pinpointing its object'. But philosophy's aim must be to correct this: 'in this sense all philosophical language is a language in opposition to language, marked with the stigma of its own impossibility' (H:TS: 100). The reason it is not simply imprisoned in this paradox is that, like Merleau-Ponty, Adorno recognises a double character of language: one that Merleau-Ponty had defined as its latent and manifest aspects and which Adorno presents as its mimetic and classifying moments. In the previous chapter I explained how the former argued that despite language's distinctiveness from the lifeworld it has an affinity with it because, like the lived, it exhibits an existential style which allows it to convey through its internal arrangement more than it explicitly says. Adorno similarly contends that language, like reason, has a mimetic dimension in so far as it catches the form (*qua* parts and whole) of its objects. It cannot be solely mimetic, since replication of immediacy would be undialectical; rather what it mimics is the mediated, subject–object structure of its objects, and it does this by itself being, like them, internally dialectical. 'The dialectic plays itself out within the medium of language itself' (H:TS: 101). Like Merleau-Ponty, Adorno thus rejects positivist dreams of purging language of its gestural, poetic dimensions ('Thought that completely extirpated its mimetic impulse … would end up in madness' (H:TS: 40)). It is in rhetoric that we find a 'mutual approximation of thing and expression, to the point where difference fades' (ND: 56). Like his phenomenological contemporary, Adorno recognises the significance of the differences and relations between signifiers while insisting that they thereby evince their affinity (not arbitrariness) with the signified.

It follows that (philosophical) language is negative not in the sense that *différance* is, but in the dialectical sense that the object's subject–object relations are replicated in it, as mimesis/reflection. It grants clarity but only 'fragmentarily' and as 'configuration', via 'sudden flashes of illumination', rather than by stolid definitions. It thereby conveys the heterogeneity of its material (where Merleau-Ponty's styles evinced its operative rationality). This is what Adorno tries to capture in his own style which, like Nietzsche's flirtation with a musical, Dionysian creative–destructive becoming, often resorts to short essays and aphorisms as well as to syntactical experimentation. Buck-Morss describes this style thus:

Adorno didn't write essays, he *composed* them, and he was a virtuoso in the dialectical medium. His verbal compositions express an 'idea' through a sequence of dialectical reversals and inversions. The sentences develop like musical themes: they break apart and turn in on themselves in a continuing spiral of variations. The phenomena ... are 'overdetermined,' so that their contradictory complexity needs to be disentangled through interpretation. But there is no affirmation, no 'closing cadence.' The contradictions are unravelled; they are not resolved.[36]

The reader cannot therefore passively assimilate the text or gain mastery over it. She must engage dialectically with it and, in doing so, she actively experiences the subject–object relation Adorno is also conveying discursively. This is then the antithesis to the way we allegedly receive the products of the culture industry. But it is also where Hegel failed. Despite his 'flowing' style (where a mimetic character overcame a significative one and a 'kind of gestural, curvilinear writing' emerged and negativity was at its deepest) he paid insufficient attention to its linguistic means, believing that vagueness and equivocation would suffice. Adorno suggests nevertheless that Beethoven's music, which must be heard multidimensionally and in a temporally-complex way, offers an analogue to Hegel's (anti-)texts (although a better one, no doubt, to his own): not because philosophy can be reduced to art, but because it shares with art the aim of rescuing the mimetic moment the concept represses (H:TS: 123, 136–7). It is only in this practising of negativity, where identity and non-identity incessantly fulminate, that philosophy can overcome the idealistic paradox: that even where non-identity is recognised, the act of defining it would render it identical so that 'the nonconceptual becomes the concept of the nonidentical' (H:TS: 147). For Adorno the movement beyond classifying thought is not an embrace of the irrational, not simply aesthetic, but a process immanent to thinking. He concludes by commending such a practice for the reading of Hegel himself, as an experimental process. Like the earlier 'exact fantasy' which produces constellations, this procedure of immanent critique is defended against charges of relativism. It surrenders to its material in the same way Hegel and Adorno would like to (with fearless passivity). Ideas 'that have confidence in their own objectivity have to surrender *va banque*, without mental reservation, to the object in which they immerse themselves, even if that object is another idea; this is the insurance premium they pay for not being a system' (H:TS: 146).

It is this tracing and practising of internal mediations that is undertaken in *Negative Dialectics*, where the paradox of negative thinking is again addressed explicitly.[37] Among adventurers in negativity, I have frequently noted a tendency to negotiate its paradoxes by means of a dual strategy: they sketch in the negative sufficiently by discursive means to indicate its critical significance while also conveying its internal logic performatively. Adorno struggles valiantly to synthesise this duality within a single discursive process; to render his reasoning inherently negative. Yet his philosophy remains a discursive practice, even where it communicates stylistically, and in principle its experiential efficacy must therefore await completion in another medium, in collectivist praxis. Adorno approaches this terrain in so far as his work criticises society but it can go no further unless it incites some political response, as he had recognised in 1931.

As far as philosophy itself is concerned, in principle the performative practising of negativity, as social criticism, should take over from the preparatory meta-critique once the latter's lessons have been assimilated. Until then philosophy and its linguistic resources are necessary, yet they harbour a threat of identification at odds with the negativity alluded to. This is why charges of performative contradiction are levelled with monotonous regularity. Adorno, as I have interpreted him, deployed this dual strategy in a highly self-conscious, dialectical way. His own work is both reflective and aesthetic and in this sense it replicates and reflects upon the rational and mimetic moments that are identified with philosophical language and reason themselves, as well as with the subject–object composition of every object. But he is also well aware of the fragility of this complicated resolution. 'A surplus of method, compared with the substance, is abstract and false; even Hegel had to put up with the discrepancy between his Preface to *Phenomenology* and phenomenology itself. The philosophical ideal would be to obviate accounting for the deed by doing it' (ND: 48). Immanent critique 'does it' but in a positivist world that remains epistemologically and socially hostile to dialectics, the more militant yet abstract insistence on negativity is still required. Adorno must yet account for the deed as well as performing it and this account can only avoid the contradictions of the negative by embracing its paradoxes. This is what *Negative Dialectics* tries to do and herein lies the core of its negativity.

It is almost impossible to explain this process since, as Adorno shows, every such attempt is drawn into the multiplicitous relations it invokes. Since practising negativity exemplifies the (dialectical, not identitarian) reconciliation of subject and object, it has a utopian resonance. But since this is only a philosophical resolution it remains negatively utopian *vis-à-vis* the social totality. Moreover, in so far as philosophy's own ideal is to 'substantialize' itself, with the subject becoming 'a reflexive form of its object', a 'self-reflecting object', its own utopianism remains paradoxical (yet fertile, unlike Kant's impossible and off-limits intellectual intuition). 'The cognitive utopia would be to use concepts to unseal the non-conceptual with concepts, without making them their equal.' 'To want substance in cognition is to want a utopia' (ND: 9, 57). In aiming for the impossible, it practises negativity and dwells irredeemably in the realms of the is-not, yet it thereby practises the very non-identity thinking that exemplifies the only practicable subject–object reconciliation. Necessarily falling short of any identity, it remains once more a negative resolution. For the 'plain contradictoriness of this challenge' is philosophy itself. Its goal and its naïveté lie in unravelling the paradox that it must transcend the concept by the concept in order to reach the non-conceptual. In so doing it should not however perceive itself as inadequate in relation to some putative dream of identity, since philosophy's objects are themselves heterogeneous: it is only in non-identity thinking that 'the very objects would start talking under the lingering eye' (ND 28). In this sense negative dialectics succeeds where philosophy fails. It is the only means of avoiding the imperialist logic of reason that Hegel discerned and incarnated, short of abandoning reason altogether.

It is only then by simultaneously 'uttering the unutterable' *and* reflecting on its impossibility that the tensions necessary for dialectics and for reconciliation are sustained. For if things are non-identical with thought, reconciliation lies not in their being articulated without remainder but in the subject's self-consciously (and not just by default) entering the labyrinthine mediations that stream between them. It is here, in the reversals and overdeterminations between subject and object, that freedom and negativity are practised, and inasmuch as dialectical reason provides a model for the social, it lies in this non-instrumental, non-hierarchical subject–object relation. Until critical philosophy is replicated by an equivalent social orientation, however, 'the divergence between dialectics as a method and substantial dialectics will go on' (ND: 29, 48). The overcoming of this divergence depends on a real transformation but, in offering the immanent critique which might incite it, dialectics once more circles around the paradoxes of its own method.

> The means employed in negative dialectics for the penetration of its hardened objects is possibility – the possibility of which their reality has cheated the objects and which is nonetheless visible in each one. But no matter how hard we try for linguistic expression of such a history congealed in things, the words we use will remain concepts. Their precision substitutes for the thing itself, without quite bringing its selfhood to mind; there is a gap between words and the things they conjure. Hence, the residue of arbitrariness and relativity in the choice of words as well as in the presentation of the whole.
>
> (ND: 52f)

Conclusion: practising negativity: philosophy and politics

While it would obviously be inappropriate to conclude with any definition of negativity in Adorno's work, it is now possible to be more specific about what it is not. Among previous adventurers I associated negativity with generativity and, as such, the term at least courted ontological implications. Adorno is adamant in denying these. Even in Hegel's case, he both credits his predecessor with opposing negativity to traditional foundationalisms and denies that Hegel's sensitivity to *process* should be considered ontological at all. For he 'alters the meaning of ontology so decisively that it seems futile to apply the word ... to a so-called fundamental structure whose very nature is not to be a fundamental structure ... or substratum' (H:TS: 9). This is of course even more valid regarding Adorno's own thinking. If non-identity were presented as a first ('nonontological') concept, its negativity would be subverted through its metaphysical invocation (ND: 136). Negativity is no lacuna in Being, no primordial nothingness or diversity, no Other or efficacious force.

This is important because (like Deleuze, and as Nietzsche is often read by his critics) Adorno sometimes seems to be invoking some materialist ontology, an underlying reality in itself, as a swarming heterogeneity, a sensuous manifold, immune to classification. Like Derrida on *différance*, he however insists that negativity is no final principle from which all else is derived (H:TS: 12); no metaphysical truth regarding things in themselves (transcendental materialism), but a purely immanent movement. In the case of dialectics this is because everything we say about Being or reality is already conceptually mediated. But Adorno's is not a Kantian response because that saying is not constitutive: there is a resistance and an insistence on the part of the object, though only because it has been historically produced in all its complex relations and internal overdeterminations. It is the collective but unintentional productivity of labour, art, desire, etc. that lends things an inexhaustible significance within a network of relationships and denies them rest or positive identity. There is then no appeal to a pre-discursive, transcendental domain, but neither is negativity locked within any self-referential system of signification. For it is precisely in their imbrication that negativity plays and engenders subject and object. 'What is, is more than it is. This "more" is not imposed upon it but remains immanent to it, as that which has been pushed out of it. In that sense, the nonidentical would be the thing's own identity against its identifications' (ND: 161). This is as true of individual persons as it is of isolated objects. 'Nonidentity is the secret *telos* of identification' (ND: 149).

Like other adventurers in the negative, Adorno's version does nevertheless convey a certain productivity because the impossibility of epistemological correspondence and conceptual identification always drives reason to renewed efforts of signifying and of changing its other. Caught in the paradoxes of this hopeless yet fecund desire, negative thinking (and politics) is committed to a ceaseless, but non-teleological, becoming. In short, the secret of negativity's generativity, its creative–destructive choreography, is non-identity. This is why identity is the 'primal form of ideology' in its bid to suppress change and to stabilise the status quo, and why ideology critique is also a critique of constitutive consciousness (ND: 148).

It is tempting here to use non-identity as a synonym for negativity, but this would have to be very carefully finessed otherwise it looks either like a transcendental claim privileging dissonant facticity, or like a claim about the productivity of logic. I have already dismissed the former and in the latter case, Adorno insists that non-identity is not the same as contradiction in so far as contradiction remains a logical term indicating a failure of identity. In other words, this denial anticipates criticisms of dialectics made by Deleuze and poststructuralists, that difference is reduced here to a *lack* of consistency or unity, with negation a merely logical procedure. 'Contradiction is nonidentity under the rule of a law that affects the nonidentical as well' (ND: 5). Here it is the subject that labels non-identity as other, whereas negative dialectics aims to restore its content in more than a merely formal manner. Jarvis summarises Adorno's political aim here concisely: as 'not the liquidation of contradictions in logic, but the reconciliation of antagonisms in reality.'[38]

For, unlike Deleuze *et al.*, Adorno's goal is not to reject dialectics as irredeemably positive or idealist, nor to jettison negativity as anathema to difference, but to restore negativity, as non-identity, to dialectics as its condition of *political* engagement. As a critical thinking, negative dialectics must think against the contradictions of (capitalist) reality as a negation of reason and it is here that it practises, for political ends, a logic of disintegration (ND: 143f). This is entwined, as I said earlier, with an affirmative, speculative moment which is nevertheless still negative in that it concerns the potential of objects that have not yet realised their possibility of a richer, fuller mediation. In tracing the ruins and vestiges of reason in society, reality's potential to become different is already presaged.[39]

It is then crucial to recognise that non-identity remains for Adorno a thoroughly dialectical term, internally related to but not derived from identity. It must not be hypostatised as *The Negative* (the 'nonidentical is not to be obtained directly, as something positive on its part' (ND: 158)).[40] It is between positive and negative, identity and non-identity, that negativity's fertility flourishes, not beneath them. Non-identity is a relational term; not an other *per se*, but the otherness that confounds every identity even while it incites, and is incited by, efforts at identification. Although negativity is suggestive of mobility and fluidity, the excessive and residual, it is also therefore inseparable from form and identity, reason and meaning, in the same way that subject and object (or Merleau-Ponty's visible and invisible) are equally co-dependent. Negativity is instantiated objectively through the historical, material process but it is only redeemed, in its turn, by critical thought and action. It is precisely because negativity operates where positive and negative, experience and philosophy, meet that in its dialectical form it remains engaged with real structures of power and their (potential) negation. This then brings us, finally, to the question of the relation between negativity and politics in Adorno's thinking.

In tracing the political implications of negativity in Adorno's work, I have argued that it neither invokes a pre-lapsarian unity to be recovered nor evokes any utopian synthesis to be won. Rather, the undertaking of an immanent critique of existing subject–object relations is simultaneously a demonstration of a reconciled alternative of non-reductionist, non-hierarchical, non-instrumental, dialectical subject–object relations.[41] This nonetheless remained, I have pointed out, a philosophical resolution and as such it seems to leave two political questions unresolved. The first concerns how, strategically, change might occur and the second, whether Adorno's practising of reconciliation figures any equivalent practice for collective life.

Regarding the first question, Adorno's antipathy towards instrumentalist thinking suggests that he would have opposed any understanding of his critiques as merely strategic interventions preparing the way for radical acts. In practising negative thinking, critical means and reconstructive ends are combined (as they were in Merleau-Ponty's model of praxis) and this suggests that political change should entail an ongoing process of creative–destructive practices, even if in Adorno's case this would include periodic ruptures. Having inferred this choreography of political change, however, it remains the case that the immanent critique of late modernity yielded Adorno no reliable agency for breaking up the positivity and fore-closure of a system which precluded this dialectical rhythm. Aspirations regarding the galvanising force of demystification tended to yield in his thinking to images of critical philosophy merely as a repository for hopes and memories.

It is not however valid to conclude that the critical theorists discerned no openings or rays of hope in late capitalism. Even *Dialectic of Enlightenment*, as I mentioned earlier, is somewhat less unrelenting than critics suggest, and one can find various glimmerings of optimism within the ruins of late modernity scattered throughout the Frankfurt School writings. Horkheimer, for example, refers to maternal care and the bourgeois family as cultivating an anti-authoritarian dream of better conditions, while he and Adorno point to aspects of mass culture that yet harbour vestiges of unrepressed pleasure.[42] Adorno himself invokes magical, mimetic, aesthetic and intuitive residues that yet bespeak subject–object reciprocity. If these hardly add up to a dialectical *rapprochement*, they do sustain memories and negations that might yet clear and figure spaces for an alternative to domination. Critical thinking is itself exemplary in this context. 'Today, with theory paralyzed and disparaged by the all-governing bustle, its mere existence, however impotent, bears witness against the bustle' (ND: 143). As I have argued, such thinking does not just criticise the positive, but its own negativity is indicative of an emancipatory logic. It is true that its practising remains unavailable to the majority who have been, like the Nietzschean herd, thor-oughly subjected, so it cannot itself be the (collectivist, democratic) solution to social domination. But nor does the latter so preclude its continued existence that it forces critical theory into performative contradiction. For negative thinking remains available, Adorno insists, to those who by a 'stroke of undeserved luck' remain 'not entirely molded', 'not quite adjusted to the prevailing norms', and it is up to them to make the 'representative effort to say what most of those for whom they say it cannot see'. If there is an element of elitism in this judgement, blame lies in the fully-administered world (ND: 41).

As long as a few remnants of alternative subject–object relations remain and inspire critique, it is not then contradictory for Adorno to be among them. As far as their instantiation in experience is concerned, however, it is also quite possible that there really were (are) no social forces capable of radically challenging the impersonal logic of commodification and administration that Adorno discerned. The main purpose of tracing history's mediations was after all to glean its stifled potentialities, but no identification of material forces for their realisation can be guaranteed. The dialectical relation between material and conceptual development does not after all promise any actual synthesis of theory and practice, nor can future praxis be determined in advance.[43]

All the same, Adorno's sociological 'keys' for interpreting the present do often look rather speculative, rather than emerging from sustained sociological interrogation, and they sometimes also look both too large (regarding the capitalist totality) and too small (the minutiae of jazz performances; the details of the F-score). Postmodernists might for example suggest that greater attention to class, gender, ethnic and racial differences might have given Adorno a somewhat different perspective on the stability of the postwar democracies and the emphasis on non-identity could have pointed him in this direction. Habermasians might similarly argue that he ignored modernity's genuinely democratic potential. So the residual antagonisms and hopes he noted were perhaps less inert than he believed. Perhaps Gillian Rose explains this shortcoming when she comments that Adorno's Nietzschean understanding of power was so socially diffuse that it seemed 'to absolve him of any further examination of the political process.'[44] As such he would have fallen short of his own dialectical method while remaining faithful to its refusal of merely ideal solutions.

Certainly Marcuse's list, a decade later, of potentially radical agencies ranging from feminists and ghetto populations to hippies and third world liberation movements (in the context of his own account of one-dimensional society and his utopian vision of a new sensibility) has tended to be treated with retrospective derision. As Adorno had commented to Benjamin, the invocation of radical forces often looked simply romantic and lacked the mediations that would have anchored them historically. Whatever changes radical groups have engendered, capitalism and bureaucratisation have only strengthened their grip. Although postmodern differences have subsequently lent an appearance of fragmentation to the social and cultural landscape, as well as encouraging hopes of radical democratic pluralism as the marginalised find a voice, Adorno would surely have noted their impotence in challenging or understanding more totalising processes as well as the inadequacy of postmodernists in tracing the mediations that structure more diverse identities within the context of the whole.

This brings me to the second question. It is often claimed that when it comes to politics, negative thinking requires some vision of a positive alternative in order to ground criticism and grant it criteria for assessing where reality falls short. This has been the gist of accusations frequently levelled at Adorno by Habermas and his followers, who have variously asserted that Adorno lacked any such vision and was thus condemned to unfruitful negativity (a wandering exile lost in the discursive zone[45]); held some quasi-theological vision of redemption, or anticipated something like a discursive ethics but was too obsessed with subject–object relations to see it.

However I think there is a significant problem in the positive–negative relationship that underpins such criticisms. Just as negativity or non-identity remained philosophically situated where positive and negative are entwined, so Adorno wished to avoid opposing a negative totality with a vision of some positive alternative. This had already been rejected unequivocally in 1947. 'Explanations of the world as all or nothing are mythologies, and guaranteed roads to redemption are sublimated magic practices.' The 'transfiguration of negativity into redemption' is condemned as an untrue form of resistance (DofE: 24). Negative dialectics overcomes this sort of dualism; it suggests instead an ongoing process of destruction/reconstruction which renders philosophy inherently political. Yet it is true that this process does not readily translate into any politics of collective action[46] and, given critical theorists' insistence on the correspondence between cultural, material and psychological forms in any social totality, might we not expect some figuring of the dialectical correspondences which are a potential alternative to modernity's equivalences? In which case, the reconciled philosophical and aesthetic subject–object relation that Adorno's own work presages should find some commensurable expression in economic and political relations; one already prefigured in possibilities of non-instrumentalised collective life.

This is where Habermas suggests that Adorno might, and indeed ought to, have introduced something like his own intersubjective solution. Communicative action, grounded in the communicative potential of language, is proposed here both as an emancipatory rationality inherent in modernity alongside instrumentalism, and as the basis for a democratic politics that would accompany, even challenge, the powerful administrative and capitalist systems (delinguistified 'steering media'). While Habermas recognises elements of deliberative democracy already operating within liberal democracies, he also grants it a more utopian dimension through its association with an ideal speech situation wherein all power-induced distortions would be eliminated and difference would be transcended in the achievement of procedural consensus through rational argument. As we saw earlier, Adorno indeed associates an authentic politics with a democracy composed of critical participants, just as in the previous chapter I suggested that deliberative democracy might have had some attraction for Merleau-Ponty. But I also argued there that Habermas's version would have fallen short of his insistence on an enduring negativity and I think this is even more valid in Adorno's case.

First, Adorno did not see any genuinely democratic potential within late modernity. While its formal practices are institutionalised, they merely reproduce the ethos of one-dimensional society and legitimise the existing state of things. If all contributions to debate are untrue, then their proliferation is not in itself helpful. 'Direct communicability to everyone is not a criterion of truth. We must resist the all but universal compulsion to confuse the communication of knowledge with knowledge itself' (ND: 41). This leads to a second point: Adorno would surely have found Habermas's solution insufficiently mediated. The conditions for genuinely free, fair and open debate, as well as the possibility of a language devoid of ideological distortion, are simply not historically available according to his analysis. In Habermas's work the is and the ought, the substantive and the normative, fall apart; his procedural model thus looks both uncritical and utopian. The appeal to new social movements, as agencies which might defend the lifeworld (where communicative reason is nurtured) against its colonisation by bureaucracy and capital (which operate instrumentally) looks as insubstantial as Benjamin's or Marcuse's romantic invocations; or, at best, a 'struggle at the margins'.[47] In short this is a formalised, Kantian discourse *ethics* but not a *politics*.

Third, Adorno would surely have rejected, as I suggested Merleau-Ponty would, Habermas's challenge to the subject–object framework ('the paradigm of the knowledge of objects', Habermas insists, 'has to be replaced by the paradigm of mutual understanding between subjects capable of speech and action.'[48]). In so far as this replacement is predicated on Habermas's rejection of Kant's transcendental subject – which gets caught in the aporias of radical self-reflection versus its other *qua* 'incomprehensible element that cannot be reflectively retrieved' – then Adorno would presumably have been sympathetic. But for him the object is not an other, not a 'primordial element' or thing in-itself, but the dialectical object with which subjectivity is always in a reciprocal relationship. It is therefore a subject–object *dialectic*, not intersubjectivity, that is the necessary response. In targeting the Kantian version, Habermas accepts its account of objective inertness and himself puts all activity on the side of subjects, thereby bracketing the resistance of the material domain which calls for interpretation and engagement. This is why his analysis of and challenge to the steering media, which are needed if the public spheres where communicative action occurs are to regain their efficacy, look too thin. While politically 'a change of paradigm from subject-centred to communicative reason' suggests a salutary shift from liberalism to democracy, this cannot substitute for an ongoing dialectic that situates politics within its material situation. Ironically it is for precisely their insensitivity to this dialectic that Habermas chides poststructuralists: 'Any interaction between world-disclosing language and learning processes in the world is excluded.'[49] But by rendering this interaction communicative, where the lifeworld is a domain of pre-reflective intersubjectivity needing rational reconstruction, as opposed to materially recalcitrant structures, Habermas's solution also looks undialectical.

Here, for example, is Albrecht Wellmer's gloss on Habermas's proposed paradigm change: modernity's differentiation of value and validity spheres (into objective, normative and aesthetic) brings to awareness, he argues,

> the sphere of symbolically mediated human praxis as the only possible source of meaning and validity, and therefore as the only possible frame of reference for intersubjective validity claims. Without external guarantees for meaning or validity, every belief becomes a potential validity *claim* for which no intersubjective redemption is possible except through arguments.[50]

From Adorno's perspective this non-foundationalist move still looks subjectivist and Kantian. Not only is the rational subject unreconstructed, merely pluralised, but the praxis cited denies precisely that interaction with the objective domain which would permit a process of verification and material change. The merely formal criterion of the unforced force of the better argument, of which Habermas speaks, imprisons subjects in a discursive domain without situating their claims within the density of history. Moreover the formal differentiation of validity claims into three spheres, which Habermas associates with modernity's continuing emancipatory potential, would for Adorno be less significant than their actual equivalence in the social totality.

Fourth, Adorno would surely have agreed with the judgement I imputed to Merleau-Ponty: that Habermas represses the operation of negativity within language, subjectivity and communication. There is no real identity/ non-identity dialectic in Habermas's idealised account, only the communicative disagreement of rational interlocutors in pursuit of consensus. Even in the unlikely event of all individuals having access to democratic procedures on a free and equal basis, there would in principle be no basis for anticipating the ideal speech situation Habermas grounds in a universal pragmatics. The overdetermination of meanings; the ambiguities, limits and mimetic or rhetorical elements of language, and the (unconscious) opacities of subjectivity, as well as the profound ideological successes of positivism and the structural imperatives of the market, are all bracketed here. Furthermore, the ideal of consensus itself suggests a desire for unity and identity which presents difference, non-identity, as a problem to be over-come. Habermas's inclinations thus remain positivist, identitarian, against the ineliminable negativity that Adorno proposes.

Finally, Adorno would surely have found Habermas's idea of emancipa-tion a very limited one. Formal procedures for intersubjective deliberation are proposed by the latter as a political solution to the subjectivist aberra-tions Habermas traces to the erroneous ontological and epistemological positions of his predecessors. But for Adorno, as I said earlier, re-ordering subject–object relations is a multi-faceted quest entailing economic, existen-tial and aesthetic dimensions as well as political and philosophical ones. Habermas insists on differentiating cognitive–instrumental from norma-tive–practical knowledge in order to save emancipatory ethical life from the instrumentalist totality described by his predecessors. But Adorno is suggesting that a new kind of epistemological and existential relation is needed between subjects and objects, otherwise instrumentalism will drive out other possibilities. In other words, instrumental reasoning is already an existential relation and as such it cannot safely be bracketed as a separate domain, since its logic is to colonise and infect the ethical and aesthetic realms – as Habermas indeed fears. Wellmer's own somewhat expanded agenda of material justice under the slogan 'to each according to his needs', coupled with a parts–whole model of 'dialogical relationships between human individuals in a liberated society', is not inimical to Adorno's sense of reconciliation. But it fails to encompass all the resonances of subject–object relations that Adorno also hoped for and still discerned in surrealistic, instinctual, magical and aesthetic objects, and in the redeemed sensuality he associated with the subject's happiness. Nor does its instantia-tion seem plausible without some more robust assault on the steering media than communicative action accommodates. If Habermas is valuable in fleshing out a democratic politics, his methodology and the practices he advocates would both, then, need to be rendered far more dialectical; more attuned to an ineliminable negativity *and* to its contemporary suppression.

It is undoubtedly true that the mobile rhythms and heterogeneous forms that Adorno chases in constellations and ruins offer an inappropriate model for a collectivist alternative and were not intended to offer one. Negativity must refuse any institutionalisation as a positive model of power; instead it implies a permanent process of critique. Here it remains forever the other side of, yet ineluctably tied to, power's positivist tendencies. It is not an alter-native to them. But negativity is not merely abstract negation or nihilism. As I have argued, its own practice reveals affirmative dimensions, while the contextuality of its immanent critiques suggests that where resistances are possible, it will discern and guide, even provoke, them. Nor is negative thinking tied to the particular situation Adorno addressed. Dialectical thinking itself entails certain indices (regarding relations between the mater-ial and conceptual, identity and non-identity, positive and negative, parts and whole; an insistence on sustaining difference while tracing the mediations that link each part to the totality and underpin an immanent critique of the latter), but the connections and possibilities it elicits will inevitably change. If liberal democracies today harbour emancipatory potential then dialectical thinking should discern them, but their realisation will depend on immanent criticism and efficacious interventions.

Similarly, while poststructuralists have rejected dialectics as insufficiently negative, the fluidities of postmodernity are yet amenable to dialectical analysis.[51] Because of the latter's attention to subject–object relations, such analysis can give weight to the sociological and economic analysis that poststructuralism has tended to preclude in its suspicion of the Real/real. But, given the fragmentation of postmodern society, dialectics would need to incline in the more genealogical direction that Adorno's methodology implies, acknowledging the impossibility of origins, the plurality of the strands it traces, the discontinuities of history and the undesirability of equating reconciliation with identity. Far from being anachronistic today, Adorno's negative thinking offers an agenda and a model for critical engagement in the present.

6

SUBJECTIVITY AND THE SEMIOTIC

Gendering negativity

In the previous chapter I considered Adorno practising negativity in pursuit of the primacy of the object. In this chapter I will explore the way psycho-analytically-informed theories infer negativity in relation to the subject. The focus will be primarily, although not exclusively, on Julia Kristeva, since in her earlier work especially (and in particular in her *Revolution in Poetic Language* (*La Révolution du Langage Poétique*, 1974)) she explicitly invoked negativity and related it to a radical politics.[1] Kristeva is usually read as a structuralist with poststructuralist tendencies. As such her work falls within an anti-humanist problematic. Despite a fascination with structural linguistics she was, however, reluctant to abandon the speaking, ethical subject, whose fate lies at the centre of her political interests. But, while her work engages with both Marxist and feminist concerns, the politics she advocates looks more postmodern in terms of the transgressive strategies and aesthetic practices she proposes, as opposed to their more collectivist concern with mass movements.[2] So far in this book I have implied that poststructuralist negativity is inimical to a politics, but discussion of Kristeva's work will allow me to present a more enthusiastic assessment of postmodern interventions. What is also novel in Kristeva's writing as far as the negativity discussed in previous chapters is concerned, is that her psychoanalytic approach provokes questions regarding its gendering. Is there any sense in which negativity might be designated feminine? And if so, what are its implications for sexual difference and for feminist politics? These questions will be addressed in the latter part of the chapter.

A materialist negativity

Subjects and objects

In chapter 2 I cited Kristeva's association of negativity with a 'fourth term' of the Hegelian dialectic. Beneath the triadic logic of negation she invokes a more mobile generativity, albeit one she credits Derrida and Freud with inciting more radically. Despite the importance to her work of Derridean *différance* and Lacanian psychoanalysis she nevertheless charges both with ignoring the instinctual bases of language, whose materiality she derives from a Freudian understanding of the drives (*pulsions*). If we recall from the previous chapter how Adorno had traced the historical mediations of subjectivity's appearing, then Kristeva defines her own task in part as evoking a more monumental process whereby subjectivity emerges from, and remains convulsed by, the rhythmic spasms of the organic. There is no onto-logical subject but a process which emanates from 'the *very movement of heterogeneous matter*' (RPL: 113). Subjects emerge psychically from this material world via processes of organisation and splitting which will eventu-ally allow them to posit and name a distinct domain of objects. But Kristeva shows that the way, and the degree to which, severance occurs will have profound implications for subjects' relations with themselves, with others and with their world. The process of establishing subjecthood is thus redo-lent with existential and ethical consequences; an alteration of its hegemonic patterning would have significant social effects.

It is essential to the interpretation pursued in this chapter that Kristeva's concerns here should be recognised as pertaining to two related levels. On the one hand she does focus on those pre-Œdipal, pre-symbolic stages where the infant remains in various states of symbiosis with the maternal body. This is what she calls the *semiotic*: a process where there is as yet no subject–object severance but where there is a pulsing of small fluctuations and splittings rather than undifferentiated plenitude. This is the forerunner to that more dramatic diremption which will eventually yield subjecthood with the acqui-sition of language and entry into the symbolic. It is in this semiotic mobility of pre-subject and pre-object that a bodily negativity plays as material gener-ativity; one whose rhythms are unconscious, pleasurable, destructive.

On the other hand, Kristeva is insistent that the semiotic is not simply infantile and pre-symbolic, nor is it wholly repressed with entry into the symbolic. If it were, it could not be invoked by the theorist since it would remain too radically other to the symbolic realm that thinking subjects inhabit. But the music of semiotic negativity yet haunts the mature psyche, such that the specular illusion of a unified ego succumbs to what Kristeva calls the subject-in-process (*un sujet en procès*), one infected with its own otherness. The instabilities it introduces are especially evident in certain borderline mental states and practices, among them avant-garde writing. The symbolic realm is thus prone to irruptions of the negativity that is its pre-condition (just as metaphysical language is vulnerable to the play of *différance*). Since Freud, Kristeva contends, the self has indeed been recog-nised as a 'strange land of borders and othernesses ceaselessly constructed and deconstructed' (SO: 191). Its invocation calls into question the (repres-sive, sacrificial) boundaries of subjectivity that two millennia of western culture have imposed and which capitalism and patriarchy both rely upon and reproduce.

Kristeva accordingly situates negativity both prior to and within the epistemological and political questions that arise from subject–object dualism. She asks about the process of that dyad's diremption and emergence rather than how knowledge might deal with an opposition which is for her a symptom of both theoretical misrepresentation and psychological denial. But the material anchoring of the movements and spacings that render negativity productive also distinguishes her work from poststructuralist approaches that locate negativity solely in the structure of language as a play of signifiers. This is why she is critical of deconstructive accounts that reduce negativity to its linguistic forms. Without recognition of instinctual heterogeneity, '*différance* would be confined within a nonrenewable, nonproductive redundancy, a mere precious variant within the symbolic enclosure: contemplation adrift' (RPL: 145). Ignoring the splittings that are outside the signifier, Derrida cannot account for ruptures in subjectivity and social structure, even a madness that might engulf them.

The structure of language nevertheless lies at the heart of Kristeva's thinking. For it is its acquisition that defines subjecthood and marks entry into the symbolic, whereupon the subject unconsciously submits to the social and signifying law, the Law of the Father, that governs it. The disruption of language and the deconstruction of identity are therefore intimately related. This in turn has political significance because different cultures register particular modulations of the symbolic law: the 'socio-symbolic contract' wherein the conditions of subjectivity and sociability are established.[3] Because instinctual economies and social systems are thus intimately linked, so are semiotic and political negativity. The psychic and symbolic status of subjects underpins the possibilities of intersubjective life.

Freudian energetics

In order to appreciate Kristeva's materialist negativity, an excursus into Freudian theory will be helpful. I will emphasise a number of arguments relevant to negativity here: Freudian energetics; the derivation of the psychic from matter; the language of the unconscious. Although critics usually focus on the inflection of Kristeva's psychoanalytic theory through Lacan's, the materialist premises of his predecessor remain crucial to her thinking.

In 1895 Freud had worked briefly on a pre-psychoanalytical *Project for a Scientific Psychology*, where he attempted to explain mental phenomena in physiological terms.[4] He was hoping, as he explained to Fliess, 'to discover what form the theory of psychical functioning will take if a quantitative line of approach, a kind of economics of nervous force', is pursued.[5] The system he tried to explain in such terms is set in motion by the efficacy of a force, Q, that flows along nerve cells, exciting (cathecting) them as it charges up or passes through them according to the laws of motion. This mobile quantum had been anticipated the previous year, when Freud had noted in *The Neuro-Psychoses of Defence* that

> in mental functions something is to be distinguished – a quota of affect or sum of excitation – which possesses all the characteristics of a quantity (though we have no means of measuring it), which is capable of increase, diminution, displacement and discharge, and which is spread over the memory-traces of ideas somewhat as an electrical charge is spread over the surface of a body.[6]

This hypothesis, he had added, 'can be applied in the same sense as physicists apply the hypothesis of a flow of electric fluid.'[7] It is this 'fluid' that appears in the *Project* as a displaceable energy that activates the nervous system. Although what it is a quantity of remained unspecifiable, mental phenomena were interpreted as its effects.

Freud speaks here of the nervous system as heir to 'the general irritability of protoplasm' and as especially receptive to intercellular stimuli that 'have their origin in the cells of the body and give rise to the major needs: hunger, respiration, sexuality'.[8] Although these operate continuously, they accumulate periodically to produce pain, thus inciting a response. Freud concludes that everything the nervous system inherits biologically is reducible to the threat of unpleasure, which 'remains the only means of education'.[9] In psychoanalysis proper, Q would reappear as specifically psychic energy and its force would be designated instinctual, with the instincts providing a bridge between psyche and soma. But Freud could never decide whether he was speaking of a real, efficacious force that might one day be measured and whose origin was bio-chemical (a 'not-yet'), or a heuristic and figurative idea (an 'as-if').[10] His energetics would remain undecidable between physics and metaphysics. In 1895 he would have liked Q to combine the physical, organic and psychic realms in a single mechanics explained by Newtonian laws of motion,[11] but the challenge was to elicit the *difference* that could explain the novelty of mind. The neurological approach was soon deemed inappropriate and abandoned, but its energetics was retained.

Freud tried to identify a psychic domain in the *Project* by distinguishing between memory and perception. Hypothesising two types of neurone, he speculated that one would allow energy to pass freely through, thereby remaining unmarked and retaining a receptive capacity for new perceptions, while the other, lying closer to the body and thus unshielded from internal stimuli, would exert stronger resistance to energy flows due to contact barriers between cells. The consequent accumulation of Q would, he surmised, result in an inscription of memory traces: 'the perennially intact bareness of the perceptive surface' as opposed to 'the engraving of furrows'; the mirror versus the photographic plate.[12] Freud explains memory, then, in terms of resistances in certain cells. But if resistances were too rigid, the system would soon ossify. He thus infers a process whereby intensities and repetitions wear down some resistances to open facilitations between cells, thus yielding pathways between memory traces. Cathexes could now flow across memories, lighting them up like Christmas tree lights as they pass over permeable nerve cells. What is ungeneralisable is only *which* pathways will be established in any particular individual.

Kristeva will draw on this language of resistances and facilitations, for it is here that the generative difference which splits the unproductive swirling of matter, and forges what will become the subject, is located. But she was not the only theorist in France to take an interest in Freud's early work. The forming of psychic phenomena via plays of differential intensities had already suggested to anti-humanists that subjectivity might be explained in non-Cartesian terms, as continuous with torrential flows of energy and matter. Now consciousness and identity would remain precarious manifestations of an unconscious process whose machinic, non-representational logic was structured like a language. This is for example how Laplanche and Pontalis present the 1895 model:

> Freud attempts to account for the registration of the memory in the neuronal apparatus *without making any appeal to a resemblance between trace and object*. The memory-trace is simply a particular arrangement of facilitations, so organised that one route is followed in preference to another. The functioning of memory in this way might be compared to what is known as 'memory' in the theory of cybernetic machines, which are built on the principle of binary oppositions, just as Freud's neuronal apparatus is defined by its successive bifurcations.[13]
>
> (Laplanche and Pontalis, 1985: 248)

At each neuronal intersection, an excitation must take one path rather than the other, its 'choice' depending upon the facilitations left by preceding runs. Facilitation (*Bahnung*) is understood here 'as a process of differential opposition: a given pathway is only facilitated in proportion as the alternative one is not'. As such, the apparatus might be compared with the operation of language as analysed by structural linguistics: 'in both cases discontinuous units are organized into binary oppositions.'

Derrida is similarly interested in this equation but if the unconscious is structured like a language, it is that of *différance*. In 'Freud and the Scene of Writing', the German *Bahnung* is translated by him not as the Standard Edition's *facilitation* but as breaching (*frayage*), thereby preserving the sense of a force opening a pathway (*Bahn*), a spacing. Facilitation alone cannot explain memory, Derrida argues; what is important is its itinerary in selecting between paths of conduction. It is then 'the difference between breaches which is the true origin of memory, and thus of the psyche'.[14]

Laplanche notes that Freud's founding hypothesis of cells and energy flows comprised but 'a new version of what in Descartes, for example, is called figure and movement, or ... mass and energy.'[15] But in locating memory in an 'ungraspable and invisible difference between breaches', Derrida is able to lift Freudian energetics out of this hylomorphic model and to present it as a more radical negativity. Its rhythms are reminiscent of Nietzsche's will to power (according to the Deleuzean interpretation Derrida cites), where differential intensities between quanta describe a self-generative, self-morphing process, one whose effects remain, like subjectivity, complex and heterogeneous. In chapter 3 I identified this generativity with a specifically Nietzschean–Dionysian, productive–destructive negativity; a non-dialectical negativity whose choreography is akin to that of *différance*. In *Margins of Philosophy* Derrida indeed claims of Nietzsche and Freud that '[d]ifférance appears almost by name in their texts, and in those places where everything is at stake.' In Freud's case it is located in the 'energetics or economics of forces'. Through this energetics with its delays, discontinuities, repetitions and intervals, Derrida is then able to de-ontologise Freud's ambiguous scientism. 'Force is never present; it is only a play of differences and quantities.'[16] In this sense the unconscious is a radical alterity, another scene that never was, and could never be made, present.

When Freud mapped the psyche, he translated the distinction between neuronal types into id and ego and distinguished between two modulations of energy, as primary and secondary process. The primary process, which described the energetics of the unconscious, is the unregulated pleasure principle at work: freely-mobile energy moving across the system; the frenetic circulating of affect seeking rapid discharge and hence the diminution of pain. This is distinguished from a secondary process, associated with the ego and reality principle, where energy is bound, quiescent and inhibits the mobility of the primary process while itself 'obeying quite different mechanical conditions'. Freud suggests that 'thinking' is originally of the former type; pre-verbal and unconscious, it merely establishes relations between impressions of objects. But ideas that are subsequently pushed–pulled into the unconscious will also have their associative links subjected to the strange logic of the primary process, as revealed in dreams. In the dynamic unconscious as it is constituted by 'repression proper', ideas take on 'extreme forms of expression' since they are charged with impulsive intensities and released into an uninhibited play of phantasy.[17] Although pure primary process thinking would be inimical to survival itself, Freud insisted that it persists in maturity and civilisation despite being overlain by the secondary process.

Energy that obeys the pleasure principle will follow associative connections that yield the shortest route to discharge; it will not linger over the bonds which grammar or logic insist upon in the secondary process, but flash across images associated with the object of desire, perhaps by contiguity or symbolic similarity. Its morphology looks more aesthetic than rational, for such is the poetics that tracks the economics, where a bizarre, imagistic syntax corresponds with the flows of freely-mobile energy.[18] The most characteristic feature of this primary process is displacement. Psychic intensity is displaced from one idea to another, so an image and its affect become mismatched, and there is also a metonymic process of substitutions along the associative chain, such that images can stand for one another. Condensation feeds off displacement to compress several images into one, thus granting them an intensity and multi-dimensionality lacking in the original. 'It is this that is mainly responsible for the bewildering impression made on us by dreams, for nothing at all analogous to it is known to us in mental life that is normal and accessible to consciousness.'[19] The unconscious knows no space/time; no contradiction or negation ('in analysis we never discover a "no" in the unconscious'[20]). It is radically un-Kantian.

Dream interpretation tries to reconstruct the dream's pathways through free association (the mode of conscious analysis whose logic most resembles the primary process), in order to explain the origin of symptoms. Freud sometimes suggested that dreams pose 'no greater difficulties to their translators than do the ancient hieroglyphic scripts to those who seek to read them'.[21] Their symbols only require transcription. Although the unconscious favours superficial linkages ('assonance, verbal ambiguity, temporal coincidence without connection in meaning, … any association of the kind that we allow in jokes or in play upon words', where no 'connection is too loose, no joke too bad, to serve as a bridge from one thought to another'), he insists that such associations always correspond to deeper but resisted connections that can be reconstructed to yield their underlying significance. Even so, since the psyche is a 'factory of thoughts' and since each association is overdetermined, it is impossible to exhaust the strange and myriad chains of association the dream deploys.[22]

There is moreover some tension between this representational logic and the energetics (i.e. precisely where Freud's materialism and Cartesianism, body and mind, impulse and image, meet; a hiatus papered over yet revealed in his shifting formulations of the instincts, which in this sense play a bridging role similar to the imagination in Kant's account of the faculties). For Freud also suggests that memory traces are only vehicles, or empty signifiers, that switch and facilitate energy flows in an economy of desire. This is an inaccessible language, immune to transcription; one that speaks the chaotic and impulsive language of the body. 'The dream-work is not simply more careless, more irrational, more forgetful and more incomplete than waking thought; it is completely different from it qualitatively and for that reason not immediately comparable with it.'[23] He now claims that the primary process less obtrudes an irrational or inexhaustible mode of association than replaces association itself with a jumble of unrelated bits and pieces. Memory traces merely provide the raw stuff of the dream, its '*subject-matter*' but not its '*mutual relations*'. Now the content and meaning of psychical elements are 'treated as of little consequence' and words are regarded as things, not signs. In the dream work, 'elements are turned about, broken into fragments and jammed together – almost like pack-ice'.[24] Freud goes on to present the loss of logical (and temporal) connection not merely as the consequence of representational difficulties but, also, as characteristic of the unconscious itself, which marks a break in the signifying or causal chain. As Deleuze and Guattari would summarise its Lacanian version:

> The chains are called 'signifying chains' (*chaînes signifiantes*) because they are made up of signs, but these signs are not themselves signifying. The code resembles not so much a language as a jargon, an open-ended, polyvocal formation ... . These indifferent signs follow no plan, they function at all levels and enter into any and every sort of connection ... .[25]

The hermeneutical, as opposed to the energetic, dimensions of the primary process remain ambiguous, as does the significance of its negativity. Does this enrich and supplement meaning by speaking a corporeal music of desire – one that might be decoded, even liberated for creative, sensuous purposes of social renewal – or mark the ruin and limit of meaning, since the desiring machine is fundamentally inhuman? Is unconscious negativity more aesthetic or sublime? The ambiguity itself seems to harbour the tension between Eros and the death drive.

In any case, the secondary process is quite different. Now energy is more bound to particular objects; satisfaction, if more secure, is also more attenuated since the original drive has been both delayed and neutralised. Laplanche writes:

> If it is not forgotten that what is at stake here are chains of ideas, the ego turns out to be what introduces into the circulation of fantasy a certain ballast, a process of *binding* which retains a certain energy and causes it to stagnate in the fantasmic system, preventing it from circulating in an absolutely free and mad manner. Such is the appearance of the *secondary process* ... .[26]

The conscious mind is constituted by negation – taboo, denial, repression – and it is also here that negation operates as logic and judgement. In other words, *if the primary process is a register of negativity, the secondary one is the order of negation*. For it is here that thinking follows the laws of syntax, reason, causality. In Kantian terms it thinks categorically, even though it still falls indirectly under the motivation of the pleasure principle and its hegemony remains a hazardous process rather than a transcendental principle. It must try to avoid primary process associations with their excess even if, as Freud notes, this aim 'is rarely attained', so that 'our thinking always remains exposed to falsification by interference from the unpleasure principle'.[27]

The dynamics of, and relations between, the primary and secondary processes are in turn broadly equivalent to those between the semiotic and the symbolic in Kristeva's work, where Freud's insistence on the unresolved relationship between unconscious and conscious is caught in her definition of the split subject as 'in-process'. Freud himself came to regard the unconscious as a virtual reality he could only infer negatively through its absence of conscious phenomena,[28] but he also insisted that its logic of wish fulfilment is apparent to rational thought because it irrupts there, in for example the parapraxes that disturb language but, also, in creative (sublimated) practices where primary process logic is put in the service of culture. As Lacan explains: 'Impediment, failure, split. In a spoken or written sentence something stumbles. Freud is attracted by these phenomena, and it is there that he seeks the unconscious. There, something other demands to be realized ... .'[29]

Regarding the negative/positive trope of critical thinking, it is now possible to be more explicit about the ways the unconscious figures negativity: a negativity that primary process logic evinces in a constellation of senses. Like will to power or dialectics, its rhythmic mobility marks the possibility and subversion of all static, reified identities; of every fixed position or unity. But this is a wilder negativity than dialectics since it engenders and refuses any law. Here is generativity through difference; a radical alterity which is at once other and lack, incomprehensible yet interruptive, virtual regarding its ontology yet actual in its effects; both a repressed or unrealised potential and a transgressive force with destructive as well as reconstructive sociopolitical implications. If the unconscious knows no negation, its cultural irruption has a negative force since it subverts its own exclusion as off-limits: the denial (and its failure) on which the symbolic, like Kantian knowledge, depends.[30]

Some of these senses underlie Deleuze and Guattari's *Anti-Œdipus*. If they are hostile to the figure of the negative here, this is in the senses that psychoanalysis both locates negation in the secondary process and allowed this negation to distort its own description of the unconscious. So much is clear from Foucault's Preface, where he writes that '*Anti-Œdipus* is an *Introduction to the Non-Fascist Life*' and lists among its principles: withdrawal of allegiance 'from the categories of the Negative (law, limit, castration, lack, lacuna)' and preference for 'what is positive and multiple, difference over uniformity, flows over unities, mobile arrangements over systems.'[31] The authors want to free this latter negativity ('positive' *qua* generative, affirmative in a Nietzschean sense) from the more positivist formulation the later Freud gave it, as well as from its own repression in philosophy and society. Freud's own suppression of desire under the triangulated Œdipal drama is viewed here as analogous to Hegel's subordinating the 'fourth term' of the dialectic to its triadic structure. Via their schizanalysis, Deleuze and Guattari would accordingly release an *anœdipal*, molecular unconscious and its desiring production from the castrated state and restricted economy to which Œdipus condemns it. Such was, they insist, the unconscious invoked in *The Interpretation of Dreams*: 'what Freud and the first analysts discover is the domain of free syntheses where everything is possible; endless connections, nonexclusive disjunctions, nonspecific conjunctions, partial objects and flows. The desiring-machines pound away and throb in the depths of the unconscious.'[32]

With Freud's 'discovery' of the Œdipus complex, however, this negativity was crushed: the productivity of the unconscious was subordinated psychically to the Law (the incest taboo and the repressions it entails) and psychoanalytically, to a hermeneutics which reads its effects as representations of a familial drama under the sign of the phallus.

> Free association, rather than opening onto polyvocal connections, confines itself to a univocal impasse. All the chains of the unconscious are biunivocalized, linearized, suspended from a despotic signifier. The whole of desiring-*production* is crushed, subjected to the requirements of *representation*.[33]

The anœdipal unconscious remains factory rather than theatre and is again reminiscent of will to power (and Freud's *Project*) in its circulating intensities and affects. This is an unconscious free of the Œdipal drama; 'it does not symbolize any more than it imagines or represents; it engineers, it is machinic.' Just as it never wholly disappeared from Freud's work, so its dynamism remains irrepressible: 'flows ooze, they traverse the triangle, breaking apart its vertices. The Œdipal wad does not absorb these flows, any more than it could seal off a jar of jam or plug a dike.'[34] The schizo who follows its decoded flows intrudes a profoundly subversive process into the social, scrambling all its codes as it shifts rapidly between them. It is a way of refusing the established order with its repressions and bureaucracies, its territories, codes and boundaries. For Œdipus is not just an inner event but the figure of power as such: an inner colonisation that penetrates the unconscious so that social authority will be better recognised outside. 'The prime function incumbent upon the socius has always been to codify the flows of desire, to inscribe them, to record them, to see to it that no flow exists that is not properly dammed up, channelled, regulated.' The schizo that rejects such codification remains at that 'unbearable point where the mind touches matter and lives its every intensity'.[35]

Kristeva cites Deleuze and Guattari as inspiration in her introduction to *Revolution* (RPL: 17). There are indeed similarities in their psychopolitical projects and in the unconscious dyamics they invoke to this end. But while their aim was to take Freud somewhere he glimpsed yet refused to go – beyond the Law, beyond guilt, beyond the father – Kristeva would remain more Lacanian in her insistence that negativity means transgression, not rejection, of the phallocentric Law (this will also distinguish her work on sexual difference from, for example, Irigaray's or Cixous's). Like the social contract theorists, she believes that without the Law there is only a destructive state of nature, with madness its psychic equivalent. Cultural and political radicalism will take place along the porous boundary where the Law and its other meet, not on its other side. This is where Kristeva's thinking remains closer to dialectics: negativity is socially efficacious only where positive and negative meet and, if subjectivity entails sacrifice, liberation does not entail its dissolution into the flows of the virtual.

Semiotic negativity

It should now be more evident why Kristeva calls pre-Œdipal operations a negativity. The differentiations, splittings and repetitions from which subjectivity will emerge are already materially operative through the drive energy that pulses in what she calls the semiotic *chora*. This is a 'rhythmic space', 'an essentially mobile and extremely provisional articulation constituted by movements and their ephemeral stases' (RPL: 25; PH: 14). It is, in other words, the site of a negativity whose dynamism comes from the drives' 'rupture and articulation' as they invest the organs and orifices of the fragmented body with instinctual resonance and lend the flows of desire a somatic patterning. This semiotic process

> is articulated by flow and marks: facilitation, energy transfers, the cutting up of the corporeal and social continuum as well as that of signifying material, the establishment of a distinctiveness and its ordering in a pulsating *chora*, in a rhythmic but nonexpressive totality.
>
> (RPL: 40)

This dynamic is facilitated by the drives' own dualistic, contradictory nature: as life and death instincts they are respectively assimilating and destructive, positive and negative, oral and anal, such that the semiotised body is itself 'a place of permanent scission' (RPL: 27, 28). There is therefore a fundamental tension although one as yet yielding no more than a monotonous process of charge and discharge – a 'mere scattering of traces' (RPL: 68) – where no enduring form (subject) is yet engendered but where expenditure is modified by repetition and hence a certain inertia. The

> term 'drive' denotes waves of attack against stases, which are themselves constituted by the repetition of these charges; together,

charges and stases lead to no identity (not even that of the 'body proper' [*corps propre*]) that could be seen as a result of their functioning. That is to say that the semiotic *chora* is no more than the place where the subject is both generated and negated, the place where his unity succumbs before the process of charges and stases that produce him. We shall call this process of charges and stases a *negativity* ... .

(RPL: 28)

Recall for a moment Freud's derivation of the psychic in his *Project* but, also, the early Nietzsche's sense of the Dionysian, where life's formless excess required differentiation in order to appear. Without this Apollinian dimension it would have remained mere expenditure, and so it is with the drives. They would merely circulate as energy quanta were they not to acquire some organisation and this begins with the discontinuity and repetition that Kristeva refers to as movement and stasis, where the drives are both energy charges and '"psychical" marks' (RPL: 25).

Despite this organic fecundity, the drives are also socially structured and never simply biological. For it is the maternal body that divides to nurture then release the corpus which will over time become a new subject under the Law of the Father. Preparatory to that stage, the mother regulates the drives. There is both fusion and refusal of mother and child, since the presence or absence of the breast, and more generally the mother's control over what enters or leaves the infantile body, already organises the oral and anal drives, inscribing there the patterns that will yield to symbolism but which are as yet more musical, spatial. Because the mother is herself situated within the Law and brings familial, cultural norms to bear, the drives have a social dimension from the start, but their organisation occurs first through a bodily, gesturing, signing operation made possible by the joining of the flesh and the intonations and rhythms of the mother's voice. In other words, there is already a material prohibition and identification operative prior to language, a bio-logic, a maternal law that 'logically and chronologically' precedes the paternal law and which is the register of the semiotic.[36] Here there is a literal singing of the flesh, where 'meaning' (*significance*) and matter, sign and desire, are not (yet) severed but where negativity does entail a certain rhythmic lawfulness that lends to energy flows an economy of libidinal/sadistic patterning and to pre-linguistic life, a musical cadence.

> What I call 'the semiotic' is a state of disintegration in which patterns appear but which do not have any stable identity: they are blurred and fluctuating. The processes which are at work here are those which Freud calls 'primary': processes of transfer. We have an example of this if we refer once again to the melodies and babblings of infants which are a sound image of their bodily instability.[37]

This pre-Œdipal negativity is paradigmatically exhibited during the anal phase, through a process of *rejection* which is one of the primary material splittings portending the subject. The infant experiences an excess of matter within itself and expels it, thereby establishing an outside to its body yet one which comes from within and therefore remains ambiguous. Rejection is 'the key moment shattering unity' (RPL: 147) but it is not simply a moment of loss, because the process of discharge eroticises the body's sphincters such that the rejection of bodily substances is also an experience of pleasure. It is therefore a stage *en route* to the subject's separation from the object world, where absent objects will be replaced by abstract signs and their loss will be devoid of *jouissance*. But it also indicates a more hazardous, reversible subject–object relation than the symbolic will sanction, where the pre-Œdipal child struggles to come to terms with an exteriority that is not yet definitive but endlessly repeated. This negativity is then a rhythm of small differences; a drama not of lack but of recuperable losses and repetitions. The oppositions and spaces of negation, identity and difference, are as yet only prefigured within the density and mobility of the flesh, but the resurrection of its rhythms subsequently will endanger the clear boundaries society insists upon.

Kristeva later added a further process of pre-symbolic splitting to rejection, which she called *abjection*. Abjection is even more archaic and adverse to definitive boundaries.

> We are no longer within the sphere of the unconscious but at the limit of primal repression that, nevertheless, has discovered an intrinsically corporeal and already signifying brand, symptom, and sign: repugnance, disgust, abjection. There is an effervescence of object and sign – not of desire but of intolerable significance; they tumble over into non-sense or the impossible real, but they appear even so in spite of "myself" (which is not) as abjection.
>
> (PH: 11)

Closer yet to a union with matter, abjection suggests a primitive attempt at forging corporeal boundaries and remains a pre-condition of narcissism. But separation is painful and undertaken only reluctantly, since the death drive always pushes for the passive plenitude of uterine symbiosis, even the inorganic. In the symbolic, abjection will again intrude in experiences of what 'disturbs identity, system, order. What does not respect borders, positions, rules. The in-between, the ambiguous, the composite' (PH: 4).

If rejection as negativity will interrupt the symbolic as a radical promise of transgression and pleasure, abjection is a more sinister reminder to subjects of their uncanniness, the point at which death infects life and life dissolves into 'heterogeneous flux'. Neither subject nor object, the abject is a frontier which both repels and fascinates: it 'draws me toward the place where meaning collapses'. It confronts us with our fragility, 'where man strays on the territories of the *animal*' (PH: 2, 12). It fills us with primal dread (as conveyed by Sartre's *Nausea*) as a permanent threat to the clean and proper body of Œdipalisation; as such it is held at bay by various rituals and taboos. Kristeva relates it to xenophobia, arguing that we will begin to accept foreigners only when we learn to love the stranger within ourselves; when we remain open to the ambiguities of our subjective identities rather than finding them threatening and projecting them on to others.[38] But abjection threatens annihilation rather than the fecundity of splitting and inscribing that marks rejection (PH: 6f). The abject character is a deject, a stray who neither belongs nor refuses, as opposed to the subject-in-process who lives a semiotic–symbolic dialectic, accepting the Law in order to transgress it and thus adopting a more political stance.

Before it can enter the symbolic, the infant's drive energy must become organised. Fleeting, cathected psychical imprints will be transformed into abstract signs organised grammatically and more or less devoid of instinctual investment. Following Lacan, Kristeva acknowledges that the mirror and Œdipal phases will be crucial in the evolution of this speaking subject. During the mirror phase, semiotic negativity begins to surrender to a process of identification and unity as the fragmentary proto-subject mis-recognises itself in its specular image. The crucial rupture however occurs during what she calls a thetic phase, which is a break between the semiotic and symbolic registers that occurs between the mirror and Œdipal phases. In the thetic, the subject acquires the secondary process. The rupture it brings between semiotic and symbolic is also the severance of subject and object and of signifier and signified, oppositions that will subsequently be frozen in the subject-predicate, metaphysical structure of grammar and the (partial) repression of negativity. The thetic is thus the deepest structure of the possibility of enunciation according to Kristeva, the threshold of language and constitutive of the subject (RPL: 44f, 62). But crucially, it is also a traversable boundary. Kristeva suggests that disorders in the mirror stage, or a resistance to the discovery of castration, will be conducive to this transgression. The dialectics of fragile boundaries that are made and unmade, already prefigured in abjection and rejection where negativity figures as ambiguity and transgression, thus continues in the symbolic where it is the latter's own limits that are ceaselessly challenged.

Why, in conclusion, does Kristeva call the semiotic a negativity? I have partially answered this question by associating it with the promiscuous, self-generative rhythms described by Freud and Nietzsche; rhythms whose pulsing both subverts illusions of subjective unity and threatens the symbolic's boundaries which sustain identity by repressing desire and the body. There is however a further dimension to be considered, since Kristeva herself says she derives the term from Hegel. As we saw in chapter 2, it is precisely a generative mobility she credits Hegel with recognising; such is the dialectic's 'fourth term' that 'reformulates the static *terms* of pure abstraction as a process, dissolving and binding them within a mobile law' (RPL: 109). As such, Hegel presented a radical and subversive philosophy. 'Hegelian negativity prevents the immobilization of the thetic, unsettles doxy, and lets in all the semiotic motility that prepares and exceeds it' (RPL: 112). He glimpsed the instability that negativity's process guaranteed and, in this sense, Kristeva presents her own work as 'the direct successor of the dialectical method'.[39]

His idealism however prevented Hegel from eliciting 'the scission that exceeds and precedes the advent of thetic understanding' (RPL: 115). This is where Freudian materialism allows negativity to be thought as 'the trans-subjective, trans-ideal, and trans-symbolic movement found in the *separation of matter*' (RPL: 113). Yet not just any generativity is negative in the dialectical sense that Kristeva signals by using the term. Since the negative cannot be positively conceptualised and no final synthesis is possible, it is in fact resistant to the Hegelian project and in this sense Kristeva confesses that it is a poor name for the semiotic process, precisely because of its association with logical negation, where it is strictly thetic.[40] It is primary process negativity in its economic, not logical, sense that she invokes: a spatial, non-symbolised negativity operative not via contradiction but through '*infinitessimal differentiation*' (RPL: 121).

But what Kristeva retains from dialectics, besides its emphasis on a process whose modulations are those of identity and difference, is the equation between this choreography and the production of the ethical subject, as well as its related insistence on a dialectical interweaving of the conceptual and the real, reason and its other. For the matrix of the *chora* is not constituted by simply random and repetitive flows, but is a site of processes that will yield the (reasoning, social) subject and the realm of meaning. The infant must deny part of itself in order to become a self. On thereby entering culture, the subject nevertheless remains internally dialectical inasmuch as the thetic boundary is porous. The subject in-process/on trial is caught in the psychical and social dynamics of the Law and its other: a dynamic in which radical philosophy and avant-garde culture(/postmodern literature) participate at a meta-level.

It is this dialectic between reason and alterity which then allows Kristeva to negotiate the representational problem negativity poses, while presenting the (postmodern) challenge of signification as being 'to blaze a trail amidst the unnamable' (PM?: 141). When negativity is provoked from within the symbolic it marks a transgression of the Law and Kristeva clearly wants to keep this politically radical sense of the dialectic as a critical, negative politics. As she laments of Melanie Klein: despite recognising the importance of the pre-Œdipal body, she failed to link it dialectically with the post-Œdipal subject (RPL: 22). It is then the engagement of the negative in the positive, not negativity *per se*, as sheer process, that interests her. Although

semiotic functioning can be defined as the articulation of facilitations and stases that mean nothing, this mechanism must
immediately be considered within the signifying chain instituted by
the thetic. Without this new *dialectic*, a description of this functioning might eventually be related to the semiotic *chora* preceding
the mirror stage and the Œdipal stage, but not to *a signifying practice that is anti-Œdipal to the extent that it is anti-thetic and
para-doxical.*

(RPL: 81–2 (final emphasis added))

This is where psychoanalysis and politics, negativity and negation, meet.

Negativity and its representation

Kristeva's invocations of negativity present a familiar problem: how to avoid
either the Kantian aporia (to rule this alterity off-limits, even while positing
it) or the Hegelian reduction (to render it rational and thereby suppress its
alterity). How is the subject positioned within the symbolic to recognise or
express this pre-linguistic negativity and by what means might it be repre-
sented theoretically? I propose to explain how Kristeva negotiates this
dilemma by using the two frames of reference mentioned above: one dialectical and the other Nietzschean.

The difficulty is that while negativity is a concept, hence an idealisation
produced by the subject whose 'indelible trace' it bears, it is a concept that
nevertheless points back to the heterogeneous place of its own production.
When language struggles to articulate this, it finds itself confined to a terminology of identity and difference that cannot replicate the semiotic's
dynamism and heterogeneity. Derrida recognises this, for example, in
conceding that *différance* can never replace metaphysical language which is
at best displaced by deconstructive interventions. Hegel had confronted a
similar problem in trying to present dialectics: as we saw, Adorno claimed he
tried to finesse it stylistically (chapter 5), while Kojève suggested Hegel
resorted to a distinction between three dialectical tiers (chapter 2). Although
both finally judged Hegel's strategies a failure, it will be helpful to begin by
interpreting Kristeva as deploying the latter tactic, describing a dialectic of
materiality and 'meaning' on three levels while presenting each as dialectically related overall. For her there is no bar between signifier and signified
because the subject-in-process bridges the gap.

First, there is then the pre-thetic, material negativity where the drives are
already semiotically patterned to evince a pre-symbolic *signifiance*, an
economy of pleasure and loss sustained through a logic of small differences
as a 'fairly rudimentary combinatorial system'. It is true that subjects cannot
regress to it without becoming mad, but it is not simply a mute plenitude
and nor are its rhythms wholly absent from the symbolic. Second, there is

the transition to language, whereby the child chronologically enters the symbolic but, because it is an embodied subject-in-process, enters a signifying order which still evinces a dialectic between abstract and semiotic registers, both of which are in some sense potentially available to it (grammatically in the first case, musically and sensuously in the second). The latter can still be heard in the cracks and silences, the rhythms and confusions, which betray the split, incomplete nature of the ego. In short, there is a rudimentary dialectic internal to both semiotic and symbolic levels and the two are also dialectically linked because *we* are in-process, embodied as well as rational, unconscious and conscious. There is no simple, linear progression that cuts the spoken or conceptual off from what preceded it. This dialectical resolution is then structurally similar to Merleau-Ponty's or Adorno's: for them, too, language operated in two registers, the latent/mimetic and the manifest/classifying. These are equivalent to what Kristeva respectively calls its 'genotext' and 'phenotext'. Within the system of abstract signs, the materiality of the flesh still sings the rhythms of rejection and desire, as exemplified by avant-garde literature.

The *theorisation* of this negativity, however, entails a third level, where a phenotextual meta-language conceptualises the entire process (whence Hegel allegedly succumbed to positivism and Adorno practises a negative dialectics while acknowledging its paradoxes). The problem of this tier has been revived by poststructuralists in so far as they have adopted a broadly Kantian and anti-Hegelian position, placing the Real off-limits to conceptual thinking (although not necessarily to alternative performative strategies) in order to preserve its negativity as alterity, heterogeneity, while denying it ontological or originary standing.

It is from this perspective that Judith Butler has criticised Kristeva, accusing her of presenting the semiotic as a 'prediscursive libidinal economy'. In so far as its negativity enjoys an 'ontological status prior to language', Butler challenges its credibility or knowability, arguing that Kristeva both posits the drives as causes of the poetic language from which they are then elicited, thereby engaging in an illegitimate circularity, and transgresses the prohibition on accessing the pre-discursive.[41] She thus poses a question that goes to the heart of negativity, namely, is it a real, efficacious process which we struggle to understand and articulate because it is outside reason, or is it a discursive construct that reason itself proposes and reproduces in various forms, as the excluded other required to guarantee its own identity? Butler raises the political stakes of this question by showing its implication in games of power and I will return to her challenge later, when discussing sexual difference.

Kristeva is certainly aware of the problems of regressing to pre-critical metaphysics and performative contradiction, for she addresses them several times. Most baldly, she is emphatic that, even if the affective can only be grasped via discourse, it 'would be semantic empiricism to believe that it does not in some fashion exist outside it' (RPL: 162). But she generally follows Freud's agnosticism regarding the instincts, acknowledging that 'the semiotic that "precedes" symbolization is only a *theoretical presupposition* justified by the need for description', although denying that it is 'solely an abstract object produced for the needs of theory' (RPL: 50, 68). Rather than trying to satisfy some realist criterion of scientific evidence, I think she has in mind that objectivity is best established at this metapsychological level by reference to the internal logic of the theory. Thus she presents castration fantasy and penis envy as 'a priori hypotheses intrinsic to the theory itself': while they can attract no empirical proof, and in this sense remain an 'article of faith', they are the pre-condition for understanding (and treating) the neurotic discourse whose identification presupposes and replicates this logic (WT: 197). In this sense the truth of psychoanalysis both is and is not internal to it.

Further reflections appear where Kristeva considers her own approach of a scientific semiotics (*sémanalyse*) and these are reminiscent of Merleau-Ponty's call for a phenomenology of phenomenology. Kristeva argues here that any theory of signification must work self-critically and reflexively (i.e. dialectically), aware that it is part of, and subject to, the process it articulates. Semiotics is thus described as an 'endless theoretical process'; 'an open form of research'; a 'constant critique that turns back on itself and offers its own autocritique.' In presenting a theory it must consider the very conditions of theoretical production, within which process it then situates itself, such that 'semiotics can only exist as a *critique of semiotics*.' Neither systematic nor teleological, it is 'a place of dispute and self-questioning, a "circle" that remains open.'[42] In seeking a productivity prior to the laws of production governing communication or commodity exchange, a new science is needed for exploring this other scene. Focusing on the very dynamics of generativity itself, semiotics 'rebels against representation even as it uses representative models, and overthrows the very formalization that gives it substance with an unstable theory of the unrepresentable and the unmeasurable.'[43] It simultaneously emphasises the alterity of its object and enacts an epistemological upheaval, calling into question the very idea of meaning with the 'intensity of white heat that set categories and concepts ablaze – sparing not even discourse itself' (DL: vii).

Kristeva is aware nevertheless that even such self-reflexive pursuits remain problematic in so far as they use communicative means to invoke a non-communicable register. In response she suggests an irreducible plurality of signifying processes, each with its own productive logic. Avant-garde literature exemplifies one such process and a privileged one, too, since its texts demonstrate performatively the process of meaning production as it is enacted in writing. A dual strategy is therefore summoned: a scientific but dialectical process of theory production on the one hand; a textual practising/exhibiting of meaning production on the other. Each is in its own way both a self-conscious presentation of negativity (the third dialectical level, facilitated by the second) *and* a demonstration of its generativity (the first level dialectic from within the second). Literary practice is more exemplary, but it still needs a scientific supplement in order to bring out negativity's radical significance. This is why

> a semiotics of production must tackle these [literary, modernist] texts precisely in order to join a scriptural practice concerned with its own production to a scientific thought in search of production. And it must do so in order to bring out all the consequences of such a confrontation, that is, the reciprocal upheavals which the two practices inflict on one another.[44]

It is only after all for the already-constituted subject (i.e. at the second-level dialectic) that the semiotic's repression appears as a sacrifice to be reconfigured. It is because of this dialectic and its different, but interwoven, levels that Kristeva's work does evince a circularity but not of the vicious and contradictory type that Butler charges. As she warns early on, repeating Merleau-Ponty's and Adorno's strictures against naming the dialectic,

> since it is itself a metalanguage, semiotics can do no more than postulate this heterogeneity: as soon as it speaks about it, it homogenizes the phenomenon, links it with a system, loses hold of it. It specifically can be preserved only in the signifying practices which set off the heterogeneity at issue ... .[45]

These practices are aesthetic and this is where I discern a more radical response to the problem of representation, one that is closer to Nietzsche's. In chapter 3 I associated his quest for the Dionysian with a dual strategy: on the one hand a discursive approaching of negativity via a variety of language games; on the other, the beginnings of a Dionysian singing in *Zarathustra*, which performs negativity by emulating its rhythms of creativity and destruction. In Kristeva's terms, these suggest two different signifying practices, or economies, each evincing its own particular semiotic–symbolic dialectic but with the latter giving considerably more voice to the semiotic. Similarly in her own work, she argues that the provisional theorisation of negativity must be supplemented by its performance: the aesthetic practices she associates with the avant-garde(/postmodern).

To some extent psychoanalysis already practises this dualism, in so far as it is both a (metapsychological) theory and a clinical practice wherein the analyst hears the genotext speaking through the analysand's faltering prose:

> semiotic functioning is discernible before the mirror stage, before the first suggestion of the thetic. But the semiotic we find in

213

signifying practices always comes to us after the signifying thesis, after the symbolic break, and can be analysed in psychoanalytic discourse as well as in so-called 'artistic' practice.

(RPL: 68)

Accordingly, the 'theory of the unconscious seeks the very thing that poetic language practices within and against the social order: the ultimate means of its transformation or subversion, the precondition for its survival and revolution' (RPL: 81). The political import of Kristeva's concerns is explicit here, but where she differs from Nietzsche is that she merely directs our attention to performances of negativity and their significance rather than enacting them herself (although she does begin to experiment stylistically, for example in 'Stabat Mater'). In her Preface to *Desire in Language* she draws readers' attention to the essays' changing style, but notes that 'this does not go so far as identifying theoretical discourse with that of art – causing theory to be written as literary or para-literary fiction' – since while there is a strong 'post-Heideggerian temptation' to do so, 'the choice I have made is entirely different.' While acknowledging that her discourse might be labelled metaphysical, she nevertheless insists that it evinces a passion, a desire, for language (DL: ix). When asked subsequently what makes her work that of a woman, Kristeva refers precisely to a dual approach of performativity and theorisation: it is to 'draw attention to that aspect of avant-garde work ['experimentation with each of the dual boundaries of sexual difference'] which dissolves identities (including sexual identities) and try in my theoretical work to oppose those metaphysical theories that censure what I have just defined as "woman".'[46]

Since the ideological contents of discourse, as well as the structures of syntax, legitimise and sustain binary oppositions and repressions, subversion must proceed on both fronts. Both approaches are political in exposing and rendering vulnerable the sociosymbolic foundations of western culture. Practising negativity through semiotic irruption both prepares the way for more rational interrogation and social movements, and presents itself as a symptom of modernity's foundational crisis which it pushes further. For just as among Freud's patients analysis had no significant e(/a)ffect if its results were accepted merely on an intellectual level, so in radical aesthetic productions their message inscribes the signifying material with a drive investment that summons the subject's alterity in a way critical theory alone cannot (or, to put it in more explicitly political terms: it provokes questions about rational or gendered identity which deliberative democracy must take for granted).

Kristeva thus speaks of a 'third-degree negativity' (one that her favoured third generation of feminists will exemplify): not the absence of a no (as in the unconscious and difference feminism), nor a negative judgement (such as theory and consciousness, and egalitarian feminists, enact), but an irruption of negativity into the symbolic. Poetic language (and deconstructive gender performances) infuses another economy (semiotic rejection), recalling through its spatial and musical arrangements those processes prior to language and definitive subject–object splitting, when *signifiance* was first engendered within the body and its pleasures. Theorisation helps to explain why avant-garde or postmodern aesthetic practices are both an invocation of negativity and a politics of transgression. But in an important sense theory is always secondary to practical demonstrations and performances of negativity, even while itself containing traces of them. Avant-garde performativity is not simply regressive here: it evinces 'a "second" return of instinctual functioning within the symbolic, as a negativity introduced into the symbolic order and as the transgression of that order' (RPL: 69). 'This practice cannot be understood unless it is being carried out. To do so, the subject must abandon his *"meta-"*position, the series of masks or the semantic layer, and complete the complex path of *signifiance*' (RPL: 103). In renewing language, the speaker also renews the subject position within it.

In conclusion, then, we can see how the question of negativity's representation is not about Truth or an ability to reach the thing-in-itself, but concerns a dialectical circling through the very becoming of knowledge and subjectivity as they are practised. Kristeva's speaking subject can finesse this challenge precisely because it is in-process/on trial. The framework for understanding the problems of representing negativity is Hegelian (rational, dialectical, secondary process), but the strategies for doing so, and the rhythms they invoke, are more Nietzschean–Freudian (aesthetic, excessive, primary process).

Language, negativity and politics

In addressing the question of representation it has become evident that Kristeva's interest in negativity is primarily political. At this stage it will be helpful briefly to contextualise her politics as well as looking more explicitly at its connection with negativity. Kristeva shares the Frankfurt School's concerns about the positive, worrying that modernity has succumbed to cultural conformity and an 'over-encoding of economic rationality'; that its social and political institutions have become uniquely reified in their techno-cratic, capitalist orientation (PM?: 141). Indeed she agrees with Adorno *et al.* that capitalism has rendered direct incursions into its materially and socially oppressive structures almost impossible. But rather than perceiving a totality immune to negativity and endlessly reproducing itself, she argues that the terrain of radical politics has merely been displaced: onto signifying practices. Fortuitously, the development of imperious forces of production has allowed a relative relaxation of the *relations* of production and repro-duction, such that the sociocultural shackles which usually suppress subversive cultural movements are loosened. 'Imperialism produces its true grave digger in the non-subjected man, the man-process who sets ablaze and transforms all laws, including – and perhaps especially – those of signifying structures' (RPL: 105). This might be called the system's weakest link, since these practices are not ultimately separable from production, exchange and social order, which they underpin. This is then where scriptural negativity marks an efficacious intervention: the social function of avant-garde, or postmodern, texts is 'the production of a different kind of subject, one capable of bringing about new social relations, and thus joining in the process of capitalism's subversion' (RPL: 105). In this sense the avant-garde displaces the proletariat as the privileged 'agency' of negation for Kristeva but its wager is even more audacious: to prompt a renegotiation of the sociosymbolic contract itself.

The displacement of politics into the psychocultural realm, coupled with an emphasis on transgressive strategies and a timeframe that sees late modernity as only the culmination of a whole history of repression, renders Kristeva's politics recognisably postmodern. Like poststructuralists, she situates her antipathy towards capitalism within a broadly Nietzschean frame, discerning a nihilistic crisis that witnesses the crumbling of social and subjective structures whose foundations lie in two millennia of western culture. It is its metaphysical and sacrificial symbolic with its rigid binary (and especially sexual) oppositions, its representational ambitions, its repressive subjectivity, its theological delusions and sacrificial asceticism that for Kristeva, as for Nietzsche, is collapsing and summoning revaluation. The malaise of late modernity is manifest in the destabilisation of religion, state and family but it is underpinned, Kristeva insists, by a more pervasive fragmentation of the myths and 'master discourses' that sustain social cohesion and the unified, disciplined self (DL: 140). She shares this contention, that a politics of (inter)subjectivity is now at the top of any radical agenda, with other poststructuralists, such as Foucault. The challenge is to prevent this politics from collapsing into ethics.[47]

The politics of negativity Kristeva advocates finds itself historically facilitated and summoned by the new spaces and exigencies that a lethal combination of fragmentation and closure opens up. Although she privileges poetic language, she also cites psychedelic drugs, youth cultures, new music, comic strips, the awakening of non-western cultures, the non-verbal aesthetic practices of American experimental art and even artificial insemination, as symptoms and harbingers of this crisis.[48] For it is such activities, she contends, that are destabilising the symbolic systems wherein 'the Western subject, officially defined as a transcendental subject, has for two thousand years lived out its lifespan.'[49] No sociopolitical transformation is possible, she adds, that 'is not a transformation of the subject: which is to say its relation to social control, to *jouissance* and more fundamentally to language.'[50]

It is in precisely this context that Kristeva will then locate the women's movement at the forefront of politics, as even its 'most radical component'. For in challenging the boundaries of sexual difference, it also throws into question relations of reproduction, life and death, consciousness and body; that is, those boundaries which the western sociosymbolic contract has policed and the limits beyond which it has not dared previously to venture. Like other critical thinkers, Kristeva believes the symbolism that facilitates social order is intimately related to sacrifice: what 'is violent is the irruption of the symbol, killing substance to make it signify' (RPL: 75).[51] In asserting the poverty of discursive resources for expressing women's experiences of pleasure, pregnancy and motherhood, feminists accordingly contest the 'murder of soma' that founds subjectivity and intersubjectivity. Scriptural performances of semiotic negativity offer one strategy of contestation while at the same time injecting corporeal resonances into the patriarchal symbolic. In this sense feminism and the avant-garde have much in common. For what is revolutionary in poetic language is not simply its transgression of grammatical rules, but its subversion of the subject's positioning within the thetic. It re-enacts the very process whereby subjectivity and signification emerge out of the semiotic, although from within the safety of the symbolic. It thereby replaces the reified, post-Œdipal ego with the subject-in-process: one that might be positioned differently, speak from a different place, and enjoy a different, less dichotomous, relationship with the body, its objects, others. It 'sketches out a kind of second birth' (RPL: 70).

Kristeva always insists that this is an audacious but dangerous wager, since it plays along the very boundaries of subjectivity and could topple the artist into psychosis or the revolutionary into terrorism. Accordingly, 'textual experience represents one of the most daring explorations the subject can allow himself, one that delves into his constitutive process. But at the same time and as a result, textual experience reaches the very foundation of the social' which it might thereby transform or destroy. Such an aesthetics

> does not relinquish the thetic even while pulverizing it through the negativity of transgression. Indeed, this is the only means of transgressing the thetic, and the difficulty of maintaining the symbolic function under the assault of negativity indicates the risk that textual practice represents for the subject.
>
> (RPL: 69)

It is this risk that Kristeva subsequently identifies with postmodern literature. In touching the biological reservoir beneath language, it plays at the limits of communicable language and sexual identity, reaching into the primary narcissism where meaning and symbolism are themselves engendered in those first pulsings of splitting and negativity. Here is a 'practical knowledge' of the imaginary which does not reduce language to the abstractions of the sign. But Kristeva always insists that this is no romanticised

217

regression to archaic plenitude. In venturing into the 'darkest regions where fear, anguish, and a defiance of verbal clarity originate', contemporary writing dares to provoke the death drive (PM?: 137, 141). Its adventurers illicitly set sail, in the language of chapter 1, on Kant's 'wide and stormy ocean': in search of the dark continent. Yet, just as the theorist must avoid hypostatising either the pre-Œdipal (noumenal) phase it cannot know, or a symbolic register whose instinctual origins it denies, so the subject who practises negativity must avoid madness once he or she has avoided the immobilising effects of too firm a positioning in the symbolic. Kristeva makes this latter point, which amounts to an insistence that negativity should be practised only within the Law, many times. Closer to Lacan than to the anti-Œdipalists here, she insists that

> the subject must be firmly positioned by castration so that drive attacks against the thetic will not give way to fantasy or to psychosis but will instead lead to a 'second-degree thetic,' i.e. a resumption of the functioning characteristic of the semiotic *chora* within the signifying device of language. This is precisely what artistic practices, and notably poetic language, demonstrate.
>
> (RPL: 50)

Primary process, instinctual generativity cannot itself offer any alternative symbolic or redemption (its operations always remain heterogeneous to meaning and signs), nor a new foundation for intersubjectivity.[52] In a political, as well as a representational, sense it must remain a negativity. Within the symbolic its role is transgressive. Nevertheless the displacements it forges do open subjectivity and its sociosymbolic contract to a different symbolic–semiotic economy and if this would be less repressive, sacrificial, then negativity also plays an affirmative role in releasing less oppositional, more fluid relationships, a new ethics.[53]

Negativity and sexual difference

Kristeva's credentials as a feminist are not especially robust: critical of the limitations of the mainstream women's movement, she is in turn accused by its exponents of remaining both too Lacanian in her theory and too deconstructionist in her politics. In fact it is difficult to conclude that her interest was ever specifically feminist. But her theory is suffused with sexual difference because of its psychoanalytical approach, while the women's politics she commends is in many ways an application of the transgressive interventions she was extolling, to the movement temporarily in the vanguard of such a politics. Once this is acknowledged, her work does have interesting implications for gendered politics while posing some difficult questions regarding negativity and its relation to sexual difference, ontology and discourse.

What is psychoanalytically crucial in the establishing of sexual difference is that, on the one hand, subjectivity is engendered unconsciously through imaginary relations with the mother and father and, on the other, that the mark of difference is the phallus. Girls and boys do not therefore enter culture under the same terms and nor does culture grant them an equivalent place. Sexual difference thus enters into the history of each subject twice. First, the maternal body is repressed in accordance with the prohibitions of the Law of the Father (the incest taboo). What remains outside this Law is invoked (by it) as Other: a supplementary, excessive *jouissance* that resists the phallic logic of Œdipus (thus it is feminine). Second, the girl enters the symbolic at a relative disadvantage. This is in part because her Œdipal identifications are more difficult to negotiate, since to become a speaking subject she must identify with her father. But because the symbolic defines sexual difference according to the binary logic of the phallus, which recognises only the plus or minus of masculinity, she is also defined by it as castrated, as a lack. Accordingly Woman, as both excess and lack, is unrepresentable.[54]

Kristeva more or less follows this Lacanian schema, whose interpretation has itself remained controversial. Is it a narrative that successfully conveys the precarious psychic itinerary of the emergent subject and explains misogyny? Or is Woman's unrepresentability actually a discursive means of exclusion that patriarchal cultures sustain and in which psychoanalysis colludes? Moreover, the connections between unconscious codings, discursive schemas, cultural stereotypes, metaphors and actual women have been notoriously hard to establish. On some readings, Lacanian theory is dangerously binary and rigid, its message for women deeply fatalistic. But on others, its invocation of a *jouissance* outside the Law both promises transgression and points to a non-binary mobility that reveals the fragility of phallic and metaphysical definitions of sexual difference. Kristeva's work seems simultaneously to encompass each of these judgements, in particular by identifying negativity with the feminine. It is this latter association that now requires consideration.

The maternal body

The equation between negativity and the feminine is mediated by Kristeva through the figure of the maternal. To avoid misunderstanding, it seems crucial to distinguish between two aspects of it. For while on the one hand there is the maternal body, that material container which produces the foetus and nurtures the infant, on the other there is the woman's experience of motherhood. Despite a certain symmetry between them, the first operates in the semiotic register and is theoretically described from the perspective of the evolving subject, for whom the body remains as yet ungendered, while the second concerns the experiences of pregnancy and care that a gendered subject undergoes from her position under the Law. Although both dimensions are associated with negativity it is important not to conflate them, otherwise Kristeva seems to be anchoring negativity in an ontology of the mother's body and glorifying motherhood as a privileged destiny for women (charges feminists often indeed make).

Kristeva designates the semiotic *chora*, that space of generativity, maternal. But the maternal body is not itself the *ontological* limit of this rhythmic productivity, which flows from the differentiation of matter where the psychic fades into the somatic and the body sinks into the flux of genes and atoms in the void, 'the eternal recurrence of a biological rhythm which conforms to that of nature'. If this process is called feminine, it is only through convention (WT: 191). From a *psychoanalytic* perspective it is not, however, insignificant that it is the mother's body that nurtures and encodes the infantile corpus, and which must be surrendered. For the infant this is the specific site of semiotic processes of pleasure and loss. Kristeva worries about confusion between the maternal and the female body, since this results in a misogynist culture where the necessary abjection of the former becomes the fear and hatred of the latter. But it is nevertheless the maternal body each subject must relinquish, so when she refers to semiotic irruptions in the symbolic, Kristeva does speak of a 'reinstatement of maternal territory', where the 'presymbolic and trans-symbolic relationship to the mother' introduces an 'aimless wandering within the identity of the speaker and the economy of its very discourse' (DL: 137).

Yet this aimless wandering is precisely the meandering of the pre-gendered, unbounded pre-subject when it reactivates again the rhythms of the drives. As such, it is available to either male or female subjects-in-process. The semiotic is feminine in the relational sense that it is not yet phallic, or refuses the phallic, while developmentally it is a '"feminine" pre-Œdipal phase' because the child is still identified with the maternal body. But it is only during its Œdipal phase that the child itself recognises the mother (and itself) as sexually-specific (as castrated) and identifies with her or not in taking up its position within the symbolic. Prior to this the semiotic's feminine epithet signifies not one axis of a sexual binary, but its ruin: multiplicity, excess. It is not an identity that could be assumed, but a mobility that transgresses the symbolic's boundaries of dualistic sexual difference and the unity of the phallocentric Law. 'No "I" is there to assume this "feminine," but it is no less operative, rejecting all that is finite and assuring in … the life of the concept'.[55] In sum: semiotic, negativity and feminine are synonymous terms. But they are linguistic terms applied retrospectively, from within the symbolic, whence they bear all the metaphorical and conventional weight they have acquired there.

The subject-in-process will sustain both father and mother identifications: not as an androgynous synthesis, but as both a phallic-identified, sexed subject (as castrated/not-castrated, according to the symbolic's binary distinction between man and woman) and as one whose unrepressed feminine residues assault that sexual identity as an alien imposition on its gender mobility and a repression of its polymorphous pleasures. It is in this transgressive sense that femininity is negativity and that subjects who retain access to their feminine dimension have available a variety of signifying processes. It is subversive not *qua* an anti-symbolic but as a disruption of its boundaries; it is called feminine not ontologically but by the conventions it subverts. All subjects have an interest in this disruption to the extent that the Law is sacrificial in entailing the 'privation of fulfilment and totality; exclusion of a pleasing, natural and sound state' (WT: 198) and in imposing the rigid either/or of sexual difference.

Negativity and the feminine

Before looking at the relation of the mother, as subject, to this negativity, it will be instructive to consider some criticisms of Kristeva's equation between the semiotic and the feminine. For these raise more general questions about the status of negativity in her work and, indeed, about the status of negativity as such. Judith Butler is typical in her concern that Kristeva's insistence on the Law's necessity leaves its hegemony unchallenged despite an appearance of subversiveness. She argues that her theory is 'self-defeating' in allowing a merely 'temporary and futile disruption'. What troubles her is that the Law in psychoanalysis seems to have a quasi-biological, universal and necessary status and 'Kristeva does not seriously challenge the structuralist assumptions that the prohibitive paternal law is foundational to culture itself.'[56]

The question of psychoanalysis's status *vis-à-vis* its validity claims is clearly a complex one, which I have partly considered above, but for Butler it is not a question of establishing its 'truth'.[57] Instead she advances the Foucaultian claim that the Law, like its other, is discursively generated in a context of power. In this case its effect is a sustaining of heterosexual order and binary sexual difference. In other words, metapsychological claims are to be understood genealogically and as such they, like the Law they describe, can only be internally deconstructed – 'when the law turns against itself' – since any forces that are posited as outside and potentially destructive (such as the feminine) are actually of its own construction. The paternal Law generates the very desire it represses. Similarly, it is according to Butler the Law (and the psychoanalytic discourse that is part of its arsenal) that constructs the maternal body, which she accuses Kristeva of presenting as 'a true body before the law'.[58] As such, Kristeva allegedly supports representations of the natural female body that oppress women while reducing negativity to 'female generativity'.[59] For her, Butler charges, the maternal body is the Real, the 'lost originary presence' that 'resists and compels symbolization' (following Lacan). If Kristeva invokes its materiality as pre-discursive she can do so, paradoxically, only *'within language'*.[60]

221

I have already discussed this charge in the context of the representational difficulties it poses and exonerated Kristeva by interpreting her more dialectically than Butler allows. The criticism that Kristeva ontologises negativity as maternal is also problematic in so far as, as I have argued, the mother's body is not a terminal site of negativity for her but slips into the heterogeneity of matter. Moreover, this is where the distinction between the maternal container that the infant abjects, and the mother's body which the female subject might acquire, is important. The latter is indeed a cultural and discursive construct, but one that Kristeva is eager to free from the defences operative against the former. In other words, the generativity of the organic and the fecundity of the mother should not be elided, psychically or discursively.

Inasmuch as there is a prediscursive negativity in Kristeva's work, its traces thus lie in the pulsings of matter that I have associated with Nietzsche's will to power and implicated in a variety of negativities.[61] But Butler's underlying quarrel with Kristeva does ultimately hinge on the equation of negativity with materiality (*qua* corporeality, alterity), as opposed to its discursive constructedness (thereby replaying the quarrel between the early Foucault and Derrida regarding the status of madness (see chapter 1 note 3)). Although I have associated negativity with a *rhythmic* generativity that is invoked across various fields, rather than with metaphysical claims regarding its ontology, and its inside/outside dialectic must remain ultimately undecidable (in-process), it is always vulnerable to the sort of accusations Butler levels. It is also true that the dominant psychoanalytic enframing of this process, as it subtends sexual difference, does lend some credibility to Butler's anxiety about negativity's gendering despite Kristeva's careful dialectical finessing of her validity claims.

This credibility arises in Kristeva's case, I suggest, because of a tension within her thinking: between the Hegelian and dialectical way she tries to negotiate the different levels of semiotic–symbolic intertwining on the one hand, and her Freudian–Nietzschean inclination to anchor the semiotic in some effervescent life force (the drives, the Dionysian) on the other. Indeed, this is one of the major tensions that has appeared within my excursus through negativity, where negativity's invocation wavers between the unrepresentable ferment attributed to splits, differentiations, contradictions and lacunae on the one hand, and the temptation to infer some vital, efficacious energetics on the other (an ambiguity self-consciously paraded by Freud). The latter responds to a dangerous invitation to seek out some positive force that would guarantee or free negativity against its psychopolitical reification, while the metaphors used to invoke it (often derived from physics or biology) are themselves seductive. In Kristeva's case her Freudian–Nietzschean inclinations leave her vulnerable to criticisms like Butler's even while she contests them via the Hegelianism that encourages a more dialectical formulation.

Jacqueline Rose registers Kristeva's difficulties rather more sympatheti-
cally when she notes that, despite her denial of the semiotic as origin, brute
corporality or energy-in-itself, the term does not strictly make sense devoid
of some appeal to the outside of meaning, where it becomes vulnerable to
archaic notions of the content of the repressed. As such it is almost impossible to avoid assigning it some originary status – as the realm of the senses,
as culture's hidden underside – which is then idealised as a repressed exuberance and a lost maternal territory. Yet at the same time, Rose insists,
Kristeva recognised the illegitimate cultural idealisation, denigration and
mystification of woman that follows.

> Kristeva's work splits on a paradox, or rather a dilemma: the
> hideous moment when a theory arms itself with a concept of femi-
> ninity as different, as something other to the culture as it is known,
> only to find itself face to face with, or even entrenched within, the
> most grotesque and fully cultural stereotypes of femininity itself.
> Unlike some of her detractors, however, Kristeva knows that these
> images are not so easily dispatched.[62]

Fantasy, she might have added, again routes us through the circuits of a
dialectic between psychic and cultural histories. But however we interpret
Kristeva on this issue, Butler and Rose do alert readers to the political
dangers both of equating femininity with negativity and of romanticising or
ontologising either as an inherently transgressive force or redemptive ideal.

The mothering subject

I began this section by distinguishing between the pre-Œdipal maternal
container and the mother as a subject who has already crossed the threshold
of the symbolic. Having explored the connection between negativity and the
former, it is now time to consider its relation with the latter. Since the
mother has a place in both the semiotic and the symbolic registers, she is an
important borderline phenomenon, or mediation. This formulation again
summons cultural representations of woman as a sorceress on the border
between the supernatural and the social, life and death, both polluted and
purifier. But, more dialectically, it is this body that on the one hand organises the infantile drives and hence the *chora* (RPL: 27) and, on the other,
gives the mothering subject some immediate experience of the semiotic and
its repressed *jouissance*. As such, motherhood is a transgressive status and
has a privileged association with negativity. This is why critics often accuse
Kristeva of essentialising or glorifying motherhood. But it is important to
note that she does not see this as the only transgressive or valuable role
available to women, even if she maintains (against her deconstructive inclinations) that while we cannot name woman without succumbing to

metaphysics, we can name the mother 'since this is the only function of the "other sex" to which we can definitively attribute existence.'[63]

Although reproduction occurs under the paternal Law, the mother experiences both a *jouissance* and an instinctual memory for which the symbolic has no name, and an ambiguous relationship between herself and an other, since the foetus/infant both is and is not her body. In this sense pregnancy and giving birth are both experiences that confound boundaries, reminiscent of the more fluid splittings associated with the pre-symbolic, while putting the mother back in touch with her own maternal, material engendering. In this sense they are symptomatic of negativity both as transgressive and as an affirmation of a more mobile, dialectical relation that is achieved under the Law. Pregnancy is referred to by Kristeva as a natural yet institutionalised form of psychosis, a privileged psychotic moment and 'impossible syllogism', wherein the original process of separation is re-lived by one who is already a subject. Thus it is experienced as 'the radical ordeal of the splitting of the subject: redoubling up of the body, separation and coexistence of the self and of an other, of nature and consciousness, of physiology and speech.' It is on 'the threshold between nature and culture, biology and language' (WT: 206), since the mother 'is a continuous separation, a division of the very flesh.'[64]

In these senses motherhood performs and figures a new ethics (a 'herethics'): of love without guilt, such as transference in psychoanalysis also attempts, but which is here exemplified in the mother's love for her child (WT: 206). Such an ethic suggests a sociability that comes under the Law yet which is not grounded in the incest taboo, separation and denial. It thus implies a less sacrificial basis for the sociosymbolic contract, founded in love not sacrifice; an economy of mergings and small, shifting differentiations, rather than one of repression and severance. Motherhood is thus suggestive of a new intersubjectivity grounded in a transformed subjectivity; an ethics where the mother embraces the otherness in herself and thus the other in relation with the self, recognising that we are all *étrangers à nous-mêmes*. This is the affirmative side of Kristeva's theory of negativity, where she evokes the image of a 'paradoxical community' comprised of strangers 'who are reconciled with themselves to the extent that they recognize themselves as foreigners' (SO: 195).

In relation to a *politics* of negativity, motherhood is however analogous to the poetic language that is also a movement along the boundary between semiotic and symbolic. It is a 'second renaissance' (CW: 15) to the latter's 'second thetic'. Indeed, because poetic language relies on a recuperation of the maternal, to which motherhood is a privileged route, the latter might well lift fixations and self-denial and thereby render the mother more creative as a woman artist (Kristeva explicitly rescues motherhood from the loss of creativity with which de Beauvoir had associated it).[65] But more generally, motherhood is transgressive both because its practitioners are driven to seek new ways of expressing their undecidable, corporeal experience, which pushes language to the very limits of the signifiable, and in so far as it evades the patriarchal discourses that sanitise it, thus challenging the boundaries between referent and sign, self and other, on which the symbolic relies.

Because not all women are mothers, and they are accorded alternative routes to negativity, I think it would be wrong to accuse Kristeva of essentialising motherhood. But she does *privilege* it as a route to negativity, which only (some) women can take. Moreover she does sometimes imply that maternity alone might grant a subject some immediate sense of the heterogeneity of matter in its very generativity. In this sense there is again a hint of a romanticised alterity (reminiscent of Nietzsche's early, Schopenhauerean phase) where the mother and the maternal container fuse.

> Women doubtless reproduce among themselves the strange gamut of forgotten body relationships with their mothers. Complicity in the unspoken, connivance in the inexpressible, of a wink, a tone of voice, a gesture, a tinge, a scent. We are in it, set free of our identification papers ... . No communication between individuals, but connections between atoms, molecules, whisps of words, droplets of sentences.[66]

Feminist politics: the third generation as third-degree negativity

I mentioned earlier that Kristeva identified the Women's Movement as the 'most radical component' of a broad cultural transformation symptomatic of a crisis in the western symbolic. 'The movement, by its negativity, indicates to all the institutions of the right, and of the left, what it is that they repress' and thus operates as a 'demystifying force'.[67] This also however implied that while feminism was currently in the political vanguard, its privileged association with a politics of negativity remains a contingent one and part of a larger drama it does not itself define. For 'modern feminism has only been but a moment in the interminable process of coming to consciousness about the implacable violence (separation, castration etc.) which constitutes any symbolic contract' (WT: 203).

In 1974 Kristeva had suggested that, because of women's fragile positioning within the symbolic, their negativity took a more ethical than anarchistic form. They are unlikely to reject the Law as such, 'which might explain why our negativity is not a Nietzschean rage.' Nevertheless she stressed the importance of maintaining the linkage between ethics and negativity, lest the former degenerate into conformism and the latter, into 'esoteric perversity'.[68] By 1979 such thoughts had evolved into a typology of three different strands, or generations, of feminism. These generations correspond with the three dialectical levels of the semiotic–symbolic relation I elicited previously. Kristeva's criticisms of feminism's first and second incarnations, as well as her identification with a third, show clearly the sort of negativity she supports, as well as her refusal either to idealise regression to some feminine pre-discursive realm or to leave the Law unchallenged.

The first generation of feminists, who demand equal rights for women within state, civil society and family (liberals, socialists, existentialists), are recognised by Kristeva as continuing an important struggle. But, because they operate unquestioningly within the symbolic, their aspirations are limited. We might say that theirs is a positive politics: it identifies with the institutions of the nation state and seeks women's inclusion there, without challenging the constitution of the (gendered) subject on which it is founded. It is a thetic, positional, politics and although it criticises, it does so from the perspective of rational negation. When Kristeva is sometimes portrayed as hostile to feminism, it is on the basis of such misgivings.

> Believing oneself 'a woman' is almost as absurd and obscurantist as believing oneself 'a man'. I say almost because there are still things to be got for women: freedom of abortion and contraception, child-care facilities, recognition of work etc. Therefore, 'we are women' should still be kept as a slogan, for demands and publicity. But more fundamentally a woman cannot *be*: the category woman is even that which does not fit in to *being*. From there, women's practice can only be negative, in opposition to that which exists, to say that 'this is not it' and 'it is not yet'. What I mean by 'woman' is that which is not represented, that which is unspoken, that which is left out of namings and ideologies.[69]

But, she adds, some '"men" know something of it too'.

Given this judgement, Kristeva might be expected to side with a second generation of feminists who emphasise sexual difference, reject the politics of the nation and seek sociocultural recognition for women by considering the uniqueness of a feminine libidinal economy and its effects on syntax when it writes, or speaks, the body. Here recognition is demanded not for the female subject who is man's opposite, but for a non-oppositional difference unique to the feminine, as 'exploded, plural, fluid' and 'non-identical'; in touch with archaic memory and monumental or cyclical time. However this feminism could be seen as an indeterminate negation and is identified by Kristeva with the semiotic, to which regression can only mean psychosis, mysticism and political marginalisation.[70] This is only a paranoid counter-investment relative to its predecessor's investment in power; a utopian fantasy of harmony grounded in the myth of the archaic mother. In her rejection of this retreat into myth, archaism and alterity, as politically impotent, I think we can see both the strength of Kristeva's refusal to idealise the pre-discursive and the sense in which a politics of negativity means for her a dialectical engagement and not simply denial or renunciation.

The third generation, with which she sympathises and which practises her 'third-degree negativity', could accordingly be classified as dialectical (an 'impossible dialectic' as she acknowledges in *On Chinese Women* (CW: 38)) and it alone practises a genuine *politics* of *negativity*. It is transgressive, analogous to pregnancy or poetic language in that it both accepts and subverts the Law, entering history and the symbolic but refusing their limitations, disrupting them from within. It calls attention to what remains 'unsatisfied, repressed, new, eccentric, incomprehensible, disturbing to the *status quo*' (CW: 37f). Through it, the tabooed and unspeakable that the Law excludes confront it at its deepest levels. Women are not then at the forefront of a politics of negativity because negativity is their essence, but in so far as they 'reject everything finite, definite, structured, loaded with meaning, in the existing state of society.' As such they are 'on the side of the explosion of social codes: with revolutionary movements.'[71] But if society rests on sacrifice, then women must also explore the specificity of its sexual differentiation. Thus

> the urgent question on our agenda might be formulated as follows: *What can be our place in the symbolic contract?* If the social contract, far from being that of equal men, is based on an essentially sacrificial relationship of separation and articulation of differences which in this way produces communicable meaning, what is our place in this order of sacrifice and/or language?
>
> (WT: 199)

The women's movement is thus understood by Kristeva via her concerns with the production of subjects and we can see why motherhood, which practised a different relationship to the other and hence suggested a new ethic, is integral to a feminist politics. What is at stake is still Œdipus or, in more Nietzschean terms, the ascetic ideal, where subjectivity means guilt and loss. The remaining question is whether women, given their contingently privileged role in struggling against the sacrifice that constitutes subjectivity, have anything specific to gain, or act merely as the vanguard of a more general revaluation of all values from which all subjects would benefit equally regardless of their sexual identity.

Although she had recognised the strategic advantages of sexual identities in struggles for equality, Kristeva clearly cannot endorse a politics for her third generation which would rely on the very polarity it must deconstruct. Irruptions of the 'feminine' semiotic are transgressive in precisely this way: 'the very dichotomy man/woman as an opposition between two rival entities belongs to metaphysics' (WT: 209). Moreover since men can also reactivate this mobile, non-binary femininity (and almost all the avant-garde texts she explores were written by men), they can also share in the less repressive, less phallic identity it invokes and engage in a politics of negativity, broadly defined. Still, Kristeva clearly favours a more explicit political awareness of the way aesthetic practices challenge institutionalised power and although she acknowledges that men as well as women experience the feelings of lack, or loss, that the symbolic entails,[72] she does suggest that women experience them especially acutely, in particular where it is the woman's body and the mother's *jouissance* that are silenced. For while all subjects sacrifice their instinctual pleasures, the phallic symbolic with its unconscious codes and cultural proliferations is especially oppressive towards women.

> Sexual difference – which is at once biological, physiological and relative to reproduction – is translated by and translates a difference in the relationship of subjects to the symbolic contract which *is* the social contract: a difference, then, in the relationship to power, language and meaning.
>
> (WT: 196)

It is difficult to avoid the conclusion that Kristeva does trade on her belief that motherhood, unlike woman, is undeconstructable, to suggest that the issue of reproduction (in its widest senses) positions women uniquely within the crises of the present, so that it is *as women* that they challenge the sociosymbolic contract. But on the other hand, it is precisely here that they mount their challenge most effectively and refuse the role as it has tradition-ally been imposed. 'No longer wishing to be excluded and no longer content with the function which has always been demanded of us ... , how can we reveal our place, first as it is bequeathed to us by tradition, and then as we want to transform it?' (WT: 199) How can women do this? By discursive and performative means, and in particular by exploring the personal, where Kristeva again likens 'active research' to transgressive aesthetic practices (which she explicitly distinguishes from the 'woman's language' of the second generation): 'to break the code, to shatter language, to find a specific discourse closer to the body and emotions, to the unnameable repressed by the social contract' (WT: 200).

What should feminists then aspire to? In accessing the semiotic, they rediscover a negativity heterogeneous to the binarism of sexual difference. This is not essentially feminine or some androgynous bisexuality, but the sexual multiplicity and singularity of each woman as a subject-in-process who has many identities and identifications; multiple roles and signifying registers that defy the weary dualities of the symbolic's oppositional sexual difference. One might perhaps glimpse the Nietzschean self here, an unstable stylisation of many wills to power operative on various levels of matter, body and spirit, where it is the role of aesthetic practices 'to bring out – along with the *singularity* of each person and, even more, along with the multiplicity of every person's identifications (with atoms, e.g., stretching from the family to the stars) – the *relativity of his/her symbolic as well as biological existence*, according to the variation in his/her specific symbolic capacities' (WT: 210). Sexual identity here obeys the undecidable choreography and fluid rhythms of negativity; it is deconstructed at the point where sociability is founded.

In earlier chapters I noted the inappropriateness of such rhythms for a collectivist politics, but in terms of the project Kristeva outlines they acquire a strategic significance, albeit one that in no way precludes the egalitarian struggles occurring in the mainstream. Although the aesthetic acts she privileges have been criticised (like Foucault's) as individualistic and elitist, their effects are allegedly intersubjective since they would transform the conditions of social and political association themselves.[73] It is in this context that the sort of aesthetic practices and transgressive performances that have more recently been associated with postmodernism acquire their political negativity. The question that remains is nevertheless whether this politics of negativity, practised at the level of the subject, will translate at some point into a more collectivist project capable of challenging the social and economic reifications of late capitalism – as the early Kristeva, at least, clearly hoped – or whether this is a politics of another scene.

CONCLUSION
Politics and negativity

The idea of a conclusion that would sum up, define and clarify what might have remained equivocal in the preceding text is obviously antithetical to the negativity I have been discussing. Nevertheless some general claims and judgements can be elicited from the foregoing tracking of negativity's adventures. More especially, a final consideration of negativity's implications for politics must now be undertaken, although I would certainly not wish to *reduce* the fascinating philosophical questions it poses to their political indices alone.

If negativity has emerged across the preceding pages as irreducibly polymorphic and polynomial, I have elicited a persistent sense of *generativity* that clings to its different forms and names. This remains continuous across its more dialectical or Dionysian modulations, challenging the way in which these are often today reduced to a simple modern versus postmodern or poststructuralist opposition. At this level negativity suggests an ontological process since it indicates *becoming*, a productivity that engenders and ruins every distinct form as a creative–destructive restlessness. Architectural metaphors about foundations are, however, inappropriate to this shifting, sometimes aleatory, process while the idea of logically deducing conclusions from premises about negativity is continually subverted by throwing the rational and linguistic chain into the cauldron of its fermentation, too. It is for such reasons that some adventurers, notably Adorno or Derrida, have resisted labelling negativity ontological. For there is always a danger of ontologies slipping into transcendent claims and, even if negativity is the ruin of the metaphysics of stable Being as Truth, it is always tempted by theological, mystical or realist slippages. To ask whether negativity is material or ideal movement is ultimately inappropriate since generativity suggests a univocal immanence of rhythms rather than substances, albeit one expressed in multiple forms and on different levels. Being, thinking, politics, perception, and so on are all modulations of becoming and in this sense they are unavoidably related.

Despite insisting on a continuity within negativity's adventures, I have nevertheless identified a differential rhythm that divides its exponents. This

230

is especially evident in Hegelian as opposed to Nietzschean modulations, where the more teleological and lawful unfolding traced by the former – where the appearing of forms is a synthetic process emanating from determinate negation and a dialectic of identity and difference – is at odds with the emphasis on chance and excess insisted upon by the latter (a difference I also mapped onto the psychoanalytic distinction between secondary and primary processes, respectively). Even so, many of the negative's adventurers have combined elements of these choreographies, introducing richness, tiers and tensions into their work in their efforts to convey the flows and movements as well as to account for the forms and phenomena that mark the effulgence of a world.

Beyond the philosophical challenges of eliciting negativity without destroying it, the major question posed by the preceding chapters has concerned the relationship between negativity and politics. For all the philosophers considered insist on some political significance for their work, even where that relationship remains cryptic and elusive. On a general level I have argued that negativity is already political inasmuch as it signals the vulnerability and contingency of every phenomenon that appears to be fully positive and replete. Thus a philosophical shift from a metaphysics of Being to an ontology of becoming, where it is the work and play of difference that drives the ferment of becoming, already has immense political implications. Negativity draws attention both to the instability of every form and to the contingency of all boundaries. It delivers the radical message that things could be different and that the way they are bounded or limited, divided up and identified, is not ontologically, naturally or normatively given. The formative process, the persistence or destruction of identities, the policing or transgression of boundaries: these are now indelibly marked by questions of power.[1] Indeed it is to signal this political implication that I have used the term *negativity* (as opposed to becoming, generativity and so on), while it is this political significance that has allowed me to bring a number of adventurers under its banner even where they have explicitly eschewed the figure of the negative.

The radical significance of negativity was already recognised by Marx when he encountered the Hegelian dialectic. Since then, diverse invocations of the negative have motivated a desire to challenge whatever resists appreciation of its own provisionality and particularity and to insist upon the privileging and exclusion that are implicated in such misrecognition. Not only are citations of negativity an incitement to negate blockages and closures, to transgress limits and borders, but the rhythms of negativity itself – the multiplicitous, fluid, contingent and highly dynamic process it indicates – have increasingly attracted a normative glow associated with an openness and affirmation that resist the violence and denial required to sustain unyielding institutions. Closure is associated with impoverishment, oppression, entropy, nihilism, while openness – which is

231

perceived as more consonant with the dynamics of becoming itself – is valorised.

In political and ethical terms this imperative is most often termed democracy or justice. It is possible to identify a number of distinct, if overlapping, approaches to democracy from the perspective of negativity. First of all there is mainstream political theory which, since the beginning of the social contract tradition in early modernity, has inclined to a rather formal, analytical approach. It has nevertheless played a critical role in challenging all forms of authority which are unjustifiable on rational grounds. The most radical contemporary discourses here, and the ones that are most sensitive to a certain negativity, are those focusing on deliberative or discursive democracy and associated with Habermas. Procedures for negotiating intersubjective rules are engendered here through communication rather than being prescribed via deductions of objectively correct principles. The strength of this approach is that it appears, especially through the work of some of Habermas's followers (such as Seyla Benhabib or Iris Young), to engage with some of the limitations of existing liberal-democratic systems while accommodating a certain contingency, difference and openness. However I have discussed its own limitations from the perspective of negativity in preceding chapters. Briefly: it acknowledges negativity only in a weak sense of disagreement and difference between discursive participants while aspiring to transcend these, via rational argument, in consensus or depoliticisation. Thus it limits negativity to discursive disagreement between rational interlocutors and negation to the force of the better argument (although even Habermas's supporters, feminists in particular, have been critical of him here). It also pays insufficient attention either to criticising existing political structures or to the means for instantiating the processes and procedures it advocates. In short, it rather neglects its own sociological context and the dialectical mediations between history and concepts that the first generation of critical theorists had insisted on. Instead it is built on assumptions about the rationality and relative transparency of language, subjectivity and lifeworlds in modernity.

Second, there are more dialectical approaches to democracy, although I want to distinguish here between classical, teleological versions and those which acknowledge greater contingency. For Marxists, democracy signals a future politics that reconfigures the very meaning of the political in so far as historically, the latter is equated with (class) domination. Voluntary association and self-government, themselves the rational culmination and transcendence of history and dialectical negativity, remain a vague intimation of a future destiny. The sources of difference or agonism that would impart becoming to this democracy-without-conflict, as well as the procedures for negotiating intersubjective life, are deliberately left untheorised lest they be modelled on specifically bourgeois assumptions. But it remains ambiguous as to whether this would be the open society, practising generative immanence, *par excellence*, or the incarnation – as Kojève suggests – of an immobile and boring positivity.

In any case, once faith in the wholesale negation of bourgeois society subsides, this theoretical deficit begins to look deeply problematic, especially if democratic processes are themselves credited with a transformative role. On the one hand it is this gap that thinkers like Habermas are working to plug; on the other, a dialectical methodology – albeit one now more attuned to contingency and the ineradicability of negativity – is deployed to analyse the historical forces and contingencies at work within global capitalism, patriarchy, (post)colonialism, etc. Here democratisation emerges as a hazardous process enacted through struggle and resistance. This approach then concerns itself with the sociology and praxis of social transformation. It is the one with which I have had most sympathy in this study, where I have traced its credentials through the adventures in negativity undertaken by Merleau-Ponty and the first generation of critical theorists (and to some extent by the earlier Habermas via his concerns with the steering media and the resurrection of a public sphere).

If Merleau-Ponty also valorises democracy as a process of unremitting openness under the sign of the interrogative, he also insists that democracy involves forging structures within a violent and contingent milieu, where a reading of events and of historical opportunities and constraints is essential to political efficacy inasmuch as values are to be made concrete rather than remaining phantoms of the beautiful soul. In short, a political commitment to openness and to practices of negativity must also involve a commitment to negation, to praxis, and the tragedy of political life is precisely that such interventions are without guarantees or final justification, while political acts and decisions must sometimes be definitive if they are to be effective. Fortunately for the dialectician, such acts are not arbitrary either. For Merleau-Ponty, like Adorno, the choreography of negativity is not dominated by chance but by contingency, where exercising *virtù* means engaging with adversity by tracing the mediations that make sense of events and inform political action. Practising negativity thus involves an intense involvement with one's times that is at the same time hermeneutical and critical, creative and audacious. It is at odds either with the formalism of discourse ethics or with the abstractness of democracy *à-venir*.

Merleau-Ponty also gave some thought as to how democracy might be practised in a manner informed by ontological negativity. The challenge in this context is to instantiate a political style which would emulate the creative–destructive rhythms of negativity in a manner appropriate to political life. In other words – to put it rather crudely – it is to find some negotiation between openness and closure, opposition and institutionalisation; between resistances to illegitimate power and an empowerment constructed through agreement. It is to recognise negativity as integral to the political process rather than entertaining rationalist fantasies of its transcendence or imagining that its wilder modulations of becoming can substitute for politics and the inertia of intersubjective life.

The difficulty here is analogous to the discursive paradox that haunts expositions of negativity. As I have shown time and again, its exponents acknowledge the need to communicate negativity as a philosophical undertaking while denying the possibility of its representation. Accordingly they adopt what I identified as a dual strategy: combining discursive invocations with stylistic performances. Similarly, in political life, the negative cannot in principle be institutionalised without becoming positive, yet some exemplary practising of a political style that accommodates the contingency and self-critical nature of collective life is summoned by its acknowledgement. This again suggests an open, democratic process but one which is afraid neither of opposition and conflict nor of judging these according to criteria of their openness. Yet it is surely naïve, ultimately – as poststructuralists recognise – to believe that negativity can be incorporated without remainder into the polity. Besides negotiating its own internal antagonisms, it is where the polity meets its other(s) that an irreducible negativity takes place.

Practising negativity as an exemplary political style entails less an affirmation of its generative exuberance *per se*, than a difficult and ongoing engagement along that porous and unstable line where positive and negative meet. For dialectical approaches, the relationship between ontological and political negativity is not in principle problematic since it is a matter of historical mediation. In oppositional politics this is classically resolved into a relation between theory and practice, the praxis discussed in chapter 2. In the democratic polity it suggests an art of politics, a certain self-critical pragmatism that is nevertheless obliged to confront more radical practices (transgressions, resistances, subversions as well as unexpected innovations) where its own limits are thrown into question. Although there may be contingent historical difficulties in actually identifying forces of progress and change, criticism and analysis are ongoing since concepts and history mediate one another.

In the context of the early twenty-first century, the challenge for this dialectical approach is to make sense of the diverse changes associated with postmodernisation. Shifting social patterns, as well as radical discursive and technological innovations, pose a far-reaching challenge to the concepts and methodological refinements that will be called for. But it is here that a third approach to democracy and questions of negativity and politics must be addressed. For, according to poststructuralists, vitalists and deconstructionists, dialectical criticism does not and cannot go nearly far enough. It is implicated in modern assumptions it fails to question (for example regarding rational subjectivity, political agency and linear history) while the sort of negations it encourages are always limited precisely because they remain implicated in the positivity they oppose. There is always furthermore a threat of instrumentalism and rationalism. The nature of the political, democracy, historicity, even the human, thus call for the sort of transfiguration summoned for example by Derrida or Deleuze.

For deconstructionists, democracy is always deferred, *à-venir*, an incitement and spacing that haunt the present yet can never be brought into presence. It is not a question of instantiation in the historical future but of a critical intervention, a promise of openness that marks a responsibility to the other. Otherwise, Derrida insists, 'justice risks being reduced once again to juridical-moral rules, norms, or representations, within an inevitable totalizing horizon'.[2]

It is from this perspective that Geoffrey Bennington elicits the ethico-political implications of deconstruction, where the latter depends upon 'a certain affirmation of the undecidable'.

> A decision worthy of its name thus takes place in a situation of radical *indecision* or of undecidability of the case in question in terms of any rules for judging it. The decision must therefore involve a measure of *invention*, and that invention entails both an uncertainty and the affirmative projection of a future. A decision is like a performative which has both to perform and to invent the rules according to which it might, after the event of its performance, be received as 'happy.'[3]

(It is interesting that much of this quote could refer equally well to Lyotard's definition of postmodern art or to Merleau-Ponty's comments on statesmanship.) If openness is not ethical *per se*, it does then yield a principle of judgement: 'any ethical or political judgment that closes off this condition of undecidability is *ipso facto* suspect'. It is in this sense that Derrida speaks of justice and democracy: not as institutions or programmes but as 'the ethico-political figure of the never-absolute, never present dispersion of *différance.*' Far from preventing specific, concrete decisions, Bennington insists, this democracy *à-venir* 'would be the condition of possibility of all such decisions, and simultaneously the condition of impossibility of any self-righteousness about them.'[4] In this sense one might perhaps speak less of a democratic regime or style than a democratic ethos.

The provocative question that Derrida or Deleuze pose is this: if linguistic or ontological negativity is already in a sense political, intrinsically deconstructive or critical, how might the political and its practices be rethought from the perspective of multiplicity, difference, constitution, becoming, the event? What would a politics of negativity look like where negativity assumes a more Dionysian than dialectical tempo?

As I noted in chapter 2, at least some of poststructuralism's hostility towards the figure of the negative is derived from a Deleuzean reading of Nietzsche. Negation, especially in its dialectical mode, is associated here with *ressentiment* and a merely nihilistic denial of life, as opposed to the affirmation which joyfully asserts difference without opposition. Affirmation here is nevertheless what, in discussing Nietzsche, I called a celebration of negativity: of the creative–destructive generativity sometimes conveyed by the terms will to power, Life, Dionysus. It is this affirmation – which celebrates the aleatory, the experimental and inventive, radical differ-ence – that finds its way into political philosophies such as those of Deleuze, Derrida or Lyotard[5] as well as into some recent feminisms, postcolonialisms and postmodernisms. The politics that emerges from this orientation is undoubtedly different from an emphasis on negation, praxis, solidarity and collective, material interventions. Indeed the failure of such a politics (in particular in its Marxist guises), with its own infidelities to the negative, has also influenced distrust towards the figure of the (dialectical) negative. But in what sense, if any, is what emerges here recognisable as a politics? Can it yield any vision of a reconfigured intersubjectivity or transformative efficacy?

Deleuzean interlude

The philosophical fascination of purifying negativity as pure generativity, as well as the difficulties that ensue if that negativity is yet discerned as politi-cally significant, are illustrated brilliantly by Deleuze and Guattari's *What is Philosophy?* (1991).[6] The main argument here concerns the nature of philos-ophy as an experimental creation of concepts and in the process the authors could be said both to offer an ontology of negativity and to describe philos-ophy as an exemplary practising of that negativity. Despite their insistence on the autonomy of philosophy, Deleuze and Guattari nevertheless grant it certain political dimensions. It plays a critical role *vis-à-vis* the territorialisa-tions of modern capitalism and the state; it exhibits a utopianism that is politically resonant; its very possibility is somehow implicated in contingent sociohistorical conditions. Implicit, too, yet perhaps the most intriguing but problematic aspect of their cryptic references to a 'people to come', is the implication that philosophy has an ethical mission. It is to think, or open the way towards, a politics which might also emulate negativity as a self-generative, autopoetic becoming. But the figure invoked here is less democracy than revolution.

In the excursus that follows I will look more carefully at Deleuze and Guattari's ontology of negativity in order to ask about the relationship between philosophy and politics in *What is Philosophy?* But I am also suggesting that this text be taken as indicative of problems – and virtues – that pure negativity poses for the political, once the historical mediations insisted upon by dialectics have been rejected. In this sense the concerns raised here have implications for post-Nietzschean, and especially decon-structive, thought more generally.

Philosophy as Deleuze and Guattari define it could be described as the sort of Dionysian/Apollinian, destructive/creative ferment that I associated with will to power in chapter 3: it 'is the art of forming, inventing, and fabricating concepts' (WiP: 2). Concepts resonate together (rather than being associated rationally or referring to external states of affairs) in an open field which is consistent but not systemic. They cohere to configure a field, re-cutting the distribution of subject and object, figure and ground, margin and centre. As such they come to inscribe a plane of consistency, referred to as a plane of immanence.

The plane of immanence grounding any particular philosophy is its pre-philosophical horizon. This is where the philosopher sieves out a plane within the infinity of chaos and prior to its conceptualisation this must be engendered by a more Dionysian, primary, process.

> Precisely because the plane of immanence is prephilosophical and does not immediately take effect with concepts, it implies a sort of groping experimentation and its layout resorts to measures that are not very respectable, rational or reasonable. These measures belong to the order of dreams, of pathological processes, esoteric experiences, drunkenness, and excess.
>
> (WiP: 41)

Not all planes of immanence are however equal. Deleuze and Guattari offer vitalist criteria for judging them. Philosophy is not to be viewed in any historicist (dialectical, phenomenological) sense, as progressing over time towards truth, or in terms of its utility in addressing historical problems. For it is of an other order than history and becomes according to another temporality altogether. 'Philosophy is becoming, not history; it is the coexistence of planes, not the succession of systems' (WiP: 59). Its possible criterion of value is immanent, not transcendent, and concerns life itself in its movements and intensities: philosophy as a tenor of existence, an 'intensification of life' in its creative ardour. In thinking immanence, the philosopher must demonstrate its generativity through the creative productivity of his or her own work. This intensification is rather poorly exemplified or conveyed where the plane of immanence is still discerned in transcendent terms (where immanence is handed over to 'Something = X', as for example in Kantian noumena).

> We will say that THE plane of immanence is, at the same time, that which must be thought and cannot be thought. It is the nonthought within thought. It is the base of all planes, immanent to every thinkable plane that does not succeed in thinking it ... . Perhaps this is the supreme act of philosophy: not so much to think THE plane of immanence as to show that it is there, unthought in every plane ... .
>
> (WiP: 59)

It is Spinoza who is credited in this 1991 text with achieving the 'best' plane: 'that is, the purest', the most resistant to illusions of transcendence. His is 'a plane traversed by movements of the infinite, filled with intensive ordinates'. His *Ethics* attains 'incredible speeds, with such lightning compressions that one can only speak of music, tornadoes, of wind and strings' (WiP: 48, 60). The achievement might be Spinoza's but the language is more evocative of Zarathustra, and Nietzsche's plane of immanence is indeed described as one of 'infinite movements of the will to power and the eternal return' (WiP: 65).

The concepts that populate the plane of immanence in thinking are similarly evaluated: not according to their referential truth value but '[i]f one concept is "better" than an earlier one, it is because it makes us aware of new variations and unknown resonances, it carries out unforeseen cuttings out, it brings forth an Event that surveys [*survole*] us'. It is not truth but 'categories like Interesting, Remarkable, or Important that determine success or failure' (WiP: 28, 80). The philosopher who creates concepts must institute certain limits or boundaries but at the same time philosophy must cross over every particular limit: in particular, perhaps, those erected by Kant. But even Kant had recognised reason's *desire* to transgress its own boundaries and when Deleuze and Guattari acknowledge the metaphysical illusions and mirages the plane of immanence inevitably engenders, the thick fog that surrounds it, they deliberately and passionately set sail for the stormy seas that Kant (himself a victim of metaphysical hallucination) had proscribed.

Presumably then Deleuze and Guattari must also credit their own venture with thinking the(/THE) plane of immanence 'well' since their ontology, like Spinoza's or Nietzsche's, presents being as pure generative immanence. Like other experimenters in the negative, being is no metaphysical substance or ultimate foundation for them but a becoming: the virtual. It is univocal but dynamic due to its internal fissuring and multiplicity; a movement expressed through high-velocity becoming and whose normativity lies in an imperative to generate, create, experiment. Thus Being/Thinking, Nature/Thinking, are one and are not to be presented in terms of subject and object. Thinking is itself an expression of being as it becomes. As in other adventures in negativity, mind constructs itself from the flux of matter and is not of another ontological order.

In Deleuze and Guattari's terms, thinking takes place materially in the relationship between territory and earth (as the forming and reterritorialising of organic and inorganic intensities and flows). Like Merleau-Ponty's flesh, the deterritorialising earth is an element embracing all others; even, here, the inorganic.

> Chemical affinities and physical causalities themselves refer to primary forces capable of preserving their long chains by contracting

their elements and by making them resonate: no causality is intelligible without this subjective instance. Not every organism has a brain, and not all life is organic, but everywhere there are forces that constitute microbrains, or an inorganic life of things.

(WiP: 213)

There is accordingly an ethics of being, of life, even of matter or energy, which extends to all spheres of becoming. This ethics is especially incumbent on philosophy, since it is here that generativity is adumbrated and absolute deterritorialisation practised in an exemplary way. Yet it must also, it would seem, fall to politics. What, then, is the significance of philosophy for politics here and what is their relationship?

To begin with it seems important to mention a distinction made by the authors between *concepts*, which are self-referential and the domain of philosophy, and *propositions*, which are referential to states of affairs and the domain of science. In this sense the sort of sociohistorical engagements I have attributed to dialectical politics might at least in part be attributed to a *social science* and the kind of methodology insisted upon for example by the Frankfurt School, where sociology, political economy and philosophy were to be brought together, would appear to be confused. Certainly in opposing phenomenology, the vitalists are adamant that philosophical concepts do not refer to the lived (WiP: 33).

It might be helpful at this point to recall Merleau-Ponty's definition of truth as the opening of a field that is fecund in terms of the possibilities and novelties is offers, as advent. This seems to capture something of the reconfigurative criterion concepts must meet according to Deleuze and Guattari if they are to be valuable. But Merleau-Ponty's dialectical approach, like that of the critical theorists, does not envisage philosophy as pure, creative novelty since its innovations emerge from a reading and reinscription of the vectors of past and present: it has historicity, it is *virtù*. It learns from past errors, eliminates false (closed, infertile) detours and offers possibilities for the future on the basis of a hermeneutical exercise that inspires a praxis. The event for Deleuze and Guattari on the other hand eschews the sedimented weight of history and while 'new concepts must relate to our problems, to our history', they seem to do so by rupturing the continuities of lived history by introducing something wholly new and unexpected there. In other words, this is the time of becoming, of philosophy, not the plodding of historical time. But given this disjuncture how, or when, can philosophy and politics meet?

As I mentioned above, there are several places in *What is Philosophy?* where the relationship is broached. In the fourth chapter on 'geophilosophy', for example, Deleuze and Guattari compare relative and absolute deterritorialisation. Unlike the Oriental empires, the Greeks established their cities as a milieu of immanence: that is, rather than the sovereign-headed imperial

239

hierarchies, the Greek state was relatively deterritorialised due, in part, to its maritime geography. There were independent cities, distinct societies, where artisans, merchants and philosophers found freedom and mobility. In this Greek milieu there existed then the *de facto* conditions for philosophy to flourish: sociability and association (as a milieu of immanence); pleasure in forming associations (friendship) and destroying them through rivalry (agonism); a taste for exchanging opinions in conversation. In other words, these were sites of negativity where conventions and opinions were generated immanently through contingent, multiplicitous processes.

Accordingly Greece offered a geographical and political deterritorialisation ('*relative*, insofar as it concerns the historical relationship of the earth with the territories that take shape and pass away on it') which was conducive to philosophical deterritorialisation, where the earth passed onto the pure plane of immanence of a Being–Thought (WiP: 87f). But what was the connection between these relative historical, and absolute philosophical, deterritorialisations? Clearly the latter is not ideological or determined, it is not a question of some base–superstructure relationship, yet neither is the bond between democracy and philosophy gratuitous. When

> relative deterritorialization is itself horizontal, or immanent, it combines with the absolute deterritorialization of the plane of immanence that carries the movements of relative deterritorialization to infinity, pushes them to the absolute, by transforming them (milieu, friend, opinion). Immanence is redoubled.
>
> (WiP: 90)

Is it then a case of the political (etc.) gaining philosophical expression, as opposed to causing or facilitating it? The authors leave the question in abeyance. Absolute deterritorialisation 'can only be thought according to certain still-to-be-determined relationships with relative deterritorializations that are not only cosmic but geographical, historical, and psychosocial' (WiP: 88). Deleuze and Guattari nevertheless use terms like 'encounter', 'conjunction', alignment and connection, the congeniality of a milieu, its necessity if philosophy were to appear at all (WiP: 93). The implication is that, if the affirmative philosophy they advocate is to flourish, then conducive geo-political conditions must also be available. But if philosophy has an ethical task of intensifying life, must it not bear some imperative to instantiate the historical conditions of its own possibility? These conditions would not however be merely a means to an end, but would themselves approach the sort of deterritorialisation and immanence, in a sociopolitical milieu, that generativity entails. Such is the utopian element of philosophy.

Modern capitalism is in fact cited as being relatively congenial to the contingent recommencement of philosophy since it too functions through immanence (its intensities and flows are restricted by no external limits; it reconstitutes itself and expands). Yet in this context Deleuze and Guattari are swift to insist on philosophy's critical position: it is no friend of capital because it recognises its only relative deterritorialization and its limits; it pushes them to the absolute in order to 'summon forth a new earth, a new people' (WiP: 99). The text demonstrates at several points that philosophy is not very friendly to even radical versions of modern democracy, either. In particular the vitalists are at pains to distance themselves from the poor generativity they attribute to Habermasian communicative action and discourse ethics. Thus philosophy finds no 'final refuge in communication' since consensus emerges here from opinion rather than creativity or concepts. As communicative reason it is merely part of the machinery for constituting universals. It in no way credits philosophy to present it in terms of 'Universals of communication that would provide rules for an imaginary mastery of the markets and the media (intersubjective idealism)' (WiP: 6). The critique here is very close to Adorno's: 'We do not lack communication. On the contrary, we have too much of it. We lack creation. *We lack resistance to the present*' (WiP: 108). But what does this mean for a politics? Deleuze and Guattari insist that philosophy's summoning of a new people and earth moves beyond propositions, consensus, opinion, communication; it remains closer, they insist, to Adorno's negative dialectics and utopianism. It 'is with utopia that philosophy becomes political and takes the criticism of its own time to its highest point' (WiP: 99).

In implicit response to their earlier circumspection, Deleuze and Guattari are thus suggesting that it is utopianism (and its political expression as revolution) which links relative and absolute deterritorialisation: '*utopia is what links* philosophy with its own epoch, with European capitalism, but also already with the Greek city.' Etymologically utopia stands for absolute deterritorialisation, 'but always at the critical point at which it is connected with the present relative milieu, and especially with the forces stifled by this milieu' (WiP: 99f). Here then is the *political* sense I have attributed to generativity in order to justify calling it a negativity. Yet it does seem to me that the allusion to Adorno is somewhat mischievous inasmuch as his utopianism was always, like Merleau-Ponty's, *dialectical*: immanent to a historical criticism and emanating from determinate negation. As cited in chapter 5, Adorno condemned Benjamin's 'immediate' materialism as merely romantic, unmediated and lacking 'real historico-philosophical weight'. Would he not have invited Deleuze and Guattari to join Benjamin 'at the crossroads of magic and positivism' despite the messianic fascination he shared in rupturing the continuum of history?

Good utopias are described in *What is Philosophy?* as non-authoritarian; as 'immanent, revolutionary, libertarian'. Revolutions seem to be privileged moments of pure generativity, negativity, autopoesis; events whose enthusiasm seems to emulate the Greeks' madness in constructing a deterritorialised plane of immanence. If revolution is the political practising of utopia it is not as an instrumental negation preparatory to a new, positive state (this is the authoritarian, positivist model associated with Marxism) but as intrinsically creative and experimental, figurative of a new people.

> ... the success of a revolution resides only in itself, precisely in the vibrations, clinches, and openings it gave to men and women at the moment of its making and that composes in itself a monument that is always in the process of becoming ... .
>
> (WiP: 177)

Its victory is immanent, consisting of the new bonds it installs, even if only briefly, between people (recall here Marx's insistence on the importance of the revolutionary experience in substituting solidarity for bourgeois egoism). The task of revolution, like that of art or philosophy, is then '*the constitution of an earth and a people that are lacking as the correlate of creation*' (WiP: 108, emphasis added).

Revolution is not then envisaged as some apocalyptic futural event of collective life towards which history progresses. It is always a possibility of the now and it is related to the limits and closures of the present. It is infinite movement but only 'to the extent that these features connect up with what is real here and now in the struggle against capitalism, relaunching new struggles whenever the earlier one is betrayed' (WiP: 100). In this sense struggles are contingent and multiple, yet they seem to participate fleetingly in a sort of revolutionary essence (the political 'correlate of creation'). Although they are presented here in negative terms (as resistance) it is their affirmative power, the intensity of their enthusiasm, that marks a permanent, if intermittent, revolutionary becoming out from the disappointments of its specific incarnations in history (revolution as event, as opposed to being a state of affairs).

If the new people which political philosophy summons cannot be a product of majoritarian democracies, nor can they be created by philosophy. It is through their resistance to nihilistic forces, through their suffering, that they (unlike the Nietzschean herd) revolt. 'They have resistance in common – their resistance to death, to servitude, to the intolerable, to shame, and to the present.' But their resistance is also affirmation, not simply negation, because 'to create is to resist: pure becomings, pure events on a plane of immanence' (WiP: 110). If such people ('oppressed, bastard, lower, anarchical, nomadic, and irremediably minor') have an effect on the historical state of affairs and lived experience, the event escapes History since the latter is 'only the set of almost negative conditions' that makes possible experimental becoming (WiP: 111).

Nevertheless, and again, those negative conditions surely have to be rendered conducive, relatively deterritorialised, before experimental becomings can flourish and this is a historical, political ambition. Does it require nothing of the hermeneutical, strategic and mediating work of dialectics? And if not, is it not condemned to a romantic faith in spontaneous uprisings or to a fatalistic waiting? Is the price of escaping the past not to repeat it? Yet, on the other hand, might this repetition not in fact be the destiny of critics who still think historically and thus remain imprisoned by the past? If life, as Nietzsche had insisted, is permanent self-overcoming, then is it not the case that vitalists, like other philosophers of negativity, are warranted in assuming unassailable resistances, unexpected creations, unpredictable contingencies, lines of flight? Is it not their theoretical mission to rethink the political from this perspective? And is it not their ethical task to assert an affirmative, life-enhancing becoming beyond the nihilism of modern politics? It is true that in this sense Deleuze and Guattari's utopianism yields no image of a future polity *qua* association of individuals under shared rules, any more than Nietzsche envisioned a collective of *Übermenschen*. In this sense vitalism is more existential than political. Yet even a Dionysian people must have its Apollinian moment. As Keith Ansell Pearson asserts in a different context: 'it is important not to neglect the role played by the existence of limits and the constitution of boundaries in any viable conception of "creative evolution". Closure is not contra "evolution" but one of its conditions of possibility.'[7] What will these closures and boundaries then look like politically? How will they be instantiated? How are the swift and infinite movements of thought or ontology to be brought to bear on, much less serve as a model for, the slow tempo of collective life?

These comments show, I think, the difficulties and ambiguities that arise in thinking through the relationship between a philosophy of pure negativity, generative immanence, and politics. Insisting on the affirmative, life-enhancing powers of generativity entails an ethical commitment to purging it of nihilistic positivity, where the latter includes dialectical negation, historicism and history itself. In the exhilaration of experimentation it alludes to a new people which serves as utopia and critique, the *à-venir* of re-creation. Yet its purchase on the 'real here and now' remains at best elusive, since philosophy is resolutely untimely.

This ambiguity is conveyed well by Ansell Pearson's assessment of Deleuze. Despite his sympathy for an ethics of speculative vitalism – where the 'virtual potentiality of the concept is an emancipatory one in that it does not restrict philosophy to imitating, or being faithful to, what is given to it' – he also notes the difficulties with Deleuze and Guattari's conception of philosophy, 'which might be said to stem from the immense power credited to the concept and its lack of mediation by social and historical forces.'[8] This narcissism is the great danger for any philosophy of pure negativity if it *also* insists on its *political* radicalism.

Deleuze courts the risk of rendering the event of thought and the tasks of philosophy not simply indeterminate but without connection to anything other than philosophy's own desire as it floats abstractly on a plane of immanence uninformed by historical praxis and the historically specific predicaments of modern thought.[9]

Yet again, he adds, there is critical merit in opening history to 'more radical transformation and transmutation through novel alliances and becomings', where 'the tasks of thought can never be restricted to a comprehension of the antinomies of the present.'[10] Indeed, Ansell Pearson concludes that going beyond what history has made us entails less a disavowal of history and politics than their reconfiguration, their opening to 'the vital possibilities of what one might call a rhizomatics of historical time'.[11] This is then a history made on many, traversal levels; one resolutely anti-teleological, linear, dialectical; one modelled on a Dionysian generativity rather than on the intricate positive/negative imbrication traversed by dialectics. But is this a politics or an ethics? And even if we accept the political dimensions of its utopian and critical thinking, is it not still incumbent on the critic to consider their historical efficacy?

For, in considering negativity, I have argued that differential tempos mark out a diversity within the generative process and I think this recognition is especially important regarding the political. While the swift-flowing fluidities of a negativity purified of positivist residues might be especially congenial to the sort of aesthetic, ethical and philosophical experimentation often associated with poststructuralism, political life seems destined to limp according to a slower beat. The politically-motivated desire to defamiliarise, deconstruct and challenge all reified institutions, coupled with an affirmation of a fleet-footed exuberance, comes into conflict here with a more specific notion of the political as the arena where collective life is negotiated. A certain inertia and turgidity are surely inevitable and even desirable in this domain where coexistence is forged as well as contested. For without some shared habits, values and procedures; without the formation of some enduring institutions and agreed-upon rules, it is difficult to imagine collective life surviving in a ferment of permanent revolution.

Democracy must then entail a formative, creative, as well as a destructive, process and it is this aspect that has been chronically under-theorised among many post-Nietzscheans. While I have insisted on the political significance of their work, the relationship between negativity and politics is indeed difficult to sustain once a dialectical sense of mediation is abandoned. Indeed politics sometimes looks here as if it were merely imagined through an analogy with the flows and heterogeneity associated with wilder modes of generativity. Of course from this perspective it can be retorted that politics has historically been precisely a means for controlling negativity: for disciplining desire, regulating excess and controlling nature, legitimising sacrifice.

One has only to look at classical social contract theories and the transition from the state of nature to civil society they describe, to see the truth of this assertion. But this has not been all that politics has entailed and it issues a challenge to political theorists who are in a position to mediate between the formalities of analytic approaches and the abstractions of poststructuralism.

The challenge for political theory, then, is to rethink the basis of collective life and political association, challenging not only the conventions of social contract theory but, also, the assumptions about political subjects on which it relies. In Kristeva's terms, it needs to rethink the sociosymbolic contract as such; the very possibility of subjectivity and intersubjectivity as well as the more concrete bases for political association. As in the seventeenth century, political theory needs again to be radically inventive, now in the context of the global shifts that will mark a new millennium. It needs to focus on the creative side of politics inasmuch as institutions which facilitate the possibility of collective life, however diverse its agents and heterogeneous their values, will have to be forged anew. Equally, it will neglect the dialectic between theory and practice, reason and violence, negative and positive, at its peril. Theory cannot replace political action but it can help to configure its discursive field. Such is the challenge of practising negativity politically and of a politics which acknowledges the irreducibility of the negative.

NOTES

INTRODUCTION: NEGATIVITY AND POLITICS

1 This was broadly the approach I took in my *Women in Political Theory. From Ancient Misogyny to Contemporary Feminism*, Hemel Hempstead: Harvester Wheatsheaf and Boulder, CO: Lynne Reinner, 1988; 2nd edn, 1993. It is an approach whose more rigorous pursuit is associated with Quentin Skinner.

2 See especially J. Habermas, *The Philosophical Discourse of Modernity*, Cambridge: Polity, 1987. Although Habermas was not the first to level charges of performative contradiction, they are commonly made against postmodernists by writers more sympathetic to Habermas's position, such as Benhabib, Dews and Wellmer. This is also a common mode of attack on Nietzsche. See D. Coole, 'The Politics of Reading Nietzsche', *Political Studies*, vol. 46, no. 2, June 1998.

3 R. Bernstein, 'Negativity: Theme and Variations', *Praxis International*, April 1981.

4 This is for example the drift of Christopher Norris's *Reclaiming Truth*, London: Lawrence & Wishart, 1996 (although he exempts deconstruction from his criticism by reclaiming it for the Enlightenment). Stephen White contends that a 'thoroughly post-structuralist approach to political thinking would be one dominated by what is in effect a perpetual witholding gesture.' (*Political Theory and Postmodernism*, Cambridge: Cambridge University Press, 1991, p. 19.) Many other examples could be cited, although Derrida himself explicitly defies such equations in 'Jacques Derrida. In Discussion with Christopher Norris', in A. Papadakis *et al.*, *Deconstruction. Omnibus Edition*, London: Academy Editions, 1989, p. 74, when he asserts that

> not only I but many people insist on the fact that Deconstruction is *not* negative, is not nihilistic ... . Deconstruction is or should be an affirmation linked to promises, to involvement, to responsibility ... . So when people say it's negative, nihilistic or so forth, either they don't read or they are arguing in bad faith.

5 The otherwise very commendable Routledge series *Thinking the Political* seems to me to have exemplified, rather than resolved, this problem. See also, among many possible examples, W. Schroeder's Afterword to the excellent *A Companion to Continental Philosophy*, Oxford: Blackwell, 1998, where he criticises continental philosophy's lack of socially-transformative efficacy in light of the critical project that his co-editor, S. Critchley, had identified with it in his Introduction.

246

6 S. Clegg, *Frameworks of Power*, London: Sage, 1989, pp. 5, 22. Clegg draws on Bauman's distinction between legislators and interpreters in developing this contrast.

7 S. Critchley, *The Ethics of Deconstruction*, Oxford: Blackwell, 1992, pp. xii, 189, 199.

8 H. Marcuse, *Reason and Revolution. Hegel and the Rise of Social Theory*, Boston, MA: Beacon Press, 1960, p. x. As Bernstein writes, for 'Marcuse, the battle between negativity and positivity is the most consequential and decisive battle in the contemporary world.' (R. Bernstein, 'Negativity: Theme and Variations', p. 87.)

9 T. Adorno, *Negative Dialectics*, London: Routledge & Kegan Paul, 1973, p. 159.

10 M. Foucault, 'What is Enlightenment?' in P. Rabinow (ed.), *The Foucault Reader*, Harmondsworth: Penguin, 1984, p. 45.

11 J-F. Lyotard, *The Postmodern Condition*, Manchester: Manchester University Press, 1984, pp. 73, 80f.

12 D. Cornell, *Transformations*, London and New York: Routledge, 1993, p. 1.

13 White, *Political Theory and Postmodernism*, 1991, p. 20.

1 NEGATIVITY AND NOUMENA: CRITICAL REASON AT THE LIMIT

1 G. Deleuze, *Difference and Repetition*, London: Athlone Press, 1994, p. 135.

2 All references to the *Critique of Pure Reason* are to the English translation by Norman Kemp Smith, Basingstoke and London: Macmillan, 1929. These are incorporated into the text as CPR. Numbers accompanying the citation refer to the standard First (A) and Second (B) Edition pagination.

3 It is implicit, for example, in the debate that took place between Derrida and Foucault regarding the latter's *Madness and Civilisation*, where madness enjoys something of the status of the noumenon. Derrida both points out the impossibility of speaking this silence (its 'words without language'), unless Foucault is himself mad, and criticises Foucault's ahistoricity. For if Foucault wants to make madness the cipher of nonreason itself (where, as Derrida puts it, 'the concept of madness overlaps everything that can be put under the rubric of *negativity*' (in *Writing and Difference*, London: Routledge, 1978, p. 41)), then its splitting from reason occurred not in the eighteenth century, as Foucault claims, but has been occurring within 'a reason divided against itself since the dawn of its Greek origin' (p. 40). In other words, nonreason has always existed as reason's other, but it exists as such only because reason circumscribes itself in its quest fully to represent the world, while it can be accessed only from within that reason. It is not an outside independent or available to us although it is, as Derrida's own work suggests, an alterity to be invoked. The conundrum posed by the quest to represent a negativity that is beyond reason shows exactly why Kant's strictures against speculative metaphysics remain so potent. As for Foucault: he subsequently restricted his notion of the other to that which is engendered within regimes of power/knowledge by a splitting off and exclusion within particular disciplines. In *The Order of Things* he dutifully defines the history of madness as 'the history of the Other – of that which, for a given culture, is at once interior and foreign, therefore to be excluded (so as to exorcize the interior danger) but by being shut away (in order to reduce its otherness)'. (*The Order of Things. The Archaeology of the Human Sciences*, London and New York: Tavistock Publications, 1970, p. xxiv.

4 I. Kant, 'An Answer to the Question: "What is Enlightenment?"' in H. Reiss (ed.), *Kant. Political Writings*, Cambridge: Cambridge University Press, 1970. See also Foucault's response, 'What is Enlightenment?' (in P. Rabinow (ed.), *The Foucault Reader*, Harmondsworth: Penguin, 1984) where Foucault presents the challenge of enlightenment as one of identifying and analysing limits in order to 'experiment with the possibility of going beyond them' (p. 50).

5 T. Adorno, *Negative Dialectics*, London: Routledge & Kegan Paul, 1973, pp. 383, 388.

6 G. W. F. Hegel, *Works* 4, quoted by Adorno in *Negative Dialectics*, p. 383n. See also T. Adorno, *Hegel: Three Studies*, Cambridge, MA: MIT Press, 1994, p. 6.

7 Adorno, *Negative Dialectics*, 1973, p. 383. S. Körner, *Kant*, Harmondsworth: Penguin, 1955, p. 46.

8 See Foucault, *The Order of Things*, 1970, pp. 241f.

9 Körner points out that in part IV of his earlier *Metaphysical Foundations of Nature*, Kant had defined matter as 'the mobile in so far as it fills a space, has moving power and can become an object of experience.' Quoted in *Kant*, 1955, p. 85.

10 As Deleuze writes: 'In Kant, the problem of the relation of subject and object tends to be internalized', as one between the (passive and active) faculties. G. Deleuze, *Kant's Critical Philosophy. The Doctrine of the Faculties*, Minneapolis, MN: University of Minnesota Press, 1984, p. 14. Lyotard refers to the irreconcilability of language games, 'which, under the name of faculties, Kant knew to be separated by a chasm'. *The Postmodern Condition*, Manchester: Manchester University Press, 1984, p. 81.

11 Deleuze, *Kant's Critical Philosophy*, 1984, p. 22. See also Horkheimer and Adorno, *Dialectic of Enlightenment*, New York: Seabury Press, 1972, p. 18: 'In the relationship of intuition (i.e. direct perception) and concept, philosophy already discerned the gulf which opened with that separation [between subject and object, image and sign], and again tries in vain to close it: philosophy, indeed, is defined by this very attempt.'

12 Adorno, *Negative Dialectics*, 1973, p. 188.

13 Ibid., p. 389.

14 Adorno, *Hegel: Three Studies*, 1993, p. 11.

15 I. Kant, *Analytic of the Beautiful* from the *Critique of Judgement*, Indianapolis, IN: Bobbs-Merrill, 1963, p. 52.

16 Deleuze, *Kant's Critical Philosophy*, 1984, p. 24.

17 Adorno, *Negative Dialectics*, 1973, pp. 386–8.

18 Ibid., p. 186. See also Horkheimer and Adorno, *Dialectic of Enlightenment*, 1972, p. 26. For an excellent discussion of Adorno's relation to Kant *vis-à-vis* the former's materialism, see S. Jarvis, 'The Coastline of Experience. Materialism and Metaphysics in Adorno', *Radical Philosophy*, 1997, no. 85.

19 F. Nietzsche, *Beyond Good and Evil*, Harmondsworth: Penguin, 1973, section 11.

20 This distinction is emphasised and explored by H. Allison, *Kant's Transcendental Idealism. An Interpretation and Defense*, New Haven, CT and London: Yale University Press, 1983, p. 295. I have drawn on Allison's excellent analysis here.

21 Ibid., pp. 272f.

22 Foucault, *The Order of Things*, 1970, p. 318.

23 Allison, , *Kant*, 1983, p. 272.

24 Deleuze, *Difference and Repetition*, 1994, p. 135.

25 Allison usefully distinguishes between two lines of argument that get confused here. The first relies on a dogmatic assertion entwined with Kant's faculty psychology, regarding the imagination's incapacity to produce data of the inner

self because it is discontinuous with it; the second, which he identifies as sketchy but more promising, relies on an equally dogmatic acceptance that we are conscious of our existence as determined in time. (Allison, *Kant*, 1983, p. 303.) As he adds: in any case, the possibility of outer experience in this latter case is not correlatively conditioned by inner experience; it has primacy insofar as it provides the data necessary for the determinate representation of time (p. 304).

26 C. Battersby, *The Phenomenal Woman. Feminist Metaphysics and the Patterns of Identity*, Cambridge: Polity, 1998, p. 67. Battersby herself argues for a metaphysics of 'self-morphing' matter, which she identifies as a female paradigm.

27 See for example Allison, *Kant*, 1983, p. 239; H. Allison, *Kant's Theory of Freedom*, Cambridge: Cambridge University Press, 1990, pp. 3f.

28 The topographical metaphor, with its clear message of conquest, is taken up again in the Preface to the *First Critique*'s 'sequel', where Kant claims for his critical philosophy a 'perfectly new science' previously unknown. Even Hume, his most worthy predecessor, 'ran his ship ashore, for safety's sake, landing on scepticism, there to let it lie and rot',

> whereas my object is rather to give it a pilot who, by means of safe navigational principles drawn from a knowledge of the globe and provided with a complete chart and compass, may steer the ship safely whither he listeth.
>
> (Kant, *Prolegomena to Any Future Metaphysics that will be able to Come Forward as Science*, Indianapolis, IN and Cambridge: Hackett Publishing Company, 1977, p. 7)

29 Thus for example the mechanical process of nature is also the regulative idea of purposeful design: one whose laws are unknowable (it is fate) yet purposeful (it is providence). We cannot know this agency but we attribute it through analogy with human artifice. Kant, 'Perpetual Peace', in H. Reiss (ed.), *Kant. Political Writings*, 1970, pp. 108–9.

30 Adorno, *Negative Dialectics*, 1973, p. 392.

31 J. McTaggart, *Studies in the Hegelian Logic*, Cambridge: Cambridge University Press, 1922, p. 27. See also Körner, *Kant*, 1955, p. 95.

32 Kant, *Prolegomena*, 1977, p. 33, emphasis added. See also CPR, A251–3 and B307.

33 M. Merleau-Ponty, *The Phenomenology of Perception*, London: Routledge & Kegan Paul, 1962, p. 61.

34 Deleuze, *Difference and Repetition*, 1994, pp. 274f.

35 This ambiguity is also apparent in the different interpretations by Kant's critics. Compare, for example, Körner, *Kant*, 1955, p. 41 with Allison, *Kant*, 1983, p. 252.

36 Kant, *First Introduction to the Critique of Judgement*, 1965, p. 14.

37 Ibid., p. 14.

38 Ibid., pp. 16–17.

39 Ibid., p. 18.

40 Ibid., p. 22.

41 Ibid., p. 16.

42 F. Nietzsche, *Will to Power*, New York: Vintage Books, 1967, section 513.

43 Merleau-Ponty, *The Phenomenology of Perception*, 1962, p. 219.

44 T. Adorno, 'Subject and Object', in A. Arato *et al.* (eds), *The Essential Frankfurt School Reader*, New York: Continuum, 1982, p. 507.

45 J-P. Sartre, *Nausea*, Harmondsworth: Penguin, 1965, p. 184.

46 J-P. Sartre, *Being and Nothingness. A Phenomenological Essay on Ontology*, New York: Washington Square Press, 1966. The in-itself is positive, brute facticity; it is consciousness, the for-itself, which endows it with meaning and which is negativity.

47 Sartre, *Nausea*, 1965, p. 192.

48 Deleuze, *Kant's Critical Philosophy*, 1984, p. 20.

49 Sartre, *Being and Nothingness*, 1966, pp. 3–4.

50 Stanley Rosen writes: 'Kant makes the dual error of attributing the actualization of order and intelligibility, and so necessity, to the spontaneous activity of our cognitive faculties, and of identifying order on the basis of Newtonian physics, Euclidian geometry, and Aristotelian logic.' (In *Mask of Enlightenment. Nietzsche's Zarathustra*, Cambridge: Cambridge University Press, 1995, p. 3.)

51 I. Kant, *Critique of Judgement*, London and New York: Hafner Press, 1951, p. 105.

52 For example Foucault in 'What is Enlightenment?', or Derrida in discussion with Christopher Norris, in A. Papadakis *et al.* (eds), *Deconstruction. Omnibus Edition*, London: Academy Editions, 1989, where he responds: 'Of course I am "in favour" of the Enlightenment: I think we shouldn't simply leave it behind us, so I want to keep this tradition alive. But at the same time I know that there are certain historical forms of Enlightenment, certain things in this tradition that we need to criticise or deconstruct.' Turning the critical instruments and ethos of enlightenment against itself, as an ongoing process, is a project shared by most exponents of negativity.

53 See Foucault, *The Order of Things*, 1970, p. 244, where he explains such developments archaeologically:

> Opposite this opening to the transcendental, and symmetrical to it, another form of thought questions the conditions of a relation between representations from the point of view of the being itself that is represented: what is indicated, on the horizon of all actual representations, as the foundation of their unity, is found to be those never objectifiable objects, those never entirely representable representations, those simultaneously evident and invisible visibilities, those realities that are removed from reality to the degree to which they are the foundation of what is given to us and reaches us: the force of labour, the energy of life, the power of speech. It is on the basis of these forms, which prowl around the outer boundaries of our experience, that the value of things ... attain our representations and urge us on to the perhaps infinite task of knowing.

54 Deleuze, *Difference and Repetition*, 1994, p. xxi.

2 HEGEL AND HIS CRITICS: DIALECTICS AND DIFFERENCE

1 References to the two main texts considered in this chapter will be incorporated as follows: (Logic) *Hegel's Science of Logic*, trans. A. V. Miller, London: Allen & Unwin, 1969; (Ph) G. W. F. Hegel, *Phenomenology of Mind*, trans. J. B. Baillie, London and New York: Harper & Row, 1967.

2 Hegel, quoted by T. Adorno in his *Hegel. Three Studies*, Cambridge, MA: MIT Press, 1993, pp. 67f.

3 Similarly, poststructuralists will condemn Marxism for translating multiple antagonisms into the dyadic structure of two opposing classes. See E. Laclau and C. Mouffe, *Hegemony and Socialist Strategy: Towards a Radical Democratic Politics*, London: Verso, 1985.

4 Adorno, *Hegel. Three Studies*, 1993, pp. 102f.

5 See Foucault's comment in 'The Discourse on Language' in *The Archaeology of Knowledge*, New York: Pantheon, 1972, p. 235, where he anticipates finding Hegel awaiting the anti-Hegelians who merely perform one of his dialectical tricks. Judith Butler similarly refers to Hegelianism's 'inadvertent reappearance even when subject to its most vehement opposition.' *Subjects of Desire*, New York: Columbia University Press, 1987, p. 15.

6 Adorno, *Hegel. Three Studies*, 1993, p. 141.

7 G. W. F. Hegel, *Philosophy of Right*, trans. T. M. Knox, London and New York: Oxford University Press, 1952, p. 34.

8 Adorno, *Hegel. Three Studies*, 1993, p. 80.

9 L. Althusser, *Montesquieu, Rousseau, Marx*, London: Verso, 1982, p. 183.

10 *Relève* is Derrida's translation of *Aufhebung*, which captures its sense of lifting up.

11 W. T. Stace, *The Philosophy of Hegel*, Toronto and London: Dover Publications, 1955, p. 101.

12 Robert Young identifies this process too in the master/slave relation. See his *White Mythologies*, London and New York: Routledge, 1990, p. 6.

13 Deleuze condemns formulae like 'the object denies what it is not' as 'logical monsters ... in the service of identity. It is said that difference is negativity, that it extends or must extend to the point of contradiction once it is taken to the limit. This is true only to the extent that difference is already placed on a path or along a thread laid out by identity.' *Difference and Repetition*, 1994, pp. 49f.

14 Where it is other subjects who are the object, the consequences of asymmetry are revealed as positive in Hegel's master/slave dialectic but negatively in Simone de Beauvoir's man/woman opposition in *The Second Sex*.

15 W. T. Stace, *The Philosophy of Hegel*, 1955, p. 179.

16 Stephen Houlgate, lecture and accompanying précis, presented during the Royal Institute of Philosophy's 1997–8 lecture series in London on 16 January 1998.

17 Hegel discusses contradiction in ch. 2 book 2 of the *Logic*, 1969.

18 Adorno, *Hegel. Three Studies*, 1993, p. 57.

19 L. Althusser, *The Spectre of Hegel*, London: Verso, 1997, p. 38.

20 A. Kojève, *Introduction to the Reading of Hegel*, New York and London: Basic Books, 1969, p. 170.

21 Ibid., p. 178.

22 Hegel, *Philosophy of Right*, 1952, section 31, pp. 34f.

23 Adorno, *Hegel. Three Studies*, 1993, p. 6.

24 Ibid., p. 6.

25 Ibid., p. 121. Stephen Houlgate (in his *Hegel, Nietzsche and the Criticism of Metaphysics*, Cambridge: Cambridge University Press, 1986, pp. 153ff.) writes: 'Both Hegel and Nietzsche want their style to reflect the shift they make from understanding the world in terms of things to understanding the world in terms of processes and activities.' He contrasts Hegel's language – 'the sober dialectical movement of thought generated by definite contradictions' – with Nietzsche's 'protean restlessness and excitement' conjured by streams of unconnected or associatively-connected metaphors. Houlgate then presents their differing styles as reflecting their basic philosophical differences: differences I would identify as emblematic of the differential rhythms and tempo of negativity they struggle to

convey. In this way, both thinkers perform stylistically the process of which they speak.

26 Ibid., p. 122.
27 H. Marcuse, *Reason and Revolution. Hegel and the Rise of Social Theory*, Boston, MA: Beacon Press, 1960, p. ix. Foucault echoes this critical intent in his 'The Ethic of Care for the Self as a Practice of Freedom', *Philosophy and Social Criticism*, 1987, vol. 12 no. 1, p. 131: 'On the critical side – I mean critical in a very broad sense – philosophy is precisely the challenging of all phenomena of domination on whatever level or under whatever form they present themselves ... .'
28 Althusser, *Montesquieu. Rousseau. Marx*, 1982, p. 184.
29 J. Derrida, 'The Ends of Man', *Philosophy and Phenomenological Research*, 1969, vol. 30 no. 1, p. 37.
30 Kojève, *Introduction to the Reading of Hegel*, 1969, p. 155.
31 See for example M. Merleau-Ponty, *Sense and Nonsense*, Evanston, IL: Northwestern University Press, 1964, pp. 81, 133.
32 M. Merleau-Ponty, 'Philosophy and Non-Philosophy since Hegel', *Telos* 29, Fall 1976, p. 68.
33 Merleau-Ponty, *Sense and Nonsense*, 1964, pp. 65, 127.
34 Merleau-Ponty, 'Philosophy and Non-Philosophy since Hegel', 1976, p. 81.
35 M. Merleau-Ponty, *Themes from the Lectures at the Collège de France 1952–1960*, Evanston, IL: Northwestern University Press, 1970, p. 58.
36 Merleau-Ponty, 'Philosophy and Non-Philosophy since Hegel', 1976, pp. 69, 81.
37 Kojève, *Introduction to the Reading of Hegel*, 1969, pp. 190f.
38 Ibid., p. 176.
39 Ibid., p. 54. See also the long footnote on the end of history, pp. 157–62n.
40 G. Lukács, *History and Class Consciousness. Studies in Marxist Dialectics*, Cambridge, MA: MIT Press, 1971, p. 154. R. Gasché writes: 'A totality ... amounts to a medium of mediation, a middle of intersecting lines.' In *The Tain of the Mirror*, Cambridge, MA: Harvard University Press, 1986, p. 57.
41 Deleuze, *Difference and Repetition*, 1994, p. 147.
43 K. Marx, *Economic and Philosophical Manuscripts* in L. Colletti (ed.), *Marx. Early Writings*, Harmondsworth: Penguin, 1974, p. 379. This follows his 'A Contribution to the Critique of Hegel's Philosophy of Right'.
44 Ibid., pp. 384f.
45 K. Marx, *Capital*, vol. I, Moscow: Progress Publishers, 1954, p. 29.
46 Marx, *1844 Manuscripts*, 1974, p. 396.
47 Ibid., p. 386.
48 K. Marx, Afterword to the Second German edition of *Capital*, vol. I, Moscow: Progress Publishers, 1954, p. 29. Here, too, Marx insists that the 'mystification which dialectics suffers in Hegel's hands, by no means prevents him from being the first to present its general form of working in a comprehensive and conscious manner.'
49 Ibid., 1954, p. 20.
50 K. Marx, *The German Ideology* in R. Tucker (ed.), *The Marx-Engels Reader*, New York: W. W. Norton, 1978, p. 149; *1844 Manuscripts*, in L. Colletti (ed.), 1974, p. 389.
51 Marx, *1844 Manuscripts*, in L. Colletti (ed.), 1974, p. 390.
52 Ibid., p. 329.
53 Ibid, p. 353; *Capital*, 1954, p. 168.
54 One might nevertheless wonder whether Marx is sufficiently self-critical of his own starting point, which might be accused of reflecting the particular perspective of a capitalist society as expressed in political economists' obsession with

scarcity and production. In this sense it is dogmatic, insufficiently mediated, and this flaw might be held accountable for the reductionist tendencies in Marx's account of history and its overcoming in an abundant, rationally-planned economy.

55 Marx, *Capital*,1954, p. 50.
56 K. Marx, *Critique of the Gotha Programme* in R. Tucker (ed.), 1978, p. 525; *Capital*, 1954, p. 179.
57 Marx, *German Ideology*, 1978, p. 157.
58 Ibid., p. 159.
59 Ibid., pp. 154f.
60 Marx, *Capital*, 1954, p. 77.
61 Ibid., p. 84.
62 K. Marx, Preface to *A Contribution to the Critique of Political Economy*, in R. Tucker (ed.), 1978, p. 4.
63 Althusser writes of Marx and Engels: 'Of the dialectic, triplicity, alienation, or negativity, they claimed to have retained only the *form* of Hegelian truth.' He presents this as paradoxical, given their criticism of Hegel's formalism, but I am suggesting that it is particularly appropriate to the impersonal logic of reified capitalist structures. Althusser, *The Spectre of Hegel*, 1997, p. 140.
64 Marx, *Capital*, 1954, pp. 293f.
65 K. Marx, *Grundrisse*, Harmondsworth: Penguin, 1973, pp. 692f.
66 K. Marx, *Contribution to the Critique of Hegel's Philosophy of Right*, in L. Colletti (ed.), 1974, p. 250.
67 Ibid., p. 256.
68 As Foucault will insist, liberation will be needed to escape the closures of domination, but this only opens a field for practices of liberty, which are once again possible where power and freedom are interwoven. These have then to be invented. 'The Ethic of Care for the Self as a Practice of Freedom', 1987, pp. 113f.
69 Marx, *Capital*, 1954, p. 115.
70 Ibid., p. 28.
71 Ibid., p. 29.
72 Marx, *Grundrisse*, 1973, p. 100.
73 E. Balibar, *The Philosophy of Marx*, London: Verso, 1995 (orig: *La Philosophie de Marx*, 1993), pp. 100f.
74 J. Zelený, *The Logic of Marx*, Oxford: Blackwell, 1980 (orig: *Die Wissenshaftslogik bei Marx und das Kapital*, 1968), p. 38.
75 Marx, *Grundrisse*, 1973, p. 102.
76 Ibid., p. 278.
77 Althusser had already insisted that what 'irremediably disfigures the Hegelian conception of History as a dialectical process is its *teleological* conception of the dialectic, inscribed in the very *structures* of the Hegelian dialectic at an extremely precise point: the *Aufhebung* (transcendence-preserving-the-transcended-as-the-internalized-transcended), directly expressed in the Hegelian category of the *negation of the negation.*' In *Montesquieu, Rousseau, Marx*, 1982, p. 181.
78 J. Kristeva, *Revolution in Poetic Language*, trans. M. Waller, ed. L. S. Roudiez, New York: Columbia University Press, 1984.
79 Ibid., p. 109.
80 Ibid., p. 111.
81 Ibid., p. 114.
82 J. Kristeva, 'The System and the Speaking Subject', in T. Moi (ed.), *The Kristeva Reader*, Oxford: Blackwell, 1986, p. 31.

83 The two main works of Derrida's that are cited in this chapter are incorporated into the text as follows: (P) *Positions*, London: Athlone, 1981; (M) *Margins of Philosophy*, Hemel Hempstead: Harvester, 1982. A Hegel of irreducible *différance* is further engaged by Derrida in *Glas*, Lincoln, NE: University of Nebraska Press, 1986.
84 Kristeva, *Revolution in Poetic Language*, 1984, p. 140.
85 For an extended discussion of Derrida's confrontation with Hegel, see the essays in S. Barnett (ed.), *Hegel after Derrida*, London and New York: Routledge, 1998. Because the Hegel confronted here is the one re-worked by Derrida, however, he is scarcely recognisable as the one discussed in this chapter.
86 In G. Deleuze, *Nietzsche and Philosophy* (orig. 1962), London: Athlone Press, 1983, which Derrida himself cites in his footnotes.
87 J. Derrida, *Writing and Difference*, London and New York: Routledge, 1978, p. 292.
88 Deleuze, *Difference and Repetition*, 1994, pp. 204f.
89 J. Derrida, 'Choreographies', in P. Kamuf (ed.), *A Derrida Reader. Between the Blinds*, Hemel Hempstead: Harvester Wheatsheaf, 1991.
90 Derrida, *Glas*, 1986, pp. 5a, 97a.
91 J. Derrida, *Specters of Marx*, London and New York: Routledge, 1994, pp. 33ff, 75.
92 Ibid., p.31.
93 J-L. Nancy, 'The Surprise of the Event' (orig: 'Être Singulier Pluriel', 1996), in S. Barnett (ed.), *Hegel after Derrida*, London and New York: Routledge, 1998, pp. 91–105.
94 Ibid., p. 96.
95 Ibid., pp. 92, 98, 100.
96 Ibid., p. 98.
97 Ibid., p. 102.
98 Ibid., pp. 96–7, 99.
99 G. Deleuze, *Negotiations 1972–1990*, New York: Columbia University Press, 1995, p. 6.
100 Deleuze, *Nietzsche and Philosophy*, 1983, pp. 157f.
101 Deleuze, *Difference and Repetition*, 1994, pp. 266f.
102 Ibid., p. 263.
103 Ibid., pp. 63f, 202.
104 Ibid., pp. 65, 202f.
105 Derrida, *Writing and Difference*, 1978, p. 292.
106 Deleuze, *Difference and Repetition*, 1994, p. 268.
107 Ibid., p. 208.

3 NIETZSCHE: NEGATIVITY AS WILL TO POWER

1 The following references to works by Nietzsche are incorporated into the text:
BGE *Beyond Good and Evil*, trans. W. Kaufmann, New York: Random House, 1966.
BT *The Birth of Tragedy*, trans. W. Kaufmann, New York: Random House, 1967.
EH *Ecco Homo*, trans. R. J. Hollingdale, Harmondsworth: Penguin, 1979.
GM *The Genealogy of Morality*, trans. C. Diethe, Cambridge: Cambridge University Press, 1994.
GS *The Gay Science*, trans. W. Kaufmann, New York: Random House, 1974.

WP *The Will to Power*, trans. W. Kaufmann & R. J. Hollingdale, New York: Random House, 1967.

Z *Thus Spake Zarathustra*, trans. R. J. Hollingdale, Harmondsworth: Penguin, 1961.

2 J.-F. Lyotard, *The Postmodern Condition*, Manchester: Manchester University Press, 1984, pp. 79ff.

3 Deleuze states this opposition starkly: 'Nietzsche's "yes" is opposed to the dialectical "no"; affirmation to dialectical negation; difference to dialectical contradiction; joy, enjoyment, to dialectical labour; lightness, dance, to dialectical responsibilities.' In *Nietzsche and Philosophy*, London: Athlone Press, 1983, p. 9. A more nuanced version appears in *Difference and Repetition*, where Deleuze distinguishes between two conceptions of the affirmation/negation relationship, one conservative and the other creative, and favourably links the creative version to the poet and a state of 'permanent revolution' equated with the eternal return. G. Deleuze, *Difference and Repetition*, London: Athlone, 1994, pp. 53f.

4 S. Rosen's comparison is incisive here: 'In Hegel, the internal excitation of chaos or negativity organizes itself to produce the totality of genesis, or Becoming. In Nietzsche, chaos organizes itself into perspectives or worlds, which also recur perpetually.' In *The Mask of Enlightenment*, Cambridge: Cambridge University Press, 1995, p. 22.

5 1886 Attempt at a self-criticism, included in Kaufmann edition of BT, section 3.

6 Deleuze, *Difference and Repetition*, 1994, p. 8.

7 See the 1886 attempt at a self-criticism written for Nietzsche's new edition of BT, and contained in the Kaufmann edition; the section in EH (1888); notes in WP such as 853 and 1050. The third of Zarathustra's discourses, 'Of the Afterworldsmen' (Book 1, Z 1882), is also perhaps an allusion to it.

8 P. Poellner, for example, refers to an 'apparent metaphysics' and contends that in some passages Nietzsche does claim 'a causal efficacy or power of some kind, a "will" with which, it is claimed, we are introspectively familiar.' *Nietzsche and Metaphysics*, Oxford: Clarendon Press, 1995, pp. 15, 46. Many critics, including Heidegger, similarly ascribe to will to power a metaphysical status. Even Deleuze has no qualms in attributing an ontology to Nietzsche here.

9 In H. S. Thayer (ed.), *Newton's Philosophy of Nature*, New York: Hafner Publishing Co., 1953, p. 54.

10 If one ignores Newton's theological nostalgia, one can interpret gravity simply as a self-sustaining field of forces. For according to the third law of motion, no isolated particle can experience or exert force: rather there is a relational, interactive process (of push/pull) between at least two entities: an action/reaction, credit/debit, where it remains undecidable which body pushes and which pulls and the causal connection is only introduced artificially. See Holton and Brush, *Introduction to Concepts and Theories of Physical Science*, Princeton, NJ: Princeton University Press, 1985, pp. 127–8. This bears a much closer resemblance to interpretations of will to power as differential forces. See also Poellner's illuminating discussion of Boscovichean forces in *Nietzsche and Metaphysics*, 1995. 'Boscovich's reduction of matter to centres and fields of force forms an essential part of the background from which Nietzsche's own dynamist "hypothesis" emerges and against which it has to be understood' (p. 51).

11 See Rosen's interesting assessment here in *The Mask of Enlightenment*, Cambridge: Cambridge University Press, 1995, where he attributes 'cosmological nihilism' to Nietzsche. According to his interpretation, which takes the cosmology as the privileged discourse, what look like creations of value, and

what can be spoken of only in metaphorical language, are only in fact 'the accumulation and discharge of points of force'; the random and inhuman modifications of chaos; the 'regular pulsation or fluctuation between the expansion and contraction of the physical universe' (pp. 13–16; 20; 58). As he acknowledges, however, this is problematic in terms of the value Nietzsche insists on. The *Übermensch* could be no more than the supreme metaphysical comfort and illusion – 'an empty celebration of the accumulation and discharge of points of force' – and the last man, the equivalent of physical entropy (p. 47).

12 A. Nehamas, *Nietzsche: Life as Literature*, Cambridge, MA: Harvard University Press, 1985, pp. 81–2.

13 J. Kristeva, 'The Maternal Body', *m/f*, 1981, nos 5 and 6, p. 159.

14 M. Foucault, *The Care of the Self. History of Sexuality* Volume 3, New York: Random House, 1986.

15 S. Freud, Fragment of analysis of a case of hysteria, *Standard Edition of the Complete Works of Sigmund Freud*, vol. 7, ed. J. Strachey, London: Hogarth Press, 1905, p. 50.

16 See Deleuze and Guattari, *Anti-Œdipus. Capitalism and Schizophrenia*, Minneapolis, MN: University of Minnesota Press, 1983, for discussion of Nietzsche and Œdipus along these lines.

17 Nietzsche's explicit political pronouncements have anyway been well documented elsewhere. See for example Keith Ansell Pearson, *Nietzsche. The Perfect Nihilist*, Cambridge: Cambridge University Press, 1994.

18 See for example M. Warren, *Nietzsche and Political Thought*, Cambridge, MA: MIT Press, 1988, and D. Conway, *Nietzsche and the Political*, London and New York: Routledge, 1997. For further discussion of my scepticism regarding such interpretations see D. Coole, 'The Politics of Reading Nietzsche', *Political Studies*, vol. 46 no. 2, June 1998.

19 T. Strong, 'Nietzsche's Political Misappropriation' in B. Magnus and K. Higgins (eds), *The Cambridge Companion to Nietzsche*, Cambridge: Cambridge University Press, 1996, p. 142.

20 M. Foucault, *The History of Sexuality* Vol. 1, New York: Random House, 1978, p. 102.

21 Ibid., p. 96.

22 The phrases in this and the preceding paragraph are derived from a number of Foucault's works: Foucault, *History of Sexuality*, 1978, pp. 92ff; 'The Subject and Power' in H. Dreyfus and P. Rabinow, *Michel Foucault: Beyond Structuralism and Hermeneutics*, Chicago, IL: University of Chicago Press, 1982; 'The Ethic of Care for the Self as a Practice of Freedom', *Philosophy and Social Criticism*, Spring 1987, vol. 12 no. 1, pp. 114, 123.

23 M. Foucault, *Discipline and Punish*, Harmondsworth: Penguin, 1977, pp. 215f; 'The Subject and Power', 1982, p. 224.

24 Foucault, 'The Ethic of Care', 1987, p. 131. In 'What is Enlightenment?', Foucault argues that what connects us still to the Enlightenment is the 'permanent reactivation of an attitude – that is, of a philosophical ethos that could be described as a permanent critique of our historical era.' In P. Rabinow (ed.), *The Foucault Reader*, Harmondsworth: Penguin, 1984, p. 42.

25 Foucault, 'The Subject and Power', 1982, p. 223.

26 Foucault, 'The Ethic of Care', 1987, p. 123.

4 NEGATIVITY AS INVISIBILITY: MERLEAU-PONTY'S
DIALECTICAL ADVENTURES

1 Merleau-Ponty's writings are referenced in the text under the following abbreviations:
AD *Adventures of the Dialectic*, London: Heinemann, 1974.
CAL *Consciousness and the Acquisition of Language*, Evanston, IL: Northwestern University Press, 1973.
HT *Humanism and Terror*, Boston, MA: Beacon Press, 1969.
IP *In Praise of Philosophy*, Evanston, IL: Northwestern University Press, 1963.
Ph.P *The Phenomenology of Perception*, London: Routledge & Kegan Paul, 1962.
PNP 'Philosophy and Non-Philosophy since Hegel', *Telos*, Fall 1976, no. 29.
PP *The Primacy of Perception*, Evanston, IL: Northwestern University Press, 1964.
PW *The Prose of the World*, Evanston, IL: Northwestern University Press, 1973.
S *Signs*, Evanston, IL: Northwestern University Press, 1964.
SB *The Structure of Behaviour*, London: Methuen, 1965.
SNS *Sense and Non-Sense*, Evanston, IL: Northwestern University Press, 1964.
TL *Themes from the Lectures*, Evanston, IL: Northwestern University Press, 1970.
VI *The Visible and the Invisible*, Evanston, IL: Northwestern University Press, 1968.
2 Heidegger refers to Heraclitus's account of an original conflict that broke up Being such that a world arose. Without this splitting – 'cleavages, intervals, distances, and joints opened' – he implies that there would have been no meaning or history. In *An Introduction to Metaphysics*, New York: Anchor Books, 1961, pp. 51f. See also his 'Letter on Humanism': 'Nihilation unfolds essentially in Being itself, and not at all in the existence of man – so far as this is thought as the subjectivity of the *ego cogito*. Dasein in no way nihilates as a human subject who carries out nihilation in the sense of denial; rather, Da-sein nihilates inasmuch as it belongs to the essence of Being as that essence in which man ek-sists. Being nihilates – as Being.' In *Martin Heidegger. Basic Writings*, New York: Harper and Row, 1977, p. 238. Deleuze credits Merleau-Ponty with 'Heideggerian inspiration in speaking of "folds" and "pleating" (by contrast with Sartrean "holes" and "lakes of non-being")' and, in the later work, with 'returning to an ontology of difference and questioning'. G. Deleuze, *Difference and Repetition*, London: Athlone, 1994, p. 64.
3 Foucault makes the claim in an interview conducted by G. Raulet, 'Structuralism and Post-Structuralism: An Interview with Michel Foucault', *Telos*, 1983, no. 55, pp. 197f. Here he recalls lectures where Merleau-Ponty spoke about Saussure, in the context of explaining the importance of the latter to the shift from phenomenology to structuralism (but where he nevertheless associates Merleau-Ponty with phenomenology's affirmation of a constituting subject and attributes most importance in that subject's demise, to the influence of Nietzsche).

There has been considerable debate regarding Merleau-Ponty's structuralist credentials. See, for example, J. Edie, 'Was Merleau-Ponty a Structuralist?', *Semiotica*, 1971, vol. 4; C. Smith, 'Merleau-Ponty and Structuralism', *British Journal of Phenomenology*, 1971, vol. 2 and J. Daly, 'Merleau-Ponty: A Bridge between Phenomenology and Structuralism', in the same volume; V. Descombes, *Modern French Philosophy*, Cambridge: Cambridge University Press, 1980; H.

Silverman, 'Re-Reading Merleau-Ponty', *Telos,* 1976, vol. 29; J. Schmidt, *Maurice Merleau-Ponty. Between Phenomenology and Structuralism,* London: Macmillan, 1985. As the titles reveal, Merleau-Ponty has often been read as combining the two traditions of phenomenology and structuralism, which became so polarised after his death.

4 Referring to *Humanism and Terror* in her autobiography, Simone de Beauvoir suggests that Merleau-Ponty tipped the balance against moralism in a way novel among existentialists. 'He subordinated morality to history much more resolutely than any existentialist had ever done. We crossed the Rubicon with him, conscious that moralism ... was the last bastion of bourgeois idealism'. *Force of Circumstance,* Middlesex: Penguin, 1964, p. 115.

5 This tension had already been recognised as an 'internal difficulty' in 1945 (SNS: 120f).

6 J-P. Sartre, *Being and Nothingness,* New York: Washington Square Press, 1956, pp. 128f.

7 Compare this with Sartre:

> Presence to self ... supposes that an impalpable fissure has slipped into being. If being is present to itself, it is because it is not wholly itself. Presence is an immediate deterioration of coincidence, for it supposes separation. But if we ask ourselves at this point *what it is* which separates the subject from himself, we are forced to admit that it is *nothing* ... . This fissure then is the pure negative ... .
> This negative which is the nothingness of being and the nihilating power both together, is nothingness.
>
> *Being and Nothingness*, pp. 124f.

8 Ricoeur argues (and I agree) that the theory of perception already contains a whole theory of action and politics. P. Ricoeur, 'Hommage à Merleau-Ponty', *Esprit*, June 1961, vol. 29, p. 1117.

9 As Hegel had written of the work of art, it 'occupies the mean between what is immediately sensuous and ideal thought'. Hegel, *On Art, Religion and Philosophy*, New York: Harper and Row, 1970, p. 66. Similarly, Merleau-Ponty suggests that Kant's Third Critique should have taken epistemological precedence over the First, where in experiencing beauty 'I am aware of a harmony between sensation and concept, between myself and others, which is itself without any concept' (Ph.P: xvii). I have explored the connections between Merleau-Ponty and Kant's aesthetics further in my 'The Aesthetic Realm and the Lifeworld: Kant and Merleau-Ponty', *History of Political Thought*, 1984, vol. 5.

10 Descombes claims that Merleau-Ponty confuses structuralist structures with *Gestalten*, in *Modern French Philosophy*, p. 73. More charitably, I am suggesting that he interpreted the former in such a way that the existentialist, political project could continue. P. Dews observes: 'This "tenderness" towards the perceived world, a *parti pris* which lies at the heart of Merleau-Ponty's philosophy, is clearly irreconcilable with structuralist and early poststructuralist thought, where there can be no doubt that, even granted the existence of a language-independent reality, it is language which segments it and determines its meaning.' *Logics of Disintegration*, London: Verso, 1987, p. 117.

11 M. Foucault, 'What is Enlightenment?', in P. Rabinow (ed.), *The Foucault Reader*, Middlesex: Penguin, 1984.

12 Lévi-Strauss had argued: 'We need only recognize that history is a method with no distinct object corresponding to it to reject the equivalence between the

notion of history and the notion of humanity which some have tried to foist upon us with the avowed aim of making historicity the last refuge of a transcendental humanism.' *The Savage Mind*, Chicago, IL: University of Chicago Press, 1966, p. 262. The book as a whole was dedicated to Merleau-Ponty's memory. Lyotard's two grand narratives of Enlightenment correspond broadly with Merleau-Ponty's two rationalist politics (of understanding and reason). See Lyotard, *The Postmodern Condition*, Manchester: Manchester University Press, 1984.

13 I take aspects of the comparison further, criticising Habermas generally for an occluding of negativity in his work, in my 'Habermas and the Question of Alterity' in M. Passerin D'Entrèves and S. Benhabib (eds), *Habermas and the Unfinished Project of Modernity*, Cambridge: Polity Press, 1996.

K. Whiteside concludes his book, *Merleau-Ponty and the Foundation of an Existential Politics*, Princeton, NJ: Princeton University Press, 1988, by comparing Merleau-Ponty's approach to politics with those of Walzer and Rawls. This study usefully brings out the relevance, given Rawls's (and in my case, Habermas's) Kantianism, of Merleau-Ponty's objections to Kantian politics: on the grounds that it 'undervalued consequences, overestimated rationality, ignored social structures, and misunderstood the nature of human motivation' (p. 293). Like other critics, Whiteside nevertheless notes Merleau-Ponty's rather abstract account of the political. 'His failing is that he neglects to engage in the concrete investigations that might impel him to identify previously unsuspected structures of constraint, to limit his claims about the extent of structures, and to appreciate the difficulty of reconciling different ethical systems.' As such, Merleau-Ponty's tendency towards holism is contrasted unfavourably with Foucaultian genealogies of power, pp. 297f.

14 T. McCarthy, 'Habermas', in S. Critchley and W. Schroeder (eds), *A Companion to Continental Philosophy*, Blackwell: Oxford, 1998, p. 399.

15 Habermas, *The Philosophical Discourse of Modernity*, Cambridge: Polity, 1987, p. 317.

16 Merleau-Ponty's insistence that we all open onto a common lifeworld is intended, I think, to refute Kantian ideas that the world needs constituting, and any idealist scepticism regarding our attunement to it. However, from our more postmodern perspective, this premise seems jarringly oblivious to the diversity of lifeworlds different groups occupy. This theme is taken up in terms of gender by E. McMillan in 'Female Difference in the Texts of Merleau-Ponty', *Philosophy Today*, 1987. Given subsequent feminist equations between *différance* and the feminine, Merleau-Ponty's work opens itself to some interesting speculation here. However given his own refusal to link negativity and gender, I have postponed consideration of this theme until my discussion of Kristeva.

5 SUBJECT–OBJECT RELATIONS AGAIN: IDENTITY, NON-IDENTITY AND NEGATIVE DIALECTICS

1 References to Adorno's work are abbreviated and incorporated in the text as follows:
AtoB E. Bloch *et al.* (eds), *Aesthetics and Politics*, London: New Left Books, 1977.
AE *Against Epistemology*, Oxford: Blackwell, 1982.
AP 'The Actuality of Philosophy', *Telos* 1977, 31.
AT *Aesthetic Theory*, Minneapolis, MA: University of Minnesota Press, 1997.

NOTES

CIR 'Culture Industry Reconsidered', in J. M. Bernstein (ed.), *Adorno. The Culture Industry*, London: Routledge, 1991.
DofE *Dialectic of Enlightenment* (with Horkheimer), New York: Seabury Press, 1972.
FTFP 'Freudian Theory and the Pattern of Fascist Propaganda', in A. Arato *et al.* (eds), *The Essential Frankfurt School Reader*, New York: Continuum, 1982.
H:TS *Hegel: Three Studies*, Cambridge, MA: MIT Press, 1993.
MM *Minima Moralia*, London: New Left Books, 1974.
ND *Negative Dialectics*, London: Routledge & Kegan Paul, 1973.
S&O 'Subject and Object', in *The Essential Frankfurt School Reader* (see FTFP).
2 M. Merleau-Ponty, *The Visible and the Invisible*, Evanston, IL: Northwestern University Press, 1968, p. 92.
3 M. Merleau-Ponty, *The Phenomenology of Perception*, London: Routledge and Kegan Paul, 1962, p. xvi.
4 Critics note the continuity and coherence of Adorno's work overall. See for example M. Jay, *Adorno*, Cambridge, MA: Harvard University Press, 1984, p. 57 and S. Jarvis, *Adorno. A Critical Introduction*, London and New York: Routledge, 1998, p. 1.
5 Peter Dews has usefully compared Adorno's thinking in this context with post-structuralist approaches. See his 'Adorno, Post-Structuralism and the Critique of Identity', *New Left Review*, May/June 1986, no. 157. Although I do not completely agree with Dews' argument that Nietzsche and his poststructuralist followers ontologise non-identity, with the implication of performative contradiction this entails, I do agree with his central argument that Adorno cannot be read as a deconstructionist *avant la lettre* inasmuch as for him, 'non-identity cannot be respected by abandoning completely the principle of identity' (p. 42).
6 Max Horkheimer, 'Traditional and Critical Theory. Postscript', in his *Critical Theory*, New York: Herder and Herder, 1972, p. 246.
7 See for example the way Rorty develops his critique of epistemology in *Philosophy and the Mirror of Nature*, Cambridge: Cambridge University Press, 1980, into cultural and political critique in *Contingency, Irony and Solidarity*, Cambridge: Cambridge University Press, 1989. On the other hand, Rorty seems quite happy to eliminate negativity from the public sphere.
8 'Marx very clearly discerned the interdependence between the fact of thinking an "order of the world" (especially in the social and political register) and the fact of *valorizing order* in the world: both against "anarchy" and against "movement".' E. Balibar, *Marx and Philosophy*, London: Verso, 1995, p. 24.
9 H. Marcuse, *One Dimensional Man*, London: Routledge, 1964, p. 33.
10 Horkheimer, *Critical Theory*, 1972, p. 200. Compare Adorno's intimation of the illegibility of the American landscape, whose shortcoming is 'that it bears no traces of the human hand', where even roads are 'unrelated and violent', 'expressionless' (MM: 48).
11 K. Marx, *Economic and Philosophical Manuscripts* in L. Colletti (ed.), *Marx. Early Writings*, Harmondsworth: Penguin, 1974, p. 351. Adorno compliments Benjamin on a passage from his *Arcades* project 'about the "liberation of things from the bondage of being useful" as a brilliant turning-point for the dialectical salvation of the commodity' (AtoB: 119).
12 S. Freud, 'On Negation' *Standard Edition of the Complete Works of Sigmund Freud*, ed. J. Strachey, London: Hogarth Press, 1966, vol. 19, p. 237.
13 S. Freud, 'The Ego and the Id', in *The Penguin Freud Library*, Harmondsworth: Penguin, 1984, vol. 11, p. 378.

260

14 See especially his FTFP, where Adorno draws on Freud's *Group Psychology and the Analysis of the Ego*.

15 Freud, 'On Negation', 1966, p. 238.

16 Freud, 'Instincts and their Vicissitudes', in *The Penguin Freud Library*, vol. 11, p. 119.

17 F. Jameson, *Marxism and Form*, Princeton, NJ: Princeton University Press, 1974, p. 99.

18 See Horkheimer's 'Authority and the Family' in *Critical Theory*, 1972, especially p. 98.

19 Elsewhere Adorno offers a more nuanced account of the Enlightenment (ND: 29).

20 Habermas surely overstates their rejection of reason when he concludes that his predecessors succumbed to 'an uninhibited scepticism regarding reason', in *The Philosophical Discourse of Modernity*, Cambridge: Polity, 1987, p. 129.

21 F. Nietzsche, *Will to Power*, New York: Random House, 1967, section 1019.

22 See J. Schmidt, 'Language, Mythology, and Enlightenment: Historical Notes on Horkheimer and Adorno's *Dialectic of Enlightenment*', *Social Research*, Winter 1998, vol. 65 no. 4.

23 For a very similar claim, see Lukács, *History and Class Consciousness*, Cambridge, MA: MIT Press, 1971, p. 162, although Adorno rejects Lukács' final identification of subject and object in the proletariat (or anywhere else).

24 J. Habermas, 'Theodor Adorno: The Primal History of Subjectivity – Self-Affirmation Gone Wild', in J. Habermas, *Philosophical-Political Profiles*, London: Heinemann, 1983 (originally 1969), p. 107.

25 See for example J. Habermas, *The Theory of Communicative Action* vol. 1, Cambridge: Polity, 1984, p. 384. If all meaning falls within instrumental reason, a version of identity thinking, then how, Habermas asks, could critical theory itself 'transform mimetic impulses into insight, discursively, in its own element, and not merely intuitively, in speechless "mindfulness"?' Here he charges that cognitive competence migrates into art and philosophy regresses into gesticulation, a charge endlessly repeated against first generation critical theorists and postmodernists by his supporters, although one I have in most cases rejected. See also *The Philosophical Discourse of Modernity*, Cambridge: Polity, 1987.

26 Jay, *Adorno*, 1984, p. 78.

27 Walter Benjamin, *Ursprung des Deutschen Trauerspiels* (1928), translated as *Origin of German Tragic Drama*, London: New Left Books, 1977.

28 See for example S. Buck-Morss, 'Walter Benjamin – Revolutionary Writer I & II', *New Left Review* 128 and 129, July/Aug. 1981 and Sept./Oct. 1981. Also her *Origin of Negative Dialectics*, Sussex: Harvester Press, 1977.

29 W. Benjamin, 'Surrealism: the last Snapshot of the European Intelligentsia', *New Left Review*, March/April 1978, pp. 50, 55.

30 Benjamin's challenge to Kantian experience has recently been explored by Howard Caygill in his splendid *Walter Benjamin. The Colour of Experience*, London and New York: Routledge, 1998.

31 Merleau-Ponty, *Adventures of the Dialectic*, London: Heinemann, 1974, ch. 1.

32 Buck-Morss, *Origin of Negative Dialectics*, 1977, p. 102.

33 Merleau-Ponty, *The Visible and the Invisible*, 1968, p. 132.

34 Merleau-Ponty, *The Phenomenology of Perception*, 1962, p. xviii.

35 A similar point had already been made in *Dialectic of Enlightenment*, where Hegel's lapsing into mythology is said to replicate the totalising logic of Enlightenment and capitalism (DofE: 6, 24).

36 Buck-Morss, *Origin of Negative Dialectics*, 1977, p. 101.

37 Habermas's summary of Adorno's project in *Philosophical Discourse*, 1987, p. 186, is most astute here.
38 Jarvis, *Adorno*, 1998, p. 170.
39 As Gillian Rose puts it, 'given the present state of society (the capitalist mode of production), the concept cannot identify with its true object. The consciousness which perceives this is *non-identity thinking* or *negative dialectic*.' In *The Melancholy Science. An Introduction to the Thought of Theodor W. Adorno*, Basingstoke: Macmillan, 1978, p. 44. Seyla Benhabib's comments are closer to Habermas's judgement when she writes that 'negative dialectic is the unending transformation of concepts into their opposites, of what is into what could be but is not.' This is a 'dialectic of pure negativity' since there is no end point of reconciliation; a 'permanent defiance of the actual.' In *Critique, Norm and Utopia. A Study of the Foundations of Critical Theory*, New York: Columbia University Press, 1986, p. 173.
40 'The non-identical is not itself negative, except from the standpoint of identificatory thinking.' Jarvis, *Adorno*, 1998, p. 212.
41 I therefore agree with Jay when he writes that the reversal of forgetting for Adorno means the 'restoration of difference and non-identity to their proper place in the non-hierarchical constellation of subjective and objective forces he called peace' (*Adorno*, 1984, p. 68).
42 Horkheimer, *Critical Theory*, 1972, pp. 114, 118. See Adorno FTFP, p. 137.
43 Both Bernstein and Jarvis insist on the necessity of leaving this opening for genuinely creative acts and thought. See J. Bernstein, *Recovering Ethical Life. Jürgen Habermas and the Future of Critical Theory*, London and New York: Routledge, 1995, p. 20; Jarvis, *Adorno*, 1998, p. 222.
44 Rose, *Melancholy Science*, 1978, p. 55.
45 Habermas, *Philosophical Discourse*, 1987, p.186. A similar criticism is also made by Lyotard: 'the critical model in the end lost its theoretical standing and was reduced to the status of a "utopia" or "hope," a token protest raised in the name of man or reason or creativity'. *The Postmodern Condition*, Manchester: Manchester University Press, 1984, p. 13.
46 Adorno's 'morality', Rose argues, is ' a praxis of thought not a recipe for social and political action.' *Melancholy Science*, 1978, p. 148.
47 This is Stephen White's judgement in S. White (ed.), *The Cambridge Companion to Habermas*, Cambridge: Cambridge University Press, 1995, p. 10.
48 Habermas, *Philosophical Discourse*, 1987, pp. 295f.
49 Ibid., p. 319.
50 A. Wellmer, 'Reason, Utopia and the *Dialectic of Enlightenment* in R. Bernstein (ed.), *Habermas and Modernity*, Cambridge: Polity, 1985, pp. 42f.
51 See for example Fredric Jameson's call for a dialectical reading of postmodernism, which he calls 'cognitive mapping', in his 'Postmodernism, or The Cultural Logic of Late Capitalism', *New Left Review* 146, 1984.

6 SUBJECTIVITY AND THE SEMIOTIC: GENDERING NEGATIVITY

1 I have integrated some of the references to Kristeva's work into the text using the following abbreviations:
CW *About Chinese Women*, New York and London: Marion Boyars, 1977.
DL *Desire in Language*, Oxford: Blackwell, 1981.
PH *Powers of Horror. An Essay on Abjection*, New York: Columbia University Press, 1982.

PM? 'Postmodernism?', *Bucknell Review* vol. 25 pt 2, 1980.
RPL *Revolution in Poetic Language*, New York: Columbia University Press, 1984.
SO *Strangers to Ourselves*, New York: Columbia University Press, 1990.
WT 'Woman's Time', in T. Moi (ed.), *The Kristeva Reader*, Oxford: Blackwell, 1986.
Other references are referenced below. Where specific essays from the *Kristeva Reader* are cited, it is referenced below as KR.

2 Although Kristeva speaks enthusiastically about postmodern literature, her analysis suggests that what she values is its avant-gardism. While there are affinities between her position and some radical postmodernisms, she remains more obviously a critical modernist than a postmodernist as such (rather like, for example, Lyotard).

3 Kristeva, 'The System and the Speaking Subject', KR, 1986, pp. 25–6.

4 S. Freud, 'Project for a Scientific Psychology' (1895) *Standard Edition of the Complete Works of Sigmund Freud*, ed. J. Strachey, London: Hogarth Press, 1966, vol. 1. References to Freud's work will be referenced below either as coming directly from the Standard Edition, as *S.E.* followed by volume then page number, or as it has been reproduced in the *Penguin Freud Library*, Harmondsworth: Penguin, 1984, as *PFL*, with volume and page number.

5 Letter of October 20 1895 in J. Masson (ed.), *The Complete Letters of Sigmund Freud to Wilhelm Fliess 1887–1904*, Cambridge, MA and London: The Belknap Press of Harvard University, 1985. Also quoted in *S.E.* 1, p. 283.

6 Freud, *S.E.* 3, p. 60.

7 Freud, *S.E.* 3, p. 61.

8 Freud, *S.E.* 1, pp. 296f.

9 Freud, *S.E.* 1, p. 370.

10 Freud *S.E.* 1, p. 371; 'Beyond the Pleasure Principle', *PFL* 11, p. 324; 'An Outline of Psychoanalysis', *S.E.* 23, p. 163. As Freud concedes in the former work:

> The most abundant sources of this internal excitation are what are described as the organism's 'instincts' – the representatives of all the forces originating in the interior of the body and transmitted to the mental apparatus – at once the most important and the most obscure element of psychological research.
>
> (*PFL* 11, p. 306)

He admits that 'we know nothing of the nature of the excitatory process that takes place in the elements of the psychic systems' and are therefore 'operating all the time with a large unknown factor, which we are obliged to carry over into every new formula' (*PFL* 11, p. 302; similarly, in 'Three Essays on the Theory of Sexuality', *S.E.* 7, p. 168n and *Civilisation and its Discontents*, *S.E.* 21, p. 117). Indeed he even confesses that 'the theory of instincts is so to say our mythology.' *New Introductory Lectures on Psychoanalysis*, *PFL* 2, p. 127. Deleuze and Guattari would be less circumspect in their materialist monism: 'in reality the unconscious belongs to the realm of physics; the body without organs and its intensities are not metaphors, but matter itself.' Deleuze and Guattari, *Anti-Œdipus*, Minneapolis, MN: University of Minnesota Press, 1983, p. 283.

NOTES

11 Freud had attended Maynert's lectures where the latter, like most of his contemporaries in the scientific world, had replaced Kant's thing-in-itself with the
notion of force. E. Jones, *Sigmund Freud. Life and Work* vol. 1, London: Hogarth
Press, 1961, p. 402.

12 The first summary is in fact Derrida's, in *Writing and Difference*, London:
Routledge, 1978, p. 200. The second is Freud's in *Studies in Hysteria*, PFL 3, p.
263n.

13 Laplanche and Pontalis, *The Language of Psychoanalysis*, London: Hogarth
Press, 1985, pp. 248 (emphasis added), 42.

14 Derrida, *Writing and Difference*, 1978, p. 201.

15 J. Laplanche, *Life and Death in Psychoanalysis*, London and Baltimore, MD:
Johns Hopkins University Press, 1976, p. 54. See also Laplanche, *New
Foundations in Psychoanalysis*, Oxford: Blackwell, 1989, p. 38.

16 J. Derrida, *Margins of Philosophy*, London: Athlone, 1982, pp. 17–21.

17 Freud, *Interpretation of Dreams*, PFL 4 p. 759; 'An Outline of Psychoanalyis',
S.E. 23, p. 163ff; 'Two Principles of Mental Functioning', PFL 11, p. 39;
'Repression', PFL 11, pp. 147f.

18 Freud, 'An Outline of Psychoanalysis', *S.E.* 23, p. 151; 'Instincts and their
Vicissitudes', PFL 11, p. 119.

19 Freud, *Interpretation of Dreams*, PFL 4, p. 754.

20 Freud, 'Beyond the Pleasure Principle', PFL 11, p. 191; 'On Negation', *S.E.* 19 p.
239.

21 Freud, *Interpretation of Dreams*, PFL 4, pp. 477, 381.

22 Ibid., p. 672. This is then the logic of non-identity Benjamin and Adorno saw in
Surrealism, as discussed in the previous chapter.

23 Freud, *Interpretation of Dreams*, PFL 4, p. 650.

24 Freud, *Interpretation of Dreams* PFL 4, pp. 422, 423, 597, 693.

25 Deleuze and Guattari, *Anti-Œdipus*, 1983, p. 38.

26 Laplanche, *Life and Death*, 1976, p. 63.

27 Freud, *Interpretation of Dreams*, PFL 4, p. 762.

28 Freud, 'Beyond the Pleasure Principle, PFL 11, pp. 299f.

29 J. Lacan, *The Four Fundamental Concepts of Psycho-Analysis*, London and New
York: W. W. Norton, 1977, p. 25.

30 As John Lechte puts it: 'Negativity, then, and not negation, would also open the
way to an understanding of the nature of the repression as both constitutive and
disruptive of the social order.' In *Julia Kristeva*, London and New York:
Routledge, 1990, p. 75.

31 M. Foucault, Preface to Deleuze and Guattari, *Anti-Œdipus*, 1983, p. xiii.

32 Deleuze and Guattari, *Anti-Œdipus*, 1983, p. 54; cf. p. 24. Also Kristeva: 'Freud
(in *The Interpretation of Dreams*) revealed (primary process) production itself to
be a *process* not of exchange (or use) or meaning (value), but of playful permutation which provides the model of production.' 'Semiotics' (KR: 83).

33 Deleuze and Guattari, *Anti-Œdipus*, 1983, p. 54. Laplanche argues similarly in
'Psychoanalysis as Anti-Hermeneutics', *Radical Philosophy*, 79, Sept/Oct 1996.

34 *Anti-Œdipus*, 1983, pp. 60, 53, 67.

35 Ibid., 1983, pp. 33, 20. Marcuse makes somewhat similar claims regarding inner
colonisation versus an unconstrained unconscious, even if he draws more
humanist, romantic conclusions for a new sensibility. See for example *Five
Lectures*, Boston, MA: Beacon, 1970, pp. 38f.

36 See Kelly Oliver, *Reading Kristeva. Unravelling the Double-Bind*, Bloomington
and Indianapolis, IN: Indiana University Press, 1983, chapter 1.

37 Kristeva, 'A Question of Subjectivity – An Interview', reprinted in R. Rice and P. Waugh (eds), *Postmodernism*, London: Edward Arnold, 1989, p. 129.

38 After Freud, 'we know that we are foreigners to ourselves, and it is with the help of that sole support that we can attempt to live with others' (SO: 170). Kristeva's solution is more psychoanalytical than political, but see Iris Young's attempt to politicise abjection by linking it to a projection structured by cultural stereotyping. In *Justice and the Politics of Difference*, Princeton, NJ: Princeton University Press, 1990, chapter 5.

39 'The System and the Speaking Subject' (KR: 31).

40 See P. Lewis, 'Revolutionary Semiotics', *Diacritics*, Fall 1974, p. 29 n.1.

41 J. Butler, *Gender Trouble. Feminism and the Subversion of Identity*, London and New York: Routledge, 1990, pp. 80, 88.

42 'Semiotics' (KR: 77f).

43 Ibid. (KR: 85).

44 Ibid. (KR: 86).

45 'The System and the Speaking Subject' (KR: 30).

46 'Interview – 1974. Julia Kristeva and Psychanalyse et Politique', in *m/f*, 1981, nos 5 and 6, p. 166.

47 See for example Foucault, 'The Subject and Power', in H. Dreyfus and P. Rabinow, *Michel Foucault: Beyond Structuralism and Hermeneutics*, Chicago, IL: University of Chicago Press, 1982, p. 216; 'What is Enlightenment?', in P. Rabinow (ed.), *The Foucault Reader*, Harmondsworth: Penguin, 1984; 'The Ethic of Care for the Self as a Practice of Freedom', *Philosophy and Social Criticism* vol. 12 no. 1, Spring 1987.

48 'The System and the Speaking Subject'; 'Why the United States?'; 'A New Kind of Intellectual: The Dissident' (KR: 31, 275, 295ff); 'Talking about Polylogue', in T. Moi, (ed.), *French Feminist Thought. A Reader*, Oxford: Blackwell, 1987, p. 115; 'Interview – 1974', 1981, pp. 166f.

49 'The System and the Speaking Subject' (KR: 31).

50 'Interview – 1974', 1981, p. 167.

51 See Nietzsche, *The Genealogy of Morality*, Cambridge: Cambridge University Press, 1994, II 3, 15.

52 'The System and the Speaking Subject' (KR: 29).

53 See K. Oliver (ed.), *Ethics, Politics and Difference in Julia Kristeva's Writing*, London and New York: Routledge, 1993, p. 19.

54 J. Lacan, in J. Mitchell and J. Rose (eds), *Feminine Sexuality: Jacques Lacan and the Ecole Freudienne*, Basingstoke: Macmillan, 1982, pp. 124, 144, 147.

55 'Oscillation between Power and Denial' in E. Marks and I. de Courtivron (eds), *New French Feminisms. An Anthology*, Brighton: Harvester Press, 1981, p. 167.

56 Butler, *Gender Trouble*, 1990, p. 86.

57 Although see Butler, *Bodies that Matter*, London and New York: Routledge, 1993, p. 71, where she argues that the primacy of the maternal body in generating signification 'cannot be shown' and is therefore 'questionable'.

58 Butler, *Gender Trouble*, 1990, p. 93. She goes on to condemn Foucault himself for appealing, like Kristeva, to a pre-discursive realm of the body and its pleasures, and thus for infidelity to his own genealogy. 'Occasionally ... Foucault subscribes to a prediscursive multiplicity of bodily forces that break through the surface of the body to disrupt the regulating practices of cultural coherence imposed upon that body by a power regime.' Here, according to Butler, he indulges in a sentimental, emancipatory discourse that would replace 'sex' with a 'prediscursive libidinal multiplicity', a primary polymorphousness before the Law (pp. 130,

96ff). Kelly Oliver similarly accuses Kristeva of yearning for 'some pre-linguistic bodily experience' in her *Reading Kristeva*, 1983, p. 103.

59 Butler, *Gender Trouble*, 1990, p. 91. See *Bodies that Matter*, 1993, too, where Butler condemns Kristeva for affirming the maternal/semiotic association and asserting its pre-symbolic status. My own interpretation places Kristeva closer to Irigaray, who is Butler's main interest here, but the latter is also implicated by her in the discursively-constituting exclusions that identify the feminine with the other in order to define the same (pp. 41f). Butler (implicitly) criticises Kristeva's abject on similar grounds (p. 3).

60 Butler, *Bodies that Matter*, 1993, p. 70.

61 Christine Battersby has argued that this 'self-morphing' metaphysics of fluidity is more woman-friendly than its Aristotelian alternative, since it is modelled on the female (the body that gives birth). In this sense 'negativity' (a term not used by Battersby herself) is discursively figured as female although in a sense quite different from the one I am advancing here. See *The Phenomenal Woman. Feminist Metaphysics and the Patterns of Identity*, Cambridge: Polity, 1998.

62 J. Rose, *Sexuality in the Field of Vision*, London: Verso, 1986, p. 157.

63 'Stabat Mater' (KR: 161).

64 'Stabat Mater' (KR: 178). See also 'A New Type of Dissident: The Intellectual' (KR: 297) and 'Motherhood according to Bellini' (DL: 240).

65 'A New Type of Intellectual' (KR: 298).

66 'Stabat Mater' (KR: 181).

67 'Interview – 1974', 1981, p. 167.

68 Ibid., p. 166.

69 Ibid., p. 166.

70 'A Question of Subjectivity', 1989, p. 131.

71 'Oscillation between Power and Denial', p. 165.

72 'A Question of Subjectivity', 1989, p. 131; WT p. 199.

73 Even Spivak, who is often associated with the former types of criticism, acknowledges that 'there is in Kristeva's text an implicit double program for women which we encounter in the best of French feminism: *against* sexism, where women unite as a biologically oppressed caste, and *for* feminism, where human beings train to prepare for a transformation of consciousness.' In G. C. Spivak, 'French Feminism in an International Frame', in her *In Other Worlds. Essays in Cultural Politics*, New York and London: 1988, p. 144. Spivak approvingly quotes Catherine Clément's remark in this context: that feminist action means changing the imaginary in order to act on the real (p. 145).

CONCLUSION: POLITICS AND NEGATIVITY

1 See for example Foucault's provocative Preface to *The Order of Things*, London and New York: Tavistock Publications, 1970.

2 J. Derrida, *Specters of Marx*, New York and London: Routledge, 1994, p. 28.

3 G. Bennington, 'Derrida', in S. Critchley and W. Schroeder (eds), *A Companion to Continental Philosophy*, Oxford: Blackwell, 1998, p. 556.

4 Ibid., p. 557.

5 For an excellent analysis of Lyotard's politics, and one which is most provocative in terms of my own analysis of negativity, see J. Williams, *Lyotard and the Political*, London: Routledge, 2000.

6 G. Deleuze and F. Guattari, *What is Philosophy?*, London and New York: Verso, 1994 (original: *Qu'est-ce que la philosophie?*, 1991). Referred to in the text hereafter as WiP.

7 K. Ansell Pearson, *Germinal Life. The Difference and Repetition of Deleuze*, London and New York: Routledge, 1999, p. 209.
8 Ibid., pp. 201, 208.
9 Ibid., p. 202. For similar comments see also pp. 19, 203, 204, 222, 223, 224.
10 Ansell Pearson, *Germinal Life*, p. 208. Paul Patton notes: 'It is possible to translate some of this terminology into the language of anglophone political theory, and to find in the work of Deleuze and Guattari conceptions of freedom, power and domination, or even theories of the state and revolution. But there is always a remainder that does not translate ... . For example, they appear to be unconcerned with issues of political community; they are more interested in ways in which society is differentiated or divided than in ways in which it is held together.' P. Patton, 'The Political Philosophy of Deleuze and Guattari', in A. Vincent (ed.), *Politial Theory. Tradition and Diversity*, Cambridge: Cambridge University Press, 1997, p. 238. This latter distinction is a crucial one, it seems to me, and one that needs some *rapprochement*.
11 Ansell Pearson, *Germinal Life*, p. 223. See also Derrida's comments on history and the event in *Specters*, p. 15.

INDEX